RELIGION, THE MISSING
DIMENSION OF STATECRAFT ▪

Religion, The Missing Dimension of Statecraft ▪

edited by

Douglas Johnston
and Cynthia Sampson

Center for Strategic and International Studies

New York   Oxford
OXFORD UNIVERSITY PRESS

Oxford University Press

Oxford   New York
Athens   Auckland   Bangkok   Bombay
Calcutta   Cape Town   Dar es Salaam   Delhi
Florence   Hong Kong   Istanbul   Karachi
Kuala Lumpur   Madras   Madrid   Melbourne
Mexico City   Nairobi   Paris   Singapore
Taipei   Tokyo   Toronto

and associated companies in
Berlin   Ibadan

Copyright © 1994 by the Center for Strategic and International Studies

First published in 1994 by Oxford University Press, Inc.
198 Madison Avenue, New York, New York 10016

First issued as an Oxford University Press paperback, 1995.

Oxford is a registered trademark of Oxford University Press, Inc.

Library of Congress Cataloging-in-Publication Data
Religion : the missing dimension of statecraft / edited by Douglas
Johnston and Cynthia Sampson.
p.   cm.
"Center for Strategic and International Studies."
Includes index.
ISBN-13 978-0-19-508734-5; 978-0-19-510280-2 (pbk.)
ISBN 0-19-508734-8; 0-19-510280-0 (pbk.)
1. Christianity and international affairs.   2. Religion and
international affairs.   I. Johnston, Douglas (Douglas M.)
II. Sampson, Cynthia.   III. Center for Strategic and International
Studies (Washington, D.C.)
BR115.I7R45   1994
291.1′787 – dc20   93-21648

Printing (last digit):   10

Printed in the United States of America

In tribute to Christa Konrad and James Laue,
two of the great spirits of our time

Foreword ▪

JIMMY CARTER

Historically and currently, we all realize that religious differences have often been a cause or a pretext for war. Less well known is the fact that the actions of many religious persons and communities point in another direction. They demonstrate that religion can be a potent force in encouraging the peaceful resolution of conflict.

Personal experience underlies my conviction that religion can be significant for peacemaking. The negotiations between Menachem Begin, Anwar el-Sadat, and myself at Camp David in 1978 were greatly influenced by our religious backgrounds. This was evident in the fact that a joint appeal for prayer preceded our discussions at Camp David and that each of us worshiped separately throughout our stay together. But the role of religion was perhaps greater than is commonly recognized or easily quantified. Begin and Sadat were deeply religious men. Their religious beliefs shaped their personalities, historical perspectives, and political convictions. If the talks at Camp David engaged statesmen in the search for a political settlement, in the final analysis they also involved religiously committed men. Each of the principals at Camp David recognized peace to be both a gift from God and a preeminent human obligation. As the mediator of the talks, I am convinced that to have overlooked the importance of religion for both Sadat and Begin would have resulted in a failure to understand these two men. Such a failure could have had a pervasive and incalculable impact.

Religious communities have also rendered critical support for movements toward democracy around the world. Zambia, which returned to multiparty democracy with elections on October 31, 1991, is a case in point. At the invitation of the Zambian government and the major opposition parties, I led an international team of election experts to assist in the preparation and monitoring of the elections. In the process, I worked closely with many sectors of Zambian society, including the churches. Even as late as July 1991, elections were threatened by a political impasse: Frederick Chiluba's Movement for Multi-Party Democracy was determined to boycott the elections unless important sections of the constitution were redrafted and adopted. In August of that year, Zambian President Kenneth Kaunda of the United National Independence Party and Mr. Chiluba agreed to meet in the Anglican Cathedral in Lusaka. The church provided an acceptable meeting place for both parties. Their meeting, which began with shared prayer, resulted eventually in a redrafting of the constitution that opened the way for the elections. Later, during the actual election, members of churches provided invaluable cooperation in the training and deployment of Zambian election monitors for virtually every polling site. The churches carried the trust of the Zambian people and made a decisive contribution to the reestablishment of democracy.

The case studies in this book reinforce my conviction that religion can play a constructive role in the world's trouble spots. In the case of Nicaragua, in fact, the work of the Interfaith Conciliation Commission laid the groundwork for the agreement I was able to secure from the Sandinistas that permitted the leaders of the East Coast Indians to return from exile. These cases suggest that the world's religious communities possess moral and social characteristics that equip them in unique ways to engage in efforts to promote peace.

This book poses a challenge to diplomats and politicians, religious figures and laypersons, analysts and academics alike. Religious representatives need to exercise their moral authority and mobilize the vast human resources of their communities in the service of peacemaking. The rest of us, in turn, must recognize the growing importance of religious factors for peacemaking and develop ways, both informal and formal, to cooperate with religious leaders and communities in promoting peace with justice. I urge anyone concerned about conflict in today's world, in reading this book, to take into account the import of its message.

Acknowledgments ∎

This book is unusual in the extent to which there are so many people to acknowledge for bringing it to fruition. In its genesis some seven years ago, the Religion and Conflict Resolution Project evolved from my own emerging awareness that there was a great deal being accomplished in the world in reconciling differences on an informal and often spiritual basis. At the same time, there was virtually no public recognition that this was the case. It struck me that the good being done might be further enhanced if officials who operate at the front lines of conflict resolution, particularly foreign policy practitioners, could be made aware of what was taking place on these other fronts. Perhaps they could then seek and exploit opportunities for mutual reinforcement.

I shared this idea with Carl Oglesby, a good friend, who expressed great support. Somehow his support seemed all the more significant because of our seemingly divergent political views. While I had spent the 1960s serving in the U.S. Navy aboard nuclear submarines, Carl had been head of Students for a Democratic Society, the embodiment of the New Left's protest against the Vietnam war. We both concluded, however, that for me to launch such an undertaking would require a unique blend of job and circumstance (certainly different from that which existed in my life at the time).

This thought process crystallized even further upon hearing an account of a trip taken to Asia and Africa in 1987 by three friends associated with the National Prayer Breakfast in Washington, D.C.: Douglas Coe, Congressman Tony Hall, and David Laux. As Laux tells the story, they were visiting with the prime minister of Mauritius, a Hindu whom none of them had met before, and started discussing the difficulties of reconciling differences among people. They suggested that because mankind's normal methods did not seem to work very well, perhaps Christ's approach might offer a useful model. At this point, according to Laux, the American Ambassador, who was also present, "displayed obvious discomfort." In spite of the ambassador's uneasiness, the prime minister responded positively, and an interesting discussion ensued on the relevance of religious values in the reconciliation process. An almost identical sequence occurred in a meeting a week later with the president of the Senate of Malaysia, a Muslim.

From this recitation, I concluded, rightly or wrongly, that the rigorous separation of church and state in the United States had so relegated religion to the realm of the personal that it left many of us insensitive to the extent to which religion and politics intertwine in much of the rest of the world. Such an insensitivity, I further speculated, could lead, and probably had led, to uninformed and potentially costly foreign policy choices.

It was at about this time that I changed jobs and found myself in a position at the Center for Strategic and International Studies from where I could launch a project that would explore these issues. I did so, and the next three years had a distinct "voice in the wilderness" feeling to them. In those early days, Paul Cook, my executive assistant at the time, and Anne O'Donnell, an expert on liberation theology, helped as I struggled to capture the vision conceptually and secure the funding to support it. Early on, it became clear that the scope of the emerging project was such that it would require a team effort. There were simply too many dimensions for any one person to treat in a comprehensive fashion. Accordingly, an advisory group was formed from a range of disciplines including theology, religious studies, political science, sociology, conflict resolution, foreign policy, and military strategy. Among those early participants were Alberto Coll, Bryan Hehir, Robert Hennemeyer, Shireen Hunter, Amos Jordan, Robert Neumann, Brad Roberts, Andrew Schmookler, George Tanham, and George Weigel. Their advice and counsel proved invaluable during the early stages of conceptualization.

A modest seed grant from the U.S. Institute of Peace (USIP) gave a needed boost and, among other things, enabled me to engage Cynthia Sampson as research coordinator for the case studies. Cynthia is a conflict resolution specialist whose work on this subject dates from 1987 when she did a survey of religiously motivated peacemaking activities for the Harvard University Program on Negotiation. Her scholarship and editorial skills proved impeccable and are reflected throughout this book.

The USIP funds were soon exhausted, and the project inched along for a time on faith. It was only after the revolutions in Eastern Europe in the late 1980s in which the churches played such a vital role that foundations began to respond favorably to the project concept. With history having thus caught up with us, a major grant followed from the Pew Charitable Trusts, which enabled us to launch the research on a full-scale basis. Kevin Quigley, Pew's program director for public policy, and Joel Carpenter, director of Pew's religion program, were particularly helpful and encouraging in this regard. Supplementary grants from the Lilly Endowment (James Wind) and the Springer Foundation in Germany (Ernst Cramer) rounded out the funding base.

At this point, a smaller steering group was formed to help shape the total effort and to author individual pieces, as appropriate. This group of world-class scholars and practitioners had also been a part of the earlier advisory group and included Stanton Burnett, James Laue, David Little, Edward Luttwak, Joseph Montville, Abdul Aziz Said, Harold Saunders, William Vendley, and William Zartman. In addition, other experts often sat in on steering group meetings, making highly valuable contributions. These included Wilson Dizard, Thomas Jones, Christa Konrad, Harry Radday, and David Wendt.

The project was also fortunate in engaging the services of Ron Kraybill, Edward Luttwak, Bruce Nichols, Cynthia Sampson, David Steele, and Henry Wooster to author the case studies. The same is true for Harvey Cox, who with the support of a group of religious scholars including Masao Abe, Moshe Idel, Harjot Oberoi, Abdulaziz Sachedina, and Arvind Sharma, crafted a valuable research piece on selected world religions and the theological basis that each provides for pursuing conflict resolution as a religious goal. A special note of thanks is also due

Hizkias Assefa, Ronald Heifitz, John Paul Lederach, Thomas Princen, and Richard Ruffin, who appeared before the steering group to share their insights on past conflict resolution initiatives with which they were familiar or on theories they had developed about conflict resolution in general.

Also important were the efforts of Alexander Nacht and Bruce McKenney, who provided valuable research assistance in support of the case study on South Africa, and those of Anthony Gaeta, who did the same for the case study on postwar Franco-German reconciliation. Nancy Eddy was extremely helpful in eliciting interest from prospective publishers, while Elizabeth Calkins, Deborah Luebke, and Shirley Collamer played the role of unsung heroes in providing the clerical support that made it all possible. And, as valuable as Carl Oglesby's support was at the beginning of the project, it was even more so at the end when he provided important commentary as an outside reviewer of the manuscript for this book. At least equivalent to all of the rest combined were the forbearance, moral support, and keen eye of my wife, Norvell, throughout the course of the project.

The final tribute is to the Stewardship Foundation (George Kovats) for providing the funding to send the steering group to a conference on "Regions in Crisis, Regions in Recovery" in Caux, Switzerland. Sponsored by the Swiss-based Moral Re-Armament Foundation (MRA), this conference provided an opportunity for the steering group to present its initial findings to about 600 individuals from different crisis spots around the world: Cambodia, Burma, Ethiopia, Algeria, the former Yugoslavia, Northern Ireland, South Africa, and the Middle East to name only a few. At the end and with Richard Ruffin's valuable assistance, the steering group met with 30 experts from a range of countries to discuss the conclusions. Typical of this group of seasoned practitioners were Rajmohan Gandhi, the grandson of Mahatma Gandhi and a significant political figure in his own right; Allan Griffith, a key foreign policy adviser to five Australian prime ministers; Joseph Lagu, ambassador-at-large for Sudan and past leader of the guerrilla movement that led to autonomy for the southern Sudan in the 1970s; and James Lester, a leading parliamentarian on foreign affairs in the British House of Commons. The feedback from this group proved highly instructive in informing both the analytic and prescriptive dimensions of this volume.

In short, there were many who contributed to the total effort. And therein lies its strength. As Harold Saunders commented at one point along the way, "In my experience, the collaborative nature of this project is unprecedented."

Washington, D.C.   Douglas Johnston
January 1993   Project Director

Contents ∎

CONTRIBUTORS ▪

Stanton Burnett* is senior adviser and former director of studies at the Center for Strategic and International Studies. Educated at the University of Washington and the New School for Social Research, Dr. Burnett previously served as counselor of the U.S. Information Agency and prior to that taught political philosophy at Hobart College and William Smith College. His most recent publication is *Investing in Security: Economic Aid for Noneconomic Purposes* (Washington D.C.: Center for Strategic and International Studies, 1992).

Harvey Cox is the Victor S. Thomas Professor of Divinity at Harvard University. He was educated at the University of Pennsylvania and the Yale Divinity School and earned his doctorate at Harvard University. An ordained American Baptist minister, Professor Cox has held a number of positions relating to the global ministry of the church. In addition to assignments at Temple University, Oberlin College, and Andover Newton Theological School, he has been a visiting professor at Seminario Bautista de Mexico and at Naropa Institute (Buddhist), Boulder, Colorado, and a visiting International Fellow in Japan. Professor Cox is the author of numerous books on religion and ethics, among them *Religion in the Secular City* (New York: Simon and Schuster, 1984), *Turning East* (New York: Simon and Schuster, 1977), and *Many Mansions: A Christian's Encounters with Other Faiths* (Boston: Beacon Press, 1988).

Douglas Johnston* is the executive vice president and chief operating officer of the Center for Strategic and International Studies, in addition to serving as project director of the Religion and Conflict Resolution Project. Educated at the U.S. Naval Academy and Harvard University, Dr. Johnston has held senior positions in government, the military, academia, and the private sector. In government, he formerly served as director of the Office of Policy Planning and Management in the Office of the Secretary of Defense and later as deputy assistant secretary of the U.S. Navy. He has taught international affairs at the Kennedy School of Government, Harvard University, where he was also founder and director of the school's Executive Program in National and International Security. Author of numerous articles on a range of subjects, Dr. Johnston's interest in this project stems from his involvement with the National Prayer Breakfast Fellowship.

Ron Kraybill is the director of training at the Centre for Conflict Resolution (formerly Centre for Intergroup Studies) at the University of Cape Town in South

*Members of the Religion and Conflict Resolution Project steering group.

Africa. Educated at Goshen College and Harvard Divinity School, Mr. Kraybill is currently a Ph.D. candidate at the University of Cape Town. He is an experienced mediator who served from 1979 to 1988 as director of the Mennonite Conciliation Service, Akron, Pennsylvania, where he wrote regularly for the *Conciliation Quarterly*. He is the author of *Repairing the Breach: Ministering in Community Conflict* (Scottdale, Penn.: Herald Press, 1981).

David Little* is a senior scholar at the U.S. Institute of Peace and a former professor of religious studies at the University of Virginia. Educated at the College of Wooster, Union Theological Seminary, and Harvard University, Dr. Little is author of numerous books and articles relating to religion. His most recent works are *Ukraine: The Legacy of Intolerance* (Washington, D.C.: USIP Press, 1991) and (with John Kelsay and Abdulaziz Sachedina) *Human Rights and the Conflict of Cultures: Freedom of Religion and Conscience in the West and Islam* (Columbia: University of South Carolina Press, 1988).

Edward Luttwak* is director of the Geoeconomics Project at the Center for Strategic and International Studies and former holder of the Center's Chair in Strategy. Educated at the London School of Economics and Johns Hopkins University, Dr. Luttwak has taught at Johns Hopkins University (Baltimore campus and the Paul H. Nitze School of Advanced International Studies) and Georgetown University and has consulted on military strategy with the U.S. government. His most recent book is entitled *The Endangered American Dream* (New York: Simon and Schuster, 1993). Among his other publications is *Strategy: The Logic of War and Peace* (Cambridge, Mass.: Belknap Press of Harvard University Press, 1987).

Bruce Nichols is a specialist in religious and humanitarian issues in U.S. foreign policy. Educated at Hamilton College and the University of Pennsylvania, Mr. Nichols was formerly the director of education and studies at the Carnegie Council on Ethics and International Affairs, New York City. He is the author of *The Uneasy Alliance: Religion, Refugee Work, and U.S. Foreign Policy* (New York: Oxford University Press, 1988) and coeditor with Gil Loescher of *The Moral Nation: Humanitarianism and U.S. Foreign Policy Today* (South Bend, Ind.: University of Notre Dame Press, 1989).

Barry Rubin is a fellow at the Johns Hopkins Foreign Policy Institute and a professor at the Paul H. Nitze School of Advanced International Studies, Johns Hopkins University. Dr. Rubin was educated at Richmond College, Rutgers University, and Georgetown University. Among his published works relevant to this study are *Paved with Good Intentions: The American Experience in Iran* (New York: Oxford University Press, 1980), *Secrets of State: The State Department and the Struggle over U.S. Foreign Policy* (New York: Oxford University Press, 1985), and *Islamic Fundamentalists in Egyptian Politics* (New York: St. Martin's Press, 1991).

Cynthia Sampson is currently an associate with the World Conference on Religion and Peace. Educated at the University of Michigan, University of

Wisconsin, and Columbia University, Ms. Sampson is a Ph.D. candidate in conflict analysis and resolution at George Mason University. She formerly served as research coordinator of the Religion and Conflict Resolution Project of the Center for Strategic and International Studies; as a foreign affairs editor at the *Christian Science Monitor*; and as a research associate at the Program on Negotiation, Harvard Law School, where she authored a study entitled "The International Conciliation Work of Religious Figures."

David Steele is currently working with the International Conciliation Service of the Mennonite Central Committee (USA) on the facilitation of interfaith dialogue in the former Yugoslavia. Educated at Syracuse University, Gordon-Conwell Theological Seminary, Andover Newton Theological School, and the University of Edinburgh, Dr. Steele is also an ordained minister in the United Church of Christ, having served churches in metropolitan Boston and Washington. His dissertation is entitled "Role of the Church as an Intermediary in International Conflict: A Theological Assessment of Principled Negotiation."

William Vendley* is interim secretary-general of the World Conference on Religion and Peace. Educated at Purdue University, Vidyodia University (Colombo, Sri Lanka), Maryknoll School of Theology, and Fordham University, Dr. Vendley has also served as a professor of systematic theology at the Maryknoll School of Theology and at the Seminary of the Immaculate Conception in the New York City area. He has written and lectured widely on religion, society, and peace.

Henry Wooster currently works at the U.S. Department of State in the Bureau of International Narcotics Matters. He was educated at Amherst College and received an M.A. in religion from Yale University. Mr. Wooster formerly served as a program associate at the Carnegie Council on Ethics and International Affairs, where he worked on programs related to foreign policy and defense.

ADDITIONAL MEMBERS OF THE STEERING GROUP

In one way or another, the steering group's deliberations are reflected in every chapter of this book. The steering group was integrally involved in each aspect of the Religion and Conflict Resolution Project, from the design of the research; to the selection, review, and evaluation of the case studies; to the analysis of the study's implications for the practice of foreign affairs and conflict resolution. These additional members are acknowledged for their highly significant contributions to this volume.

James H. Laue (since deceased) was the Lynch Professor of Conflict Resolution at George Mason University. Educated at the University of Wisconsin–River Falls and at Harvard University, Dr. Laue was an experienced mediator and the former president of the Conflict Clinic, Inc. Prior to that, he served in the U.S. Department of Justice Community Relations Service and as director of the Center for

Metropolitan Studies at the University of Missouri–St. Louis. Dr. Laue's publications focused on the ethics of intervention, getting parties to the negotiating table, and on policy mediation.

Joseph Montville is a Senior Associate at the Center for Strategic and International Studies and Director of the Center's Conflict Resolution Project. He is a consultant to both the U.S. Department of State and the Department of Defense, a lecturer on psychiatry at Harvard University Medical School, and a visiting professor of psychiatry at the University of Virginia. Educated at Lehigh, Columbia, and Harvard universities, Mr. Montville is a retired foreign service officer and a specialist in Middle Eastern affairs. He is also a leading architect and practitioner of track II (nonofficial) diplomacy. He is the editor of *Conflict and Peacemaking in Multiethnic Societies* (Lexington, Mass.: Lexington Books, 1990) and editor (with Vamik Volkan and Demetrios Julius) of *The Psychodynamics of International Relationships* (Lexington, Mass.: Lexington Books, 1990 (Vol. I) and 1991 (Vol. II).

Harold Saunders currently serves as director of international affairs for the Kettering Foundation and is a participant in the continuing Dartmouth Conferences on U.S.–Russian (formerly Soviet) relations. Educated at Princeton and Yale universities, Dr. Saunders worked for 20 years (1961–1981) at the center of U.S. policy-making on the Middle East and Southwest Asia as a former assistant secretary of state and a member of the National Security Council staff. He was one of the principal architects of the Camp David Accords. Among his many publications is *The Other Walls: The Arab-Israeli Peace Process in a Global Perspective* (Princeton, N.J.: Princeton University Press, 1991).

Abdul Aziz Said is the senior ranking professor at the School of International Service, American University, an affiliation that dates from 1957. Educated at the American University of Beirut and the American University in Washington, D.C., Dr. Said was a member of the White House Commission on the Islamic World, has been a consultant to the U.S. Information Agency and the Department of State, and has participated in Arab-Israeli peace dialogues. He has authored a number of publications in the field of international relations with a focus on human rights, ethnicity, peace and conflict resolution, and American foreign policy.

I. William Zartman is the Jacob Blaustein Professor of International Organization and Conflict Resolution and the director of African Studies and Conflict Management Programs at the Paul H. Nitze School of Advanced International Studies, Johns Hopkins University. Educated at Johns Hopkins and Yale universities, Dr. Zartman is the author or editor of more than 20 books on North African politics and African international relations and has made major contributions to the conceptual development of the field of negotiation and conflict management.

I ▪ THEORY

1 ▪

Introduction: Beyond Power Politics

DOUGLAS JOHNSTON

Those who start by storming bastilles will end up build-
ing their own.

Adam Michnik

As the twentieth century draws to a close, one is struck by the degree to which the relative calm in the West during the four decades of the Cold War contrasts with the all but unprecedented brutality of the preceding 50 years. Clearly, the sobering constraints on geopolitical adventurism imposed by the advent of nuclear deterrence represented a major watershed in the relations of nations. Now a watershed of a different sort is emerging: the composition of conflict itself is changing.

With the decline of the East-West confrontation and most of its regional manifestations, few of the conflicts that evolve will be rooted any longer in the old Cold War ideologies. Instead, most will derive from clashes of communal identity, whether on the basis of race, ethnicity, nationality, or religion. Such disputes tend to occur at the fault lines between rival nationalities or in situations where societies are suffering from the strains of economic competition and rising expectations. These are the most intractable sources of conflict, and they are the sources with which conventional diplomacy is least suited to deal.

The classical tools of diplomacy typically include an exchange of information, the often manipulative signaling of positions, and one or more forms of negotiation. These measures are normally quite suitable for dealing with conflicts that relate to power politics and tangible material interests. Such interests are inherently divisible and thus subject to compromise. Nonmaterial "identity-based" conflicts, on the other hand, are often not well understood by practical-minded diplomats accustomed to operating in the old East-West context of nation-state politics. What is required is not a shrewd understanding of the interests of both sides, but rather an understanding of the emotional stakes of the parties, which are often deeply rooted in history, and their respective interpretations of first principles such as self-determination, justice, and freedom.

Until very recently, this challenge to diplomacy was exacerbated by the restrictions that international organizations placed on themselves against becoming involved in the internal conflicts of member states. This vacuum, coupled with the changing nature of conflict, resulted in an observable expansion of the role played by citizens outside of government—religious figures and spiritually motivated laypersons among them—in the conduct of various forms of mediation and conflict resolution.

Because individuals operating on a religious or spiritual basis have been particularly neglected in the study of international relations, their experience is the focus of this study. Such persons are often better equipped to reach people at the level of the individual and the subnational group—where inequities and insecurities are often most keenly felt—than are most political leaders who walk the corridors of power. They are also better attuned to dealing with basic moral issues and spiritual needs, at times extending beyond the boundaries of their own faith traditions.

Among the more prominent spiritual leaders of our times are those who have led significant nonviolent movements for socio-political change, such as Mahatma Gandhi, Dr. Martin Luther King, Jr., and Archbishop Desmond Tutu. There is, however, a growing cadre of spiritual actors at a different level: people who have sought to promote peaceful change "from the middle." Sometimes in the realm of official mediation and sometimes in the anonymous, behind-the-scenes realm of track II (nonofficial) diplomacy, these third-party intervenors are making their mark in the world of negotiation and conflict resolution.

While the divisive character of religion is widely recognized, its obverse contributions to resolving conflict are all but totally unknown (as Edward Luttwak points out in Chapter 2). The purpose of this book is to help fill a telling gap in the literature and to provide insights that will enable policymakers and others to comprehend and reinforce the positive contribution that religious or spiritual influences can bring to peacemaking.

Although the terms are used somewhat interchangeably in this work, it is important to recognize the distinction between religious and spiritual phenomena. Simply put, the term *religion* is meant to imply an institutional framework within which specific theological doctrines and practices are advocated and pursued, usually among a community of like-minded believers. *Spirituality,* on the other hand, transcends the normal parameters of organized religion, suggesting a less bounded and, at times, more far-reaching scope of human involvement. For the individual, it often implies action born of a faith commitment that may or may not be informed or circumscribed by an allegiance to any particular religious tradition. As will be seen in later chapters, nonsecular involvement in a conflict situation can derive from either a religious or a spiritual motivation: from the authority of a religious institution or from the personal commitment of individuals acting independently of organized religion.

BACKGROUND

This study, though more global in its implications, was prompted in part by a concern that the rigorous separation of church and state in the United States has desensitized many citizens to the fact that much of the rest of the world does not operate on a similar basis. Foreign policy practitioners in the United States, for example, are often inadequately equipped to deal with situations involving other nation-states where the imperatives of religious doctrine blend intimately with those of politics and economics. At times, this has led to uninformed policy choices, particularly in our dealings with countries of the Middle East. This aspect is explored by Barry Rubin in Chapter 3.

Because of the degree to which we as Americans separate our spiritual lives from our public lives, we face a certain difficulty in comprehending the depths to which religious and political considerations interact in shaping the perceptions and motivations of individuals from other societies. We also inadequately appreciate the transformational possibilities that exist when the parties involved in a conflict can be appealed to on the basis of shared spiritual convictions or values. Implicit in the latter is the prospect that, under the right conditions, the parties can operate at a higher level of trust than would otherwise be possible in the realm of realpolitik. This is not to suggest that it is necessarily an "either-or" proposition with regard to the spiritual and the secular. More likely, it is a "both-and" phenomenon in which a breakthrough at the spiritual level is made possible once the political, economic, and security "planets" have been brought into some kind of proximate alignment.

METHODOLOGY

To explore the positive potential of religious or spiritual influences in conflict resolution, this book offers a series of case studies that illustrate specific situations in which such factors have played a helpful role in preventing, ameliorating, or resolving a dispute. While estimates of how influential these factors may have been are inherently subjective, they have been attempted. The final judgment, however, must rest with the reader.

To establish credibility with the skeptic or the uninformed practitioner, it was deemed necessary that some form of closure have been achieved in each case situation selected so that it would be possible to assess whether the religious or spiritual dimension had made any real difference. The assumption was that if a positive contribution could be demonstrated, thoughtful practitioners should then feel compelled to understand the phenomenon and develop an appreciation for where and when it might be brought into play or usefully reinforced.

A concerted effort was made to identify cases that would be representative of a range of situations and religious traditions. Although the first objective was largely achieved, the second was not. Other than Christianity, in which the peacemaking mandate is clear and has been pursued with some frequency, examples of similar attempts in other religious traditions have been more difficult to find. Situations that initially appeared promising either had not yet achieved closure or had occurred so long ago that the principal actors were no longer alive to provide researchers with the kind of confirmation and insights that would be required to support sound scholarship.

Perhaps equally significant is the fact that, within certain other religious traditions and settings, peace-related activities do not usually take the form of political activism and, thus, do not lend themselves to analysis on a comparable basis to the cases presented here. Nevertheless, it is hoped that by examining the precepts of other religious traditions, as Harvey Cox and his colleagues have done in Chapter 12 and upon which William Vendley and David Little have built in Chapter 14, one can extrapolate the potential for a range of peacemaking activities equivalent to those examined in this work.

Finally, many of the principles treated by the case studies have important implications for the conduct of foreign policy. While these principles clearly have broader application, the analysis by Stanton Burnett in Chapter 13 focuses on the U.S. foreign policy community because it is this community with which the participants were most familiar.

THE CASES

The case studies presented here span the globe (Europe, Central America, Asia, and Africa) and were chosen to illustrate a broad spectrum of involvements by religious actors. The case dealing with the Philippines (Chapter 8), for example, reflects a situation in which the temporal power of the Roman Catholic church was brought to bear in defusing a potentially violent transition from the Marcos to the Aquino regime. In somewhat similar fashion, churches in East Germany (most particularly Lutheran) provided the instrumental forum for civil opposition, which led to that country's peaceful political revolution in 1989 (Chapter 7). These two cases, as treated here, explore the spiritual dimension of the churches' roles, in addition to the better documented political aspects. Nicaragua (Chapter 5), on the other hand, involved third-party mediation on the part of Moravian church and other religious officials in helping resolve a major conflict between the Sandinista regime and the East Coast Indians.

The case relating to Rhodesian independence (Chapter 10) illustrates the impact of several religious actors in bringing about a negotiated end to a bitter civil war and facilitating a peaceful transition of power, while the Franco-German case (Chapter 4) relates to reconciliation in the wake of World War II. And, although the Nigerian civil war was settled on the battlefield instead of at the bargaining table, the efforts of the Quakers in that conflict may have contributed to what was a remarkably conciliatory aftermath (Chapter 6).

Perhaps more than any of the above cases, the unfolding abandonment of apartheid in South Africa (Chapter 9) illustrates the transformational potential of the religious factor. The recent reversal by the South African Dutch Reformed church of its stand on apartheid has effectively removed the theological justification for such a system for most Afrikaners. The examples of spiritually motivated individuals operating on a personal (rather than an institutional) basis cited in Chapter 15 also illustrate this transformational dimension. These range from an inspired initiative on the part of a Southern Sudanese guerrilla leader that contributed to the breakthrough settlement with the North in 1972, to the personal contribution of a Catholic cardinal in Rome to relieving the persecution of Christians in East Germany, to the role played by a chairman of the U.S. Joint Chiefs of Staff, acting in his capacity as a member of a prayer fellowship group, in resolving a border dispute between two African countries.

THE CHALLENGE

As one looks to the end of the century and beyond, the challenges of preventing or resolving conflict are likely to prove even more formidable than they have in the past. The problems posed by today's ethnic and nationalistic hostilities, whether inter- or intrastate, have shown themselves to be peculiarly resistant to diplomatic compromise. If the goal of achieving peace in meaningful terms is to prove any less elusive, different approaches will be required—approaches that key to deep-rooted human relationships rather than to state-centered philosophies. Far greater insight into the human dimensions of conflict and its resolution will be required on the part of foreign policy and religious practitioners than has been demonstrated to date. Perhaps this book can contribute to that end.

2 ∎

The Missing Dimension

EDWARD LUTTWAK

*Two species of blindness easily combine; of those
who see not what is, and of those who see what
is not.*

Quintus Septimius Tertullianus
Apologeticus IV, 20

ANTECEDENTS

In Homer as in the Bible, the vicissitudes of war and peace are unfailingly attributed to divine intervention, yet though the entire discourse of the classical world was pervaded by Homer's metaphors, his teleology was not shared by most Greek and Roman writers on politics and conflict. Both Thucydides and Tacitus, among many lesser lights, freely invoked geographic, economic, psychological, social, and technical primary causes to explain the course of human events, attributing nothing to divine intervention.

That, however, was an explanatory freedom no longer wanted (and if wanted, denied) once Christianity fully evolved from a perilous faith to the pervasively authoritative ideology of European civilization. For a thousand years and more, just as philosophy was only admitted as the daughter of theology, historiography could only register the unfolding of the divine will, remaining firmly teleological when it transcended mere narrative.

There was still a search for explanations, of course, because the proximate or apparent causes of human events were still in dispute, but the primary cause was always the same.

It was not until the eighteenth-century Enlightenment that the teleological barrier to free inquiry, already breached since the Renaissance, was entirely slighted. Yet even as the Enlightenment swept away clerical obscurantism and discredited all ascriptive dogma, it imposed its own restrictive prejudice on the scope and content of scholarship as on literature and the arts.

Enlightenment publicists and philosophers wielded none of the torture instruments of the Catholic inquisitions, nor did they burn dissenters under some Protestant dispensation. But when it came to religion in all its aspects, they strangled free inquiry just as effectively by the commanding force of the fashion they imposed.

8

Because thinkers had been preoccupied by devotional matters and the affairs of the church throughout the millennium then labeled medieval and vehemently denigrated as an unrelieved dark age of religiously contrived ignorance, the newly compelling fashion prohibited any sustained intellectual interest in religion itself, in religious institutions, and even in the role of religious motivations in secular affairs. Thomas à Kempis and Pascal had each been celebrated as intellectual ornaments of their very different ages as Kierkegaard and Newman[1] would be again; but, in between, the Enlightenment denied intellectual respectability to all such spiritual explorations. Even ecclesiastical historiography, though subject to the same standards of scholarship as any other historiography and the source of important evidence for "general" history, was condemned as the province of mere church chroniclers. As for religious motivations in secular affairs, they were disregarded or dismissed as mere pretense, and because this could not be done in the case of the entire history of Byzantium, the quandary was resolved by simply abandoning its study.

A century after Du Cange[2] and Mabillon[3] had greatly advanced all historiography by their novel methods of textual analysis and paleography (*diplomatia*) precisely because they were so interested in Byzantine texts and Byzantine history, both were scorned simply because of the dominating importance of religion for the Byzantines and their empire. Its history, Voltaire declared, was "a worthless collection of orations and miracles"; Montesquieu dismissed it as "a chaotic tissue of rebellions, insurrections and treachery"; Lebeau[4] treated it entirely as a tragically extended decadence from Roman glories, and Gibbon roundly denounced it as "the triumph of barbarism and religion," hardly concealing his opinion that religion itself was only a species of barbarism. Such judgments from such eminent voices had a powerful effect: Byzantine scholarship, publication, and teaching was so effectively dissuaded that it did not fully recover until after World War II.

Despite the prevailing intellectual view, religion, of course, continued to play a large role in the lives of individuals and societies. Thus began an extraordinary separation between those who studied polities and those who engaged in the practice of politics, the conduct of war and diplomacy, and the acts of everyday life.

THE STATE OF THE ART

Astonishingly persistent, Enlightenment prejudice has remained amply manifest in the contemporary professional analysis of foreign affairs. Policymakers, diplomats, journalists, and scholars who are ready to overinterpret economic causality, who are apt to dissect social differentiations most finely, and who will minutely categorize political affiliations are still in the habit of disregarding the role of religion, religious institutions, and religious motivations in explaining politics and conflict, and even in reporting their concrete modalities. Equally, the role of religious leaders, religious institutions, and religiously motivated lay figures in conflict resolution has also been disregarded—or treated as a marginal phenomenon hardly worth noting.

To be sure, the widespread refusal to extend recognition to the entire religious dimension of politics and conflict has nothing to do with *personal* attitudes toward religion; in fact, it is shared by those who may themselves practice religion quite seriously. And, of course, a positive hostility to religion as such, once quite common in intellectual circles, has become something of a rarity.

One is therefore confronted with a learned repugnance to contend *intellectually* with all that is religion or belongs to it—a complex inhibition compounded out of the peculiar embarrassment that many feel when faced by explicit manifestations of serious religious sentiment; out of the mistaken Enlightenment prediction that the progress of knowledge and the influence of religion were mutually exclusive, making the latter a waning force; and sometimes out of a willful cynicism that illegitimately claims the virtue of realism. The following examples illustrate the tendency.

Lebanon

Ordinary prejudice denigrates, but absolute prejudice ignores (cf. "The Invisible Man"), and when inadmissible facts cannot be ignored, they are instead transmuted by secularizing reductivism. Thus, for example, during the first several years of the Lebanese civil war, the antagonists were routinely described as "rightists" and "leftists" in countless press accounts, even though in most cases Lebanese political affiliations were religiously determined, as they still are.

True, the persistent alignment of many "Greek Orthodox" Christian Arabs (as opposed to Maronite Catholics) with the leading Arab-nationalist faction of the day (itself a religion-protective stance, designed to shield a minority faith by stressing membership in the majority nationality) meant that the Lebanese civil war was not exactly a Christian-Muslim conflict. But even that brutal simplification would have distorted Lebanese realities far less than the persistent Right-Left obfuscation, so clearly a product of secularizing reductivism and so clearly absurd when leaders on both sides were quintessential feudal lords and tribal chieftains.

The Intifadah

After the most inappropriate Right-Left categorization was renounced in the case of Lebanon, and confessionalism was at last plainly recognized as the salient factor in its civil war, it was the turn of the Palestinian Intifadah to be misreported because of the influence of secularizing reductivism. The Catholic Arabs who had their own excellent reasons for remaining as little involved in the unrest as possible, and who were therefore subject to Muslim hostility, were mostly ignored; the Orthodox-traditional Muslim alliance mostly enrolled by the Fatah movement was described as "moderate," as if it were the center of a typical political spectrum, and not at least as violently extremist as the Irish Republican Army.

Vietnam

Before the Lebanese civil war and the Intifadah, secularizing reductivism restricted the otherwise exhaustive journalistic reportage and diplomatic reporting of Vietnamese affairs.

From the later 1950s, every demographic, economic, ethnic, social, and, of course, military aspect of the conflict was subjected to detailed scrutiny, but the deep religious cleavages that afflicted South Vietnam were hardly noticed. In fact, the acute tensions between the dominant Catholic minority, a resentful Buddhist majority, and several restless syncretic sects were largely ignored until Buddhist monks finally had to resort to flaming self-immolations in public squares, precisely to attract the attention of Americans so greatly attentive to everything else in Vietnam that was impeccably secular. Only then did it occur to the responsible U.S. policy officials that religion was an important factor in popular perceptions of the Saigon leadership and that a Buddhist identity might be a desirable attribute in a president of the Republic of Vietnam.

Sudan and West Irian

Currently, the same perceptual syndrome has been manifest in places as disparate as Sudan and West Irian; in both cases, missionary-converted Christians and animists have been resisting Muslim governments that combine inherent official support for proselytization with straightforward forced conversions and, in the Sudanese case, with attempts to impose Islamic law, which allows only a choice between conversion and death to unbelievers and a degraded status for "peoples of the book" such as all Christian denominations.

Here again, struggles in which religion is the central factor are misreported as primarily racial, regional, or colonial by secularizing reductivism. Thus in Sudan, the antagonists are described as "Northerners and Southerners" as if they were the antagonists of the American Civil War, or as "Arabs and Negroes" (with the latter often rendered as "Blacks," in a grotesque misapplication of U.S. terminology). In fact, a vast majority of Sudanese Muslims are dark-skinned Nilotics (and not uncommonly darker than many sub-Saharan Africans), and most of the Christians and animists of Sudan are also Nilotic, not Negroid. True, especially after years of fighting, there are relatively few Muslims in the southern parts of the country and fewer Christians in the northern parts, but it is not the geographic distinction that induces the struggle.

In West Irian, the Indonesian authorities, their military and police personnel, and the Javanese settlers who arrive with official assistance are all Muslim and naturally inclined to treat native animists with contempt (though at least no effort appears to have been made to impose the radical choice between conversion and death). On the other hand, native Christians, the product of missionary activity under Dutch rule, are repressed because they once formed an emerging elite and have thus been prominent in the resistance to Indonesian colonialism. Religion is thus a central factor in West Irian's greatly underreported travails (as in Timor's extended agony), but once again as in the case of Sudan, the bashful refusal to contend with religion obscures local realities.

Iran

When secularizing reductivism distorts not the detail but the core of policy, a disastrous outcome should not be a surprise. Even nonspecialists, with only a generic interest in the region, could hardly ignore the most salient feature of Iran's history: the unique alternation of its clashing identities, with "Iranic" periods under rulers at least tolerant if not actually secularizing (whose favorites were often Christian Armenians, Assyrian Nestorians, Zoroastrians, or, lately, Baha'is), giving way to "Islamic" periods dominated by Shii orthodoxy and punctuated by outbreaks of religious fanaticism.

Given this well-known background, U.S. monitoring of Iranian politics should always have included their religious dimension, at the very least to keep abreast of the attitudes and activities of the more prominent religious leaders. But in a particularly dogmatic example of secular reductivism, the one recorded attempt to do just that within the Central Intelligence Agency before the revolution was vetoed on the grounds that it would amount to mere "sociology," a term used in intelligence circles to mean the time-wasting study of factors deemed politically irrelevant.[5]

When the popular revolt against the shah of Iran became threatening enough to attract U.S. attention, secularizing reductivism intervened again, to greatly distort U.S. analyses and then U.S. policies. What the participants themselves explicitly proclaimed as an Islamic revolutionary movement, and what was so transparently a perfectly typical if unusually violent religious reaction to Westernizing modernization by an authoritarian regime, was variously ascribed to (a) political/constitutional opposition to autocracy (although then, as now, it was rather the norm in Iran's political culture, as in the region as a whole), (b) economic resentment at wealth inequalities especially on the part of newly urbanized masses (another norm, which causes no serious uprisings elsewhere), (c) anger at the regime's corruption (yet another norm, also compatible with political stability elsewhere), (d) the specific social resentment of the traditional (Bazaari) merchant class at the rise of a new class of large-scale entrepreneurs, and (e) "normal" repression. In other words, political, economic, and social motives were all considered important, while the religious motive, though salient, was slighted as a surface phenomenon.

Characteristically, a constrast was drawn in U.S. reporting between "pious" (traditional, therefore necessarily in decline) and "modern" Iranians (the "wave of the future"), when in fact it was the most earnestly pious who were the most modern in their ability to control Iran's fate, while Westernizing "moderns" and their attitudes were being made obsolete by the course of events.

It must be admitted that the situation probably allowed no successful policy, but false diagnosis was inevitably followed by false prescriptions: at various times during the intensifying crisis, the shah was enjoined by U.S. officials, including the president himself, to "broaden the basis" of his regime by accelerated constitutional reforms and immediate ministerial changes; he was advised to improve income distribution as quickly as possible and to urgently implement highly visible measures against corruption.

A demoralized and physically debilitated shah duly complied by forming a new cabinet, promising constitutional reform and redistribution, and ordering the arrest of some prominent court-connected financiers and former ministers not especially venal. Naturally, these efforts failed to have the desired effect (though they were lethally effective for the former favorites imprisoned at U.S. instigation on corruption charges, who were tortured and executed once both the shah and his U.S. mentors left the scene). The mass agitation, quite otherwise motivated, duly continued until it was fully successful with the advent of the Ayatollah Khomeini's regime.

Confounding the secular reductivism that imprisoned U.S. analysts—official, journalistic, and scholarly alike—it turned out that the new regime could easily remain in power in the years that followed even though it was less "broadly based," no more redistributive, and if anything more corrupt than its predecessor, because of the purely religious authority of its leadership and because of the pervasive religiosity of its public conduct.

IGNORING THE INTRACTABLE

The Iranian case suggests yet another motive for secularizing reductivism: unlike political problems at least theoretically amenable to political reforms and socioeconomic travails remediable by appropriate social engineering, religion is an intractable force that can be quite unresponsive to all the normal instrumentalities of state power, let alone the instrumentalities of foreign policy.

Had U.S. analyses admitted Iranian reality in 1979—that the revolt was motivated not by conventional political, economic, and social dissatisfactions but by religious hatred for the Westernization (always perceived as Christianization) that sudden oil wealth had suddenly made pervasive—U.S. policy would have been left quite impotent, unless, of course, it would have been deemed fit to appease the revolt by actually promoting the sort of Islamic obscurantism and outright religious oppression that characterizes Saudi Arabia (where conversion to Christianity is only one of the many crimes of free expression punishable by execution). By refusing to admit that the culprit was Westernization itself, which the Muslim masses found so profoundly disorienting and so corrosive of traditionally authoritarian relationships between men and women and between parents and children (as well as crypto-Christian), U.S. analysts could imagine that the revolt was not aimed at the West and thus at the leading Western power, the United States.

It was this "preferred reality" that guided U.S. policy. Hence the disastrous quality of the advice given to the shah (who had more than a whiff of grapeshot at his command until quite late in the day but no will to use force) and the fatal delusion revealed by the upkeep after his departure of a still-numerous U.S.

diplomatic mission in Tehran, the most tangible manifestation of the mistaken belief that the revolt was only religious in form, while being actually (anti-shah) political in content.

Throughout the final crisis of the regime, the unpleasant reality that the shah was opposed because he was seen as too close to the United States of America, and thus to the (Christian) West, was reversed in prorevolutionary apologetics, which held that anti-U.S. sentiment was only caused by past U.S. support for the shah. This reversal of the terms of the question, the central theme of anti-shah propaganda aimed at U.S. opinion and at responsible U.S. officials before the final success of the revolt, and, of course, calculated to inhibit U.S. efforts to save the shah's regime in extremis, was widely accepted by U.S. observers (and still is, in some quarters).

True, Khomeini's Paris-based propagandists were skillful, indeed. As always, however, those who believed them were predisposed to being deceived—in this case by the secularizing reductivism that would not admit the importance of a religious movement as such and much preferred the alternative depiction of a conventional political reaction to autocracy and its foreign patron. The result was to magnify hugely the true importance of the shah and of U.S. assistance to his regime, both in fact secondary in the context of the far broader struggle between entrenched religion and societal innovation. Typically, even in the aftermath, belief in the reductivist reversal still persisted, notwithstanding the evident hostility of the new Islamic regime toward other Western powers that had done nothing to support the shah and toward the Soviet Union, which had long sustained the anti-shah Tudeh party; quite rightly, Khomeini always regarded communism as a Christian heresy and the Soviet Union as merely another manifestation of the hated West.

MATERIALISTIC DETERMINISM AND ITS LIMITATIONS

At a time when religious figures are playing leading roles in some of the most travailed parts of the world (for example, Polish prelates, the pope himself, Archbishop Tutu, and the Dalai Lama), when religiously motivated conflicts are all too prevalent, and when a variety of international mediation and reconciliation efforts explicitly based on religious values or carried out by religious leaders or institutions have been sufficiently plausible to attract governmental participation, it is clearly urgent to overcome the varied inhibitions that continue to obscure and distort both official and unofficial analysis when religion is involved.

There is no generic remedy for prejudice other than a greater personal awareness of its reach and of its sometimes very subtle forms. But there is also a quasi-methodological aspect to the question, which transcends the scope of explicitly religious phenomena. It has been widely noted that materialistic determinism remains prevalent in American political discourse, even as (dialectical) materialism is being so broadly repudiated in the lands in which it remains the official ideology. As soon as it is noted that X country is afflicted by political instability or social unrest, economic amelioration is immediately offered as the sufficient remedy; as soon as the prospect of Y secessionism in country X is discussed, the diseconomies-to-scale of separation are suggested as compelling reasons that will inhibit separatism. Of course, economic incentives are routinely suggested as the sovereign remedy to all forms of conflict.

In such cases, a crude materialistic determinism slights nonmaterial motivations, always important and not infrequently decisive. Such motivations are often ethnic, but as often they are spiritual; the latter in turn are often personalistic and socially inchoate (as in the May 1968 Parisian uprising), but as often they are constituents of structured religious beliefs.

Now that the Marxist-Leninist challenge to democratic, free-market capitalism has virtually collapsed, it is easier to recognize that the latter is faced by more fundamental "communitarian" and spiritual challenges, though of course there is no Great Power ready to instrumentalize them for its own strategic purposes, as the Soviet Union long instrumentalized Marxism-Leninism.

Even as the wholly superior performance of democratic capitalism in providing widespread prosperity is being universally accepted, more attention is being focused on the alienating effect of its integral free-market dynamics, which disrupt established communities and social relations by the ceaseless change they cause. Although the competitive stimulation of novel ideas and fashions is the greatest achievement of democratic capitalism, it is also inherently corrosive of the customs, norms, and values that integrate individuals in families, communities, faiths, and elective affinity groupings.

Labor-market dynamics, to cite the most obvious example, promote the efficiency-maximizing flow of individuals to new employments in localities perhaps quite distant by offering greater individual remuneration; in this process, residential stability is only a "rigidity," a harmful impediment to efficiency routinely blamed for structural unemployment. Yet residential stability is essential for the growth and preservation of most social relationships, which in turn provide a reinforcing framework for the stability of family life. In that regard, "economic man" is fully alienated man, ready to abandon friends, neighbors, and perhaps his (extended) family for incremental material rewards.

Equally, in democratic capitalism it is the market that is supposed to determine the development of new infrastructures, housing, and industrial facilities—but the logic of the market ignores the resulting mutilation of neighborhoods and dilution of established communities.

The inherent conflict between economy and community has, of course, long been recognized (Weber's formulation is classic), but when democratic capitalism first intervened to feed the hungry, clothe the naked, and liberate individuals imprisoned in narrowly restrictive traditional societies, its alienating side effects were properly regarded as well worth the price. The very success of democratic capitalism, however, depreciates its continued achievements. The greater the supply of goods and services, the less likely are the already prosperous to accept increments of prosperity as sufficient compensation for the disruptive social effects of free-market forces. And the greater the scope of the individual liberty already assured by democratic capitalism, the greater the perceived cost of its corrosive effects on customs, norms, and values.

What can perhaps be best described as a *communitarian* reaction to democratic capitalism is already manifest in many ways, from the worldwide rise of fundamentalisms (Buddhist, Christian, Hindu, Islamic, and Jewish) to the antigrowth policies of an ever-increasing number of local authorities throughout the industrialized world—policies seemingly motivated by purely localized considerations yet paralleled so widely, and seemingly preoccupied with the material (X highway versus Y housing), yet countermaterialist in their essence. Environmentalist resistance to the logic of the market, also at least in part an expression of communitarianism, is frequently rationalized in materialist terms (health impacts, the flooding of coastal areas by the melting of polar ice caps, etc.) but it, too, has a large spiritual element, if only in the form of nature worship.

Whatever interpretation may be imposed on these ambiguous and complex phenomena, it seems quite certain that materialistic determinism, always a poor predictor, is even less likely to be predictive in the future.

REMEDIES

For governments, even administrative remedies may not be inappropriate in all cases. For example, "religion attachés" could be assigned to diplomatic missions in those countries where religion has a particular salience, to monitor religious movements and maintain contact with religious leaders, just as labor attachés have long been assigned to deal with local trade unions.[6] Intelligence organizations that already have specialists in many functional areas could usefully add religion specialists as well. Certainly one should not perpetuate administratively the misconception that religion with its institutions and leaders is necessarily a marginal factor, or necessarily a diminishing force, or necessarily a purely political (or social, or economic, or ethnic) phenomenon in religious guise.

That, clearly, is a misconception especially distorting in the case of Islam, now the source of violent agitations in the entire arc from West Africa to East Asia, which reflects an inner and *purely religious* crisis. Islam is unique, of course, in that it is the only major faith whose validity was historically affirmed by military victories;[7] theologically, it still utterly depends on the promised martial superiority of its adherents—but that is a superiority that has often been disproved in the contemporary world at the hands of Christians, Hindus, and Jews alike, raising well-concealed but clearly exasperating doubts that, in turn, induce conflictual stances. This one factor alone should warrant a belated repudiation of secular reductivism by area scholars and students of conflict.

RELIGION AND CONFLICT RESOLUTION

In contrast to the millennial role of religion as a source of conflict, the increasing role of religious leaders, religious institutions, and religiously motivated lay figures in conflict resolution[8] is a modern phenomenon.[9]

The chapters that follow examine a variety of specific cases, both in their particularities and broader implications. Others will have to judge the analytical merits of the individual studies, but precisely because of the widespread tendency to slight the significance of religious factors in conflict resolution as in other secular affairs, even the basic information presented in these may have more value than would otherwise be the case: in an era of exhaustive documentation, indeed over documentation, this remains an under documented aspect of international relations. It is symptomatic, for example, that only the very recent appearance of a collection of essays on East-West relations by Giulio Andreotti,[10] Italy's long-serving minister of foreign affairs and past prime minister, has disclosed the significance of the mediation/communication efforts undertaken over the years by the Belgian Dominican Merlon and his Union of International Research for Full Development; it turns out that the important Norman Cousins-Khrushchev dialogue was only one of Merlon's initiatives. To be sure, the quasi diplomacy of religious leaders, religious institutions, and religiously motivated lay figures, all lacking in the instrumentalities of state power, can only function within the context created by the relevant balances of power; it may therefore be argued, of these as of all conflict-resolution efforts, that they can only yield results already preordained by the balance of power.

But even a minimalist interpretation of what is feasible must acknowledge that frictional factors, institutional barriers, and sheer suspicion can prevent communication—let alone conciliation—even in situations when both sides seek to communicate, and that religious third parties, as any other third parties mutually acceptable, can overcome such impediments to actualize what was theoretically possible yet unachieved.

This minimalist interpretation, however, is insufficient—indeed, it may be said to be politically naive. As is well known, rulers and governments engaged in international disputes tend to lose their negotiating freedom of action as disputes become more intense, because the increasing attention thereby attracted raises the perceived value of what is at stake, along with the internal political costs of concessions.[11] Depending on the degree of political participation, it may be an aroused electorate, or the competitive extremism of rival factions in a ruling elite, that makes assets less negotiable and demands more inflexible.

In the context of this familiar syndrome, the conflict-resolution efforts of religiously motivated third parties can do more than merely offer a negotiating mechanism, a method of communication, or any other such purely procedural assistance. By introducing the authority of religion into the negotiating equation, they enable the parties, if they so desire, to concede assets or claims to that authority itself so to speak, rather than to their antagonists. Concessions previously regarded as intolerable evidence of a lack of fortitude, may become politically acceptable if they can be presented as acts of deference to religion—always assuming that the religion in question is not itself viewed with hostility.

By thus reducing the vulnerability of rulers and governments on each side to accusations of weakness, the range of politically feasible negotiating positions is expanded, more options for solution become available, and the chances of reaching a settlement are increased accordingly. Hence in the degree that the invoked authority of religion has internal political validity for the parties, warranting a deference that neither side may show to the other, religiously based conflict resolution can ameliorate the objective circumstances of the conflict and not merely operate within unchanging constraints.

Religion, to be sure, is only one of the possible sources of third-party authority; most notably, the U.N. Security Council has often fulfilled that function,[12] though its permanent membership of Great Powers can itself inhibit deference in some cases.[13] Again, parties in conflict in need of relief may choose to invest the U.N. secretary general with an individual authority that they may have utterly denied until then.

That this dimension of religiously based conflict resolution is not unique does not diminish its importance, however; it warrants further study, as do the other dimensions, none of which can claim methodological exclusivity either. Certainly, secularizing reductivism should not dissuade us from examining the methods and results discussed in the studies that follow, which are in effect the interim reports of a continuing project.

Notes

1. John Henry, Cardinal, Newman (1801–90), the Anglican convert to Catholicism whose *Apologia pro vita sua* is an indispensable autobiography.

2. Charles Du Fresne, sieur Du C. (1610–88), French historian, numismatist, philologist, genealogist, and topographer, author, inter alia, of the still invaluable *Glossarium ad scriptores mediae et infimae graecitatis*.

3. The French Benedictine Dom Jean Mabillon (1632–1707); we owe the word *diplomacy* (originally the study of documents, hence treaties, etc.) to his *De re diplomatica*.

4. Charles, author of the monumental *Histoire de Bas Empire* (1757–1786), whence that periodization.

5. James E. Bill, *The Eagle and the Lion: The Tragedy of American-Iranian relations* (New Haven: Yale University Press, 1988), 417. The analyst who proposed the study was the CIA's Earnest R. Oney; following his retirement, he did carry out the study, on contract, after the revolution.

6. In smaller missions, this function could be added to the portfolio of the cultural attaché.

7. "Muhammad was his own Constantine," as Bernard Lewis has written. He and his disciples did not merely convert an empire but created one, on the sole basis of their religion, and their religion's truth was proved to its followers by their victories on the field of battle. Hence the attributes of Allah, as the giver of victories (Nasr), the giver of conquests (Fath), the giver of supremacy, and so on. The crusades, by contrast, were neither formative nor spiritually determinant for Christianity, in which the possession of secular power is at best irrelevant if not compromising ("The meek shall inherit . . .").

8. Herein used throughout to mean the resolution of conflicts by whatever means, without reference to the "conflict resolution" school of thought within the contemporary disciplines of political science and international relations.

9. It is, to a degree, a case of convergence: while secular politics are increasingly preoccupied by essentially spiritual matters (e.g., the abortion question and the varied

aspects of alienation), simply because the totality of the material is depreciated by the material abundance of post industrial societies, religious leaders and institutions are increasingly preoccupied by secular matters, because the purely devotional is likewise depreciated. To be sure, the violence of war is undoubtedly an evil to be diminished, for Christianity, at least, as is hunger and human distress in general; on the other hand, for Christianity, at least, nothing earthly is supposed to be of decisive import either—all alleviations of human suffering in the "vale of tears" being necessarily marginal when compared to the eternal life of the soul.

10. Giulio Andreotti, *L'URSS vista da vicino* (Milan: Rizzoli, 1989), 307–21.

11. This is illustrated most recently, and most dramatically, in the Falklands/Malvinas conflict. On the British side, the rather casual promise of a former minister that the wishes of the inhabitants would be respected in any disposition of the islands was transformed into a fundamental principle that could no longer be contested by any British political party.

For parties that find themselves entangled in unsuccessful warfare, it is easier to "accept" U.N. Security Council cease-fire resolutions than to admit their need for urgent relief from incipient, or actual, defeat. In the Arab-Israeli wars, this was the preferred course of the Arab belligerents in 1948, 1949, 1967, and 1973.

13. This was the case with Iran in the 1980s during the later phases of the Iran-Iraq war. Iran's government could not continue to present itself domestically as the leader of the "oppressed of the world," in effect at war with *all* Great Powers, and also accept their authority in council.

3 ■

Religion and International Affairs

BARRY RUBIN

For God doth know how many now in health
Shall drop their blood in approbation
Of what your reverence shall incite us to.
Therefore take heed how you impawn our person,
How you awake our sleeping sword of war.

Henry V to the Archbishop of Canterbury
Henry V (Act 1, Scene II)
William Shakespeare

United States foreign policy in recent decades has often misread the importance of religion as a factor in the national politics and international behavior of some countries and regions. This has sometimes led to incorrect analysis and erroneous policy responses that have proven quite costly. If previous experience is correctly evaluated, however, the United States should be able to avoid potential future disasters.

The foundation of this problem is the generally accepted reading of European history that American political leaders, policymakers, and intellectuals have applied to Third World realities, often in an uncritical manner. In this context, religion has been perceived as a declining factor in world politics. There are three principal errors in this perception:

1. In modern times religion has increasingly been seen in the West as a theological set of issues rather than as a profoundly political influence in public life. Having studied the development of religion over the centuries and having been influenced, in particular, by such events as the early Christian schisms, the Protestant Reformation, the Catholic Counter Reformation, and the European wars of religion, some Western thinkers in the past two centuries have come to believe that debate over theological questions is what makes religion political. For instance, disputes historically took place over the nature of Jesus or whether clergy should be allowed to marry. The example of the Medieval question of how many angels could stand on the head of a pin was used to ridicule the idea that religion is a key aspect of practical political disputes.

In many areas of the world, religion should be seen as a central political pillar maintaining the power of any ruler—a major pole in determining the people's loyalty—and as a key ingredient in determining a nation's stability or instability. In short, the issue is neither the content of a given religion nor one group's attempts to convert another group. Rather, religion plays its role as an important defining characteristic of politically contending communities. Yet, in the absence of a heated theological debate—or on the assumption by some modern Western scholars that such debates are trivial and abstracted from real considerations of power—religion as the prime communal identity has, until recently, been too often neglected.

2. The expectation that religion would inevitably decline in the process of Third World modernization was wrong. Noting the secularization process in most of the West during the eighteenth, nineteenth, and twentieth centuries, some observers have assumed that the rest of the world would follow the same pattern. It was expected that modern ideas, such as science, technology, secularism, and humanism, would overcome the religious concept of the universe that dominated premodern society. This position fails to comprehend several points that will be explored later in this chapter, including the fact that modern ideas came to many countries as imports, were often perceived as forcibly imposed or imperialistic, and, therefore, were viewed suspiciously and as being out of tune with the prevailing political culture.

3. The West—including the communist regimes—tended to misapply Marx's concept, accepted widely in some quarters of the Western intellectual tradition, that religion is the opiate of the masses. This concept was taken to mean that religion was a distraction from the important things of life and that the chance to improve one's existence in this world would obviate the need for a system that could only promise rewards in the world to come.

Marx himself and many others neglected the point that opiates are addictive. Heroin addicts usually can be weaned from their drug only by the use of methadone, an equally addictive drug that is dispensed by government authorities and that provides no "high." This is analogous to the role of comprehensive secular ideologies that revolutionary regimes often try to push onto the masses from above in lieu of religion. They must be imposed continually and bring relatively little satisfaction. Moreover, the substratum of religious belief often continues to exist underground, awaiting some opportunity to reassert itself as an ideology. Thus, Ayatollah Ruhollah Khomeini provided a better aphorism than Marx when he commented, "The masses are naturally drawn to religion."

Indeed, Marx's contemporary, Moses Hess, also understood far better than Marx the social function of religion. He used the word *opium* to denote a medicine rather than a drug:

> The people, as the Scriptures say, have to work in the sweat of their brows in order to maintain their lives of misery. . . . Such a people, we maintain, needs religion: it is as much a vital necessity for its broken heart as gin is vital for its empty stomach. There is no irony more cruel than that of those who demand from utterly desperate people to be clear-headed and happy. . . . Religion can turn the miserable consciousness of enslavement into a bearable one by raising it to a state of absolute

despair, in which there disappears any reaction against evil and with it pain disappears as well: just as opium does serve painful maladies.[1]

STRONG RELIGIONS, WEAK STATES

For several reasons, these points and the political importance of religion reverberate with special strength in Third World countries. First, the states of Africa, the Middle East, and Asia emerged to deal with modernity and industrialization in a way different from the West. Nationalism, for example, is largely a novel and foreign concept for these new states. Religion and clan (or ethnicity) were the primary, tightly entwined roots of ideology and loyalty in the long histories of their peoples. The nation-state is an existential notion that existed in practice before the concept was defined or accepted by the people. Moreover, religion has the form of an indigenous idea, developed or adapted through long internal practice. In contrast, nationalist, Marxist, humanist, and secularist ideas are imports that often are viewed with some suspicion, if not hostility.

Not having experienced a long period of communal fusion into a nation, these societies continue to see religion, clan, ethnicity, and other such factors as the markers of community identity. In the Middle East, national identification is still largely a function of religious affiliation. One's community is either Sunni or Shiite Muslim, Alawite, Druze, Christian (Roman Catholic, Maronite, Copt, Eastern Orthodox, or Greek Catholic), or Jewish.[2] Iran's Islamic revolution and Lebanon's civil war are only the most obvious and salient examples of this phenomenon that is present in many other situations. The Arab attitude toward the conflict with Israel is heavily conditioned by religion. Pakistan's raison d'être is its Islamic composition. Religion is also a fundamental political issue defining community in Sudan, India, Malaysia, Indonesia, and elsewhere. In sub-Saharan Africa, the Protestant and Catholic divisions often have manifested themselves along political lines as well.

Northern Ireland is a good example of a European society where religion remains the prime communal and, hence, political as well as ideological definition. Yet in formerly communist countries, the line of political community can run between believers and nonbelievers. Poland, where the Roman Catholic church has been either the backbone of or inspiration for the opposition, is the clearest example. In places where Eastern Orthodox churches are hegemonic, like Romania, the long subordination of church to state makes that faith, both institutionally and ideologically, a weaker reed.

The disintegration of Yugoslavia provides several good examples of religion's importance as a definer of communal loyalties. The armed conflicts between Serbs, Croatians, and Bosnian Muslims are not wars of religion per se. Yet the durability of such intense hatreds among people who had so long lived side by side, spoken the same language, and practiced very similar cultures can only be explained by the different identities largely generated by being Eastern Orthodox, Catholic, or Muslim.

Religion played a role on several levels in the collapse of the USSR. Despite seven decades of communism, that country's society was in many ways far more traditional than those of the West. In addition, the USSR was still an empire, with religion one of the few ways—sometimes the only way—the distinct culture and history of national groups could be manifested. Communities were still defined largely by religion and by the language in which they practiced their faith. Ukrainians, Lithuanians, Jews, and others were distinguished by loyalty to their distinctive beliefs and practices, many of which had religious origins that had been so watered down during the communist era as to become more sentimental than ritual.

As for the Russians themselves, the eclipse of communism led to an upsurge in the Eastern Orthodox church, which is still deeply rooted in their culture. Religion seems to be a central factor among conservative and right-wing nationalists, who are trying to build on Russian traditions to advocate a more chauvinistic foreign policy—including reestablishment of the USSR as a Russian empire—and a discriminatory attitude toward minority groups.

These points also hold true for the "Muslim" republics of the former Soviet Union, but in their case, speakers of Russian are often the victims of majority pressure. Religion's principal function is as a key element in the local ethnic revival—Azeri, Uzbek, Tadjik, and others—which may be predominantly secular nationalist in political form. But there are also considerable Islamic fundamentalist movements encouraged by Iran. These groups could eventually take over one or several republics, considerably recasting the politics of the region.

Clearly, religion is playing a more important role throughout the former USSR. No area of the world illustrates more clearly the fallacy of past beliefs that religion would be a steadily declining influence in society.

In most of the countries discussed here, politics is characterized by communal divisions within nation-states. In largely homogeneous countries, however, religion can be a central factor in the dominant political culture.

To create a Third World Marxist cadre requires years of training, while Islamic fundamentalism, for instance, is easily grasped by far more people, regardless of their level of urban intellectual sophistication. On a related note, national elites are often more cosmopolitan, cynical, and worldly than the masses. They are more likely to have been educated overseas, to speak foreign languages, and to admire some aspects of Western culture. Like their counterparts abroad, they tend to have contempt for, or at least a lack of identification with, religion.

The admission of the masses into politics and the recruitment of huge numbers of people into a broadened elite of professionals, business people, military officers, government bureaucrats, and teachers are hallmarks of the modernization process. Yet these changes also give upward mobility to the religious sectors of the population that have greater loyalty to a more narrow, religiously defined community.

Thus the secret of the influence of religion in contemporary world politics is that the modernization process, rather than causing religion to weaken and disappear, often makes its public role stronger and a more necessary part of the process of state-building or revolutionary transformation. On a subnational level, religion underlies the definition of communities, each of which may contend for political power or some degree of autonomy. Consider, for example, the Muslims of the Philippines, whose guerrilla war against the central government has led them as far afield as Libya in order to obtain aid.

Given the lack of other strong social institutions, the church or mosque and their clerical hierarchies and laypeople come to play an important function. They define values, social goals, and foreign linkages, providing a base of support for the rulers or a foundation for the opposition. In Latin America, the role of the Catholic church—or individual priests—on one side or the other of social and political issues has been of increasing importance, particularly because the church is the social and intellectual center of the masses. In South Africa, Archbishop Desmond Tutu and other clerics have become political figures in their own right. The importance of religious institutions is further guaranteed because they and their personnel are usually relatively immune from repression.

Finally, religious structures are some of the strongest institutions in many Third World countries that generally have a weak state apparatus. As the most real and powerful arm of government, the armed forces of Third World countries are always a prime candidate for seizing control of the state. Religious institutions, however, have the greatest presence and, often, influence among the people. Thus, they are an alternative route to mobilization, having the capacity to provide the backbone for opposition to the authorities. In this context, several specific situations can be reexamined.

LEBANON

Lebanon's modern political system rested on an agreement among elites that divided power in a proportionate way. The following factors unhinged the compromise arrangement that had been enshrined in this National Pact: migration from rural areas to the cities, which brought together separate religious communities; demographic changes, which increased the proportion of Shiite Muslims to Maronite Christians; and new radical ideologies, which made groups believe they might be able to seize control of the whole country. Foreign interference, although important, was essentially secondary.

The theology and history of the various religious denominations in Lebanon had a great impact on their ideological orientations, operational characteristics, and foreign alliances. It is first necessary to introduce briefly the differences among the communities before explaining their significance for U.S. policymaking.

Sunni Muslims, as former rulers of Lebanon and the largest religious group in the Arab world, have considered themselves to be an aristocracy. They have looked down on the Shiites as poor, backward, and fated to follow Sunni leadership. Sunnis were also more likely to support pan-Arabism, believing it would reinforce their power.

Maronites, the politically dominant group in Lebanon, are not only Christians but also Catholics directly linked to the West. This factor made them allies of

France when it ruled Lebanon, and later made France willing to reciprocate by supporting the Christians. Thus the Maronites see themselves as a besieged Western community in the Middle East whose interests are threatened by pan-Arab nationalism, and this idea is reinforced by their clergy.

Although Sunni Muslims and Maronites historically have been the two main forces in Lebanon, a third group, the Shiite Muslims, has become the largest single community there. In the past, the Shiites were uneducated, poor peasants living in Lebanon's neglected south. Then Shiites began migrating to the cities, where they gained higher level education and built communal self-consciousness. Charismatic clerics, notably the Lebanese Shiite founder of Amal, Musa al-Sadr, began to organize the Shiites in order to demand more rights. The Shiites' historic antagonism to the Sunnis began to reemerge. Theologically, the Sunnis were blamed for "stealing" in the seventh century the post of caliphate, the leadership of the Islamic state and religion, from the Shiite candidate, Ali, and from the family of the prophet Muhammad. Historically, Shiites have complained about Sunni oppression. Furthermore, the Shiites structurally were oriented more toward independent clerical leadership and charismatic leaders than were the Sunnis. Ideologically, the Shiites questioned the pan-Arabism that sought to unite the mainly Sunni Arab world under Sunni rule, providing over the decades little advantage for Lebanese Shiites.

Subsequent events made the Lebanese Shiite Muslims feel more distinct from Sunni Muslims. The Iranian revolution was the most important factor. The critical political issue was whether the Shiite community in Lebanon would see itself as being more Lebanese or more Shiite. In other words, would they identify themselves as a community within Lebanon seeking more rights or with Tehran's revolutionary Islamic fundamentalism so as to make Lebanon a Shiite-Islamic state? The former idea dominates the Amal faction; the latter is espoused by the Iran-backed group known as Hizbollah.

The Lebanese civil war, with the many shifts of alliances and advantages from its onset in 1975, has been essentially a battle among religiously defined communities, although they often divided into subfactions on other grounds. The maximal aim of each group—Maronite, Sunni, Shiite, and Druze—has been to dominate Lebanon; the minimal goal has been to achieve internal unity of the faction and to defend its own territory. The Syrians became the patrons of the Druze and of subfactions of the other three communities. During its 1982 invasion of Lebanon, Israel tried to consolidate the Maronites' grip on power. At that time, the United States became involved directly in Lebanon, but put too much stress on ideological factors. Some top policymakers in the United States viewed Christians as pro-Western moderates, saw Shiites as pro-Iranian fundamentalists, and mistakenly labeled the Syrians as Soviet surrogates. That analysis was too rigid and exaggerated Moscow's role. In fact, the main groups were primarily concerned with their own religiopolitical interests. Broader ideology or international alliances were distinctly secondary.

In this context, these same policymakers became preoccupied with the question of legitimacy of the government in Lebanon. Because Amin Gemayel was president and was battling Syrian forces, he was given U.S. support. This approach of supporting one beleaguered faction contrasts with the successful policy of the Eisenhower administration in 1958, when U.S. leverage forced Maronite concessions that reconciled the other groups, producing 17 years of relative stability and continued Maronite primacy.

In 1982 U.S. policymakers would have been far better advised to recognize the legitimacy of the concerns of other religious communities, build relations with those groups, and broker a compromise. Since many of those concerns derived from economic deprivation and lack of political power in addition to religion, compromise was possible. The old Sunni elite and Amal, along with their clerical supporters, would have been open to a deal. An accord might have included reducing Syrian influence, a larger share of power for Shiites (especially patronage and aid to south Lebanon), and Sunni reintegration into the government coalition.

Amal's faction, engaged in a struggle for hegemony with Hizbollah, would have welcomed aid in order to defeat its rivals and to bring material gains to the Shiite community. The conflict between Amal and Hizbollah for control of the Shiite community, which is the main source of anti-American terrorism, was fought as a theological battle in which both sides used religious justifications.[3] Still, the victory of Hizbollah and its radical fundamentalism was never inevitable because Amal offered equally valid theological arguments.

The Druze would have been harder for the United States to deal with—it was Druze artillery that shelled the U.S. Marines at the Beirut airport—but they, too, wanted a larger share of political participation. It is likely that Syria would have used its military power and influence over the Amal and Druze factions to try to block any United States–arranged pact. Still, given the central role of religion rather than ideology, such an effort might have succeeded and would have been preferable to the drift that led to the ensuing debacle and the deaths of so many U.S. citizens. The key then and now to Lebanon is to see its civil war not in ideological terms, but as a conflict with deep historical, social, and economic roots among groups that define themselves in religious terms.

IRAN

Perhaps the best example of the centrality of religion as a factor in international affairs lies in the recent history of Iran. Lebanon's communal rivalries are religiously based, while Iran's ideology and movements manifest themselves through religious vocabulary and institutions.

The Iranian revolution was influenced and caused by a number of specifically Iranian factors. Some of these had implications for other countries. Religion, for example, was a major factor. Although Iran has a tradition of anticlericalism, clerics were highly respected and tended to be the most articulate and educated people who had regular contact with the masses. The clergy had accepted secret subsidies from the shah, Muhammad Reza Pahlavi; nonetheless, when his government came to be considered illegitimate, the clergy was the group least compromised by collaboration with or infiltration by the government.

The ideology of Iranian religious leaders embodied large elements of traditional thought and culture and provided the only completely developed alternative to Western, Marxist, and modernist worldviews. Moreover, the clergy, mosques, and religious schools enjoyed a certain immunity from repression that other groups such as students and merchants did not have.

Western observers and, particularly, the U.S. government viewed religion in Iran under the shah as a weak and declining institution. As the Iranian people began to look for a source of identity during a period of turbulent change in the 1960s and 1970s, however, religion was being reinforced. Islam came to embody the country's ethos, filling a niche usually occupied by secular nationalism. In short, religion represented authenticity.

Just as religion was underestimated, so were its clerics. Although they were perceived as unworldly, naive ascetics, some of the Iranian clerics actually were shrewd, ruthless, worldly politicians. They were capable of maneuvering and mobilizing bases of support for themselves and were adept at propaganda.

In the Ayatollah Khomeini, the revolution had a charismatic, unbending man who used religion skillfully as a tool to manipulate power and who compared to Lenin as a compelling theorist and masterful leader. Khomeini's ideology was only one interpretation of Islam and of Shiite Islam, in particular. But it was one that lent itself to an extremist, xenophobic, and intolerant concept that became the governing ethos of Iran's Islamic republic.

The Iranian case raises a larger question about the difficulty that many members of the foreign policy community in the United States have in comprehending the role of religion in international affairs. Although religion is generally concerned with the problem of evil in the world, secular U.S. diplomatic thought is not. Holding that rational, national interests are the root of human and state motivation, many policymakers and diplomats have become incapable of understanding certain phenomena.

Motivated by transcendent beliefs, the religion-based ideology of Iranian and Lebanese Shiite fundamentalism obeys rules different from the materialism-based system of thought that dominates U.S. policy-making. Consequently, inaccurate assessments are often made of how such religiopolitical forces will behave.

With regard to Iran, the United States deemed it impossible that a fundamentalist government would take power; inconceivable that Khomeini would mean what he said; unexpected that Tehran would seize U.S. diplomats as hostages; unbelievable that Iran would continue a war with Iraq long after the battle was counterproductive; and irrational that Khomeini would call for the murder of author Salman Rushdie at the moment Iran needed Western investment for reconstruction. In addition to shortcomings of analysis—or even when analysis is reasonably accurate—policymakers face the even more difficult problem of how to deal with such situations.

The strategic, economic, and political factors that would seem to rule out the course Iran has taken during the last decade may eventually triumph. Tehran finally did release the American hostages and end the war. In any given crisis, however, the country's ideology will produce different decisions. Pragmatic choices regarding the hostages and the war were made in order to keep the Islamic government in power, enabling it to carry out its programs on every other front.

Failing to understand this principle, the administration of Jimmy Carter underestimated the radicalism of the Iranian revolution and then tried to overcome Iranian suspicion and antagonism by offering minimal concessions. Similarly, the administration of Ronald Reagan believed Tehran would be moved by appeals to its realpolitik interests. It thought that Iran must be either pro-West or pro-Soviet, while Tehran's religiously based ideology made it see the world in totally different terms. U.S. efforts in Iran failed completely, with resulting embarrassment and political costs.

The type of problem inherent in the Iranian case has broader importance. The West has often assumed that religion is shed in order to form national self-consciousness. As argued here, however, in the Third World, nation-state nationalism often is nonexistent and the state apparatus is relatively weak. In such areas, religion can be the strong institution that provides a central element in the building of a popular and national identity.

The type of religion in a region also must be understood. Politicized Christianity tends toward some form of Western ideology that may be pro-capitalist or, in the case of liberation theology, neo-Marxist. Islam, however, provides an alternative view of the world, institutional structure, and set of goals.

FUNDAMENTALISM AND INTERNATIONAL RELATIONS

The anti-Americanism of radical Islamic fundamentalism does not result from some mistaken U.S. policy or from a resolvable misunderstanding. In general, Islamic fundamentalists seek to take over Muslim countries in order to revolutionize their societies. If the United States opposes such objectives—and U.S. national interests make this inevitable—then the two forces are going to be adversaries.

It is a mistake, however, to assume that radical Islamic fundamentalism will inevitably win, just as it is a mistake to assume that all Muslims are "fundamentalists." Most individuals turning back to Islam prefer the religion's traditional form. Revolutionary fundamentalist Islam is a deviationist movement, and some of its key ideas are unacceptable to truly orthodox believers. In Sunni countries, radical fundamentalists are also anticlerical—at odds with a clergy that largely supports the incumbent government. Although it could be argued, for example, that Khomeini was in line with Islamic doctrine when he called for Rushdie's murder, a dozen other Muslim states found well-grounded doctrinal rationales for ignoring him.

Heterogeneous religious populations greatly affect the stability and foreign policy of many Middle Eastern countries. Islamic fundamentalism poses a major threat to Israel, from both its Arab citizens and residents of the occupied territories. In addition, small, ultraorthodox Jewish religious parties often hold the balance of power between the larger blocs in Israeli politics. Any understanding of Israeli policy and the Arab-Israeli peace process requires an appreciation of the depth of Israel's concern about the Islamic fundamentalist determination to destroy it and the role of Jewish religious parties in the movement to create West Bank settlements. The main opposition to the PLO and the peace accord comes from the Palestinian Islamic group Hamas.

The majority of Syrians are Sunni Muslims, but the ruling establishment is overwhelmingly Alawite. In Syria, Sunnis look down on Alawites, not even considering them Muslims. This religious antagonism is at the center of the internal power struggle in Syria and is a major motive for Syria's hard-line foreign policy. In order to forge domestic unity and prove themselves good Arabs and Muslims, the Alawites try to be the most steadfast in fighting Israel and U.S. "imperialism." This reason, among others, is why past U.S. efforts to draw Syria into Arab-Israeli peace talks or to appease Syria in Lebanon (especially in 1982–84) were doomed. Iraq's Saddam Hussein followed the same pattern. Only by understanding these religiopolitical issues to the fullest extent possible can U.S. policy deal effectively with religiously influenced states or with fundamentalist movements.

RELIGIOUS CHALLENGES IN THE FORMER EASTERN BLOC

Religion is not just a problem or issue for the West. Religious worldviews and institutions were a central force challenging Marxist-Leninist governments in the Soviet Union and Eastern Europe. The Orthodox churches in the Soviet Union, on the other hand, were purely national bodies long subordinated to the state and as such were far less likely, or were structurally unable, to develop as opposition centers than was the self-ruling, internationalist Catholic church. Nevertheless, a revived religious consciousness played some role in the Russian dissident movements leading to the collapse of communism and the Soviet Union. The real question as one looks to the future is whether the broad-scale revival of Russian Orthodoxy will be used by forces favoring a nationalist, chauvinistic political vision.

In the former Soviet Union, an impressive blending of religion and nationalism was evident in the Jewish, Catholic, and Muslim communities. For instance, a revival of Jewish and Zionist sentiment, leading to a large-scale emigration movement, became a major issue in U.S.-Soviet relations. The activity of Lithuanian, Estonian, Latvian, and Armenian church groups was an important factor in promoting effective internal nationalist movements in their respective countries. In the Central Asian states that emerged from the Soviet Union, the growing Muslim population, with the potential appeal of Islamic sentiments in both fundamentalist and nationalist versions, will be a potential threat to regional stability in the next two decades. Evangelical Protestant groups that preach an extra-state loyalty may have a smaller but interesting effect as well.

These changes will challenge U.S. foreign policy in a number of ways, posing such questions as the following: How will an internal upsurge in religion affect Russia's stability and foreign policy? Will religious movements undermine Russia, or will they ultimately strengthen civil society there? Is a Russian nationalist movement going to produce an aggressive expansionism as did Marxism-Leninism?

A sort of limited and imperfect rehearsal of the challenge took place in Poland when the Catholic church and the Catholic-oriented Solidarity trade union, with aid from Polish-born Pope John Paul II, forced the Polish government to grant them a major share in decision making. The dramatic changes included holding the first free elections in the history of any communist government. Even in Poland, some U.S. policymakers tended to underestimate the power of the church as a political factor.

RELIGION AND OPPOSITION MOVEMENTS

In other major crisis areas, religion has also played a central role in shaping opposition movements. Christian churches have become leading institutions and often the motivating philosophy in a number of countries, particularly in Central America, but also in the Philippines, South Korea, and South Africa.

During the struggle against the government of Ferdinand Marcos in the Philippines, the Catholic church, led by Cardinal Jaime Sin, was a vanguard element (see also Chapter 8). By underestimating the staying power and broad base of the church-based opposition movement, the top levels of the Reagan administration almost fell into a major foreign policy disaster. The mistake was their failure to understand that the church and allied forces provided a strong doctrine and alternative to communist elements. Fortunately, a number of mid-level officials at the departments of State and Defense and at the Central Intelligence Agency had a better understanding of the situation and were able to persuade their superiors that the anti-Marcos forces represented a powerful and moderate grouping that the United States should not oppose. Otherwise, to get rid of Marcos, the church and moderates might have been driven to support the Marxist-Leninist New People's Army.

Events in Nicaragua were similar to those in the Philippines, except that in Nicaragua the moderates were driven to support the radicals. In 1978–79 the powerful, centrist Catholic church hierarchy was in the forefront of opposition to the government of General Anastasio Somoza. Despairing of success in overthrowing Somoza, the church turned to the Marxist-Leninist Sandinistas, whose armed struggle seemed the key to victory, instead of heading up a more moderate coalition.

The Sandinistas' victory posed a major problem for U.S. policy. Their success resulted, in part, from Washington's failure to listen to the Church's warnings of revolution and to work more with it and from U.S. underestimation of the Nicaraguan clerical and lay forces of Christian Democratic orientation. In this connection, many of the Sandinistas had religious backgrounds, and several of the movement's key leaders were priests. In general, as many, or more, contemporary

Latin American revolutionary Marxists have come from Christian backgrounds as from the ranks of pro-Moscow communist parties. Especially now that the former Soviet Union does not seem an attractive model, people are motivated to support revolution through the religious view of injustice, with the vision of building a better world. Throughout Latin America, more and more leftists and those willing to engage in armed struggle have traveled this ideological path.

In contrast, Catholicism does not necessarily take this same path. In El Salvador, Archbishop Oscar Romero became the most respected political figure during the 1970s, before being gunned down by a right-wing death squad. He was a leader in demanding reform and democracy, criticizing both the military and the Marxist guerrilla groups. The Catholic church, involved in a number of grass-roots efforts to organize peasants, often collided with the extreme right. Priests and nuns were threatened, sometimes killed, or forced to leave the country. The Right's justification for these attacks was that the clerics were playing a political role, which was true. The Christian Democratic Party, which led the country during most of the 1980s, was religiously motivated in its philosophy and links.

Similarly, the church became the main public force in Sandinista-ruled Nicaragua, criticizing government policies and calling for a compromise settlement with the opposition. The Managua government, unable to repress the church itself, tried to create an alternative, state-directed Catholic infrastructure, but the effort met with little success. The Sandinistas tried to woo Pope John Paul II but failed when his visit to the country ended with his being heckled by a Sandinista-organized crowd. Church opposition subsequently played a major role in the fall of the Sandinistas in the free elections of 1990.

Whether moderate or radical, theological thinking is a central force in Latin America, and its influence in politics is likely to increase in the coming years. United States foreign policy must study the trends, comprehend the stands and demands, analyze the effect on stability, and identify reformist and revolutionary religious elements in Latin America and throughout the world.

Why have Catholic bishops, priests, and nuns come to play such an important political role in nationalist, revolutionary, or pro-democratic movements? A number of factors can be cited:

- The Catholic church's leaders and property are relatively inviolate. Although individuals may be slain or attacked by death squads, governments are loathe to court international disfavor and to risk alienating hundreds or thousands of believers by directly confronting the Catholic church.
- Catholicism's international links as a movement and its connection with the Vatican in Rome make it easier to mobilize international support and more difficult for a government to dominate it. The pope always names cardinals and bishops, which allows him to choose candidates from the opposition, if he wishes.
- The Catholic church's discipline is a powerful force that makes it a de facto political party. Its cadres are dedicated and often highly educated. The

institution controls schools, radio stations, lay organizations, property, and, of great importance, its own finances.

- Catholicism has a distinct ideology, of which an important component is social justice, although the latter may be emphasized or deemphasized, depending on the Vatican and on local leadership. No matter what the government preaches, however, the church presents a fully realized, alternative worldview.
- In Pope John Paul II, the Catholic church has a strong, charismatic leader who, in spite of opposing neo-Marxist liberation theology, is a firm supporter of democracy and activism. To this end, he is influenced deeply by his own experience in Poland and by his direct support of the Solidarity movement.
- Catholics compose the great majority of people everywhere in Latin America and form a very large bloc in several dozen countries throughout Africa and Asia.

Lacking some of these advantages, Protestant denominations have had less political influence. Their divisions among sects and philosophies, along with a looser internal organization, weaken their unity. Protestant groups still remain a minority in Latin America, but there are some signs that evangelical sects will play an important, conservative role in the future.

In parts of Africa and Asia, Catholicism and Protestantism have become new sources of identity that provide a basis for political communities. These definitions at times have supplemented kinship and ethnic distinctions, welding several smaller groups into a federated arrangement. In southern Nigeria and southern Sudan, for example, Christian affiliations were set off against the Muslim affiliations in the northern parts of those countries and became prime ingredients in the civil wars there. In Nigeria, riots on religious matters annually kill from 50 to 100 people—hundreds of lives were lost in 1992—and it is possible that Islamic fundamentalist movements will become politically important in that country.

In large areas of West Africa, deepening Christian and Muslim commitments are already influencing foreign alignments. The conversion from Christianity to Islam of Gabon's President Omar Bongo was motivated, at least in part, by the lure of aid from the Muslim world. The late Côte d'Ivoire President Félix Houphouët-Boigny built the world's largest church in his home village to strengthen Christianity in his country. His personal religious beliefs probably enhanced his links with the West.

In contrast, a relatively recent influx of Christianity in other societies brings with it new ideas about political alternatives and activism. South Korea provides a good example because Christian groups of all denominations were the main forces of the ultimately successful struggle for democracy there.

Finally, South Africa is a particularly interesting case in which religion characterized the formation of both the moderate and radical opposition to the existing system of government (see also Chapter 9). Ministers and bishops, Archbishop Desmond Tutu being the best known among them, have led much of the black opposition movement. Within the African National Congress (ANC), a strong, Christian religious orientation has been the main competitor of Marxist-

Leninist ideology and the principal restraint against using terrorism as a tactic. In the dominant white Afrikaner community as well, the Dutch Reformed church has been a central ideological and political force with both pro- and antiapartheid wings. Traditionally, the church had been a mainstay in justifying white rule and a pillar of the ruling National Party. In recent years, however, with the exception of certain hard-core elements, it has basically challenged the system and aligned itself with the antiapartheid movement. The success of a peaceful settlement of the conflict in South Africa will intertwine with the future role of these theological institutions and with their influence on the political contenders. To understand or influence the outcome, U.S. policy must be attuned closely to these factors.

CONCLUSION

For several decades, the prevailing school of thought underlying U.S. foreign policy has assumed that religion would be a declining factor in the life of states and in international affairs. However, experience has shown and projections indicate that the exact opposite is increasingly true. To neglect religious institutions and thinking would be to render incomprehensible some of the key issues and crises in the world today.

As more and more people become urbanized, educated, and politicized, they will search more consciously and systematically for identity and ideology. Prescribed status and customs increasingly will come under question, and religion will be enhanced as an answer to problems. In many Third World countries, disappointment with the postindependence course of events and the discrediting of radical and Marxist philosophies may result in religiously based or influenced political viewpoints filling the vacuum.

A number of possible outcomes may affect U.S. interests. The triumph of radical Islamic fundamentalism could destroy alliances and create new crises. Such a scenario would result not from the strength of existing fundamentalist movements, but from a breakdown of current structures, socioeconomic deterioration, and despair about lack of progress.

The political manifestations of Christianity and of Catholicism, in particular, have changed from a major force against change into a factor favoring the attainment of democracy and social justice through reformist or revolutionary means. Moreover, the Catholic church has proved to be the one organized institution that has survived years of communist rule, having an almost instantaneous mass appeal.

A few decades ago, the highest foreign commitment of the United States went to a little country called South Vietnam led by President Ngo Dinh Diem. United States citizens were startled to see Buddhist monks burning themselves in graphic protest against the Diem regime, but these events proved to be the starting point for public opposition to the official U.S. engagement in Vietnam and to the instability that would overthrow Diem and help destabilize his successors.

More recently, (a) a religiously inspired revolution in Iran unexpectedly took power and followed an unpredictable course, (b) U.S. military forces suffered their single largest loss since Vietnam from a fundamentalist car bomber in Beirut, and (c) Christian-led movements brought democracy to the Philippines and South Korea—all of which posed issues for quick and difficult decision making by U.S. policymakers. No stronger argument could be made for the centrality of religion in international affairs than this graphic experience.

Notes

Reprinted from *The Washington Quarterly*, Volume 13:2, Barry Rubin, "Religion and International Affairs," by permission of the MIT Press, Cambridge, Massachusetts, and CSIS. Copyright© 1990 by the CSIS and the Massachusetts Institute of Technology.

1. Shlomo Avineri, *Moses Hess: Prophet of Communism and Zionism* (New York: New York University Press, 1987), 102.
2. Approximately four-fifths of the world's Muslims are Sunni. Shiite Muslims comprise the majority of Iranians and sizable communities in Iraq, Lebanon, Bahrain, Kuwait, Pakistan, India, and elsewhere. Shiites argue that the post of caliph should have passed to Ali, the prophet Muhammad's son-in-law, and thus reject the line of Sunni caliphs, who ruled the Muslim world for several centuries after Muhammad's death in 632. Shiite Islam is characterized also by a more independent clergy and by the belief that 12 imams, beginning with Ali, exercise religious authority that is divinely guided and thus infallible. The Alawites, a sect that combines certain Christian and Islamic beliefs, are regarded as heretical Muslims by most Sunnis. Lieutenant General Hafiz al-Assad of Syria is an Alawite. The Druze are a breakaway Muslim sect centered in the mountains of Lebanon and Syria, which combines Shiite rites with some pre-Islamic elements of religion. Walid Jumblatt of Lebanon is one of the major hereditary leaders of the Druze. The Maronite Christians, a Roman Uniate sect, adhere to some Eastern rites but have submitted to papal authority since 1736. Copts are members of the traditional Monophysite Christian church that originated and is centered principally in Egypt.
3. Martin Kramer, *Hizbollah's Version of the West* (Washington, D.C.: Washington Institute for Near East Policy, 1989), 21–22.

II ▪ RESEARCH

4 ▪

Franco-German Reconciliation: The Overlooked Role of the Moral Re-Armament Movement

EDWARD LUTTWAK

In 1945 Germany was not merely defeated—its very identity as a nation-state was invalidated, just as much of its industry and all of its larger cities were all but totally obliterated. Facing immediate hardship and sometimes hunger, unable to imagine a better future, the Germans were far from ready to atone for the unprecedented cruelties then revealed to the world. As for the French, the deep wounds of 1940 were by then aggravated by the prolonged humiliation of the German occupation and by the sheer terror evoked by even routine encounters with German security patrols on country roads or in Paris subway stations. At the same time, the revelations of the concentration and death camps more than confirmed all possible fears. In the circumstances, any attempt to effect a reconciliation between the two peoples was seemingly premature to the point of absurdity.

Greatly respected in both Japan and Germany for successfully introducing its moral-responsibility concept of labor-management relations, highly reputed in southern Africa for its bridge-building between blacks and whites, strongly based in Switzerland and significantly present elsewhere, the Moral Re-Armament (MRA) movement, created by an American, Frank Buchman, is ironically almost forgotten in the Anglo-Saxon world where it originated. Doubly ironic is the lingering suspicion with which MRA has been viewed in British and therefore American academic circles, given its genesis among students at Oxford University in the 1920s. (It was first known as the Oxford Group.[1])

An American Lutheran pastor who always retained the appearance of a stolid man of affairs, Frank Buchman was converted to evangelism in England, albeit by a fellow American, and subsequently learned from a third evangelist the meditation technique of "silent listening to God," which he called the "secret of guidance." Obviously charismatic by nature, Buchman quickly gathered a circle of devoted followers. The conventional idealism of the age, patriotic fervor, had just been shattered by World War I and Buchman's message was especially appealing to the young because it transcended the barriers of class as well as nationality.

Why did Moral Re-Armament attract suspicion at all? It was, and is, nothing more than a loose, voluntary association whose independent national branches, each quite small and locally funded for the most part, have only a handful of full-time organizers. Moreover, MRA was never seriously accused of being a sect, let alone a fanatical one, and its founder, for all his centrality (at least in regard to the subject at hand), never became the object of a full-blown cult. Undoubtedly, the overeager zealousness of early adherents was a factor; but the sources of animosity directed against MRA varied greatly. They ranged from the general rejection of all forms of religiosity by most contemporary intellectuals to the particular dislike of Buchman's enthusiastic theism in the notably disenchanted 1930s; from the frivolous, inverted snobbery evoked by MRA's favorite setting, the country-house gathering with its misleading class connotations,[2] to the hardheaded opposition of radical class warriors alarmed by the movement's message of social reconciliation;[3] from the pre-1936 misapprehension of secrecy caused by the unadvertised spread of the Oxford Group's ideas[4] to the post-1936 perception that Buchman was an appeaser or even a Nazi sympathizer.

As a matter of fact, Buchman did consort with Germans a great deal during the final prewar years, but it was with anti-Nazis that he was in contact, although this could not be widely known at the time because, for obvious reasons, his German associates could not proclaim their true beliefs.[5] (The most prominent, Adam von Trott, both an official of the regime and its determined foe, was executed after the failure of the anti-Hitler coup of July 1944.) Buchman's surviving anti-Nazi contacts were crucial (on the German side) for MRA's reconciliation initiatives, while his deep personal interest in Germany undoubtedly was the motivating factor in giving those initiatives a very high priority for the group as a whole.

Whatever its causes, MRA's dubious reputation in intellectual circles has served to obscure its important contribution to one of the greatest achievements in the entire record of modern statecraft: the astonishingly rapid Franco-German reconciliation after 1945. That, of course, was both the precondition to, and true origin of, the (Western) European integration movement that in turn transformed European politics. The historiographical record is thereby incomplete.

Given the exceptional importance of the subject—and its vast implications in the present—the history of the Franco-German reconciliation has naturally attracted a great deal of scholarly attention. Yet no contemporary student of the published sources can be faulted for ignoring the role of Moral Re-Armament in that momentous evolution from hostility to cooperation, because there is simply no mention of MRA in the huge academic literature on the subject (mostly in French and German).[6]

There matters would stand for all eternity but for the existence of both unpublished documents and indirect evidence that prove beyond all doubt that Moral Re-Armament played an important role at the very beginning of the Franco-German reconciliation. More precisely, the documents identified in this chapter prove:

1. That MRA was responsible for the first organized and substantial activity in the field in 1946–48—that is, before the many and varied similar initiatives

eventually undertaken by trade unionists, business interests, religious groupings (notably Pax Christi—see Appendix to this chapter), local border-area officials, academic bodies, diplomats, and politicians from both sides.

2. That MRA's efforts were explicitly recognized as highly consequential by the two undisputed protagonists of the intergovernmental reconciliation, Robert Schuman and Konrad Adenauer, who both used their MRA contacts to initiate and support official activities of great moment.

Most notably, Adenauer wrote to Buchman in 1951:

> It is my conviction, too, that men and nations cannot outwardly enjoy stable relationships until they have been inwardly preparing for them. In this respect Moral Re-Armament has rendered great and lasting services. . . . Very soon after the war Moral Re-Armament reached out a hand to the German people and helped them make contact again with other nations. . . . In recent months, too, we have seen the conclusion, after some difficult negotiations, of important international agreements. Here, also, I believe, Moral Re-Armament has played an invisible but effective part in bridging differences of opinion between negotiating parties, and has kept before them the objective of peaceful agreement in the search for the common good which is the true purpose of human life.[7]

Likewise, on September 13, 1953, in a speech given at the World Assembly for Moral Re-Armament in Caux, Switzerland (see Figure 4.1), Schuman praised the efforts of Buchman's supporters around the world and commended him for what he had achieved. He stated that what impressed him most about MRA was its ability to translate the MRA philosophy "into terms of international relations between countries." France and the world needed "the fresh hope which came from Caux."[8]

Before reviewing this documentary evidence—which, in any case, is merely listed in what follows, for it still awaits a full-scale archival study—it is important to recall the attending circumstances that made MRA's aim both urgently necessary and also seemingly hopeless.

THE CONTEMPORARY CONTEXT

By 1945, the classic conditions were present for an exceptionally bitter, secular hostility between France and Germany. That the two nations had just fought a war was the least of it. War, after all, is the usual source of peace, for its destructions also destroy the motives and means of further warfare: hatreds are aroused in war but also exhausted; ambitions are expressed but also cut down to fit the possible; and war-making abilities are greatly developed but also consumed. In the particular case of the French and Germans of 1945, however, the fighting of the respective armed forces that had just ended could not achieve this beneficial result, because it had been little more than marginal in the far harsher vicissitudes that spanned three generations.

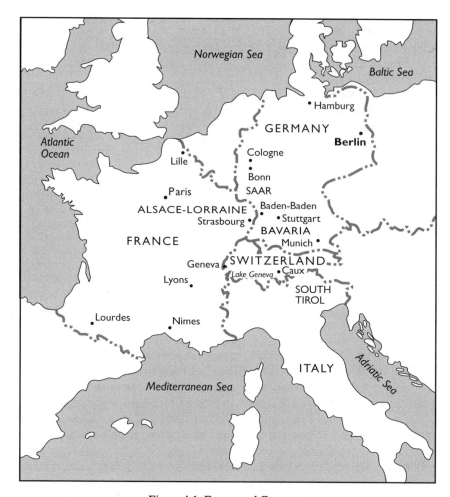

Figure 4.1. France and Germany

For the French of 1945, both World War I and the Franco-Prussian war of 1870 still lived on in vivid personal or family memories; the former had literally engulfed the entire nation (it was no Vietnam: *all* fit males had served[9]), while the impact of the latter had been exceptionally profound. France had often lost wars before without suffering any collapse of morale, but never before had her entire army been disgraced by swift, ignominious defeat, and never before had France been defeated by anything less than a multinational coalition. Hence the Prussian victory of 1870 caused the collapse of an entire collective self-image of France as Europe's preeminent martial nation. Worse still, the several weeks of regular combat were merely the prelude to a bloody insurgency marked by harsh German reprisals[10] followed, in turn, by a yet bloodier civil war.

Likewise, for the Germans 1918 had brought not only military defeat but also the end of all certitudes—from the assurance of public order to the value of the currency, and from the structure of society to its most basic mores. Moreover, because German national unity had only been achieved so belatedly in 1871, and only by the formation of the Hohenzollern empire, its downfall seemed to threaten not merely the regime but also the integrity of the nation itself.

By 1918 several million French and German servicemen had been killed, mutilated, or left as invalids from gassing in five years of combat—casualties wholly unprecedented in military history, and for the French also unsurpassed (their war dead exceeded 1.3 million, a higher proportion of all military-age males than in the case of Germany, let alone Britain[11]). The resulting aversion to renewed war was correspondingly deep, and might also have been lasting on the German side, as well, had it not been circumvented by Hitler's promise of swift, cheap, blitzkrieg conquests. Nevertheless, after the orphans of the trenches fought once more in 1940 and then again in 1944–45, the catastrophic devastation of Germany should have created a favorable climate for a reconciliation, for the Germans in their plight could only welcome it, while the French should have been inclined to magnanimity given the very small losses suffered by the French armed forces as compared to those of Germans.[12]

In reality, of course, there were no such grounds for magnanimity, for the fighting of the armed forces on each side had been almost a sideshow in the overall French experience with Germany and the Germans during World War II. On the public scene of French collective life, the swift defeat of 1940 had been followed by the humiliation of the German occupation immediately thereafter, by increasing hardships from 1941, by mounting oppression from 1942, by mass compulsory labor deportations from 1943, by episodes of outright massacre in 1944, and then, in 1945, by the stunning revelation that all known German cruelties had been only the lesser manifestations of an altogether greater evil, suddenly exposed when the slave-labor, concentration, and extermination camps were finally overrun.

Yet more vivid and emotionally significant were the personal experiences. Fully occupied after November 1942, France became a vast deployment area for the German Wehrmacht and increasingly large Waffen SS (Schutzstaffel), while the Gestapo, the yet more sinister SD (Sicherheitsdienst), and the Abwehr[13] were also present in substantial numbers. Hence many millions among the French actually lived through the terror of being herded by guns and shouts in roundups and block searches, of waiting in line for the sudden identity checks that could end in immediate labor-service deportation for any number of trivial reasons, or simply of being present when German troops were angry and looking for victims because they had themselves been bombed, strafed, or attacked by the resistance. Even those perfectly routine experiences that mostly passed harmlessly hugely amplified what was glimpsed or heard of the arrest, torture, and execution of resisters or suspected resisters and of the hunt for the Jews. Although it was French policemen and gendarmes who arrested most of them, on the routine charge of invalid identity papers, it was the sight of Germans diverted from war duties to anxiously search villages, towns, and apartment houses for men, women, and children to deport that left an indelible impression.

Thus, along with frequent memories of German troops in the guise of middle-aged conscripts plainly tired of war, visibly homesick, and all too human, there were far stronger memories that identified the very profile of the German helmet, the Gestapo's leather raincoats, and the colors of SS uniforms with an outright and genuine inhumanity, for which there was neither precedent nor mitigation. And those were the stigmata of Germans at large, not of the handful of prominent Nazi leaders known to all, or of the remote and theoretical category of Nazi party members. Finally, the revelations of 1945 combined with both the collective and personal experiences of the occupation to redefine the Germans as monsters in human form in the eyes of many, if not most, of the French people.

It was only the general belief that Germany would indefinitely remain partitioned in four zones, firmly occupied and disarmed, that stilled demands for the formal and permanent division of the country into separate states, each of them small enough to be harmless.[14] And it was only the discovery of the concentration and extermination camps that, paradoxically, dissuaded the unspoken intention of executing as many Germans as possible by invoking any sort of Nazi affiliation (in addition to those caught in SS uniform,[15] and identified war criminals, of course), of keeping German prisoners of war at forced labor till few would live to return home, and of letting famine take its course in war-devastated Germany. Had the Germans not practiced genocide so very systematically, they might have been the victims of a less thorough attempt aimed at themselves.

Strategy is stronger than politics, and the advent of the Cold War gradually altered attitudes toward the Germans all over Europe, while in France it established more and more clearly the obsolete character of the Franco-German antagonism. But that transformation of mentalities did not even begin until after 1948, when the Czech coup affirmed the symmetry between Stalin and Hitler for Europe's noncommunists, and its effects were clearly perceptible only after the 1950 outbreak of the Korean war. Even so, the rearmament of West Germany was flatly rejected by the French government and public opinion in 1955 (in the vote against the European Defense Community), and it was not widely regarded as desirable until the late 1960s.

In the immediate postwar years, by contrast, when Moral Re-Armament set out to promote management-labor harmony, only to find itself promoting Franco-German reconciliation, the notion that France might actually want to coexist with the German people, let alone with an independent German state, was too outlandish to merit discussion.

WHY MORAL RE-ARMAMENT?

MRA's resources were exceedingly modest. They amounted to Buchman's prewar contacts among surviving anti-Nazi Germans, MRA's handful of devoted French followers, and the ability of the Swiss branch to host large-scale meetings at a huge resort hotel it had just acquired at Caux, near Montreux.

These assets were particularly insignificant when compared to those of the established churches of France and Germany, whether Catholic or Evangelical. If the French and Germans were to be reconciled on the basis of their common Christianity, then the churches—with their capillary networks of parish priests and pastors, highly developed episcopal hierarchies, and numerous ancillary institutions—should have been infinitely more effective in achieving that purpose than MRA.

That was not the case, however. How effective the established churches might have been one will never know, because on an institutional basis they did little, while their affiliates and individual churchmen did not achieve much. (In addition to what follows, see the Appendix to this chapter.) Toward the end of 1945, an association devoted to Franco-German relations, the Bureau International de Liaison et de Documentation (BILD), was established at Offenburg, in the French zone of occupation, by Joseph Rovan, a Catholic activist of German origin who had survived a concentration camp, and the Jesuit Jean de Rivau. The latter was also the editor of *Documents*, a monthly journal of Franco-German relations founded by Rovan.

In fact, these were activities more governmental than religious, because both BILD and *Documents* were actually funded and controlled behind the scenes by the general secretariat for German affairs in the French foreign ministry; their goal was to influence German opinion in the French zone rather than to effect a reconciliation on a moral or religious basis.[16] In that regard, the work of the lay militant Catholic Madame Simone Veil (the future presidential candidate) was more apposite. A convert from Judaism newly released from a concentration camp, Veil manifested an astonishing altruism by almost immediately dedicating herself to alleviating the plight of the German POWs kept at forced labor in French coal mines. Such efforts were also undertaken by some local parish priests (as well as trade unionists who had access to the work camps). Finally in 1947, Rovan and de Rivau, *qua* Catholics, established a private nondenominational but religiously motivated association, the Comité d'Echanges avec l'Allemagne Nouvelle, directed by Alfred Grosser, a (Jewish) ex-refugee from Frankfurt am Main, in which the well-known Germanist, Professor Edouard Vermeil, played a leading role.

The institutional near-abstention of both the French and German churches from a task that one would have thought would have enlisted their most devoted efforts was the direct and inevitable result of a previous abstention. On the German side, both the Evangelical and Catholic churches had done very little to resist the Nazi regime. At the very least, they could have denounced known Nazi crimes loudly and early—and there was much to denounce from the start, notably the political murders of 1933–34. Their control of pulpits all over Germany, the only media of public information independent of the regime, implied in itself an obligation to witness to the truth that was largely evaded. True, resistance would have invited persecution, but that should hardly have been a deterrent to institutions that professed a martyrdom-based religion.

As far as the Evangelicals were concerned, the affirmation of the Bekennende Kirche, in contradistinction to the emergence of the Nazi-affiliated Deutsche

Christen with its unfortunate Hitler-appointed "Reich-bishop" Müller, did imply a categorical self-identification as a non-Nazi institution. But this did not, in fact, result in any strong, broad stand on absolute Christian principles. Except for its handful of martyrs, even the Bekennende Kirche's clergy muted its rather infrequent criticisms of the increasingly open brutalities of the regime. For every sermon that mildly censured the mass arrests or outright murder of political opponents, or—yet more rarely—mentioned in passing the persecution of the Jews, there were hundreds and thousands that addressed the usual themes in the usual manner, thereby implicitly affirming the normality of the situation amid increasing horrors. That vast flow of pious words quite inoffensive to the regime actually served to isolate the well-known handful of Evangelical clergymen who did speak up courageously to oppose the Nazis, and who were in any case outnumbered by those who did not conceal their enthusiasm for Adolf Hitler's achievements, if not the man or his party.

As for the German Catholic hierarchy, it enthusiastically welcomed the successful negotiation of the 1933 Concordat conceded by Hitler, which completed the reversal of the Bismarckian *Kulturkampf* by removing the last residue of the 1873 Falk Law restrictions on religious orders and religious education.[17] To obtain the Concordat (still in force) the Catholic church was evidently willing to confer legitimacy on Hitler's regime, thereby greatly enhancing Hitler's political position at a time when it was not yet consolidated and badly in need of such legitimization. In addition, several bishops and many priests explicitly endorsed aspects of Nazi policy, notably the anti-Jewish Nuremberg laws of 1934, as well as the repression of the communists. To be sure, most expressions of approval of Nazi conduct came early on, before the regime's most horrific crimes. But the moral inadequacy of the German Catholic episcopate, and of the papacy, was in any case completed by their joint failure to confront the regime in subsequent years, indeed until the very end—except when their own organizational interests were directly threatened, for example by the prohibition of Catholic youth groups. That was the burden of *Mit brennender Sorge* ("with burning concern") and the subsequent encyclical addressed to Germany, both of which studiously refrained from denouncing the murders and mass arrests of political opponents, or the increasingly more ominous anti-Jewish measures.

Actually, the institutional voices of both Evangelicals and Catholics were only raised loudly and clearly in opposition to the increasingly open promotion of "Old German" neopagan rituals under SS auspices. Yet that amounted to mere dressing up and harmless playacting as compared to most other SS activities—and was certainly insignificant on a moral plane. Of course, there were ordained chaplains with the Wehrmacht on every front, including the Eastern front where all the rules of war were simply abrogated to unleash mass cruelties not seen in centuries. The importance of that one fact cannot be overestimated.

The French Catholic episcopate, then as now more independent of the papacy than any other under its "Gallican" dispensation, was not compromised so early, of course, but it was even more deeply compromised. Petain's Vichy regime did not sponsor a rival neopagan religion, and its rendition of traditional values

(*Travail, Famille, Patrie*[18]) had an explicitly Catholic cast. More fundamentally, Petain's *l'Etat Français* may have been a puppet regime but it was not a German invention. It represented quite well the views of those among the French who were still unreconciled to the Revolution, chiefly the church-going Catholic bourgeoisie and the monarchists.[19]

The Vichy regime rejected the separation of church and state and nullified the anticlerical legislation of the Third Republic (the Combes Law) which, among other things, had ejected priests from the classrooms of state schools. The French episcopate reciprocated the favor by strongly supporting the Vichy regime until 1943, at least, when the course of the war visibly turned against its German patron. Many priests and bishops stood alongside Vichy's functionaries at countless official functions; many sermons endorsed the regime with vehement enthusiasm, not a few praised collaboration, and almost all deplored the violent acts of the Resistance, necessarily aimed at the Vichy authorities as well as the Germans.

Certainly the French Catholic church as an institution did nothing to oppose the regime, and it did not protest or resist Vichy's repression of its political opponents or its anti-Jewish legislation,[20] except for some scattered interventions on behalf of individual converts. Individual priests, nuns, and monks who helped either the Resistance or the Jews had to conceal their activities not only from the Vichy authorities and the Germans but also from their own bishops in many cases. The result was that the very few French Protestant clergy did much more good during the occupation than the vast Catholic church—and suffered correspondingly and most disproportionately.

It was in that overall context—the moral bankruptcy of the established churches—that Moral Re-Armament, for all its numerical insignificance, became a significant force when it set out to apply its own activist brand of theistic morality to the task of reconciling the French and German peoples.

MORAL RE-ARMAMENT'S METHODS

Conferences: MRA's Group Dynamics

The basic tenet of Moral Re-Armament—no different from that of most interpretations of Christianity—is that to change nations and the world, the consciousness of individuals must first change, and that in conflict situations (interclass or international) the first step in conflict resolution is to induce the parties to *listen* to one another. To do that, suitable circumstances must first be provided.

While MRA has had its occasional mass meetings, has distributed literature, and has even produced plays, Frank Buchman himself was always at his best in intimate face-to-face meetings stretching over several days, and that became MRA's preferred modus operandi. During its formative period in prewar Britain, MRA (still called the Oxford Group) found a ready-made social format for itself in the classic country-house weekend of the British gentry and aristocracy. It was in such gatherings that Buchman, from the late 1920s, first mingled followers and prospects to propagate his ideas. Subsequently, when Buchman began to concentrate on international issues, that favorite venue for Victorian political confabulations, naughty Edwardian goings-on, and literary murders of quality also became the scene of earnest MRA encounters in which trade unionists rubbed shoulders with the upper classes, and where anti-Nazi Germans met with British political figures in an atmosphere of spiritually conditioned mutual respect.

When Moral Re-Armament set out to provide a suitable venue in which German opinion makers and significant individuals could listen to their French counterparts, and vice-versa, the intimate British-style country-house gathering did not quite fit the purpose. Much larger encounters would be needed to have a significant impact in useful time. It was therefore most fortunate that in 1946, with this purpose in mind, the Swiss followers of MRA were able to acquire the enormous and enormously ornate Caux Palace Hotel, dramatically perched high above Montreux on Lake Geneva. Renamed "Mountain House," the old hotel still provides bedrooms that can accommodate several hundred, vast social rooms where visitors can all meet at once with room to spare, and all other necessary facilities, together with a most dramatic Alpine panorama conducive to elevated thinking.

When the first Franco-German encounters took place in the multinational context of the Caux conferences, MRA's new facility offered an advantage far more decisive than its beautiful Alpine view, however. At that time, and until the establishment of the Federal Republic in 1949, there was no German state-level authority, Germans were not citizens, and there was no such thing as a German passport. As enemy civilians under military occupation, Germans had few rights, and the right to travel freely was not one of them. To leave the American, British, French, or Soviet zones of occupation to visit another, Germans had to apply for a travel permit from their local military government office (*Kommandatura*, in the new-speak of the times). Badly understaffed and with no particular reason to accommodate the applicants, these local offices were invariably slow and often rejected applications for any number of reasons, or no reason at all. The American and British military governments soon broke down the barriers between their respective zones, thus creating the phantom country informally called "Bizonia." But the French and Soviet military governments had a definite policy to limit all travel that did not serve their particular purposes.[21]

The practices that applied to interzonal travel within Germany extended to foreign travel as well — except that those permits were even more difficult to obtain. Moreover, permission to leave Germany was useless without a visa that would allow Germans to enter their country of destination, and that was the far greater obstacle. Germans had no passports, only rudimentary travel documents issued by each military-occupation authority, which both consulates and border officials viewed with suspicion. The hunt was still very much on for fleeing Nazis, and the usual touristic or business reasons for foreign travel hardly applied, given the lack of hard currency and the virtual absence of external trade. Thus all German visa applicants were, at best, considered as prospective illegal immigrants; indeed, many Germans would have become economic refugees if only they could have left their devastated country (whose reconstruction was considered a matter of decades, not years). The overall result was that almost all countries simply refused to issue visas to Germans, except in unusual cases when there was some pressing intelligence, political, or economic benefit to admit them.

Nor could the problem be solved by organizing an encounter in Germany itself. Aside from the not-insignificant logistical problems—if they ran at all, trains were terribly overcrowded, and all undestroyed hotels had been commandeered by the occupiers—the zonal military governments restricted the entry of foreign citizens as much as the exit of Germans. The French authorities were especially unwilling to allow travel in or out of their zone. Even American citizens who wanted to visit the U.S. zone had to obtain permission from a special unit of the Joint Chiefs of Staff for which application delays were long, and naturally cross-travel (for example, French citizens to the British zone) was even more restricted, if allowed at all. This entire pattern of restrictions would have complicated enormously any attempt to organize MRA gatherings in Germany, what with the need to secure interzonal permits for each German and entry permits into the chosen zone for each non-German participant. In practice, it would have been impossible to obtain all those permits in timely fashion.

While a meeting in Germany would have been exceedingly difficult to organize, a meeting in France, Britain, or, say, the Netherlands was simply out of the question, even if the necessary visas had been issued. German tourists often experienced pointed acts of rudeness throughout Europe, even in the late 1950s, and in some countries (the Netherlands and Norway) they were frequently refused accommodation in smaller hotels and *pensions*. In 1946, any gathering of Germans would have invited physical attack. That is why MRA's conference center at Caux in Switzerland was of special significance, given the crucial additional fact that key members of the Swiss branch of MRA had very close ties with that country's Foreign Ministry [22] that allowed them to secure entry visas for Germans, as well as for other unfavored nationalities (a category that included virtually everybody in those days, except for Americans, Britons, and a few others). At the time, a Swiss entry visa was an impossible dream for most Europeans, let alone Germans, without serious quantities of ready cash, and yet MRA could arrange them virtually as a matter of routine. Concurrently, American, British, and French MRA disciples and sympathizers in the military governments of each zone helped German invitees obtain their exit and reentry permits. [23]

That was the second factor that allowed Moral Re-Armament to function as a far more significant force than one might have expected, a factor as important, perhaps, as the abstinence of the established churches.

MRA's modus operandi in conflict resolution was and is to engender a heightened spiritual sensitivity in both parties and to thereby induce them to enter into a genuine and deep dialogue marked by a reciprocal sense of moral obligation. In geometric terms, this amounts to a triangulation toward the desired stage of mutual moral regard, achieved by stimulating each side's religious feeling (i.e., regard for the deity). In the case at hand, if French and German invitees could both achieve an enhanced spiritual consciousness, that in itself would provide a medium in which the barriers of national antagonisms would have no place, allowing each side unobstructed access to the other's resentments, guilt, and fears, which could then, in turn, be overcome by exchanges of reassurances and expressions of repentance as well as of mutual regard, even affection. Those were the proximate aims.

In the context of the multinational Caux conferences, which were *not* primarily or explicitly dedicated to the purpose of Franco-German reconciliation,[24] the proximate aims were achieved by a variety of means. Some had a classic social-bonding character in which religion or spiritual factors played no direct part:

1. The conferences were not one-day affairs: participants came for several days at least and sometimes weeks, thereby having repeated opportunities to gradually achieve intimacy.
2. The informality that was part of the MRA style favored cohesion.
3. The lack of a housekeeping staff meant that rich and poor, French and German, among others, worked side by side in the kitchen peeling potatoes or washing up, thereby inducing the usual sense of rueful comradeship.[25]
4. The exceptional beauty of the setting induced a sort of ésprit de corps of its own (we are all privileged, because we are here).

Other means were typically of a religious character:

1. Personal declarations made in public sessions by the participants often communicated their sense of moral discovery (thereby inviting others to reveal their own) and often included a confessional element.
2. Both invocations and exhortations were made in the statements of Frank Buchman and MRA's long-time members, who were highly experienced in the subtle art of unobtrusive but effective spiritual persuasion.

To be sure, it was the combination of both sets of means that was most effective in inducing what the participants called "the spirit of Caux."[26] But at least for the 1946 and 1947 meetings, there was a further stimulant. For all the Europeans who came from formerly belligerent countries,[27] the sights and experiences offered by undestroyed Switzerland had a dreamlike character. But for those who came from devastated Germany it was sheer heaven to be in a place where bridges still stood, all buildings were intact, and hot water could be had by turning a tap. And then there was the food. In 1946 wartime shortages persisted. Moreover, the winter of 1946–47 was exceptionally harsh in Western and Central Europe, further depressing agricultural production that was already afflicted by transport difficulties and shortages of machinery, fuel, fertilizer, and both animal traction and manpower. The result was that two years after the end of the war, malnutrition still persisted, not only in Germany but even in France. Although Mountain House offered nothing resembling the old hotel's gourmet kitchen, there was no lack of food, including such great luxuries as real butter and chocolate. Early Christian ascetics had sought God by deliberate hunger. MRA's early contingents at Caux found fraternal conviviality around the dining-room tables.

Conferences: The Participants

The success of the Moral Re-Armament conferences per se was assured by the conducive atmosphere, but success in achieving the particular goal of propagating the feasibility and desirability of Franco-German coexistence (although this was not the exclusive goal) naturally depended on the nature of the invitees.

A total of 1,983 French citizens and 3,113 Germans took part in the Caux meetings of the formative postwar years of 1946 to 1950.[28] That is not an unimpressive number, but who were they? However well-meaning and spiritually responsive, participants who could play no role in shaping government policy or that of influential organizations such as trade unions,[29] nor affect the attitudes of important business entities or public opinion, would have had difficulty in applying or even propagating MRA's message. Hence a review of the qualifications of the participants is in order.

French participants from the various sectors included:[30]

Government: a total of 17, including a minister of labor, a minister of reconstruction, a minister of overseas territories (François Mitterand, the current president of France), a state secretary, two councillors of the republic, three former ministers and current members of the French parliament (Assemblée Nationale), a vice-president of parliament, six other members of parliament, and one former member.

Trade Unionists: a total of 200, including one national general secretary (farmers), one vice-president (cadres), two national secretaries (of gas and electricity workers and of electrical industry workers), a general secretary of the noncommunist CFTC Federation for the Lille area, a secretary-general (of the miners union, Nord and Pas de Calais), six members of the national executive of the CGT-FO, and two (regional) executive members of the CFTC.

Industrialists: a total of 207, including a president of the National Council of French Employers (and president of the European Employers Association), a vice-president of the National Council of French Employers, three presidents of industrial associations (textiles, jute, and artificial fibers), a regional president of the National Council of French Employers (Nord), three regional/local industry association presidents (Nord, Roubaix-Tourcoing, and Lille), a general secretary of the Young Employers Movement, a director of the (nationalized) electricity of France (EDF), a director-general of the (nationalized) SNECMA aeroengine concern, and four owner-directors of (major) industrial enterprises.

Clergy: a total of 35, including no cardinals or bishops; two monseigneurs, the director of the (highly influential, later controversial) "Témoinage Chrétien"; the dean of Strasbourg Cathedral (the border city par excellence); the dean of the Lille seminary; and a lay leader, Mrs. Marguerite Hoppenot, president of the "feminine [sic] Catholic groups."

Media: a total of 30, mainly regional press; only one national paper (*Figaro*).

Education: a total of about 100, including two university rectors (Paris and Lille) and the general secretary of the national association of French students.

German participants included:[31]

Government: a total of 82, including Chancellor Konrad Adenauer (who made a brief visit, but his adult children Paul and Georg participated in several annual conferences for extended periods), four ministers (of interior, refugees, labor, and housing), Hans Ehard, president of the Bundesrat (upper house of the federal parliament), 23 members of the Bundestag (lower house of the federal parliament), five "minister-presidents" of *Land* (regional/state) governments (Bavaria, Hesse, North-Rhine Westphalia, Württemberg-Baden, Württemberg-Hohenzollern), 18 other *Land* ministers, and 34 other members of *Land* parliaments (with 10 of the 11 West German *Länder* plus Berlin represented). (Many of those listed with their 1949 and 1950 Federal Republic titles had also attended in 1947 and/or 1948 when no such positions existed as yet.)

Opposition: three members of the national executive of the Social Democratic Party, then much more left wing than it was to become (Dr. Walter Menzel, Ernst Scharnowsky, and Dr. Elisabet Selbert).

Trade Unionists: a total of some 400, including Dr. Hans Böckler, chairman of the German trade union congress; the secretary of the above for the French zone; a regional president of the above (Berlin); a national union treasurer (mine workers); three members of the national executive of the mine workers; four other national-executive members (metalworkers, woodworkers, post office workers, and printing workers); Works Council members from I. G. Farben, Krupp, Siemens, Ford, AEG, Daimler-Benz, Bosch, and the major Ruhr mines, among other enterprises.

Industrialists: a total of 210, including the general manager, three section managers, and representatives of every pit of the Gelsenkirchen mine company (West Germany's largest with 82,000 employees and 22 percent of Ruhr coal production); the general manager of Hibernia (second largest company); the commercial director of the Hoesch coal company; the chairman of the Reconstruction Bank (Dr. Otto Schniewind); five heads of local chambers of commerce (Hamburg, Bremen, Hessen, Duisburg, and Bayreuth); the chairman of the metal industry employers association, the president of the Bavarian central bank; six chief executives (of Mannesmann, Telefunken, Siegerland Metal, Gerreshein Glass Works, Duisburg Copper, and United Rayon); and two owner-industrialists (of Girardet Printing and Goldschmidt Chemicals).

Clergy: a total of 14, including Bishop Theophil Wurm of Württemberg, president of the Council of the German Evangelical Church; Bishop Heinrich Rendtorff; Dr. Hans Schönfeld, formerly of the Ecumenical Council in Geneva (during the war); Dr. Eugen Gerstenmaier, a leading Protestant layman (and later president of the German Bundestag); Werner Schollgen, professor of moral theology in Bonn; Professor Karl Adam of Tübingen University; Pastor Hahn of Minden; Pastor Naumann of Southern Tirol; R. Egenter of Munich, a Catholic priest and professor; Georg Banasch, a Catholic prelate from Berlin-Dahlem; Pastor Herbert Fuchs of Speyer in Rheinland-Pfalz; Pastor Jörg Simpfendörfer of the Evangelische Stiftung (Foundation) in Tübingen; Oskar Daumiller of the Oberkirchenrat in Munich; and Professor Adolf Lang of the Benedictine Monastery in Munich.[32]

Media: a total of 160, including the chairman of the board of DPA, the West German press agency (Dr. Anton Betz); five publishers (of *Die Zeit, Hamburger Freie Presse, Deutsche Rundschau, Westfalenpost,* and *Münchener Merkur*); the chairman of the board of North-West German radio (British zone); the general manager of Bavaria radio; three chief editors (of *Der Abend*, DPA, and the Catholic news agency CND).

Education: a total of 35, including six university rectors (of Freiburg, Tübingen, Heidelberg, Hamburg, Kiel, and Stuttgart-Hohenheim), 19 other university professors, the chairman of the university students of West Germany, the vice-president of the above, the chairman of French-zone university students, the chairman of the university students of Bavaria, the "speaker" of the Berlin university students, and the presidents of the student councils of five universities (Heidelberg, Tübingen, Marburg, Bonn, and Stuttgart-Hohenheim).

Saar: until the 1955 plebiscite, the Saar was detached from other German lands and was indeed the scene of a French attempt to incorporate that border region. The Saar minister of justice (Heinz Braun) formed a delegation of his own, separate from the German delegation.[33]

Parallel Diplomacy

From the above it should be noted that (a) the French participation in the Caux conferences, though far from insignificant, was much weaker than the German, while obviously it was French forgiveness that was needed above all to start the process of reconciliation, as well as German confession; (b) the participation of coal industry representatives, both labor and management, was exceptionally strong on the German side, and quite significant on the French side as well; and (c) the steel industry was also strongly represented, on the French side as well via the regional exponents for the northern and northeast regions.

Actually, the imbalance in French and German participation was very well compensated by the intensive direct and indirect MRA contacts with *the* key figure on the French side, indeed the true architect of the Franco-German reconciliation, Robert Schuman, who was repeatedly the foreign minister during those years and the sometime prime minister (see the evidence in later discussion).

As for the exceptional MRA emphasis on exponents of the coal and steel industries, that turned out to be a classic case of serendipity (favorably interlinked chance, luck, providence), though it actually reflected a quite different conflict-resolution purpose,[34] because Schuman's chosen device to embody both a guarantee of nonaggression and the promise of a full reconciliation was precisely the creation of the European Coal and Steel Community (ECSC). Once considered an obscure bureaucratic-industrial phenomenon, the ECSC is now universally recognized as an initiative of world-historical importance because it was the organizational progenitor of the Common Market, itself the direct parent of today's European Community. The expressed purpose of the ECSC was to integrate the coal and steel industries on a transnational basis so as to "make war impossible," as well as to rationalize them economically (Schuman's notions of the industrial requirements of war were evidently pre-aeronautical as well as pre-nuclear). It was not Moral Re-Armament but Jean Monnet who conceived the idea, but when Schuman set out to apply Monnet's concept (publicly presented on May 9, 1950, and informally known as the Schuman Plan), it was certainly a crucial advantage for the politicians and bureaucrats on both sides that many leading French and German coal and steel industrialists and trade union leaders had already developed warm personal relationships at Caux. If MRA had done nothing else, its ancillary role in the creation of the ECSC would alone give it importance in the history of Europe.

The few French MRA disciples included some that were personally or politically close to Schuman or his associates. That is how Buchman met Schuman in 1947, and maintained contact with him thereafter, as demonstrated by the following:

1. Significant correspondence, including inter alia a Robert Schuman letter to Frank Buchman of May 31, 1948[35]
2. Robert Schuman's preface to the French edition of Frank Buchman's book *Réfaire le monde* (Editions de Caux, 1950), written when Schuman was minister of foreign affairs (it is dated March 1950) that conveys his understanding of MRA's approach to conflict resolution
3. The award of the Croix de Chevalier of the Legion d'Honneur to Frank Buchman on June 4, 1950, upon the proposal of Schuman, in recognition of Buchman's efforts for Franco-German reconciliation (this was matched by Adenauer's sponsorship of the equivalent Federal Republic decoration, the Grand Cross of the Order of Merit, for the same reason[36]).

The existence of MRA's parallel diplomacy having been proven, though the larger part was too informal to be documented, it remains to define its contents and their significance. The evidence provided by a veteran French MRA member, the presumptive devotee but credible Michel Sentis[37] — which in any case is internally very credible also — is as follows.

1. Frank Buchman did *not* suggest to Schuman the goal of reconciliation. At their 1949 meeting, Buchman asked Schuman what was the one thing that he would like to achieve before the end of his political career. To reconcile the French and Germans was the answer of the German-speaking Schuman, who was born in Alsace-Lorraine when it was under German rule, educated in Germany proper, and was once a conscript in the Kaiser's army.

2. Buchman then urged Schuman to meet with the most politically promising of his German contacts, including the former mayor of Cologne, Konrad Adenauer, who was then president of the Constitutional Assembly (Parlamentarischer Rat), which wrote the German "Basic Constitutional Law." The merits of this suggestion were *not* obvious at the time. The future chancellor and architect of Germany's renaissance — and Schuman's essential partner in the entire diplomacy of reconciliation — was still an obscure figure at the time. The British authorities (Cologne was in their zone) had briefly removed him even from his unimportant

post for "inefficiency," and they were not alone in regarding Adenauer as far too rigid and ultra-conservative to be of much use. In any case, at age 71 he could hardly have much of a future.

3. MRA intervened directly at a critical juncture following the enunciation of the Schuman Plan. At that time, the Saar was once again separated from Germany and placed under French control (but not annexed).[38] By 1955, within the context of an already established pattern of Franco-German amity, Adenauer's CDU-CSU party proposed that the Saar become a first "European" region (though that farsighted idea was rejected, and the 1955 referendum resulted in the incorporation of the Saar as a *Land* of the Federal Republic). In 1950, however, the Schuman Plan met with opposition from members of Adenauer's government on the grounds that the amity presumed by the ECSC proposal was incompatible with the continued French refusal to return the Saar. As a result, the Schuman Plan was effectively blocked.

At that point, Moral Re-Armament arranged an unofficial meeting between Schuman and Adenauer's opponents on neutral ground in Luxembourg, at which one German and one French MRA member were present. In a classic application of the MRA concept, Schuman expressed compassion for the personal grief of refugees from the lost Eastern territories of Germany and promised that the Saar issue would be settled democratically, and thus necessarily in Germany's favor. Adenauer's opponents thereafter renounced their objections to the ECSC (although, of course, other factors were involved so no cause and effect can definitely be claimed).

CONCLUSION: POTENTIAL, POSSIBLE, AND PROVEN RESULTS

Efforts, however worthy, do not equate with results. Likewise, the documentation of efforts does not equate with the documentation of results. As far as the Caux conferences are concerned, even the documentation of the effort—let alone of the Franco-German reconciliation results actually achieved—is only fragmentary. There is not even a summary record of the discussions that took place in public sessions of the conferences, let alone of the many private dialogues, routinely more consequential in such occasions.

The Caux archives hold only the transcripts of the speeches at the public sessions, in the speaker's language and/or in translation.[39] In some cases, these were prepared statements, possibly written by assistants in the case of officials (many have a formal character, at least in part; some are set pieces throughout). In other cases, these were clearly personal speeches, even when delivered by officials. A few were emotional outbursts, although the prevailing MRA style was definitely Anglo-cool rather than confessional-emotive.

The transcripts include speeches by French participants that express their surprise at finding themselves engaged in dialogue with Germans at all, their new recognition of the feasibility of a dialogue, and their intent to strive to diminish the antagonism between the two peoples. From the German side, there are more dramatic testimonies. Often German participants would give vent to expressions of self-pity upon their first arrival at Caux, recounting their own sufferings and those of their families as if they were unique, and with no apparent recognition that others had suffered far more at German hands. Later, having absorbed the "spirit of Caux," the tone and content of the declarations would change drastically, combining expressions of intense gratitude for being received as equals and even as friends by the other participants, avowals of guilt and repentance, repudiations of past belief in Hitler and his ideology, and promises that Germans would never again be guilty of aggression.[40]

One cannot of course determine the impact of any statement in any situation on the worldview of its audience. Hence, what the documentation proves is only (a) that the Franco-German contacts established at Caux were numerous enough, and featured individuals important enough, to be *potentially* significant in achieving the overall goal, and (b) in regard to the ECSC, on the other hand, the crucial organizational framework of reconciliation, the impact of Caux must be upgraded to the *possible* category at the very least, given the fact that it was only at Caux that its industrial protagonists had met at all before the initiative was officially unveiled in the 1950 Schuman Plan.

More generally, that there was a fundamental change in the reciprocal attitudes of both nations over the years 1945–1950 is undisputed. That there were virtually no other Franco-German venues of real significance in 1946–47 and only a few venues (of uncertain importance) from 1948 is also clear.[41] But of course it was the Cold War that was decisive, because it resulted in the emergence of a radically new conflictual fault line that placed the French and (West) Germans in the same camp. That, it may be argued, made *all* voluntaristic reconciliation efforts, including the personal diplomacy of Schuman and Adenauer, let alone MRA's own initiatives, of merely marginal significance, or even quite insignificant.

Against that view, there are the facts of chronology. The Cold War may have started even before 1945 in some phenomenological sense, and Churchill made his (then very controversial) "Iron Curtain" speech in 1946. But it was not until 1948, after the Czech coup and the Berlin airlift, that its strategic reality was widely perceived and accepted to thereby shape public opinion and political attitudes throughout Europe, including France and Germany. And it was not until 1950 that the Cold War was transformed from a possibly transitory state of diplomatic tension to a permanent confrontation (the United States, for its part, did not even begin its rearmament until after the invasion of South Korea in June 1950). In other words, the Cold War did not become the decisive influence on Franco-German reciprocal attitudes until *after* the two sides were already on the verge of effecting their reconciliation by means of the Schuman Plan and the ECSC.

Further, any progress toward Franco-German reconciliation was inseparable from the adoption of a decisively Western orientation by the Germans themselves: it is now forgotten that a diffident, equidistant attitude associated with neutrality was quite common among German leaders during the first postwar years. The

Soviet Union had been courting West German opinion very vigorously since 1945 (when Stalin abruptly ordered a redefinition of the enemy as Nazi rather than German), while until the Berlin airlift of 1948, the Germans had encountered only hostility if not outright hatred from Westerners — except at Caux. And, as shown in this chapter, the "significant" Germans who went to Caux amounted to a fair proportion of the entire (West) German elite.

As far as MRA's parallel diplomacy is concerned, by contrast, the evidence cited here is literally conclusive. Its contribution was clearly limited and just as clearly of proven significance: MRA did not invent the Schuman Plan but it facilitated its realization from the start. That is no small achievement given the vast importance of every delay — and every acceleration — of the process of Franco-German reconciliation during those crucial, formative years.

Notes

1. The Oxford Group was renamed Moral Re-Armament in 1938. On the origins, see W. H. Clark, *The Oxford Group* (New York: Bookman Associates, 1951); Allan W. Elster, *Drawing-Room Conversion: A Sociological Account of the Oxford Group Movement* (Durham, N.C.: Duke University Press, 1950); and Garth Lean, *Frank Buchanan: A Life* (London: Constable and Company, 1985).

2. Actually, Buchman cultivated working-class trade unionists as ardently as dukes.

3. See, for example, Kingsley Martin, *New Statesman*, July 11, 1936.

4. It spread mainly through small, informal gatherings, but in July 1936, the then Oxford Group convened an open mass meeting in London's huge Albert Hall.

5. See letter in *The Times*, December 29, 1945, signed by Lord Ammon et al., which refers to the 126-page *Die Oxfordgruppenbewegung* report circulated by the Reich Security Department in 1942 to expose Moral Re-Armament's anti-Nazi aims.

6. Walter R. Schutze, German-born member of the Institut Français des Relations Internationales and a leading expert on Franco-German reconciliation, kindly carried out a multilingual literature search for this study. The number of titles (monographs and articles) he surveyed exceeds 10,000 (personal communication, November 14, 1991).

7. "Message from the German Federal Chancellor, Dr. Konrad Adenauer, to Dr. Frank Buchman at the World Assembly for the Moral Re-Armament of the Nations, Mackinac Island, Michigan, 3 June, 1951," MRA archives, Tirley Garth House, Tarporley, England; also reported in "Moral Re-Armament Is Credited for Role in Schuman Plan Talks," *New York Herald Tribune*, June 4, 1951, cited in Lean, *Frank Buchman*, 382.

8. Robert Schuman, untitled speech, MRA archives, Tirley Garth House, Torporley, England.

9. In World War II, 7.8 million men were mobilized, out of the total of 9.9 million males between the ages of 15 and 49; in other words, only outright invalids were exempted (B. Urlanis, *Wars and Population* [Moscow: Progress Publishers, 1971], 209.)

10. This has been overlooked in the great German historiographical debate, although the readiness of the German army to shoot civilians on mere suspicion of *Franc-Tireur* ("sniper/guerrilla") activities in 1870–71 marked a huge regression.

11. This represented 13.3 percent of all males between the ages of 15(!) and 49, as compared to 6.2 percent for Britain and 12.5 percent for Germany (Urlanis, *Wars and Population*, 209).

12. Some 250,000 as compared to 4.5 million (ibid., 221).

13. The SD was the security arm of the SS. The Abwehr (Amt Auslandsnachrichten und Abwehr) was the intelligence and counterintelligence arm of the armed forces' command.

14. One plan briefly contemplated in always antiquarian Britain was to reestablish an independent Burgundy, as a Duchy, of course.

15. They were shot on sight by Canadian, French, and Soviet troops as a matter of sanctioned routine, by British troops sporadically, and by American troops infrequently.

16. Walter R. Schutze, personal communication, November 26, 1991. Copies of *Documents* may be consulted at the Bibliotheque Nationale.

17. Cf. Gerald Manley Hopkins's "The Wreck of the Deutschland."

18. These replaced *Liberté, Egalité, Fraternité* in the coinage and all official emblems.

19. In choosing its nomenclature, the regime replaced *Republique Française* with the nondescript *État* (state), specifically to leave open the possibility of a monarchical restoration—which would have been Bourbon(!), if only because the Orleanist pretender, the Comte de Paris, was not a collaborationist.

20. At least on paper, Vichy went beyond the Nuremberg laws.

21. In addition to the Iron Curtain that marked off the Soviet zone, there was talk of a French-zone "silk curtain" at the time.

22. The brothers Daniel and Philippe Mottu were both MRA activists; Philippe was an official of the Swiss Foreign Ministry.

23. MRA member Kenaston Twitchell, through his father-in-law, U.S. Senator H. Alexander Smith, met with U.S. Secretary of State George Marshall and Secretary of War Robert Patterson, who offered to help secure permit visas. In London, Twitchell met with Lord Pakenham, who was in charge of the British Occupation Zone in Germany. Pakenham asked General Sir Brian Robertson, Commander of the British Zone, to allow 55 invitees to go to Caux. Within the U.S. military, another MRA supporter, General Albert Wedemeyer, had already spoken with U.S. Military Governor General Lucius Clay of MRA plans. When Twitchell and other MRA members met with General Clay, he in turn arranged for them to meet with the political leaders of the four states within the American Zone. Twitchell invited them (with their families) to Caux and asked them to list other prospective invitees. In Munich, the three top officials of the Bavarian government decided to go to Caux, along with the city's Catholic bishop. In August, General Clay authorized permits for repeated journeys of MRA members to the American Zone and facilitated the granting of travel documents for Germans bound for Caux (Kenaston Twitchell, *Regeneration in the Ruhr: The Unknown Story of a Decisive Answer to Communism in Postwar Europe* [Princeton: Princeton University Press, 1981], 8–15, 22–25; and Lean, *Frank Buchman*, 349–50).

24. Other purposes included the recasting of labor-management relations and the moralizing of other international relations, in addition to purely spiritual goals of individual significance only.

25. Verbal communications, Philippe Mottu and Michel Sentis of resident staff, January 6–8, 1992.

26. This and much of what follows is based on the transcripts of the collected but unpublished declarations of years 1947, 1948, and 1949, consulted by the author in the Caux archive in January 1992. Not a few are of historical value and deserve publication.

27. As early as 1946, 11 Germans came to Caux. By contrast, even one year later European trade union leaders meeting in Bern refused to accept the presence of German fellow trade unionists, old Social Democrats and presumptive anti-Nazis though they were.

28. The data that follows is from the unpublished compilation "Survey: National Delegations at Caux 1946–1950," Caux archives.

29. Trade unions were highly politicized and party-affiliated in both France and Germany, much more so than in Britain, let alone the United States.

30. See "Survey: National Delegations at Caux 1946–1950," 11–14.

31. Ibid., 19–21.

32. Lists of delegates to Caux from the years 1947, 1948, 1949, and 1950 and "Survey: National Delegations at Caux 1946–1950 [U.K. version]," MRA Archives, Tirley Garth House, Tarporley, England; also Pierre Spoerri, personal communication, April 21, 1992.

33. "Survey: National Delegations at Caux 1946–1950," Caux Archives, 18.

34. All along, MRA's *primary emphasis* was on labor-management relations and interclass, rather than international, reconciliation.

35. Copy in the Caux archives.

36. See also Konrad Adenauer's letter to Buchman of September 12, 1948 (letter no. 168 in his collected personal correspondence).

37. Interview notes, Douglas Johnston, Caux, Switzerland, September 18, 1991; and verbal communications, January 1992.

38. It was first detached in 1919 under the terms of the Versailles Treaty; it had reverted to (Nazi) Germany in the wake of a 1935 plebiscite, then was detached once again in 1945.

39. It is impossible to determine to what extent the record is complete, but the collations of personal statements made in the public sessions run to several hundred pages for each annual conference season.

40. When a large German delegation of 150 persons arrived at Caux in the summer of 1947, they were given a warm welcome (notably by a French chorus singing a German song). Buchman himself insisted that the emphasis at Caux must be on Germany's future rather then her past, her potential rather than her guilt.

During the 1949 summer conference, it was reported that the topic of Franco-German relations was dealt with "frankly and courageously," according to *L'Aube*, Schuman's MRP party paper (*L'Aube*, Sept. 20, 1949, cited by Lean, *Frank Buchman*, 378). One day during that summer, Hans Böckler, head of the German Trade Unions Federation met with Georges Villiers, president of the French Employers Federation who was sent to Caux by Schuman. Reportedly, after Böckler noted that they should be enemies on two counts, union leader/employer and German/French, Villiers added that he had been condemned to death in a Nazi concentration camp. Villiers ended by saying, "But all that is in the past. We must forget it and I simply want to offer you my hand" (Georges Villiers, speech at Caux, in *Caux Information Service*, New World News Agency no. 1 [Summer 1949], 6).

41. For the Comité d'Echanges avec l'Allemagne Nouvelle, see above; for Pax Christi, inter alia, see the Appendix.

Appendix: The Role of Other Religious Networks in Franco-German Reconciliation

DAVID STEELE

Other religious networks, in addition to Moral Re-Armament, actively promoted Franco-German reconciliation during the postwar period. Their approaches varied with regard to their level of political activity, although none approximated the level of interaction with and among government, industrial, and labor leaders achieved at Caux.

WORLD COUNCIL OF CHURCHES

In October 1945, while still in an embryonic stage of development, the provisional World Council of Churches (WCC) sent a delegation of American, British, Scandinavian, Dutch, Swiss, and French representatives to meet with leaders of Germany's Confessing Church in Stuttgart. The German delegation to Stuttgart included future political leaders such as Gustav Heinemann and Eugen Gerstenmeyer, as well as a number of prominent church leaders.[1]

At a meeting in Baden-Baden held a few days before the session, the non-German delegates together with one member of the German delegation determined that a confession of guilt by the German church leadership would be necessary in order to begin a reconciliation process between the churches of France and Germany. A discussion paper was prepared that subsequently became the basis for the "Stuttgart Declaration of Guilt," which was signed by all members of the German delegation. In return, the German church was again extended an invitation to join the ecumenical movement.[2]

After the war, the WCC gave its active support to efforts by local organizations—such as the German Kirchentags and the Student Christian Movement in Holland, France, and Germany—to bring together thousands of citizens from France, Germany, and other European nations to work on Franco-German reconciliation and in the context of European unity. At the first WCC Assembly in 1948, the WCC itself addressed this issue, calling on all governments to curtail hatred and hostility toward other nationals and to develop economic policy sensitive to the needs of other nations.[3]

Such concerns led the WCC to create, in 1950, the Ecumenical Commission on European Cooperation (ECEC, renamed the Committee on the Christian Responsibility for European Cooperation in 1953). This was an independent advisory group, organized in cooperation with the Study Department of the WCC. It drew upon WCC's capacity to convene distinguished religious and political leaders but had no authority to speak for the WCC or its member churches.[4] Membership was drawn from most of the countries of Western Europe and included noted lay experts on European cooperation. Among the German representatives were the minister president of Lower Saxony, the president of the Bundestag/Parliament, an industrialist, the president of the German Protestant Church Conference, and Heinemann, who was at that time president of the synod of the Protestant churches in Germany and who had recently resigned as Adenauer's minister of the interior over the issue of German rearmament. French representation included a law professor, a theology professor, and commission chair André Philip, a representative to the Council of Europe and a close colleague of Schuman's who did much to launch the Schuman Plan. Another influential member of the commission was Max Kohnstamm from Holland, who also was the first secretary of the new European Coal and Steel Community and, later, under Monnet's leadership, became vice-president of the Action Committee for the United States of Europe.[5]

The commission's primary purpose was to help the Christian churches examine the problems of European cooperation and find ways by which the churches could exert a creative influence on governments and peoples to seek the "common weal." These aims were pursued primarily by formulating statements on the need for cooperation, which were publicized extensively and discussed by various church bodies during 1951. The commission made a special attempt to encourage the people and churches of Germany and France to set aside hatreds and fears and affirm the need for unity within the framework of European cooperation and economic reconstruction.[6]

Although the discussions and debates generated by ECEC on the Schuman Plan were designed primarily to instruct the churches on these matters, they also gave support to the plan during the critical months between May 1950 and April 1951, when commission chair Philip was assisting Schuman in drafting the plan and was building support for it within the French Socialist Party. Even after the plan's inception, Philip helped devise and implement various details, while some groups (e.g., the French Right) were attempting to rescind it altogether. Thus the ECEC's support, together with active participation in the search for further expressions of European unity, was significant at a point when it was widely agreed that even the Schuman Plan would collapse unless further coordination of political, economic, and military policy was achieved.[7]

INTERNATIONAL FELLOWSHIP OF RECONCILIATION

The International Fellowship of Reconciliation (IFOR) is a pacifist, para-church organization that began in Britain in 1914 and was internationalized in 1919. By World War II, it had a network of members within both France and Germany. After the war, IFOR reestablished branch organizations within these and other European countries. The initiative began in France with public meetings in Lyon and Nimes in 1945. A significant addition to IFOR's membership, in 1949, was Jean Lasserre, a Reformed pastor with years of experience working with the coal miners and steel operatives of Northern France.[8]

Outreach to Germany began in 1947 with the appointment of French Reformed Pastor André Trocme as a traveling secretary for IFOR. That August he and two other IFOR members visited German members throughout southern Germany with the stated desire of being reconciled with the German people. The following year the German branch began to rebuild. Leaders of the informal movement known as the Confessing Church, along with leaders of both the Protestant and Catholic churches, became active in the membership.[9]

Unlike the other religious organizations involved in Franco-German reconciliation, IFOR had major reservations about the direction of European cooperation. In keeping with long-standing convictions, the IFOR opposed the rearmament of Europe. It was, however, solidly in favor of European integration, emphasizing a supranational federalism as the best alternative for Western Europe.[10] IFOR pursued its long-standing goal of developing a nonviolent, international federalism by focusing primarily on grass-roots peace building; it chose to work on enlarging the core of people committed to its movement and specific agenda rather than on developing extensive relationships with political figures in an attempt to influence the politics of the moment. At the same time, Franco-German reconciliation was identified as one of the urgent needs of that period at an IFOR Consultation on Federalism and Nonviolence, held in France in July 1949.[11]

PAX CHRISTI

The Roman Catholic organization, Pax Christi, began as an attempt at Franco-German reconciliation through prayer services, pilgrimages, annual convocations, and "peace and reconciliation retreats." In early 1945, a few French Catholic laypersons who were formerly Nazi victims approached Bishop Pierre-Marie Theas of Montauban with a request to lead a "prayer pilgrimage for the conversion of Germany." Bishop Theas, who subsequently became the first president of Pax Christi, gave episcopal sanction to this movement when he announced the pilgrimage on Easter Sunday of that year. The archbishop of Toulouse gave his support on Whitsunday (Pentecost), while on March 10, 40 French bishops signed a summons to participate in the pilgrimage. News of this event was communicated to Germans in the French-occupied Saar and, from there, spread throughout Germany.[12]

In November 1945, the name of the pilgrimage was changed by deleting the word *conversion*, a recommendation made by Vatican Cardinal Nuncio Roncalli (later to become Pope John XXIII). "Prayer pilgrimage for Germany" was deemed to put both nations on a more equal footing. In November 1946, the name was changed again to "prayer pilgrimage for all nations," reflecting a concern to broaden the reconciliation efforts to include other nations that had suffered at the hands of the Nazis.[13]

Relations between French and German Catholics, however, continued to be of central importance in the development of Pax Christi. The organization's first newsletter, published in 1945, praised two German bishops for their support. A newsletter later that year carried a long list of French bishops who had committed themselves to the developing organization. In 1946 the archbishop of Fribourg-En-Brisgau welcomed the movement to Germany through a letter published in the newsletter and invited other leaders of the German Catholic Church to participate.[14]

German participation became active in 1946, when Germans joined with French members of Pax Christi in numerous secular and religious events. Pilgrimages to Bezeley and to Lourdes, as well as international meetings between French and Germans, became regular occurrences, with Germans increasingly participating in leadership roles.[15] Pax Christi finally established itself in Germany in 1948, with an international congress held in Germany, ending the period of predominantly French initiative.[16]

The character of Pax Christi underwent some transformation with the naming of Archbishop Feltin of Paris as the movement's first international president in 1949. Feltin undertook to expand the vision of the organization from being solely a "prayer crusade" to having a broader agenda, including prayer, study, and action. Pax Christi–initiated aid organizations in Germany were one result of the new focus on social and political action.[17]

Prior to 1950, however, the primary focus of Pax Christi activity had been on spiritual and devotional events. Even the international congresses were designed to promote interpersonal reconciliation rather than specific policy changes in the international order. French and German church leaders were amply represented in virtually all activities, but there were few government, labor, or industrial leaders in attendance. One exception to this was contact made in 1946 with Joseph Foliet, who became vice-president of France in 1951.[18] It was not until 1952, after the Schuman Plan was history, that Pope Pius XII would describe Pax Christi as having social and political needs at the heart of its mission. That year the pope assigned Pax Christi the objective of "countering closed nationalisms," by encouraging nations to abandon policies of isolation and to build toward European unity. At its international congress of 1953, the organization finally adopted the theme, "The Building of Europe," in order to advance this new sense of mission.[19]

Notes

1. Gerhard Besier, "Zur Geschichte der Stuttgarter Schulderklärung vom 18./19. Oktober 1945," in *Wie Christen ihre Schuld bekennen: Die Stuttgarter Erklärung 1945*, ed. Gerhard Besier and Gerhard Sauter (Göttingen: Vandenhoeck & Ruprecht, 1985), 27–28; "Die Stuttgarter Erklärung," in ibid., 62; and *The Work of Action Reconciliation* (Berlin: Aktion Sühnezeichen/Friedensdienste, n.d.), 5.

2. The German churches turned down the first invitation in 1933, but accepted this post–World War II offer (Besier, "Zur Geschichte der Stuttgarter Schulderklärung," 28–32; and *Work of Action Reconciliation*, 5–6.

3. Paul Abrecht, unpublished letter, February 19, 1993; and "Report of Section IV of the First Assembly of the World Council of Churches," *The Church and the International Disorder*, an ecumenical study prepared under the auspices of the World Council of Churches (London: SCM Press, 1948), 224.

4. Paul Abrecht, unpublished letter, March 30, 1992; and Ecumenical Commission on European Cooperation (European Commission, World Council of Churches Study Department), "Second Statement on European Cooperation," July 20, 1951, World Council of Churches archives, Geneva, 3.

5. Committee on the Christian Responsibility for European Cooperation, *The Future of Europe and the Responsibility of the Churches* (Geneva: Committee on the Christian Responsibility for European Cooperation, 1954), back cover; R. C. Mowat, *Creating the European Community* (London: Blandford Press, 1973), 57, 73–74; Paul-Henri Spaak, *The Continuing Battle: Memoirs of a European 1936–1966*, trans. Henry Fox (Boston: Little, Brown, 1971), 207–11; Konrad Adenauer, *Memoirs 1945–53*, trans. Beate Ruhm von Oppen (Chicago: Henry Regnery, 1965), 183, 291–92; Abrecht, unpublished letter, February 19, 1993; and Ecumenical Commission on European Cooperation, European Commission, World Council of Churches Study Department, cover letter for "A Statement on Germany and European Cooperation," January 29, 1952, World Council of Churches archives, Geneva.

6. Ecumenical Commission on European Cooperation, "Report on the Consultative Meeting at Treysa, August 11th 1950," 1–2; Ecumenical Commission on European Cooperation, European Commission, World Council of Churches Study Department, "Minutes of the Meeting of the Provisional Steering Committee, Hotel Terminus, Paris, September 14, 1950," Study 50 E/16, September 1950, World Council of Churches archives, Geneva, 1–2; Ecumenical Commission on European Cooperation, "European Issues," document drawn up at the first meeting of ECEC on January 13–14, 1951, 4–6; Ecumenical Commission on European Cooperation, "Second Statement on European Cooperation," July 20, 1951, 1; and Ecumenical Commission on European Cooperation, "Minutes of the Meeting Held at Gästerhaus der Stadt Frankfurt, Schönberg i.Ts., Germany, January 13th and 14th, 1951," Study 50 E/23, March 1951, World Council of Churches Archives, Geneva, 4.

7. The primary influence of the ECEC came through the relationship between its chair, Philip, and Schuman (telephone interview with C. L. Patijn, vice-chair of ECEC, February 11, 1992; Mowat, *Creating the European Community*, 24, 57, 72–75, 86–88, 115; Committee on the Christian Responsibility for European Cooperation, "Minutes of the Meeting of the Committee on the Christian Responsibility for European Cooperation with a Group of European Church Leaders, Paris, February 28–March 1, 1953," *European Issues: Bulletin of the Committee on the Christian Responsibility for European Cooperation*, 2 [May 13, 1953], 14–19; and Committee on the Christian Responsibility for European Cooperation, *Future of Europe and Responsibility of the Churches*, 4).

8. Vera Brittain, *The Rebel Passion: A Short History of Some Pioneer Peace-makers* (Nyack, N.Y.: Fellowship Publications, 1964), page facing the title page, 148, 158–59.

9. Ibid., 63, 124, 127–28, 153–54; and Christian Baccuet, *De l'evangile à la non-violence: Les cahiers de la réconciliation 1946–1963* (Montpellier: Institut Protestant de Théologie, Faculté de Montpellier, 1991), 116.

10. Baccuet, *De l'evangile à la non-violence*, 117–19; and "Fédéralisme et non-violence (Troisième consultation fraternelle du Chambon)," *Cahiers de la réconciliation*, 1 (1950), 3, 25.

11. "Fédéralisme et non-violence," 3–4, 21–22, 25.

12. Pierre-Marie Theas, "Pax Christi: A Crusade of Prayer for All Nations," *American Ecclesiastical Review* 121 (July 1949), 7; Von Hermann Pfister and Waldemar Ruez, "Lebendiges Zeugnis für Frieden und Gerechtigkeit: 40 Jahre Pax Christi, deutsche Sektion," *Internationale Friedensbewegung Pax Christi: Ziele–Schwerpunkte–Geschichte* (Frankfurt: Pax Christi, Deutsches Sekretariat, 1988), 38–39; Joseph Fahey, "Pax Christi," in *War or Peace?: The Search for New Answers*, ed. Thomas A. Shannon (Maryknoll, N.Y.: Orbis Books, 1980), 59–60; and Bernard Lalande, "The Birth of a Peace Movement, (1945–1965) in *Reflections by Two Pioneers* (n.p.: Pax Christi International, n.d.), 3–4.

13. François Mabille, untitled text on the history of Pax Christi, trans. Margaret Wehrer and Vivetta Petronio, available from Pax Christi France, Paris, 4–7.

14. Telephone interview with Valerie Flessati, author of Ph.D. thesis, "Pax: The History of a Catholic Peace Society in Britain 1936–71", June 4, 1992; and Mabille, untitled text, 9.

15. Mabille, untitled text, 4–9; Gordon C. Zahn, *War, Conscience and Dissent* (New York: Hawthorne Books, 1967), 91; and Theas, "Pax Christi: A Crusade of Prayer for All Nations," 9.

16. "Chronik der deutsche Sektion der Pax Christi," *Internationale Friedensbewegung Pax Christi: Ziele–Schwerpunkte–Geschichte* (Frankfurt: Pax Christi, Deutsches Sekretariat, 1988), 52.

17. Lalande, "Birth of a Peace Movement," 5–6; and P. Manfred Hörhammer, "Pionierarbeit in den ersten Jahren," *Internationale Friedensbewegung Pax Christi: Ziele–Schwerpunkte–Geschichte* (Frankfurt: Pax Christi, Deutsches Sekretariat, 1988), 34.

18. Mabille, untitled text, 7; and Zahn, *War, Conscience and Dissent*, 90.

19. Lalande, "Birth of a Peace Movement," 18, 27.

5 ▪

Religious Conciliation Between the Sandinistas and the East Coast Indians of Nicaragua

BRUCE NICHOLS

Successive colonial interventions in Nicaragua by Spain, Britain, and the United States left a legacy of chronic domestic instability. Throughout the 1980s, one of the surrogate conflicts of the Cold War pitted the Soviet-supported Sandinista government against the U.S.-backed contras. Sometimes developing in parallel to that confrontation, sometimes intersecting it was a different type of conflict. The Sandinistas, upon coming to power in 1979, had failed to comprehend the culture of the Indians of the East Coast and had infringed on their sovereignty. Many Indians fled to neighboring Honduras and Costa Rica from which they waged a war of resistance, a fight for regional autonomy from the Sandinista government.

"It is without historical precedent," Interior Minister Tomás Borge told Nicaragua's National Assembly with characteristic forcefulness in September 1987. "Autonomy [for the East Coast Indians] is part of our principles of national liberation."[1] His speech praised the progress that Nicaragua had made in passing a new autonomy law designed to end seven years of armed conflict between the Sandinistas and the indigenous East Coast tribes. Among the world's most liberal efforts at granting political autonomy to an ethnic enclave within a nation-state, the new law appeared just weeks after the enactment of a new Nicaraguan constitution that also spoke of the East Coast's two "autonomous regions."

Borge hoped that these legal steps would strengthen his position in upcoming negotiations with a team of East Coast Indian leaders. He badly needed a cease-fire that would free limited Sandinista resources and troops for use against the U.S.-supported contras. So far the best efforts of the Sandinista government had failed to end the armed conflict between the Sandinistas and the East Coast peoples over who would be the primary masters over roughly half the territory of Nicaragua. This area had been occupied, farmed, fished, and mined for centuries by the Indians.

In moves they would later publicly regret, the Sandinistas imposed controversial reeducation and relocation programs on the Indians in the early 1980s, leading the Indians to organize militias and flee to the fledgling contra training grounds in neighboring Costa Rica and Honduras. Their participation in contra resistance and their own personal war against the Sandinistas became the subject of a protracted dispute that lasted for most of the decade, and which followed its own path quite apart from the wider contra war.

The Indians cared little about who ruled in Managua (see Figure 5.1); the fundamental issue for their leaders was always their freedom to carry on their lives on the East Coast as they best saw fit. There was frequent conflict among Indian factions on how to live together, but they could all agree that their world was a different one from the Spanish-dominated mestizo and Latino world of those who ran the country. This central political and ethnic gulf was articulated in the early 1980s as a forceful demand for political autonomy. Borge had, he hoped, given them enough of what they sought to secure the cease-fire he needed.

Four months after the Autonomy Law came into effect, in January 1988, leaders of the Indian rebellion, themselves banned for years from entering the country, stood in the dark on the tarmac at Managua's airport, invited by Borge to negotiate a settlement of their disputes. They were met by members of the new Conciliation Commission charged with organizing and presiding over the negotiations. After months of preparation and false starts—including a last minute "36-hour phone call"[2] between Indian and Conciliation Commission leaders in San Jose, Costa Rica, and Sandinista authorities in Managua—they had arrived, only to be told that they were to remain outside the airport until they agreed that they would greet Borge, in his official capacities as interior minister and National Autonomy Commission president, in his office the next morning. The Indians, who had received a commitment that their negotiations would not take place in any government offices or buildings, balked at the symbolism of Borge's demand, believing that Sandinista manipulation of the planned negotiations had already begun. It was not, they argued, the government's autonomy that was being discussed; it was the East Coast's autonomy, and they intended to enforce their view by declining a meeting at the Ministry of the Interior.

Brooklyn Rivera, leader of the Indian delegation, was eventually put on the phone with Borge. Very well, he was told, if that was his view, the negotiations were off. The Indians would be taken to a hotel and put on a plane to Costa Rica the next morning. They were provided a military escort to a nearby hotel, and soldiers took them individually to their rooms. It was not an auspicious start; only with the assistance of members of the Conciliation Commission was a compromise reached by which the negotiations were allowed to proceed. Rivera then shook hands with Borge in front of a government public relations office.[3]

This chapter will explore the contributions of the Conciliation Commission in bringing about a negotiated accord in the midst of the emotional firestorm that had grown between the Sandinistas (FSLN, or the Sandinista Front for National Liberation) and leaders of the Indian East Coast. Over a period of several years in the 1980s, the commission, comprised of a small group of Protestant church leaders, became the moving force in bringing the Sandinistas into negotiations with the Indian and Creole leaders who sought political and economic autonomy for their peoples. Their efforts, which led to a series of formal negotiations in

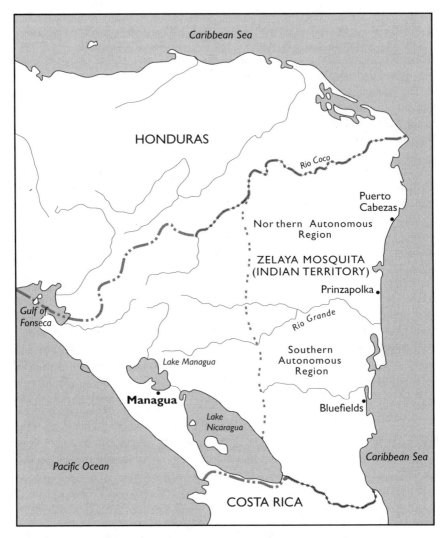

Figure 5.1. Nicaragua

1988, substantially contributed to ending a difficult conflict within the wider armed struggle that engulfed the nation for nearly a decade.

Three central lessons emerge from Nicaragua's experience with the Conciliation Commission. First, religious leaders were able to effectively serve in formal negotiations between a national government and a rebellious ethnic enclave. This was remarkable in this case because most of the members of the Conciliation Commission were themselves East Coast Indians and Miskito pastors. Second, the effectiveness of religious leaders was contingent on developments in existing political and economic issues; the Indians' struggle, after all, was taking place in the midst of the wider contra war, with all of its Cold War overtones and superpower interests. Third and finally, the ability of the religious conciliators to create an environment of trust and communication was directly tied to their standing as local spiritual leaders.

In isolating a single set of negotiations in order to understand the contribution of religiously based mediation in resolving a lengthy conflict, it is possible to overvalue the negotiations and to undervalue the wider process within which they were embedded. To avoid this, we begin with an overview of the struggle that led to the necessity of formal negotiations in early 1988.

SANDINISTAS ARRIVE ON THE EAST COAST

The 1979 revolution in Nicaragua that brought the Sandinista Front (FSLN) to power revealed a surprising fact: the leaders of the junta knew virtually nothing about the life and cultures of the Indians who occupied the eastern half of the country. The Indians, a mix of Miskito, Creole, and smaller tribes that had occupied Nicaragua's East Coast well before British traders and explorers arrived in the eighteenth century, had long been accustomed to insular lives lived in local pursuits or in the service of outside wealth, largely from the United States or the Somoza family, which had ruled Nicaragua with U.S. support for three generations.

The lives of the Miskitos revolved around the village and the Moravian church, which had been brought to the region by missionaries in the 1840s. With their own indigenous language, culture, and Protestant leadership, the Miskitos represented a challenge to the new FSLN leaders eager to integrate them into the country's new culture of Soviet-funded, Latin-inspired socialism known as *Sandinismo*. In the absence of organized local governments, the Moravian parson was the unelected mayor of most Miskito villages.

The peoples of the eastern coast of Nicaragua have for centuries built villages and towns on the ocean and inland, usually along the banks of rivers that run through dense jungle and relatively open lowlands. The Miskito Indians also live in neighboring regions of Honduras and Costa Rica and have cared little about how mestizo governments drew their maps. Smaller, older tribes, the Sumos and Ramas, and the Creoles, born through intermarriage of Indians with colonial British and Caribbean peoples, were often more at home with visitors who came from the sea than with those who came overland from Managua.

Poor roads ensured that access to the region by most Hispanic Nicaraguans would be relatively limited. Nonetheless, the Somoza family developed extensive fruit production and gold mining in the region. With much of the production leaving Nicaragua via the Caribbean Sea, little direct interaction with the rest of the country was required. Since the Indians had only limited local government or political culture through which they could respond to the Somozas, they were easily dominated. One of the early Indian efforts at a political movement, ALPROMISU (Miskito for Alliance for the Development of the Miskito and Sumu People), did bring forward various leaders and interests in the early 1970s, yet it was widely perceived as a tool of Somoza interests.

Following the Sandinista revolution of early 1979, the FSLN commandantes began a process of consolidating their victory at the local level across the nation. When they sought to seize the economic infrastructure of the East Coast in August, their ignorance of Indian life led to many painful mistakes that eventually broke much of the Indian enthusiasm for the new government.[4] Cuban doctors and teachers were brought in, the teachers to impose Spanish language education. That November, the Indians formed a new political organization, MISURASATA (an acronym based on names for the Miskito, Rama, and Sumu tribes), which began with the goal of structuring support for the Sandinista government. Although Moravian parsons from Miskito villages were active participants in the effort, the confrontations grew increasingly heated and deadly.

In 1980 the Sandinistas took over existing Miskito hospitals, which had been run largely by the Moravian church. This aggression pushed Indian leaders to new levels of political organization. A political rivalry that dominated the rest of the decade between two young Indian leaders, Brooklyn Rivera and Steadman Fagoth, both Miskito, dates from this early period. Though there were other less influential Indian factions at work during the period, notably one composed of those Indians who were openly supportive of the Sandinistas, these two leaders expressed contradictory approaches to Indian interests. Rivera, while openly hostile to Managua and supportive of armed conflict that served Indian interests, was to become the leader in supporting a negotiated settlement with the authorities. Fagoth, also hostile to the Sandinistas, kept a firm eye on the benefits being offered by the United States if the Indians could be persuaded to join forces with the contras and bring down the government by force.

Both leaders seized the flag of regional autonomy at an early stage of the struggle. From 1980 onward, the autonomy question—whether the Indians would participate in the Sandinista revolution or follow their own path, within or without Nicaragua—was joined. Fagoth, for instance, visited local villages to conduct a census, telling residents that his study was the precursor of a new autonomy government.[5] When in February 1981 he attempted to assert regional control by announcing new land rights at a MISURASATA meeting, Sandinistas arrested several Indian leaders, and Fagoth fled the country. Armed conflict broke out across the region; eight Miskitos and Sandinistas were killed in the Moravian church at Prinzapolka, a small East Coast town. The first large rush of refugees, 3,000 Miskitos, largely young men, fled to Honduras. The war between the Sandinistas and the Indians had begun.

By September 1981, Rivera had also left the country for Costa Rica, implicitly abandoning a political settlement. Fagoth remained at large, shuttling between eastern Honduras and Washington, D.C., building support in the Reagan administration, organizing a militia, and calling for armed resistance. In December, the Sandinistas organized armed incursions along the Coco River that separated Honduras and Nicaragua. Thousands more Indians fled, and by early 1982, the U. N. High Commissioner for Refugees estimated that 30,000 Nicaraguan Indians had been driven outside the country. Thousands more were forcibly relocated away from the combat zone along the Coco River south to detention areas where they were held by armed Sandinistas.

INTERNATIONAL ATTENTION SPURS LOCAL MEDIATION EFFORTS

The best early efforts of Protestant leaders in Nicaragua to mediate the conflict were no match for the organized interests of the U.S. government in prolonging the conflict and giving the Sandinistas one more battle they needed to fight. In the spring of 1982, Secretary of State Alexander Haig warned ominously about a new wave of "feet people" from the south, echoing public U.S. concern over the numbers of Vietnamese boat people arriving there at the time in large numbers from Southeast Asia. United Nations Ambassador Jeane Kirkpatrick made the plight of the Miskito Indians a personal cause in her diplomatic and political offensive against the Sandinistas. From the point of view of the Reagan administration, the Sandinista/Miskito rift was a welcome opportunity.

Amid these confrontations, Indian leaders of the small Moravian community in Managua joined leaders of CEPAD, an ecumenical Nicaraguan relief and development agency that provided internal assistance through existing Protestant networks, in trying to calm the waters. They met with little success. They organized an inquiry into the Prinzapolka incident, and they pleaded for protection for those Indians forcibly relocated within Nicaragua. But the Indian cause was quickly politicized beyond the borders of Nicaragua by a U.S. administration eager to build any manner of support for an armed resistance to the Sandinistas.

The Sandinistas, for their part, quickly realized that they had made major tactical errors in their dealings with the East Coast. In January 1983, the Contadora Agreement[6] raised the hope of regional mediation of conflicts, but the agreement had no serious effect in halting the conflict. The Indians had effectively created a zone of *alzados* ("armed militias") across the East Coast, and their political agenda, both internally among their own factions and externally with Managua, increasingly centered on the concept of autonomy.

Toward this end, the Indians essentially listened to two contesting sets of voices. While supportive of the efforts of Protestant leaders to mediate the conflict, Miskito leaders, most notably Rivera, were also receiving the advice of a variety of Indian and North American anthropologists and human rights attorneys. These advisors were promoting cultural and political autonomy as the best means of protecting traditional societies and assuring self-determination. Fiercely loyal to the interests of the Indians, they urged strong versions of autonomy that caught Rivera's interest.

In October 1984, following a secret visit in New York with Senator Edward Kennedy and Nicaraguan President Daniel Ortega, Rivera was given permission to return to Nicaragua to discuss ways of ending the dispute. He came to Managua with legal and anthropological advisors who brought the language of cultural and political autonomy to the heart of emerging discussions between the Indians and the FSLN. As a result of these discussions, the Managua government convened a national autonomy commission to formulate a new autonomy law for the East Coast.

At the same time, CEPAD and Moravian leaders continued their own peace-making efforts. With the agreement of leaders on both sides, a CEPAD official arranged for meetings to be held in Bogotá, hosted at the presidential palace by Colombia's President Belisario Betancur. For three days in January 1985, Rivera met with a delegation representing the FSLN Interior Ministry, which under Tomás Borge controlled the government's dreaded internal security forces. The mood was cautious and exploratory: the Sandinistas wanted disarmament, while Rivera could make no such commitment and held out for a full-fledged autonomy. The CEPAD official who organized the sessions, which produced no agreement, noted that the Sandinista delegation seemed to know little or nothing about life on the East Coast and returned constantly to basic historical questions.[7] In a move that revealed their own limited horizons, the FSLN sent two Miskito Sandinistas to study Soviet-style autonomy – in Lithuania.[8]

In spring 1985, a scheduled vote in the U.S. Congress, which would appropriate $14 million in new contra aid, brought increased pressure on the Sandinistas to reach a settlement with the Indians. While Rivera pursued negotiations when possible, Fagoth was doing what he could to draw Indians into common cause with the contras in order to tap additional U.S. assistance. In April, Rivera took a different approach and met President Ortega in Mexico City; Rivera had been offered a seat on the National Autonomy Commission in advance of the meeting. They reached agreement to "avoid offensive armed action," but acknowledged that they had "still not achieved definite accords over the fundamental issues for a solution." Both sides denied the obvious, saying that the progress they had made "was reached independently of the forthcoming vote [in the U.S. Congress]."[9] Additional negotiations were scheduled for the following month in Bogotá.

By the time of this second round in Bogotá the process had broken down, and Tomás Borge decided it was time for him to enter negotiations personally. According to the FSLN's former lead negotiator, Luis Carrion, the Indians were demanding "a state within a state." Noting that the word "autonomy" does not exist in the Miskito language, Carrion assumed that this was "a concept they picked up from various international organizations."[10] Rivera held that the Sandinistas "continually deny our aboriginal rights."[11] Looking back to this period, Rivera later reached the conclusion that Borge, his new negotiating partner, was a racist with "a warlike attitude."[12]The Bogotá meeting dissolved in acrimony, but the pressures for a negotiated settlement continued to build on both sides.

Over the next two years, the desperate need of both sides for peace forced new developments on the local and legal fronts that, in turn, led to a diminishment of the conflict. Hundreds of Indian refugees came home in response to early San-dinista offers of amnesty, and fighting was reduced to occasional skirmishes. Local peace and autonomy commissions were elected on the East Coast to work with the FSLN in developing a new autonomy law. The real breakthrough came, how-ever, with the signing of the Esquipulas II agreement in early 1987, an effort by five regional governments to extend the "Contadora process."[13] Among the provisions of the accord was an agreement that all of the five Central American countries engulfed in civil conflicts would form national reconciliation commissions.

In May 1987, 600 Indian leaders—village elders, Moravian parsons, leaders of militias, and others—met in a multi-ethnic assembly that convened just inside the Nicaraguan border with Honduras. By plenary vote they rejected U.S. offers of funds to carry on their fight. Instead, abandoning MISURASATA, they formed a new Indian political umbrella, YATAMA (from Yapti Tasba, the Miskito name for the region), with the express purpose of bringing their conflicts with the Sandinistas to an end. All major Indian factions rallied behind Brooklyn Rivera and asked him to move forward with peace talks with the Sandinistas.

The Sandinista's National Assembly in Managua passed the new autonomy law in October 1987. While Borge considered it unprecedented in the degree of autonomy it afforded, it was not enough to satisfy the Indian leaders. After all, despite the national amnesty and the regional Contadora and Esquipulas accords, the people of the East Coast were still in a state of armed conflict with the Sandinistas. With or without an autonomy law, serious face-to-face negotiations were still needed to bring an end to the hostilities.

Before this time, late that summer, Moravian church leaders who had long been active in making contacts between both sides, Rivera, and the director of CEPAD, Dr. Gustavo Parajon, had begun organizing a new conciliation commission along lines set forth in the Esquipulas II accord. Also working with the group was John Paul Lederach, a Mennonite then living in Costa Rica and conducting workshops on peacemaking and reconciliation in local settings. They broached a plan with Borge and Rivera for early formal negotiations on ending the conflict.

Getting to the negotiating table under conditions of civil war was not an easy task. The Sandinistas did not want Indian leaders to reenter the country under terms that could then be extended to contra leaders. Frustrated in its efforts to draw the Indians into the contra war, the United States opposed a settlement between the Indians and the FSLN and was thus opposed to the proposed talks. Covert agents working in Costa Rica allegedly planted information within Indian circles designed to break the YATAMA coalition, and Lederach received phone calls threatening his family with kidnapping. While the State Department denied U.S. government complicity in these activities, it put potential negotiators on notice that their moves were being watched.[14]

CONCILIATION COMMISSION MOVES INTO ACTION

Beginning in late January 1988, the Conciliation Commission launched the first of three extended negotiations between the Indians and the Sandinistas, all held in the Moravian Church of Managua or at hotels or restaurants around the city. The second and third sessions were held in March and May of that year; each session lasted several days. The high point of the sessions was the emergence at the end of the January meetings of a substantial accord addressing political, economic, and cultural aspects of a settlement. Since our primary interest here is in the role of the religious leaders in mediating the conflict, we will explore the strengths and weaknesses of this accomplishment from the perspective of the commission's emerging contributions to the overall peace process.

Analyzing his experience as an advisor to the Conciliation Commission, Lederach draws a distinction between an "outsider-neutral" third party, the standard model in most diplomatic settings, and an "insider-partial" third party, whose value lies "not in distance from the conflict . . . but rather in connectedness and trusted relationships with the conflict parties."[15] While the distinction is not absolute, it speaks directly to the way the Conciliation Commission accomplished its goals; its members, while inevitably partisan toward the cause of the East Coast, were well known and respected by Sandinista leaders as well. Lederach claims that the commission maintained the trust of all parties (with the probable exception of many of YATAMA's Indian rights and anthropological advisors), by exploiting the "insider" position of its members.

Each of the core members of the commission was a public figure. The chairman, Dr. Parajon of CEPAD, was a respected doctor and Baptist layman. His agency, organized to help raise and distribute aid following Managua's terrible earthquake of 1972, had built ties with the East Coast peoples and taken an interest in the economic development of the entire country. Commission member Andy Shogreen was a youthful superintendent of the Moravian churches in the East Coast's Northern Province. Another member, Norman Bent, pastored Managua's Moravian Church and had intervened on behalf of the Indians with the Sandinistas during the early stages of the conflict. Though only Lederach had been trained as a professional mediator, agreements reached in advance of the negotiations stipulated that as a non-Nicaraguan, he would serve as a "technical assistant" who would exchange positions between the negotiating parties rather than as a member of the commission, and he would not be allowed to sit at the table during discussions. The three core commission members, together with Lederach, were assisted from time to time by others.

The teams representing the two parties to the conflict were led by Rivera and Borge and varied in size, depending on who was available on a given date. These two leaders were the principal negotiators at all sessions; while their fellow negotiators, whose numbers ranged from two to a dozen or so at different times, were available for consultation, they rarely participated directly in the talks. Instead, their presence served a need to visibly incorporate a variety of factions in the proceedings. For Rivera, for example, there were supporters of Fagoth, Creoles, and other smaller groups represented in the YATAMA coalition; for Borge, there were various departments within the Sandinista government, as well as an articulate group of East Coast Indians, including professionals and a member of the National Assembly, who were openly supportive of an accommodation between the FSLN and the Indians. Underscoring the serious character of these negotiations, diplomats from "friendly nations," including Canada, Costa Rica, Cuba, Denmark, Finland, Holland, Norway, and Sweden, regularly attended and monitored the sessions.

The first set of formative decisions, made during the prenegotiation phase, covered procedural matters and the issue of how the safety of YATAMA leaders could be guaranteed during their stay in Managua. Once resolved, all parties to the negotiation issued a statement as the talks began in late January 1988, defining the role of the commission.[16] It was pragmatic: the commission was to coordinate the place and timing of meetings and facilitate communication between both sides. Other functions included:

- formally presiding and serving as moderator in conversations, including facilitating the discussion, clarifying subjects that could easily be misinterpreted, and writing down subjects of mutual interest for future discussions
- making sure the conversations follow "the right path"
- making recommendations
- testifying that the accords are fulfilled.

This limited mandate was essential in offsetting the partisanship inherent in the insider-partial composition of the group. The commission did not, for instance, propose the substance of accords as is common in third-party mediation. This limitation contributed to its being a conciliation commission rather than a mediation commission. "Emotionally, spiritually, they set out an impartial role," according to Rivera,[17] though the reality of their position was probably closer to what Lederach described as "balanced partiality."[18] While various members of the commission later emphasized the low-key housekeeping aspects of their mandate, they were also in this document empowered to "make recommendations" and make sure talks were "following the right path."

IMPORTANCE OF THE SPIRITUAL DIMENSION

Such bland formulations cause one to ask what difference it made that the conciliators were religious figures? That they were Christians? Could non-religious leaders have achieved the same, or even better, results?

Simply put, "religion was important because there were religious leaders in the commission."[19] Members frequently wore clerical collars and shirts to the negotiating table (in like manner, Commandante Borge always appeared in military garb[20]). They approached Sandinistas and Indians alike with pastoral sensitivity; that "right path" on which they sought to guide the talks assumed the need for progress toward Christian reconciliation among all parties, even in the midst of talks that were often raucous and confrontational. Members of the commission endured physical violence from angered constituents and governmental acts that seemed targeted against them.[21] The commission members prayed together and with members of the negotiating teams; on at least one occasion, Moravian parsons received tearful expressions of remorse from President Ortega and from Borge for the suffering the Sandinistas had inflicted on their people.[22] On several occasions, members of the Sandinista delegation requested prayer alone with the Conciliation Commission.[23] "The most important goal of the process was to bring about reconciliation," said commission member Andy Shogreen. "Many people were badly hurt."[24]

These were spiritual understandings long embedded in the cultural backgrounds of the Sandinista and YATAMA delegations alike, whether or not individual participants held explicitly Christian views. In this sense, the commission was able to draw on a common language of conciliation, and it often did so in explicit ways. At the formal level, for instance, each new session was opened with a prayer and often a reading from the Bible. On one occasion, when the commission chair forgot the morning prayer, it was Commandante Borge, himself a former Catholic priest, who interrupted him with the question, *Y la oración?* ("What about the prayer?").[25] While such elements might be dismissed as formalities, they do call attention to a fundamentally acknowledged theological framework that the Conciliation Commission used to open a window on the deeper emotional and spiritual realities contained in the conflict and in the lives of individual negotiators.

All commission members spoke of their participation as a calling, and a difficult one at that, which had long-term consequences for their personal futures. Nevertheless, each took the risks involved for the sake of ending violence in his country. From the kidnapping threats against the Lederach family in Costa Rica, to death threats to Norman Bent before and during the negotiations,[26] to physical violence endured at a rally, their perseverance in a Christian calling was essential. As insiders who themselves would live with the success or failure of their efforts, they became personally tied to the outcome of events.

The members of the commission were all Protestants, most of whom drew inspiration from the peace church influence of the Mennonite tradition (as seen in their selection of Lederach as their chief consultant). Asked to cite passages of the Bible that were particularly meaningful to the commission in its work, Lederach cited several verses from Psalm 85, a prayer for deliverance from national adversity:

> Surely his salvation is at hand for those who fear him,
>   that glory may dwell in our land.
> Steadfast love and faithfulness will meet;
>   righteousness and peace will kiss each other.
> Faithfulness will spring up from the ground
>   and righteousness will look down from the sky.[27]

The Hebrew word here translated as *righteousness* is frequently translated today as *justice*. To a Mennonite sensibility, this image of justice and peace together is not so much visionary as it is clear goal-setting.[28]

A variety of other Christian themes were explicitly set forth in opening devotions during the negotiations, both from the Bible and from the Moravian book of daily inspirational readings. These included references to the vocation of serving rather than being served; Job's acceptance of evils visited on him despite his personal integrity; the distinctions between worldly and divine wisdom and the "harvest of righteousness" awaiting those who sow in peace; and the example of Christ who, rather than exalting himself, "humbled himself and became obedient unto death."[29] While theology could not ultimately be said to control the framework of discussion around the negotiating table, neither did the Conciliation Commission hide its spiritual light under a bushel. Their Christian vocation was named and acknowledged.

SUBSTANTIVE NEGOTIATIONS BEGIN

The first negotiating session, on January 26, 1988, was held in a conference room at the Moravian Church of Managua. By mutual agreement there was no formal agenda for the talks, and both sides were free to submit proposals or initiate discussion. There were "no preconditions," but both sides had come with clear agendas. In opening remarks, Borge stated his belief that the recent passage of the autonomy law by the National Assembly had created the conditions for a new cease-fire and that this would be his primary goal. Rivera, while acknowledging progress toward peace on the East Coast, stated that a cease-fire only made sense in the context of a wider accord that covered a range of political, economic, and social aspects of the conflict, to culminate in a new relationship of autonomy. To that end, YATAMA presented a version of what it would like such an accord to contain, and made agreement on autonomy for Yapti Tasba its precondition.

In Rivera's view, the Nicaraguan autonomy law did not adequately protect the nascent rights that, on the counsel of the U.S.-based Indian Law Center and others, were due the East Coast peoples. The Sandinistas had no trouble assenting to many of these rights because, as the new autonomy law itself stated:

> In Latin America and in other regions of the world, the indigenous populations subjected to a process of impoverishment, segregation, marginality, assimilation, oppression, exploitation and extermination demand a profound transformation of the political, economic, and cultural order to effectively achieve their demands and aspirations.[30]

The law promised regional "administrative organs" that would address East Coast concerns in areas of development, new transportation, economic and social concerns, local taxation, and regional markets. But frequent references to working "in accordance with the national plan of development" or "in compliance with the Political Constitution" and the generally vague and strictly administrative character of reforms promised in the law were unsettling to the Indians. Furthermore, the new law spoke of the need for "the defense of life, the fatherland, justice, and peace to achieve the complete development of the nation," and stated that in "the Autonomous Regions . . . the defense will be directed by the Sandinista Popular Army."[31] The Indians were to be defended by their military enemies of the last seven years!

These points emerged often during the first day of the talks, but were refocused by a proposed accord offered by YATAMA that evening. Borge passed it on to his legal advisors and continued to press for a separately negotiated cease-fire. This was so important to him that he authorized FSLN military leaders to bypass the talks and approach Indian leaders on the East Coast while the negotiations were taking place in Managua.[32] Rivera continued to resist.

Though Rivera was permitted to make a brief trip to the East Coast during the talks, both sides were interested in making a longer trip to tell the East Coast peoples directly that "some accords linked to the rights of the native people and of the Atlantic Coast have been reached."[33] The Conciliation Commission supported this approach and suggested that, while there, the Sandinista and YATAMA authorities might issue a joint call for a temporary cessation of offensive activities for the duration of the talks, a plan that initially appealed to both Borge and Rivera.

An accord, signed on February 2, 1988, after much revision and discussion, covered political, economic, and cultural issues, thus including key points of interest to both sides. It offered to recognize YATAMA leaders as the political establishment on the East Coast; it granted the right of communal ownership of all Indian lands; it promised government assistance in securing foreign investment and promoting economic development; and it promised the formation of an Emergency Reconstruction Commission following the end of hostilities. A cease-fire deadline of March 1 was set.[34]

A number of points raised by YATAMA were not, however, included in the accord, so it was agreed that a second round of talks would be scheduled for late February to address these points specifically. These points pushed toward the strong version of autonomy sought by Rivera: modification of territorial boundaries; verification of compliance on both sides by a group of international observers; the integration of YATAMA militia and Indians serving in the national forces into a regional military controlled by YATAMA; freedom of YATAMA youth from national conscription; the right of the Indians to choose between the FSLN autonomy law and the YATAMA autonomy proposals; and control over all land and mineral rights.[35] These demands went well beyond the framework of the Nicaraguan constitution and (certainly in the views of Sandinista negotiators) amounted to the establishment of an armed state within a state.

The February 2 accord did not address its own implementation; it was intended by both sides as a marker toward the end of conflict rather than as an explicit road map. It was, for Sandinistas and Indians alike, a set of promises cast upon turbulent political waters. No expenditures were authorized, there was no action strategy; it was a document for public consumption that for the Sandinistas addressed a cease-fire and for YATAMA acknowledged the importance of autonomy. In this sense a point made in the introduction to this book (Chapter 1) can be clearly seen: the conflict was based on issues of identity rather than of ideology. Though Borge represented and readily defended an ideological government, the emotional concerns tied to Indian autonomy dominated all aspects of the accord.

There were pressing political, economic, and military reasons for the parties to reach an accord. But the Conciliation Commission's role was to conduct the process and maintain the integrity of the talks, not to deal with the substance.

Throughout the negotiations, members planned the sessions, scheduled locations around Managua and the East Coast, carried messages between participants, and prepared records and written documents. Since it was agreed that a key element of the second round of negotiations would be an extensive trip to the East Coast to promote the accord, commission members helped make travel arrangements. All these activities cost money, and it was through commission contacts with church bodies outside Nicaragua that much of the funding for the negotiations and related travel was obtained. With all Nicaraguans severely strapped, this financial contribution was an important dimension of what the Conciliation Commission brought to the table.

The second round of talks, which began on February 29, 1988, in Managua, got off to a poor start, with YATAMA presenting a proposal that returned directly to the matters of hard-line autonomy that had not been agreed upon in the first round. The proposal spelled out new gerrymandered boundaries for the two East Coast regions that excluded most of the non-Indian population. It refused to acknowledge the autonomy law as the basis of discussion and asked that its implementation be suspended during a proposed popular referendum. It also called for YATAMA control of the military and freedom from the national draft.

All of Borge's efforts to convince the Indians that they would have to work within the autonomy law and the Nicaraguan constitution had failed, and now they were planning a trip together to the East Coast to present their accord. After three days of discussion, it was clear that the accord had merely clarified the existence of strong and weak definitions of autonomy held respectively by Rivera and Borge. Rivera demanded that land boundaries and concepts of autonomy be settled before a cease-fire was enacted; Borge countered that YATAMA's new proposals blatantly moved the goalposts outside of Nicaragua's constitutional order.

Frustrated, Borge decided he would not accompany YATAMA to the East Coast, but let YATAMA leaders do their own "proselytizing."[36] By the third day of this round of meetings, the Conciliation Commission had been required to make numerous interventions as tempers flared; by the end, the commission had to separate the parties and speak with each team individually. The meetings ended inconclusively and acrimoniously, and YATAMA leaders prepared to embark on their own 10-day visit to the East to explain their negotiations in Managua.

While the government made good on its promise to allow air, land, and sea travel to the East Coast, the Conciliation Commission covered all costs for the 19-person delegation. Four commission members accompanied the YATAMA leaders and their advisors, seeing the occasion as an extension of its stated tasks in the negotiations. From village to town, Rivera and his colleagues held rallies announced in advance over shortwave radio. But once on the East Coast, Rivera exposed himself to the grass-roots supporters of other Indian factions. The long-term conflicts erupted again at a variety of stops. After Conciliation Commission members intervened to open a locked stadium in Puerto Cabezas so the major rally of the trip could be held, fighting broke out among Indian factions. Members of the Conciliation Commission and CEPAD were injured as they sought to assist YATAMA negotiators who fled the angry crowd.[37]

These unfortunate events brought a sober report of the trip from the commission, rebuking YATAMA for its lack of caution in presenting its case and the government for its negligence in informing its regional authorities about the accord. Now it was the commission's turn to be frustrated; with the parties apparently so willing to undermine whatever progress they had achieved, the commission asked that both affirm in writing that they were still interested in the commission's services.[38]

The third and final round of talks mediated by the Conciliation Commission was the least productive of the negotiations. With Steadman Fagoth joining the negotiating team for the first time, YATAMA again presented its strong autonomy demands. Rivera insisted that the Sandinistas could not stiffly remain within a constitutional framework that the Indians did not consider functional. The YATAMA proposals remained strong on political and human rights, YATAMA control of the military, and adjusted boundaries and weak on economic and transformational strategy beyond proposing a new reconciliation commission that would now include two members "selected by the international Indian community."[39] Rivera argued that the struggle of the coastal peoples for their own rights and their communal control of their territories long predated the current legal system of Nicaragua. He asked the Sandinistas to call in the International Court of Justice to mediate the boundary dispute, suggesting that it was beyond the Nicaraguan government's competence to do so.[40] For his part, Borge increased the tension in the negotiating sessions by bringing with him several FSLN leaders from the East Coast, as well as several *desalzados*, Indians who had accepted government offers to disarm. Borge pressed his point that a comprehensive settlement might be at hand by noting that several YATAMA military leaders on the East Coast had signed individual cease-fire agreements with Sandinista authorities. Rivera dismissed the significance of the local cease-fires and insisted that the rights of the people in general and their relation to the state was at the heart of the February 2 accord. Borge declared that without a definitive cease-fire, no further travel of the YATAMA delegation to the East Coast would be authorized.

Both sides reverted to their clashing juridical frameworks to justify their well-established views. By the end of this debate, which consumed a full eight hours, the Conciliation Commission was able to focus both sides on one point of agreement: namely, to jointly explore a humanitarian role for the International Committee of the Red Cross on the East Coast. Otherwise, hostility and mistrust was building among participants. The next day, in one last marathon session that lasted until 4:20 A.M., the Sandinista and YATAMA teams went at each other, with no visible success in reaching an accommodation. Borge indulged in several lengthy expositions of the Nicaraguan revolution, the machinations of imperialists and arms dealers in the United States and Israel, and the promise the Sandinistas held for a new indigenous life on the East Coast. If he were to take Rivera's demand for his own standing army seriously, he said, he might as well jump off the roof of the Intercontinental Hotel, where the last round of negotiations was held.[41]

There was little for commission members to do but take notes, for both sides had gone as far as they could. In the end, Borge thanked all participants for coming, reiterated his ban on further travel throughout the country, and expressed regret that no further progress was possible. The commission's chairman, Dr. Parajon, read a passage from Paul's Letter to the Romans:

> For the kingdom of heaven does not mean food and drink but justice and peace and joy in the Holy Spirit; he who thus serves Christ is acceptable to God and approved by men. Let us then pursue what makes for peace and for mutual upbuilding.[42]

With the reading and a final prayer, the formal negotiations were over. Rivera was told he could not return to the country and be part of a political party.

THE AFTERMATH

Despite the failure of the second and third rounds of negotiations to produce further accords, the preliminary agreement of February 2 was a distinct contribution to peace in Nicaragua. By 1988, U.S. support for the Reagan administration's Central American policies had eroded, and all parties were preparing for a negotiated end to the contra war and the broader regional hostilities. In a sense, the YATAMA/FSLN agreement was ahead of its time. Nicaragua's National Reconciliation Commission, created through the Esquipulas II agreement, negotiated a general cease-fire between the Sandinistas and the contras later in 1988, only to have it disintegrate. A national dialogue on peace was begun in 1989. For their part, Conciliation Commission members helped facilitate a series of reconciliation meetings between the three major Indian factions and their exiled leaders in Honduras, as factional fighting among them had resurfaced. During the same period, the Sandinistas announced a general demobilization and agreed to an international team of observers to monitor it. They also agreed to a national election.

A national election had not been on the agenda during the YATAMA talks, and it represented a new opening to the impasse between the Indians and Sandinistas. Denominational connections within the Conciliation Commission played an important role in advancing the legitimacy of the upcoming elections. Rivera, himself a Baptist, had through the interventions of commission chairman Parajon (also a Baptist) been actively building ties with another Baptist in the United States, Jimmy Carter. After Rivera visited the Carter Center in Atlanta, Georgia, the former president agreed to lead an international team that would monitor the elections. Carter scheduled a preelection visit to Nicaragua in September 1989 to discuss his intentions with the Sandinistas. While the FSLN had already eased its restrictions on the contra leaders, permitting them to return and participate in opposition politics on the condition that they give up their armed struggle, no such accommodation had been reached with the Indian leaders, who remained out of the country under Borge's ban. Carter came in 1989 ready to focus on the question of Indian participation in the process.

At a meeting held in a Moravian church in Puerto Cabezas, Carter reported that his discussions with Borge had been successful and that Rivera and other Indian leaders would be permitted to return to the country under the same conditions as the contras: no armed struggle and participation in the existing political structure. They would not be required to guarantee a total demobilization of Indian troops, which Borge had originally demanded. The road to a national election was effectively cleared.[43]

The election was set for February 1990. Most observers credit Violetta Chamorro's victory to one key promise: abolition of the national draft. YATAMA had long demanded that East Coast residents be free from the national draft, and, given their antagonism toward the Sandinistas, there was little doubt where their votes would go. Chamorro won in a landslide, and a new phase of the Indians' relations with Managua was inaugurated.

Throughout the three years following the 1988 negotiations, the Conciliation Commission continued to function, albeit in a less formalized way. When it came to actually planning how the Indians would organize their life after the Sandinistas, there still remained deep divisions. In August 1989, commission and Moravian leaders held meetings in Guatemala designed to bring factional leaders together. Following the elections, from July to August 1990, a new series of reconciliation meetings between Rivera and Fagoth attempted to heal old wounds, but without notable success.

In the meantime, the Chamorro government, supported by a loose coalition of 16 parties that ranged from conservative to communist, faced major problems of its own, starting with the fact that, before leaving office, the Sandinistas had plundered the national treasury and left the country without financial resources. In this context, the Indian problems once again fell to the bottom of the list of priorities. The 1987 autonomy law was seen as going too far in granting freedom to the indigenous peoples, and Chamorro's government sought a means of addressing the issues without taking substantive actions. To that end it formed a new Managua-based commission, INDERA (National Institute for the Development of the Atlantic Regions), which would supervise relations with the East Coast. In fall 1990, Chamorro appointed Brooklyn Rivera as the director, with Owen Hodgson, the legal advisor to the Conciliation Commission, as his assistant.

On the East Coast, INDERA was denounced as a sellout by none other than Steadman Fagoth, who in Rivera's absence was making common cause with Indians who had supported the Sandinistas. There was little doubt that Chamorro's government had continued to bypass regional authorities; a case in point was its signing away Atlantic Coast fishing rights to foreign companies and returning the tax revenues to Managua. The regional government, established in May 1990 in accord with the autonomy law, had many of its mandates and most of its funding transferred to INDERA. Fagoth argued that Managua should be bound by the autonomy law and that his old rival had gone from being an Indian leader to becoming a tool of Latino interests. "INDERA is working against autonomy," he claimed.[44] So, some 10 years after the fighting began between the Indians and the Sandinistas, just how effective was the work of the Conciliation Commission?

EFFECTIVENESS OF THE CONCILIATION COMMISSION

The Conciliation Commission contributed to a process of normalizing relations between the East Coast Indians and the Sandinistas. Over the course of the decade, its members helped the parties move from armed conflict to a cessation of hostilities. The significance of their role at the negotiating table and around the region has been assessed variously by participants in the process themselves.

Tomás Borge has a positive view of the commission's contributions, finding them a stabilizing presence when dealing with Rivera, who in the end he could not take seriously as a political leader. Borge is nonetheless also of the view that the Moravians and CEPAD had sought this engagement in order to further their own interests on the East Coast.[45]

Brooklyn Rivera believes that the commission played a limited role in the process: "Progress was more our [the YATAMA leaders'] responsibility than it was that of the mediators." He also believes that the lack of YATAMA supplies and funding in 1987–88 (when U.S. funding of the contra war was also in decline) and the signing of the regional Esquipulas II accord in 1987 were the primary political developments that moved the situation forward, eventually allowing Indian troops and refugees to return to the country. In his view, the February 2 accord was a secondary step along that way.[46]

Among members of the Conciliation Commission, there is a more positive assessment of their contributions. Legal advisor Owen Hodgson believes that they provided a necessary counterbalance to the advice YATAMA leaders were receiving from their U.S. advisors, who he thinks were offering suggestions on political autonomy based on evolving international standards of human and aboriginal rights rather than on what was actually possible in Nicaragua. In contrast to the commission members, these advisors "were not familiar with the situation inside the country."[47] "We had a knowledge of the suffering in Nicaragua, and this was important," says Commission member and Moravian pastor Norman Bent. When asked to participate in the Conciliation Commission, Bent "knew it was important that I stopped just looking at my own life, that I look at the whole situation and ask how I could make a difference."[48]

Gustavo Parajon feels the February 2 accord "was very basic to what evolved thereafter, despite the fact that there was no further agreement" at the time. He sees the inability of the Indians to settle their own differences as having been a more limiting political factor than their disputes with Managua, arguing that no matter what course evolved with the national government, the East Coast would make no serious progress toward development and ethnic autonomy without a more developed, problem-solving political culture.[49]

In John Paul Lederach's view, the talks "created a time and a place where people could meet and exchange what it was they wanted from each other. It created a foundation for what was to come." Carrying forward his analysis of the insider-partial third-party role, Lederach argued that persons in this capacity, by virtue of their local roots and ongoing presence in the situation, are able to help sustain progress over time. Longstanding relationships of trust that crossed political boundaries made such involvements possible.[50]

To pursue the question of the value of the Conciliation Commission and the February 2 accord within the wider peace process that spread through Nicaragua and most of Central America, we can turn to an objective measure of reconciliation achieved: the rate at which Indians who had fled the country in the 1980s, both civilian and military, felt safe in returning home. In assessing the figures, it is important to understand that from their earliest arrival in 1981, the Nicaraguan Indians had found Honduras and the U.N. camps established for them there inhospitable. Efforts from the U.S. Agency for International Development to create long-term development projects proved equally unpopular; the Indians retained a primal attachment to their own homes and always hoped to return. It is in this broad context that the efforts of the Conciliation Commission to build trust and confidence between the government and the Indians bore fruit.

The figures on Indians who voluntarily repatriated to Nicaragua are revealing. Of those refugees within the care of the United Nations—and for the Miskito Indians, this was the large majority of the estimated 25,000 outside the country—only 57 returned during the height of hostilities in 1984. Following the Mexico City negotiations in 1985, the number rose to 586. The FSLN's decision in 1986 to establish local peace and autonomy commissions represented the next marker toward peace, and 1,714 refugees returned home that year. The following year, when the Indians' Multi-Ethnic Assembly authorized negotiations with the government, the number jumped to 3,724, in part due to increased patrolling and harassment of Indian troops in Honduras by the Honduran military.[51]

In 1988, the year the Conciliation Commission–mediated accord was reached, 7,948 Indian refugees returned home, a significant increase. These figures suggest that while incremental progress was being made each year, the climate improved substantially inside Nicaragua following the FSLN-YATAMA accord. With YATAMA leaders again exiled and unable to move the situation forward prior to Jimmy Carter's visit, the number dropped to 1,098 in 1989. However, in 1990, once Carter had secured agreement that elections would go forward with Indian participation and Chamorro's election in February assured that the national draft would be suspended, 10,206 Indians returned.[52]

The sense of safety people feel about returning to their homes is a better measure of progress toward peace than most others; it is the emotional green light to reclaim the most basic aspects of communal and ethnic identity. In this elemental sense, the return home expresses belief that peace and normalcy are at hand. Given the fact that the same men who negotiated in Managua had the direct attention of the troops and others in exile, the positive influence of the peace process is evident in the figures. The February 2 accord made a substantial contribution to the climate of peace, but it was one element in the national political process that eventually culminated in the removal of the Sandinistas from office and abolition of the draft.

It is also useful to look at objective areas of failure in which the commission was not able to reconcile the positions of the different sides. If we consider the proposition that religious leaders are strongest at engaging "emotional meaning" in issues that touch on ethnic identity, and weakest at issues of traditional statecraft—what Douglas Johnston calls in Chapter 1 the realpolitik of "shrewd balancing of interests"—these negotiations appear to provide a case in point. The issue of autonomy is full of such emotional meanings for the Indians. In the end, the concept as they defined it was too heavily laden: it spoke to human rights, military defense, self-government, and economic independence, as well as serving as a "cloak," a political concept that masked the Indians' inability to resolve their own internal political conflicts. Nevertheless, the Conciliation Commission helped both sides engage limited versions of autonomy that included socio-cultural, political, and economic aspects.

It was in the matters that might directly impact the balance of power in Nicaragua—territorial redistricting and the freedom to maintain an independent army without being subject to a national draft—that the conciliation effort was unavailing. Such difficult issues are, of course, capable of undoing secular mediators as well.

Perhaps the most elemental measure of success for a third party in any intractable conflict is to win the acceptance of the parties for the duration of the conflict, or until some form of resolution is achieved. The commission's success in this regard can be attributed to its perceived integrity and the trust this generated among the participants. With Latino, Creole, and Indian members, the commission contained leaders from groups that each enjoyed a measure of public support. They were insiders who wanted to make a difference for peace. The trust they generated honored not only their religious convictions but also their deeply held sense of obligation as participants in Nicaraguan political life.

For all who took part in the overall peacemaking process, before, during, and after the Managua negotiations, it was a risky choice. John Paul Lederach asked the question:

> Why did these people get involved in such a draining, sacrificial, costly enterprise? For the Moravians, they knew that there had to be a better way. There had to be a practical, theological role for intermediaries in creating space for dialogue and understanding. . . . That "space" comes through people, people willing to take a risk themselves, to create the space, and to carry it with them.[53]

Their actions in coming forward were the first steps in building bridges between the Sandinistas and the Indians.

Was there anything unique about the commission that could not have been accomplished by a nonreligious actor? While there were devotional readings, prayers, confessions, and reconciliations, making explicit a Christian framework, the sincerity, truthfulness, and ultimate effect of these individual acts of private and public devotion is impossible to determine. Yet their impact must also be measured by the documented ability of the commission members to sustain religiously grounded trust among all participants throughout the peace process. Few other leaders representing public constituencies (politicians, labor and business leaders, and soldiers) would be viewed as capable of the "balanced partiality" the situation required. Religious leaders opened a window to a transcendent dimension at both the personal level (prayer, forgiveness, and reconciliation) and in political terms (peace, and political and social accords). Looking through this window, it was easier for individuals on both sides of the negotiation to speak with each other, and to see beyond their individual preoccupations to goals shared by the other.

Moreover, the conciliators were sustained by Christian hope. In the selection of Bible readings and in their prayers, as well as in private conversations, they proclaimed to the assembled negotiators a prophetic vocation for peacemaking that was deep and persistent. To quote Lederach again:

> Biblically, there is an image of Christ breaking down walls of hostility between enemies, an image that views Christ as the person in which hostilities are broken down. The cross is there in that space. That is also where the conciliator must be. When justice and peace, truth and mercy are brought together, something unique is created. In times of war, these conjunctions happen through people creating links between the camps.[54]

While the Conciliation Commission's contribution was incremental in terms of the overall process of resolving the military, political, and social issues at stake, their devotion to the task was consuming. Their infusion of Christian trustworthiness and hope into the negotiating process created unique opportunities for human contact across a great political gulf. When the gulf appeared insurmountable, as happened at several points, their Christian virtues held out a uniquely spiritual bridge to which both sides frequently resorted.

The wider contra war received most of the public attention in public reporting of Central America in the 1980s, and the struggle between the Indians and the Sandinistas emerged only on occasion. To the individuals involved on both sides, however, it was far from a sideshow; it was a conflict every bit as disruptive and deadly as the battle with the contras. The record and results of the Conciliation Commission represent a significant involvement that guided the entire process of peacemaking with the East Coast Indians. It went well beyond most nonofficial diplomacy more typical of religiously motivated peacemakers in that it involved mediation of formal negotiations between a state and a hostile ethnic enclave.

In the negotiations there was a sense in which Borge did not trust Rivera at all, and merely wanted an expedient cease-fire; by the same token, Rivera saw bad faith in all dealings with the Sandinistas and ultimately wanted an autonomy that implied some form of separate statehood. Neither man got what he wanted. Yet in the middle of this continuing hostility, the Conciliation Commission's religiously impelled perserverance—its mixture of pragmatic message-carrying, peace process maintenance, and fund-raising, together with its constant resort to confession, prayer, and scripture reading—helped link developments in the East Coast issues to the wider framework of peace that emerged in Central America. In the fragile politics of Nicaragua, that was no small accomplishment.[55]

Notes

1. Tomás Borge, speech to the National Assembly, September 9, 1987.
2. John Paul Lederach, transcript of a presentation on the Nicaragua negotiations to the Religion and Conflict Resolution Project Steering Group, Center for Strategic and International Studies, Washington, D.C., April 16, 1990, 19.
3. Interview with John Paul Lederach, Eastern Mennonite College, Harrisonburg, Virginia, January 1991.
4. See "The Treatment of the Nicaraguan Indians by the Sandinista Government," *Freedom at Issue*, 66 (May/June 1982).
5. Charles R. Hale, "Institutional Struggle, Conflict, and Reconciliation: Miskitu Indians and the Nicaraguan State," in *Ethnic Groups and the Nation State*, ed. Center for Research and Documentation of the Atlantic Coast (Stockholm: University of Stockholm, 1987), 108.
6. The Contadora Agreement grew out of a negotiating process that was initially organized in January 1983 by four Latin nations (Colombia, Venezuela, Mexico, and Panama) to promote regional peace in Central America. Under the agreement, which was eventually signed by El Salvador, Honduras, Nicaragua, Guatemala, and Costa Rica on September 9, 1983, the Central American states agreed to a loose process intended to promote internal democratization and to limit superpower intervention in the region. The United States, while publicly supportive of this Latin initiative, did what it could to block progress behind the scenes, and three U.S. allies in the region, Guatemala, Honduras, and El Salvador, eventually failed to ratify the plan. For a detailed treatment, see William Goodfellow and James Morrell, "From Contadora to Esquipulas to Sapoa and Beyond," in *Revolution and Counterrevolution in Nicaragua*, ed. Thomas W. Walker (Boulder, Colo.: Westview Press, 1991), 369–394.
7. Interview with Benjamin Cortes, former associate director of CEPAD, Managua, February 1991.
8. See Bernard Nietschmann, "Negotiating with the Sandinistas," unpublished article, June 5, 1985. Dr. Nietschmann is a Berkeley, California, geographer who has worked and written extensively on the Nicaraguan East Coast and was an observer in the FSLN-Indian negotiations until he was asked to leave the country following a riot at a YATAMA rally in the Puerto Cabezas stadium, at which some Conciliation Commission members were injured.
9. "Sandinistas Reach Pact with Indians," *New York Times*, April 23, 1985; "Sandinistas' Talks with Indians Fail," *New York Times*, May 30, 1985.
10. Ibid. Carrion was referring to such groups as the Washington, D.C.–based Indian Law Resource Center and Cultural Survival of Cambridge, Massachusetts, which were among those providing counsel to the East Coast Indians. For their views, see, for example, "Report on March 1985 Negotiations on the Indian Rights Conflict in Nicaragua," Indian Law Resource Center, Washington, D.C. [1985]. In addition to such groups, representatives of more than a dozen groups representing indigenous peoples of North and South America (including the American Indian Movement, the Indian Council of South America, and the Six Nation Confederacy) attended the talks as observers and advisors.
11. "Sandinistas' Talks with Indians Fail."
12. Interview with Brooklyn Rivera, Managua, March 1991.
13. In May 1986, the president of Guatemala convened a new regional peace initiative in Esquipulas, Guatemala, which was designed to move the Contadora process forward. Participants included the five Central American states, as well as Venezuela, Panama,

Colombia, and Mexico. The new accord, eventually signed in August 1987, was known as Esquipulas II and offered five agreements critical to bringing peace to the region: an amnesty for all irregular forces fighting their own Central American governments; a cease-fire covering all conflicted areas; movement toward pluralism and participatory democracy in each country; cessation of all aid to irregular forces from governments within and without the region; and agreement that irregular forces could not use the territory of any Central American state to attack another Central American state. All participants in the conciliation process between the Sandinistas and the East Coast Indians felt this agreement set the stage for the formal negotiations that took place in early 1988.

14. Interview with Lederach. Participants from both sides of the mediation and the Conciliation Commission members all felt that the United States covertly sponsored these activities. The kidnapping calls to Lederach allegedly came from a Cuban-American CIA contract operative; before anything happened to Lederach's family, they were returned to the United States. Additional alleged U.S. government–related activities included bribes to Creole Indian leaders to win East Coast support for the contras and misleading reports of U.S. government payments to Rivera's staff designed to fragment the YATAMA coalition. See Martha Honey and Tony Avirgan, "The C.I.A.'s War," *Nation*, February 6, 1988. After Lederach visited the State Department to report these allegations, they were denied in writing.

15. See Paul Wehr and John Paul Lederach, "Mediating Conflict in Central America," unpublished paper [1990]; also Lederach, "Transformation from Within: Peacemaking in the East Coast of Nicaragua," unpublished paper commissioned under a grant by the U.S. Institute of Peace, delivered at George Fox College, Portland, Ore., 1989.

16. "Agreement over the Functions of the Conciliation Commission Between the Government of Nicaragua and YATAMA," January 26, 1988, Managua, unpublished.

17. Interview with Rivera.

18. Lederach transcript, 15.

19. Interview with Milton Arguello, secretary to the Conciliation Commission, Managua, February 1991.

20. Ibid.

21. Andy Shogreen, superintendent of the East Coast Moravian churches, was prevented from attending several negotiating sessions in Managua by FSLN officers in Puerto Cabezas, who kept him from boarding the plane. Shogreen attributed this directly to the intervention of Tomás Borge (interview with Shogreen, Bethlehem, Pennsylvania, January 1991).

22. Testimony of Moravian pastors, as cited in Lederach transcript, 18.

23. Interview with Lederach.

24. Interview with Shogreen.

25. Interview with Arguello.

26. Interview with Norman Bent, Managua, March 1991.

27. Revised Standard Version of the Bible, National Council of the Churches of Christ, 1952.

28. For 70 years, the Mennonite Central Committee has promoted these and similar peacemaking goals in a variety of settings, from post–World War I relief in Russia through the Spanish Civil War, Vietnam, and numerous other conflict areas around the world. In 1987 Lederach was serving in the Committee's Conciliation Service.

29. Passages referenced include Mark 10:32–45; Job 2:1–10; James 3:13–18; and Philippians 2:1–11, all from the Revised Standard Version. They were quoted in the minutes of the negotiations kept by Conciliation Commission secretary, Milton Arguello.

30. *Statute of Autonomy of the Regions of the Atlantic Coast of Nicaragua, Law No. 28, La Gaceta: Diario Oficial*, Managua, October 30, 1987.

31. Ibid., Art. 13, 14.

32. Interview with Lederach.

33. "Communiqué from the Government of Nicaragua and YATAMA," January 28, 1988, unpublished.

34. "Preliminary Accords Between the Government of Nicaragua and the YATAMA Organization in a Round of Negotiations from the 25th of January to the 2nd of February [1988]," Managua.

35. Ibid., "Appendix II: Matters submitted by YATAMA neither agreed upon or discussed," Managua, February 2, 1988.

36. "Minutes of the Second Meeting Between the Government of Nicaragua and YATAMA, Second Round of Talks, Wednesday, March 2, 1988."

37. Interview with Lederach.

38. "Report of the Trip of YATAMA and the Conciliation Commission from March 4th to March 14th to the Atlantic South and North," April 4, 1988, unpublished.

39. Ibid., Sec. 10.1.

40. "Minutes of the Second Meeting Between the Government of Nicaragua and YATAMA, Third Round of Negotiations, Tuesday, May 10, 1988," Sec. 9.5.

41. Interview with Tomás Borge, Managua, March 1991.

42. Romans 13:17–19, quoted in "Minutes of the Fifth Meeting Between the Government of Nicaragua and YATAMA, Third Round of Negotiations, Friday, May 13, 1988."

43. "Deal at Hand on Miskitos, Says Carter," *Washington Post*, September 19, 1989.

44. Interview with Steadman Fagoth, Puerto Cabezas, March 1991.

45. Interview with Borge.

46. Interview with Rivera.

47. Interview with Owen Hodgson, Managua, March 1991.

48. Interview with Norman Bent, Managua, February 1991.

49. Interview with Dr. Gustavo Parajon, Managua, March 1991.

50. Interview with Lederach.

51. On the matter of Honduran military operations, see "Minutes of the Fourth Meeting of the Government of Nicaragua and YATAMA, Third Round of Negotiations, Thursday, May 12, 1988."

52. Source: Dr. Sonia Muñoz, U. N. High Commissioner of Refugees, Nicaragua.

53. Interview with Lederach.

54. Ibid.

55. In addition to the interviews already cited, other individuals interviewed for this study were Juan Amunategui, director, Central American Region, U. N. High Commissioner for Refugees, San José, Costa Rica; Mateo Collins, Moravian parson, Puerto Cabezas; Federico Lindbohm, field officer, U. N. High Commissioner for Refugees, Puerto Cabezas; Betty Muñoz, assistant director, East Coast Documentation Center, Managua; Sonia Mūnoz, legal officer, U. N. High Commissioner for Refugees, Managua; Cesar Pais, director, regional Sandinista headquarters, Puerto Cabezas; Leonel Pantín, governor, Northern Autonomous Region, Puerto Cabezas; Armstrong Wiggins, Indian Law Resource Center, Washington, D.C.; and Bishop John Wilson, Moravian bishop and participant in conciliation efforts.

6 ▪

"To Make Real the Bond Between Us All": Quaker Conciliation During the Nigerian Civil War

CYNTHIA SAMPSON

Although independence came peacefully to Nigeria in 1964, the British left a young state that was deeply divided along regional, ethnic, and religious lines. The predominantly Muslim and politically dominant North was outranked economically by the Eastern and Western regions, where Christianity and traditional religions prevailed. A flawed constitution and electoral corruption produced an explosive mix in the First Republic, until two military coups, six months apart, brought the military to power in 1966. With tensions still rising, pogroms against Easterners living in the North sent the survivors fleeing back home. Within months Eastern secessionism reached a fever pitch, and the young nation was plunged into a brutal civil war.

In early January 1970, Adam Curle received a call from Arnold Smith, secretary-general of the British Commonwealth. The Nigerian civil war was abruptly ending. Would the Quaker conciliator return quickly to Nigeria to try to secure a final-hour agreement that might prevent the feared bloodbath?

Nigeria had been locked in bitter warfare for 30 months, since May 30, 1967, when its breakaway Eastern Region declared itself the independent Republic of Biafra (Figure 6.1). In the course of the long war, the federal army had closed in on Biafra from all sides, taking the areas occupied by many small ethnic groups on the perimeter and recapturing the oil-rich lands of the coastal stretch near Port Harcourt. A succession of Biafran capitals had fallen. What was left of the secessionist region was the heartland of the Ibo people, the largest group in the East. Landlocked, in a state of siege, and with hunger widespread, their situation was desperate.

Finally federal troops succeeded in bisecting the rebel enclave. On January 10, Biafran Head of State General Emeka Ojukwu fled in the company of his top cabinet members. In his last broadcast to a beleaguered people, Ojukwu announced that he was "leaving the country temporarily to continue the search for peace." Two days later, the Biafran commanding officer instructed his troops to lay down their arms.

In a midnight broadcast on January 12, Nigerian Head of State General Yakubu Gowon welcomed back into the fold "our brothers who were deceived and misled

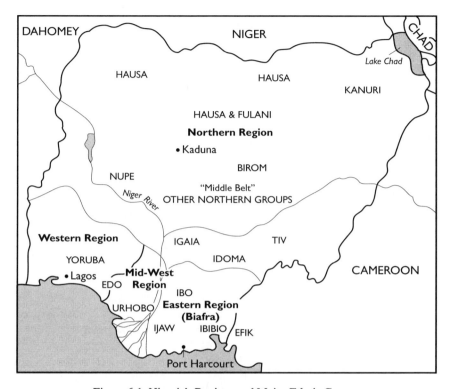

Figure 6.1. Nigeria's Regions and Major Ethnic Groups

into armed rebellion against their fatherland." Proclaiming later that there were "no victors, no vanquished" in the war, Gowon shunned any sort of victory celebration and instead called for three days of prayer. The promised amnesty for all Biafrans was put into effect; within days, many former Biafran civilians and soldiers began returning to their jobs under federal auspices, and Nigeria set off on the path of the "three Rs": reconstruction, reintegration, and reconciliation.

Adam Curle did go to Nigeria during this period, as did another Quaker conciliator, John Volkmar, several weeks later. These were the last of 12 trips made to Nigeria and Biafra by these two men and a third Quaker colleague, Walter Martin, in the course of a war whose immense tragedy took at least half a million lives through fighting and hunger. But instead of finding the widely feared violence and retribution against the defeated Easterners, they found that military discipline on the federal side prevailed, and the fighting had ended. Many of the former adversaries were in the midst of a joyful reunion, and Nigeria was beginning to rebuild in what may have been the most extraordinary post–civil war reconciliation to have occurred in modern history.

The Commonwealth secretary-general's alarmed call at the end of the war was one of many indications that the conflict might not have ended that way, however. It was also telling in other respects: it revealed something about the nature of the close working relationship that had developed over the course of the war between Secretary-General Smith, an official-level third party, and the Quaker team of nonofficial intermediaries. It also revealed Smith's awareness of the close relationship that the Quaker conciliation team had developed with top leaders on both sides in the conflict, particularly with Nigerian leader Gowon.

GENESIS OF THE CONFLICT

The roots of the conflict[1] in Nigeria could be found in ethnic and religious cleavages in the society reinforced by regional divisions dating from the colonial period. Although Nigeria has some 240 distinct language groups, three groups of approximately equal numbers—the Hausa-Fulani, Yoruba, and Ibo—make up roughly two-thirds of the population. Each of these is concentrated in one of the traditional regions, the North, West, and East, respectively. A small fourth region, the Mid-West, was created in 1964 in the culturally mixed area between East and West.

The large, predominantly Muslim, Northern Region dwarfed the other two regions in size, however, with more than three-quarters of Nigeria's territory and more than half of its total population. Thus the North dominated Nigerian politics in the postindependence civilian government. At the same time, the mixed Christian-Muslim-animist Western Region and, especially, the predominantly Christian Eastern Region surpassed the North in education, level of development, and representation in the civil service and upper ranks of the military.

Tensions had been mounting in Nigeria since before the country's independence in 1960. Intensely fought elections plagued with fraud and violence, along with widespread corruption and mismanagement by government officials, culminated in two military coups in 1966. The first was staged on January 15 by seven mid-level officers, six of whom were Ibos, the seventh a Yoruba. Although they were unsuccessful in seizing control of the government, the coup plotters succeeded in wiping out much of the country's political leadership, with assassinations of the Nigerian prime minister (a Northerner), the minister of finance, the premiers of the Northern and Western regions (the premiers of the Eastern and Mid-West regions escaped unharmed), and much of the senior military leadership, including four of the most senior Northern officers and two high-ranking officers from the Western Region. The coup attempt was quelled by another Ibo, Major-General Aguiyi-Ironsi—not one of the plotters—who assumed power as head of the federal military government.

ˈThough the new government was initially greeted with some relief and the expectation that the army would restore order and clean up corruption, several moves by the new head of state quickly turned the tide of opinion against him.[2] The coup plotters, though jailed, were never brought to trial. And while Ironsi's cabinet was ethnically mixed, he tended to surround himself with fellow Ibos as his top advisers. In time, many Nigerians, especially in the North, began to view the January coup—because of the ethnic makeup of its Ibo ringleaders and of its non-Ibo victims—as an Ibo attempt to take over the government. These suspicions were compounded by Ironsi's decree in May 1966 abolishing Nigeria's federal structure and making it a unitary state, in the interest, he said, of centralizing the administrative functions formerly divided by region and of reducing tribalism and regionalism. At the same time, he banned political activity for 30 months, giving the impression that the military planned to remain in power longer than previously indicated. Demonstrations in the North against the unification decree turned violent against the Eastern Ibos residing in the region, and hundreds were killed. Also in May, compounding suspicions still further, a round of 12 military promotions saw the advancement of eight Ibos, given that Ibos dominated the middle officer ranks; only one of the 12 was a Northerner.

A countercoup in July led by a coalition of Northern officers took Ironsi's life (many other Ibo officers were also targeted) and installed a young Northern officer, Lt. Col. Yakubu Gowon, as supreme commander. Gowon, who had not been part of the coup and who, because of his military training, firmly believed that soldiers did not belong at the helm of government, accepted the leadership role with some hesitation. He fully expected to return power to a civilian government within a matter of months.[3] Even so, from the beginning, one of the four regional military governors refused to accept his authority. Lt. Col. Emeka Ojukwu of the Eastern Region argued that 12 other officers, including Ojukwu himself, were senior to the new head of state.

Gowon immediately reinstituted the four-region federal structure and convened an ad hoc constitutional convention to make recommendations on an appropriate form of civilian government for Nigeria's future. Before it could complete its work, however, in late September and early October, pogroms broke out against Easterners living in the North (Ibos and various Eastern minorities). Retaliation against Northerners living in the Eastern Region further fed the violence in the North. In all, an estimated 6,000–8,000 Easterners were massacred[4] as the violence spread beyond the Muslim far-North into the ethnically and religiously mixed "Middle Belt" area, and this time army soldiers were deeply involved in the killings.

An estimated 1.5 million Easterners fled the North and other parts of the federation for their home region,[5] while Eastern Military Governor Ojukwu ordered the expulsion of all non-Easterners from his region, saying he could no longer ensure their safety. Already Eastern troops stationed elsewhere in Nigeria had been repatriated to their home region, and Northern troops had been transferred from the East.[6] Ojukwu refused to send the Eastern delegates back to the ad hoc constitutional convention, saying he feared for their safety, and numerous efforts to schedule a meeting of the Supreme Military Council in a location that Ojukwu would consider safe were unsuccessful.

One meeting of the Supreme Military Council, including Gowon and Ojukwu and their deputies, did take place in January 1967, hosted by Ghanaian Head of State General Joseph Ankrah at Aburi, Ghana. Though the meeting produced a set of accords that, among other measures, provided for a much decentralized, confederal form of government for Nigeria's four regions, the confederation was never fully implemented, as both sides retreated from some of the commitments made at Aburi. A second Aburi meeting was being planned for April 1967 in an attempt to salvage the accords, but a coup attempt against General Ankrah ended his efforts on behalf of the Nigerians.

Nigeria continued what by then seemed an inevitable slide toward civil war. On May 27, 1967, the Eastern Consultative Assembly authorized Ojukwu to declare a sovereign Republic of Biafra "at an early practicable date." That declaration came on May 30.

The first shots in the Nigerian civil war were fired by federal troops on July 6, 1967, initiating a "police action" that was expected to last perhaps three weeks. Not until mid-August, when the Biafran Army invaded the Mid-West Region, pushing to within 135 miles of Lagos, did the federal government declare "total war" against the secessionists. Although by early October the Biafran troops had retreated back across the Niger River into their home territory—and never again threatened areas beyond Biafran boundaries (the Eastern Region)—over the next 27 months the conflict settled into a war of attrition with an estimated 600,000 deaths on the battlefield and from starvation.[7] Despite the persistent efforts of a wide array of official and nonofficial third parties from three continents, it ended with the battlefield defeat of a Biafra so diminished in size and strength that it had long since passed the point of being able to plausibly secure its independence.

QUAKER INVOLVEMENT BEGINS

It was on the strength of Quaker contacts in West Africa and the previous experience of certain key Nigerian and Biafran officials with Quaker programs that the Quaker team gained entry as conciliators into the Nigerian conflict.[8] Quaker involvement in Nigeria had begun shortly before the country's independence in 1960 with the posting there of Paul and Priscilla Blanshard, who served as international affairs representatives for the American Friends Service Committee. Recognizing the internal stresses caused by the rivalry among the three dominant ethnic groups, Paul Blanshard launched a series of international work camps in Nigeria in 1961 to strengthen leadership across ethnic lines.

A second Quaker program, International Dialogues in West Africa, was established in Lome, Togo, in 1963 to bring together new and potential leaders of the countries of West Africa to find African solutions for African problems. It was from the Lome office that International Dialogues program head, John Volkmar, monitored the rising tensions in Nigeria. At the same time, Adam Curle, a Harvard professor with education and economic development experience in Ghana and Western Nigeria, began to wonder whether his recent conciliation experience with a Quaker mission in the India-Pakistan conflict could be of use in Nigeria.

The first contact with one of the Nigerian parties was made by the man who became the third member of the Quaker team, Walter Martin, who had joined the Quaker United Nations Office after 10 years of reconstruction and reconciliation work in Kenya. Martin arranged a meeting for himself and Curle with Joseph

Iyalla, the Nigerian deputy permanent representative to the United Nations, on January 4, 1967, six months before the outbreak of fighting. The two Quakers offered assistance as channels of communication between the different parts of the country. Iyalla, who had been the first Nigerian to attend a Quaker conference for diplomats,[9] encouraged Curle to make private, unofficial explorations on an upcoming business trip to Nigeria.

With authorization from the two Quaker service agencies, the American Friends Service Committee in Philadelphia and British Friends Peace and Service in London, Curle and Volkmar toured all regions of Nigeria for four weeks in April and May to gather information and seek ways of helping relieve tensions through conciliation or humanitarian aid. In the East they met Ojukwu and most of the other key people later involved in peace negotiations and as Biafran representatives in Western Europe and the United States. In Lagos they met two federal officials, Okoi Arikpo, soon to become commissioner of external affairs, and Hamzat Ahmadu, principal secretary to Gowon who, like Iyalla, was an alumnus of a Quaker seminar.

With the outbreak of the war in July 1967, Martin reiterated the Quaker offer of conciliatory work or relief in a meeting with Iyalla and Arikpo in New York. The Quakers decided subsequently, however, to support an African initiative: the Consultative Committee of six African heads of state, which was created by the Organization of African Unity (OAU) to deal with the Nigerian problem (discussed in greater detail later in this chapter). But the Consultative Committee, bound by its authorizing resolution, did not pursue a mediation role; at its first meeting, in November 1967, it called on Biafra to renounce secession and to accept the federal offer of peace in the context of a united Nigeria.

The decisive move for the Quakers came as a result of a meeting, on other Quaker business, between John Volkmar and Hamani Diori, the president of Niger and a member of the Consultative Committee. In light of the committee's having, in essence, taken the federal side in the conflict, Diori suggested that the Quakers, with their unofficial status and long conference experience, might be able to convene a secret meeting of lower level officials from the two sides to search for possible areas of agreement.

The American Friends Service Committee (AFSC) in Philadelphia authorized a second trip by Volkmar and Curle to Nigeria. Although there was some disagreement as to whether it should be a high-level conciliation effort (Curle's view) or a lower level meeting (favored by AFSC staff), all agreed on "proceeding as the way opened," in the time-honored Quaker fashion.[10]

This time, the two Quakers felt that an early meeting with General Gowon, whom they had not met previously, would be the key to the whole trip. When a letter to Principal Secretary Ahmadu did not open the door, it was Edwin Ogbu, minister of external affairs (later permanent representative to the United Nations) and the third federal official with a firsthand acquaintance with Quakers, who helped them gain access to General Gowon.[11]

At a meeting on February 3, 1968, the Nigerian head of state, who had himself learned of the Quakers through his schooling in British and American history,[12] listened to their proposal for a secret meeting and agreed that they should pursue the idea with the rebel side. He authorized them to travel there, although cautioning that he could not guarantee their safety as all flights into the rebel enclave were suspected of carrying arms and were therefore targets of federal antiaircraft gunners.[13]

So began the Quaker conciliation mission, which continued throughout the course of the war. Four times the team members, traveling in pairs,[14] made hazardous trips into Biafra for meetings with officials (twice with Ojukwu), and eight times they held consultations with federal officials (six times with Gowon). They also met with representatives of the two sides in New York, Washington, London, Paris, Geneva, and Lisbon and worked in a variety of ways to support other third-party efforts.

THE QUAKER APPROACH TO CONCILIATION

The exploration of a possible meeting to be convened under Quaker auspices—an idea that reemerged at a later time when, as initially, other peacemaking efforts were stalled—served as an opening point of discussion for the Quaker team with Nigerian leader Gowon and, upon receiving encouragement from him, with Biafran leader Ojukwu. It also set in motion two of the three key aspects of the Quakers' conciliation role in the conflict: opening lines of communication; reducing suspicions, misperceptions, and fears; and advocating for a negotiated settlement while supporting official mediation efforts.

Opening Lines of Communication

Gowon, although doubtful about the prospects for a Quaker meeting since so many other meeting attempts had failed, was nonetheless willing to consider it and authorized Volkmar and Curle to travel to the rebel enclave. He also said he would be very interested in hearing their report from the other side and asked them to tell Ojukwu that as soon as a cease-fire was agreed upon, he would stop the federal advance and bring in a third party to police the lines (a new and significant point, they later learned).

This was the first of at least five times during the Quaker mission when team members were specifically requested to carry a message from one leader to the other. Numerous other times they reported back, as a matter of course, to one side following a meeting with the other. It was always their practice to be entirely open about their travels and the individuals with whom they had met. They consistently shared their impressions of conditions and attitudes on the other side, to the extent possible without violating confidentiality or providing information that might give one side a military advantage. They also, on several occasions, made substantive suggestions of their own that they thought might help break an impasse in negotiations.

One episode (see pp. 101–2) found the Quakers carrying to Lagos concessions being offered by the Biafrans that they felt they could not present at formal peace talks for fear of appearing weak. The importance of the Quaker team's role of opening lines of communication was also highlighted in another incident. After an outburst against the Nigerians, as well as the United States and the United Kingdom, during a meeting with the Quakers, a Biafran official apologized saying, "You see, you are the closest we can get to Lagos."[15]

But in carrying messages, writes Curle, the Quaker conciliator does not consider himself to be a "passive postman." He acts instead as an emissary, a participant "in the total situation whose task is to try to change it in a direction that, in general *both sets of protagonists want*."[16] The conciliator also actively tries to remove obstacles to the next step in peacemaking: negotiation. This involves the second aspect of the conciliation role.

Reducing Suspicions, Misperceptions, and Fears

Writing shortly after his experience in Nigeria, Adam Curle described the suspicion, distrust, faulty perceptions, and poor communications that accompany deteriorating relations in times of war. The central purpose of conciliation, then, is to correct misperceptions, to reduce unreasonable fears, and to improve communications to an extent that reasonable discussion can take place and rational bargaining becomes possible.[17]

Curle believes that the things that separate people are relatively easy to solve. But it is necessary to change people's perception of—to help them "re-perceive"— their enemies, themselves, and the whole situation so that they can accept what might otherwise be a simple solution.[18]

Though he has described conciliation as "essentially an applied psychological tactic,"[19] the Quaker practice of conciliation is impelled and informed by Quaker faith, and Curle has himself written and spoken of its religious underpinnings. "Virtually the sole dogma," he writes, "if this word is not too emphatic, of Friends concerns 'that of God in every one'."[20] Characterized as a "divine spark" in each person,

> this gives us [the conciliators and the parties] a real relationship. Literally, we are all connected. . . . One cannot be hostile or violent toward another without being hostile or violent toward oneself. . . . In working for peace I am simply doing what I've sensed is carrying out a normal human function: to realize—make real—the bond between us all.[21]

To carry messages faithfully and to truly understand the parties' attitudes, perceptions, and fears demands of the conciliator a carefully cultivated skill at listening. For the Quaker conciliator, however, listening has a spiritual function as well. Curle has described it this way:

> To listen attentively is to act autonomously. . . . Thus as in prayer, so in listening we try to reach a deeper part of our being.
> Moreover, listening does not only lead to hearing and understanding, but also to speech. If we learn to listen, we will often find that the right words are given to us.

These do not come as a result of careful thought, but spring from our more profound sources of knowledge.

The importance of listening, then, is not only that we "hear" the other in a profound sense but communicate with him or her through our true nature. For this reason very strong and positive feelings are often aroused in both the listener and the one listened to. In this way peace makers may reach the part of the other person that is really able to make peace, outwardly as well as inwardly.[22]

Quaker conciliators strive "never [to] point the finger at a single guilty party," recognizing that "everything that happens is the product of the convergence of multiple forces of which some may only appear more directly responsible than others."[23] Quakers will engage in the practice of "speaking truth to power," however, trusting that "when the relationship is founded on real liking and the anguished words are spoken without rage they will really be heard and acted upon."[24]

In the Nigerian civil war, for example, on two occasions team members informed Gowon that hospitals and markets in the rebel enclave had been targets of Nigerian bombers. The first time, though shocked and saddened, Gowon replied to Martin and Curle that perhaps this would serve the "good purpose" of making the rebels "realize that rebellion doesn't pay and so lay down their arms." To this Curle responded that in fact, the bombing had had the opposite effect of causing people to think that the charges of genocide against the Ibo people must be true, and they might as well go on fighting as long as possible, rather than waiting to be massacred.[25] When after a visit to Biafra a month later Volkmar and Martin again raised the issue of the bombing of civilian targets, Gowon responded that he had given strict instructions for accurate bombing of military installations only, but perhaps the time had come to reissue the order.[26] On the Biafran side, on the other hand, the Quakers did what they could (although apparently to little avail) to explain that these bombings were not intentional but rather hits by inexperienced pilots.

Advocating for a Negotiated Settlement and Supporting Official Mediation Efforts

In all that the Quaker conciliators did in Nigeria, their overarching goal was to end the suffering on all sides by promoting a peaceful settlement of the conflict. As nonofficial actors, untrained in diplomacy, they had no pretensions of taking the lead in mediating formal peace talks. They saw their role as a support to such official efforts as appeared to have any chance of making progress.

The substance of Quaker discussions with the parties dealt very much with the political, economic, and military issues in the conflict—with positions and possible terms of settlement. Their message was never religious per se, but in certain respects it might be considered spiritual. The "desire of the Quakers for peace was well-known, their anti-war stance," according to former Biafran Commissioner of Commerce and Industry Sylvanus Cookey.[27] Some top advisers to Gowon, in fact, were initially concerned that a Quaker influence on Gowon—"himself a pacifist by nature, a Christian gentleman"—might lead to a deliberate slowing down of the war.[28] Their fears proved to be unfounded.

The Quaker message with regard to war, according to Volkmar, was that "no problem is ever resolved by war. War only postpones the problem, and it is destructive, expensive, and painful. Ultimately you will have to sit down together."[29] Volkmar adds that he and his colleagues were not trying to sell Gowon on Quakerism, but they did talk about peace, reconciliation, and the potential to resolve conflict nonviolently. A key theme in their discussions with the Biafran side, according to one close observer, was that Gowon's offer of amnesty could be trusted and that the Ibos would not be punished if they laid down their arms.[30]

ENVOYS, PEACE SEEKERS, AND PEACEMAKERS: OTHER INTERMEDIARY EFFORTS

The Nigerian civil war was surely one of the most mediated conflicts in recent history. Quaker conciliation efforts over the course of the conflict ran parallel to—and in a number of cases intersected with—numerous other attempts to bring a negotiated settlement to the conflict. No fewer than 16 African leaders became involved in some capacity, in addition to a number of British and American political leaders, ministers, and legislators. Numerous international, regional, and subregional organizations sought to mediate or in some way promote peace, as did a variety of religious figures and institutions, and even two Western academics.[31]

Two initiatives, those of the Commonwealth Secretariat and the Organization of African Unity, succeeded to the extent of convening formal peace talks, although none of the attempts at peacemaking proved successful in ending the war. Discussed here are the Commonwealth and OAU efforts, the Quaker interface with those efforts, and the Quaker relationship to other more limited initiatives.

Commonwealth Secretariat

The most sustained official-level peacemaking initiative in the Nigerian civil war—and the initiative with which the Quaker team cooperated most closely—was that conducted by Commonwealth Secretary-General Arnold Smith and a number of top deputies on the secretariat staff. Over the course of much of the civil war, the secretariat was active, primarily behind the scenes, in trying to establish terms for a cease-fire and enough substantive common ground to make formal peace talks viable. Smith and his colleagues had many contacts with the two sides by phone and mail and in confidential consultations in London, Lagos, and elsewhere.[32]

Smith's first overtures to the parties were made in the early months of 1967, prior to the outbreak of fighting. But although both Gowon and Ojukwu indicated they would welcome a visit from him, there was no support for a Commonwealth peacemaking mission while General Ankrah of Ghana was still trying to mediate an agreement based on the Aburi accords.[33] In addition, Biafran leaders made it clear that they would not accept any arbitration or mediation involving formal British participation; they were profoundly suspicious of British motives based on their interpretation of colonial history and the British role in establishing northern dominance in the Nigerian federation. Ojukwu also believed that the British were responsible for persuading Gowon to backtrack on the Aburi accords.[34]

In Nairobi at the time of Biafra's declaration of independence on May 30, 1967, Smith was urged by East African presidents Milton Obote of Uganda, Julius Nyerere of Tanzania, and Kenneth Kaunda of Zambia to go to Lagos to caution Gowon against starting hostilities against the secessionists. But while in London awaiting an invitation from Gowon, Smith received word that the federal government had decided to launch its police action against the East. "Any time for mediation had now passed," Gowon informed him. When Smith finally did meet with Gowon in Lagos on July 7, the Nigerian leader established a precondition that would be repeated many times in the months ahead: no negotiations could be held—and no official travel authorized to the rebel side—unless Ojukwu renounced secession. Smith learned shortly thereafter that hostilities had broken out the day before his meeting with Gowon.[35]

The secretary-general and his colleagues remained active for the next 11 months, trying to bring the parties together for talks at the ministerial level. A flurry of activity in October 1967 seemed to hold promise of progress, only to founder in a pattern that Smith portrays as illustrative of "the general flow of negotiations" as he experienced them.[36] Secret talks between officials of Nigeria and Biafra were scheduled for late October in Smith's London flat, but the two Biafran representatives were delayed for 10 days by "mechanical difficulties." Meanwhile, Ojukwu complained about the British venue and the level of representatives sent by the federal side. During the period of waiting, Smith was able to bring another Biafran emissary and a more junior Biafran together with the Nigerians for exploratory talks. But by the time the missing negotiators arrived from Biafra, their Nigerian counterparts had left. Back in Lagos, Cabinet hardliners wanted to pull out of the London talks, but Gowon and Foreign Minister Arikpo convinced them to send the team back to London. By the time the Nigerians arrived, however, the Biafrans had left for France.[37]

Writes Smith, this episode gave him

> a first sight of Ojukwu's pattern for wrecking talks. While keeping an international reputation for being ready to enter negotiations—a reputation for reasonableness he recognised as essential if he was to win sympathy and, best of all, recognition for Biafra—he was wary of entering any real discussions that might involve compromise. So he allowed them to be set up, and then played for a breakdown.[38]

Smith's continued efforts to bring the two sides together were finally crowned with success when in May 1968 formal peace talks under Commonwealth auspices, and hosted by Ugandan President Milton Obote, were held in Kampala.

Preliminary to the formal talks were days of meetings between the two parties, held in Smith's London flat, to agree on the venue and agenda for the formal negotiations to follow.

The Quakers, who by now had established a relationship of trust with leaders in both Nigeria and Biafra, as well as with members of the Commonwealth Secretariat, felt it was important to have a representative in London to be in touch with both sides and try to help in the search for a peaceful solution.[39] Walter Martin, sent by the British and American Quaker service bodies, had long talks with the chief negotiators on the Biafran side, Chief Justice Sir Louis Mbanefo and Dr. Eni Njoku, and a shorter talk with Nigeria's senior representative, Chief Anthony Enahoro. Although he made several suggestions aimed at resolving points of impasse, Martin's major contribution was to reassure the Biafrans that the Commonwealth Secretariat was impartial and to persuade them to go to the peace talks.[40]

Adam Curle and his wife, Anne, were then dispatched to Kampala to provide a Quaker presence during the nine days of talks, May 23–31, 1968. Their terms of reference, in effect, were expressed in a letter by the Philadelphia AFSC staff:

> It must be understood of course that our role in this whole process is a very humble one. We do not presume to be acting as major negotiators in any way. We are merely hoping to put our relationship of confidence to good use on both sides.[41]

Or, as Adam Curle was to write at the conclusion of the talks:

> It is not our role to arrange a conference such as this. . . . But there is a lot of persuasion, clarification, message carrying, listening, defusing, honest brokering, encouraging, and liaison with the Commonwealth Secretariat to be done.[42]

This he had plenty of opportunity to do at the talks. From the start, the public positions taken by the two sides were incompatible; therefore, much of the intermediary activity went on behind the scenes. Three sets of proposals were put forward: a cease-fire proposal by the Biafrans, a counterproposal by the Nigerians, and a compromise developed by Smith and his colleagues in separate talks with the parties. Although private talks suggested some possible flexibility, negotiations collapsed when Biafran chief negotiator Mbanefo took a hard line in a May 31 plenary speech, which was later revealed to have been drafted in Ojukwu's headquarters well before the talks had begun.[43] Smith had tried to salvage the process by talking to the parties directly and through messages carried by Curle. Curle had also given all parties copies of a Quaker paper suggesting a substantive solution to their problem.

As the talks broke down, Smith decided not to expose Ojukwu's posturing at the request of Mbanefo, who believed he could convince the Biafran leadership to resume talks in London within a month. Mbanefo then left for London to put the Biafran case before the international press. Ojukwu, as it turned out, did not allow the Biafran negotiators to return to London for further talks.[44]

It is unlikely that the Biafrans ever accepted Smith as an entirely impartial third party. The secretary-general undertook to act in a purely personal capacity, both to avoid being interpreted as conferring international legitimacy on the Biafrans and to avoid the obvious identification of the Commonwealth with Great Britain. But both Biafran and Nigerian sources suggest that the two sides considered the Commonwealth secretary-general to be "little more than a stalking horse for British interests."[45]

In any case, although Smith continued his efforts to re-start the peace talks in London for some time—and though he never ceased to monitor events for opportunities to promote negotiations, at times with the help of information gathered by the Quakers on trips to Lagos and Biafra—the peacemaking initiative was now taken up again by the OAU. Only much later, in November 1969, was there the renewed prospect of the action returning to the Commonwealth Secretariat's court. Before anything definite could be launched, however, the war had come to an abrupt end.

Organization of African Unity

Throughout the Nigerian civil war there was a strong feeling in many African quarters that there should be an African solution to the crisis. But, as with every other attempt to settle the conflict away from the battlefield, the various African initiatives attempted were unsuccessful. One group did succeed in at least getting the parties as far as the bargaining table: the Organization of African Unity.[46]

The OAU first dealt with the Nigerian crisis at a meeting of the Assembly of Heads of State in Kinshasa in September 1967, shortly after the outbreak of the war. Gowon's representative at the meeting, Chief Obafemi Awolowo, was successful in preventing formal discussion of the conflict by the assembly and in heading off a move to create an ad hoc mediatory committee. Instead, the assembly established a Consultative Committee of six heads of state (Haile Selassie of Ethiopia as chair, Joseph Mobutu of Congo/Zaire, William Tubman of Liberia, Joseph Ankrah of Ghana, Ahmadou Ahidjo of Cameroon, and Hamani Diori of Niger) with the mission of assuring the head of the Nigerian government "of the Assembly's desire for the territorial integrity, unity and peace of Nigeria." This stand in opposition to secession was reiterated at the Consultative Committee's first meeting in Lagos two months later, a position that left Ojukwu no room to maneuver and prevented the group from serving in the capacity of mediator. After the Lagos meeting, the committee did not take action again for eight months.

In July 1968, after the Kampala talks had failed, the Consultative Committee was reconvened, this time in Niamey by President Diori. Gowon and Ojukwu each addressed the group on separate days in what turned out to be preliminary negotiations for a second round of formal peace talks. Held in Addis Ababa under the chairmanship of Emperor Selassie, the talks lasted a month, from August 5 to September 6.

Present for the opening session, Ojukwu held forth in a two-hour speech that equated the physical survival of the Biafran people with the sovereign independence of the Biafran state. When Gowon himself failed to appear, however, Ojukwu abruptly departed on August 6, leaving Eni Njoku as delegation head but effectively foreclosing any possibility for substantive negotiations.[47]

The federal proposal made in Addis Ababa showed a somewhat greater sensitivity than earlier to Ibo fears of physical abuse at the hands of an occupying force and indicated new flexibility regarding the possible introduction of an "external force" after fighting ceased. The Biafran proposal was essentially the same as at Kampala: for Biafra to rejoin the Nigerian federation, it must retain responsibility for its internal security, have an armed force of its own, and have the ability to join international organizations in its own right. When, after a week and a half, the peace talks became stalemated, Selassie turned to the subject of transportation of relief supplies. He eventually adjourned the conference to prepare for an upcoming OAU summit.

Although the Quaker team members had not tried to get to the preliminary OAU talks in Niamey, they thought it would be important for them to provide support to the formal talks in Addis Ababa. Adam Curle checked into the hotel where the Nigerian delegation stayed, while John and Joanne Volkmar stayed in the same hotel as the Biafran delegation. This time the talks were conducted with a high degree of formality and tight security, making it difficult for the Quaker team to make quiet, private contacts with the parties as they had in Kampala. And there were few openings for contact with the conference organizers, the OAU Secretariat and Ethiopian government. Volkmar reported in a letter that the general atmosphere of the talks was one of propaganda warfare rather than of conciliation.[48]

After about a week of the talks, the Volkmars and Curle decided to go to Lagos to do something they had not previously done: present their own view on an issue that deeply concerned them. They (and others) had begun to fear that a disastrous guerrilla struggle would be waged by the rebels in the event of a federal victory and occupation of the major Biafran population centers. They felt they should speak out as tactfully as possible, even at risk of offending Gowon.[49]

Then, on the eve of their departure, Biafran chief negotiator Njoku revealed privately to the Quakers new terms that his government would be willing to accept but could not state openly for fear of appearing to weaken. Would Volkmar and Curle communicate these proposals to the federal government? Njoku maintained that Biafra was prepared to give up its insistence on sovereignty and would be flexible on cease-fire lines, boundaries of an eventual state, composition of a peacekeeping force, and the name of a state (implying a compromise on the name *Biafra*). But it could not compromise on the need for an independent armed force within cease-fire lines and having some degree of international standing.[50]

So on August 14, 1968, Curle and Volkmar presented the Njoku proposals to Gowon, together with suggestions of their own on ways of meeting the Biafrans' two key conditions. Apologizing for their temerity, they also expressed their hope for a negotiated settlement to avoid the threat of extended guerrilla activity, a prospect Gowon dismissed as infeasible for the rebels without a good supply line from the outside. As the Quakers left Gowon's headquarters in Dodan Barracks, they passed a group of senior field commanders gathering for an important meeting. They later learned that their report had aroused a controversy in the inner councils of government as to whether the concessions being offered were of significance. But the hawks prevailed; two days later federal officials informed Volkmar of the decision to pursue the war into the Ibo heartland.[51]

The OAU, for its part, did not pursue efforts to mediate the Nigerian conflict again until eight months later when, in April 1969, the Consultative Committee convened a round of preliminary negotiations in Monrovia, which were unsuccessful in establishing a justification for resumption of full-scale talks. A final effort was made by Selassie just one month before the war's end when, in December 1969, he hosted a round of talks in Addis Ababa. This time they broke up due to a prior ambiguity as to the nature of the auspices under which the meeting was to be conducted (Selassie acting as an African head of state, auspices acceptable to the Biafrans, versus Selassie acting under OAU auspices, which is what the Nigerians understood to be the case).

Other Initiatives

At one level, the fact that the Quakers were a religious organization helped open the door for them to Gowon, so eager was the federal side to make its case that this was not a religious war of Muslims against Christians, as the early Biafran propaganda maintained.[52] But admittance was by no means a guarantee that the federal door would remain open and the welcome hospitable as, indeed, it proved to be for the Quakers throughout the course of the war.

In this respect, the Quakers were unique among the many religious actors that became involved in the conflict. Because the Eastern Region of Nigeria is predominantly Christian, Western churches, particularly the Roman Catholic church, became deeply involved in providing humanitarian aid to the Biafrans. Most religious figures who made efforts to promote peace were therefore highly suspect on the federal side, and their peacemaking attempts were unsuccessful.[53]

Of the nonofficial third parties, only the Quakers won the acceptance of both sides and sustained their involvement for the duration of the civil war. On two occasions, however, they put their own credibility on the line by sponsoring non-Quaker initiatives that they believed held some promise for progress. Neither the effort to secure a truce by Harvard Professor Roger Fisher nor that by U.S. Representative Charles Diggs to secure agreement on opening a new airstrip for relief supplies to Biafra met with success, however. The Quakers came to realize the threat these outside involvements had posed to their own position of trust with the parties when, after the war, some Nigerian authorities privately criticized them for having aided the efforts of other parties whose neutrality the Nigerians questioned.[54]

WHY EFFORTS AT A NEGOTIATED PEACE FAILED

The Nigeria-Biafra conflict became the world's first public relations war, with Biafran propaganda proving highly effective in putting the plight of the Biafran people before the eyes of the world—and in shaping the perceptions of Biafran citizens about the threat posed by the Nigerian government and military. The most effective propaganda theme, internationally and internally, proved to be that the Biafrans were victims of a war of genocide, a charge that had more to do with the anti-Ibo pogroms that occurred before the war than with the Nigerians' conduct of the war itself.[55] With the help of Markpress News Feature Services, a Geneva public relations firm, Biafra had gained widespread press coverage—and massive popular sympathy—in Europe and the United States by mid-1968.

By the end of the war, however, the genocide charge had very little credibility, in large part due to the activities of an international observer team, which Gowon had invited into the battle zone to investigate charges of misconduct by federal troops and to observe the federal treatment of prisoners and civilian refugees.[56] But the charge had also, by then, served to internationalize the Nigerian civil war and put Western governments that supported the Nigerians—or that failed to recognize Biafran secession—on the defensive by church and civic lobbies at home.[57]

Only one Western country, France, succumbed to domestic pressures to the extent that it provided a certain measure of political support for Biafra and, ultimately, became a significant supplier of arms.[58] French support, together with diplomatic recognition of Biafra by four African states, Tanzania, Gabon, Côte d'Ivoire, and Zambia, may have been decisive in prolonging the war at a critical moment for Biafra. The support came at the nadir of Biafran fortunes, in spring and summer 1968, when its army had suffered reversals on the battlefield and church humanitarian relief efforts had not yet reached a volume that could arrest the growing starvation. So at a time when the Kampala and Addis Ababa peace talks might have held the promise of a negotiated end to the war, the diplomatic recognition by the four African states and the prospect of French recognition increased Biafran confidence and strengthened the young republic's resolve to carry on the battle. French military assistance, channeled through Gabon and Côte d'Ivoire, started to flow to Biafra that September.[59]

On the battlefield, meanwhile, it proved to be a war that Nigeria could not win early but Biafra could not win late. With the loss of Northern and Western officers in the January coup and the flight of Ibo officers to Biafra, Gowon was initially fighting with a decimated officer corps. But once the federal government could call up reservists, it had superior resources to draw upon. It was able to purchase British arms throughout, but when, shortly after the outbreak of war, Britain and the United States both declined to sell Nigeria fighter aircraft, Gowon (declaring "I'll go to any devil to get what I need to keep my country united"[60]) turned to the Soviet Union to purchase a dozen reconditioned MIG-17 fighters. Once Nigeria had begun to demonstrate the capacity to defeat the secession, and having shown its willingness to resort to Soviet suppliers, Western powers started to embrace the federal cause more openly.

Biafra, for its part, was never able to repeat the audacity of its early invasion of the Mid-West state, although it did sustain a stalemate on the battlefield for the last year or so of the war. When, 10 months into the war, its access to the sea through Port Harcourt was cut off (its border with Cameroon having already been sealed), Biafra was forced for the next 20 months to rely on airlifts of both food and military supplies. Hunger, corruption, and demoralization ultimately undermined the Biafran war effort.[61]

In light of Biafra's clear inability to secure its independence on the battlefield, by 1968 Ojukwu's overriding concern was to ensure maximum opportunities for Ibo political and economic self-determination within a united Nigeria.[62] He sought first of all an immediate and unconditional cease-fire, which would serve to halt Nigeria's military advance and freeze the status quo of two independent centers of power. Only then, according to the position taken by Biafra, could a full-scale peace conference be held that would work out Nigeria's future constitutional arrangements. Ojukwu refused to renounce secession until all other substantive matters had been resolved through negotiations; otherwise, he maintained, the Biafrans would not know what they were agreeing to.[63]

The federal government insisted that the negotiation process must begin, rather than end, with the renouncement of secession and saw the bargaining table as primarily a forum for determining the mechanics of surrender. Gowon opposed an unconditional cease-fire on the grounds that it would permit the rearming of rebel forces and thereby increase the danger of a prolonged conflict. And he never permitted the fundamental question of 12 states to be discussed in negotiations, arguing that any discussion of the country's constitutional arrangements could only take place among representatives of all of the 12 states.[64]

Yet this issue was critical to Ojukwu's effort to ensure equality for the Ibo people. He sought a return to the four-region framework with a separation of power and a high degree of autonomy, along the lines of the Aburi accords. Ultimately, concludes author John Stremlau:

> Ojukwu was certain that had Gowon been forced to accept a return to the four regions, this concession would have so undermined the viability of the wartime federal coalition that the ensuing political chaos would have opened the way for a full revival of the "Biafran spirit" and possibly the forging of an Ojukwu-dominated southern alliance.[65]

Citing a postwar interview with Ojukwu, Stremlau adds:

> However astonishing it may seem in retrospect, Ojukwu firmly believed in December 1969 [one month before Biafra's final defeat] that Biafra possessed the means to fight on long enough to force a political settlement with Nigeria, and this would allow him sufficient independence to survive in power and gradually undermine Gowon's authority in Lagos.[66]

That the recently defeated Ojukwu should so unabashedly admit to his former grand ambitions lends support to the view expressed by many who attribute the civil war—or at least the prolongation of the war—largely to Ojukwu's ambition. The Oxford-educated Ojukwu was widely known to have elected a career in the military because he saw it as the most promising path to political power. For example, Edwin Ogbu, former Nigerian ambassador to the United Nations, recounts his first meeting with Ojukwu in 1957. Ogbu was working in Kaduna, and Ojukwu came for a medical examination to join the army. Asked by Ogbu why he was joining, Ojukwu said he believed the army would take over the government of Nigeria, and he wanted to be there. After the first coup in 1966, Ogbu challenged Ojuwku about that statement, and the latter responded that he remembered it well.[68]

By Arnold Smith's assessment of him, Ojukwu

soon showed himself dominant and persuasive over his Biafran followers, but he was blindly unrealistic in the broader arena of world politics. He somehow believed he would win if he persevered until a magic number of countries recognised Biafra. Like many others, I came to the view that he was determined to play for all or nothing, although many of those around him were sincere seekers of a compromise settlement.[68]

Smith's perceptions were confirmed by Biafra's most prominent citizen, Nnamdi Azikiwe, who served from 1964 until the January 1966 coup as the first president of Nigeria. As early as October 1968, Azikiwe confided to Smith his disillusionment caused by Ojukwu's intransigence in the failed peace talks. Azikiwe said he had persuaded Tanzanian President Julius Nyerere to recognize Biafra in April 1968 on the assurance from Ojukwu that the recognition would be used to increase his bargaining power at Kampala and thereby improve the chances of an agreement, since Ojukwu planned to accept the principle of a united Nigeria as the basis for a settlement. Azikiwe said he felt he had been used to mislead Nyerere by Ojukwu's false pretenses.[69] Ten months later, in August 1969, in a dramatic reversal, Azikiwe declared his support for a united Nigeria and subsequently permitted Radio Nigeria to repeatedly beam his appeal for surrender into the Ibo heartland.[70]

In the final analysis, probably the greatest significance in the interpretation that the war could be attributed to the "personal ambition of a person and his clique" lay in the fact that this view was held by Nigerian Head of State Gowon.[71] It helped him withstand pressures within his cabinet from hard-liners who favored an occupation and punishment of the rebels in the event of a federal victory. In the words of Principal Secretary Hamzat Ahmadu, who worked closely with Gowon throughout the war: "Gowon's vision, his philosophy, was that you are fighting your brother—a misguided brother. . . . He believed this from beginning to end—almost alone. We used to say that we must separate the misleaders from the misled."[72]

Not only does this formulation of the war help explain the reserve with which the federal side prosecuted the war and the amnesty extended to Biafrans immediately following their defeat. It also helps account for Gowon's own intransigence in negotiations with the secessionists. A speech Gowon made before the OAU Assembly of Heads of State and Government on September 10, 1969, in Monrovia is illustrative:

> General Gowon spoke last. He did not appeal for support, but offered a personal account of his past association with Ojukwu since their days in military college. It was a rather shrewd attempt to personalize the enemy of Nigerian and African unity in order to convince the assembly that his regime harbored no vindictiveness toward the Ibo people. Ojukwu, he claimed, had invited him to join a budding coup against the Balewa government in January 1965 and, until the federal army repulsed the rebel blitz through the Midwest in August 1967, Ojukwu's overriding ambition was to rule all Nigeria. Deprived of this option, Gowon suggested that his adversary would exploit any opportunity to remain in power in the East. A cease-fire, he warned, would merely reward Ojukwu's intransigence and thereby prolong the suffering of the Ibo people.[73]

IMPACT OF THE QUAKER MISSION

That the Quaker conciliators won the trust, respect, and, in some cases, the affection of the Nigerian and Biafran leaders with whom they dealt cannot be in question. In the words of Joseph Iyalla, the Nigerian who from his post at the United Nations helped launch the Quaker mission, the team was successful in gaining "a good hearing and complete and uninhibited acceptability by all sides."[74]

The parties' assessment of the Quakers' motives—together with the Quakers' obvious lack of a political or denominational interest in the conflict—appears to have been central to their acceptance. Again, quoting Iyalla:

> [The] Quakers were readily perceived as friends who did not favor one side or the other but understood the underlying commitments on both sides that gave rise to all this ferment. They were obviously regarded as having no particular ax to grind, but at the same time as being genuinely concerned. They were factors in the equation.[75]

For General Gowon there was a religious element to their acceptance as well. He said he found "no difficulty in my relating to them. They were another sect of Christians, though not a formal organization. The basis is a belief in God and humanity." Gowon attributed their motivation to an "abhorrence for any war or violence."[76]

While not discounting the religious dimension, a third former federal official and one who had close contact with the Quakers, Hamzat Ahmadu, highlighted the human dimension in the Nigerians' relationship with the Quakers: "We embraced them more with an open heart than perhaps others with religious dogma, such as the Catholics, the bulk of Southern Christians, and the Muslims in the North. We saw them as a religious people but [also] as friends."[77]

From Ojukwu's point of view, it was the Quakers' nonofficial status and their denominational disinterestedness that were critical factors in their acceptance by the parties:

> It was a civil conflict therefore the element of suspicion was very large. Any political actor would be suspect; only a nonpolitical actor would have a chance of bringing the two sides together or giving the necessary type of assurance—not of security, but rather an umbrella under which you go in and you don't lose anything. Other churches . . . were suspect. With the Quakers, no one could say that Biafra was their mission.[78]

Ojukwu attributed the Quakers' motivation to their "absolute dedication to humanity" and saw the trust they achieved as based on "an infinite capacity for neutrality."[79]

The Quakers were also credited with being more modest and discreet than some of the other third parties who sought to become involved in the Nigerian conflict and with not having an agenda of their own to promote. Said Ahmadu: "The effect and confidence might be more than with publicity and ostentation as with a party doing it to get results or publicity. It was devoid of any publicity; they just wanted to do the job."[80]

But what of the Quakers' success and impact based on their own threefold set of objectives?

Opening Lines of Communication

Gowon credits the Quakers for both their constancy and their faithfulness in performing this particular task:

> They are the group that one would never forget. They persisted right the way through and were accepted. I did not feel betrayed or let down by their effort and knew that the message did get to the other [side].[81]

Allison Ayida, who served as permanent secretary to the Nigerian Ministry of Economic Development and was a member of every negotiating team fielded by the Nigerians, said he thought the Quakers' "most useful role was not so much peacemaking as the communication gap they filled."[82]

The most significant example of message-carrying was the Biafran proposal sent by chief negotiator Eni Njoku in Addis Ababa via the Quakers to Gowon in Lagos. Given a more favorable environment for negotiations, the new terms being offered by Biafra might have produced a breakthrough. For a host of reasons, however, they did not.

The value to the two parties of the Quakers' message-carrying function was perhaps best demonstrated by their *not* taking actions to prevent it. Gowon consistently refused to authorize travel to the rebel enclave by official-level actors such as the OAU Consultative Committee and Commonwealth Secretary-General Arnold Smith, insisting that this would confer political legitimacy on the breakaway region and internationalize the conflict. Nonofficial actors such as the Vatican envoys were told that they could visit the other side at their own risk, and, indeed, those were the terms under which the Quakers undertook their own hazardous trips into Biafra.[83] It appears, however, that the Quakers were the only third party specifically *requested* by Gowon to carry messages for him into the rebel enclave, and he was deeply appreciative of their willingness to incur both the hardships and dangers of such travel on the Nigerians' behalf.[84]

Ojukwu, for his part, was known to use visits from the outside to score propaganda points against his adversary.[85] The Quakers' first visit to Biafra after the war began was carefully monitored on the federal side for this type of publicity that would signal a manipulative use of the Quakers on the part of the Biafrans. When no mention was made of the Quaker visit on Biafran radio, the Nigerians concluded that the rebels were serious about using the Quakers as a channel of communication.[86]

Reducing Suspicions, Misperceptions, and Fears

The first step in performing this aspect of the conciliation role is listening empathetically to understand the parties' fears and concerns. Ojukwu eloquently expressed the way in which the Biafrans felt listened to and cared for by the Quakers:

> I saw them as highly objective and, then, being a church organization they never lacked in sympathy, which again helps in such a situation. Don't ever say to me, "Oh, 50 people were killed, oh well, that happens," and tell you let's go on. No, when you say to the Quakers, "this is what happened," there is a silence for a bit. There is a fellow human feeling for the tragedy, which is fully understood, and they then take that into consideration in their responses.[87]

The next step is to communicate this information in a way that it can be understood—and acted upon—by the other side. There is some evidence that this process occurred with both the Nigerians and Biafrans. On the federal side, the Quakers' main contribution may have been to help the leadership realize that, after a certain stage in the war, the Biafrans were motivated more by fear than by malevolence. Arnold Smith sees this as not having been so much a case of shaping Gowon's concern, for Gowon "was always concerned. But there were a lot of people [around him] with a different view." Smith believes the Quakers may have strengthened Gowon's determination to prevent a federal occupation of the Ibo heartland and vengeance on the part of federal troops—and bolstered Gowon's position in this regard among others in the Nigerian leadership who took a more hard-line position.[88]

This view coincides with John Volkmar's own sense of the Quakers' impact on Gowon: that Gowon's respect for them helped give legitimacy to his natural conciliatory inclinations.

> Gowon respected Adam as a professor and me for the work I did. You didn't have to be a freak to be for peace. Gowon was young [in his early thirties] and had little experience in the real world. . . . He took a lot of risks. His respect for us made him think about the things we talked about.[89]

In a similar vein, according to Arnold Smith, the Quakers were able to help some among the Biafran leadership believe that Gowon was "genuine in his concern for unity" and in his lack of desire for vengeance against the Ibo people.[90] Biafran London representative Ignatius Kogbara explained the effect on some Biafrans' thinking of the Quaker belief in the essential goodness of every person:

> That is, in fact, a conflict point. When you are at war and there are people in the Nigerian government with a strong Muslim background, seeing some element of goodness in them is a conflict point. . . . The Quakers would think there was something good in the federal government and in us. . . . They saw Gowon as basically a good man. It helped some of us to be sympathetic.[91]

Kogbara concluded that, ultimately, the Quakers' best contribution may have been that "they tried to resolve the hardness of the heart."[92]

This resonance between the Quakers and the more peace-oriented individuals on the Biafran side seems to have played itself out in a very practical way once the war was over. Allison Ayida credits them with having helped federal officials "identify which people on the Biafran side were most likely to assist in establishing a lasting peace. They could identify the peace lovers in influential positions."[93]

Advocating for a Negotiated Settlement and Supporting Official Mediation Efforts

The Quakers had a direct impact on the peace process, according to Biafran representative Kogbara who, from his base in London, had frequent contact with the Quaker conciliators. Kogbara acknowledges that the Biafrans were "the more recalcitrant side" when it came to negotiations, but "the Quakers did succeed in persuading us to go to the peace conferences and keep talking while the war was going on."[94] Kogbara says that during the preliminary stages prior to the Kampala talks, he had become convinced of the Quakers' sincerity and was in a position to communicate his views to C. C. Mojekwu, the Biafran commissioner of home affairs and Ojukwu's closest confidant.

Smith, the convener of the Kampala talks, supports this assessment of the Quaker contribution:

> They played a considerable part before the Kampala talks in encouraging key people around Ojukwu to favor talking—and afterwards. . . . Their total influence was

very considerable in preparing attitudes that would favor talking to Gowon's representatives.[95]

It would appear that, although the ultimate goal of peace escaped the Quakers along with the several dozen other envoys, peace seekers, and peacemakers in the Nigeria-Biafra conflict, the Quakers did achieve a measure of success in the performance of each of the specific functions of their conciliation role as they themselves defined it.

CONCLUSION

In his own study of the Quaker mission in Nigeria, C. H. Mike Yarrow, with characteristic Quaker modesty, describes the Quaker "enterprise" as a "small footnote" to a complicated story with many important actors. "In enlarging that footnote to fill many pages," he acknowledges, "there is an inevitable distortion, making the Quaker effort appear more important than it was."[96] Curle and Volkmar are themselves cautious when pressed to assess their role in the Nigeria mission.[97] Theirs was a quiet, totally behind-the-scenes effort—a support role in most respects. And the core of what they aspired to do—to get the parties to "re-perceive" their enemies, themselves, and the conflict so that progress could be made toward peace—is virtually impossible to measure.

All of that said, what can be concluded about the value, impact, significance, and replicability of their involvement? And what of the spiritual dimension?

The first conclusion to be reached is that the Quakers were genuinely appreciated and valued for what they did. Although they never spoke of religion, the people with whom the Quakers met were well aware of their pacifist convictions and assumed a spiritual motivation behind their work. Asked what he thought motivated the Quakers, Ignatius Kogbara replied, "God." For Yakubu Gowon, it was "a belief in God and humanity." For Emeka Ojukwu, "an absolute dedication to humanity." Asked whether the Quakers were seen as religious or secular actors, Arnold Smith replied, "I think people who knew them understood that their motivation was spiritual. But spiritual is not an opposite to secular, it's an attitude of values, of how you deal in secular matters."[98] The Quakers would surely endorse this view.

Perhaps with an eye to encouraging a broader interest in conciliation work, Adam Curle has suggested that there is no such thing as a Quaker approach to peacemaking:

> There is an approach based on an understanding of fears, hopes, greeds, prides, confusions, loves, hatreds, guilts, the projections of inner demons; and a strong motivation to clear up the mess these things produce. However, there is nothing specifically Quaker, or even religious, about this; any decent humanist would do and want the same.[99]

While it is probably quite true that the Quakers are not *uniquely* qualified to do conciliation of this sort, it could at the same time be argued that, as Quakers, these men were particularly well equipped spiritually for the practice of conciliation. Others might well look to their example in seeking to understand—and perhaps approximate—the sensitivities, the stamina, the humility, and the caring and respect for others required for this type of work.

Certainly the Quakers' own deep spiritual convictions about "that of God in every one" and the power of nonviolence underpinned their commitment and fortified them to endure the dangers, hardships, tensions, tedium (at times), and disappointments that were integral to this peacemaking effort, along with its accomplishments. Although it is possible to conceptualize a purely secular form of conciliation practice, it would be a mistake in the case of the Quakers to try to separate the secular from the spiritual or to assume that the same results could have been accomplished by individuals operating from a totally secular perspective.

It is difficult to reach conclusions about the efficacy of a peacemaking effort in a conflict in which peace was not achieved short of total surrender. (One cannot help but wonder, however, whether a negotiated peace in this war, given the personalities involved, could have possibly equaled the magnanimity expressed and reconciliation achieved in victory and defeat.) Nonetheless, some conclusions can be reached about the accomplishments of the Quaker mission.

The Quaker team was the sole third party that won the complete trust of both parties in the conflict, and they sustained that trust for the duration of the war. Although the Quakers insisted on being completely open about their movements, they also proved that they could be trusted with sensitive information, including the personal disappointments and fears of men in power. Their nonpolitical base of operation and their powerlessness were also ingredients in their acceptance. With nothing to gain denominationally or professionally, they were believed to be sincere in their desire to help relieve the suffering on all sides.

By their presence and availability at critical moments, the Quakers succeeded in opening lines of communication that would have otherwise remained closed. Although they were not the only intermediaries carrying messages in the Nigerian civil war, it cannot be assumed that had the Quakers not been present, an alternative emissary would have been available in every instance to perform this service. This conclusion is particularly justified given that every other intermediary who came forward was considered to be biased by one side or the other.

The Quakers had a hand in bringing about the formal peace talks that occurred by urging the Biafrans to the table. Given Ojukwu's skittishness about negotiations—particularly those mediated by third parties seen as partial to the Nigerian side—the Quaker encouragement appears to have been particularly influential. (At the same time, given the international pressures on both sides to appear reasonable and willing to negotiate, it may not have been decisive).

Finally, insofar as the Quaker conciliators had a hand in sensitizing federal officials to the genuine fears of the Biafran people and in legitimizing Gowon's stand against occupation and retribution, they might also have had a hand, however indefinable, in winning the extraordinary peace that prevailed in postwar Nigeria.[100]

Notes

1. The principal sources relied on for the history of the Nigerian civil war were John de St. Jorre, *The Nigerian Civil War* (London: Hodder and Stoughton, 1972); and John J. Stremlau, *The International Politics of the Nigerian Civil War 1967–1970* (Princeton, N.J.: Princeton University Press, 1977).

2. For a discussion of this period, see de St. Jorre, *Nigerian Civil War,* 30–64.

3. Interview with Yakubu Gowon, London, July 9, 1991.

4. De St. Jorre, *Nigerian Civil War,* 86. This is an estimate; no casualty counts were kept. De St. Jorre uses the figure of 10,000 for the total number of Easterners killed in 1966 in the disturbances of May, during the July coup, and in the September–October massacres.

5. Ibid., 87.

6. In an effort to stabilize the situation after the July coup, representatives of the regional military governors and Gowon had agreed on August 9 to order all soldiers back to their respective regions of origin. Gowon did keep federal troops of mainly Northerners in the Western Region and Lagos, however—a bone of contention with the West—until the time when their numbers could be replaced by Westerners.

7. De St. Jorre, *Nigerian Civil War,* 412 n.1.

8. This section's overview of the Quaker involvement is drawn from C. H. Mike Yarrow, *Quaker Experiences in International Conciliation* (New Haven, Conn.: Yale University Press, 1978), 188–96.

9. Launched in 1952 and extending through the 1970s, Quaker conferences for diplomats brought together young foreign service officers from different countries to discuss issues of current interest in international politics.

10. Yarrow, *Quaker Experiences,* 194.

11. In 1948, when Edwin Ogbu was a young college student in Florida, a Quaker woman (whose surname happened to be Friend) arranged a summer job for him. "I shall remain eternally grateful for that. . . . When they [Volkmar and Curle] introduced themselves as Quakers, I felt I should do the best I could" (interview with Edwin Ogbu, Lagos, August 9, 1991).

12. Interview with Gowon. Such was the case as well with the Oxford-educated Ojukwu (interview with Emeka Ojukwu, Lagos, July 17, 1991). Another Biafran leader, Commissioner of Commerce and Industry Sylvanus Cookey, had known some Quakers when he was a graduate student in London (interview with Sylvanus Cookey, Port Harcourt, Nigeria, July 23, 1991).

13. Federal officials refused to use the name *Biafra* during the war, referring instead to the "rebel enclave" or the "secessionist area." At some point after the war it became permissible, apparently well into the 1970s, to make reference to "the former Biafra" or to Ojukwu as the "Biafran rebel leader" (interview with Hamzat Ahmadu, Washington, D.C., April 25, 1991). Most of the former federal officials interviewed for this study, however, still did not utter the name of the breakaway republic.

14. In the closing months of the civil war, Curle, Volkmar, and Martin were assisted in their conciliation efforts by Kale Williams, head of the Quaker relief mission in Nigeria.

15. Yarrow, *Quaker Experiences,* 219.

16. Adam Curle, *Tools for Transformation: A Personal Study* (Stroud, U.K.: Hawthorn Press, 1990), 61 (emphasis in original). Curle goes on to explain that if there were not some desire for peace on both sides, they would not tolerate the involvement of mediators, who would "simply be a nuisance who confused the scene."

17. Adam Curle, *Making Peace* (London: Tavistock, 1971), 177.

18. Interview with Adam Curle, London, July 8, 1991.

19. Curle, *Making Peace*, 177.

20. Adam Curle, *True Justice: Quaker Peace Makers and Peace Making* (London: Quaker Home Service, 1981), 5.

21. Interview with Curle.

22. Curle, *Tools for Transformation*, 50–51.

23. Ibid., 63.

24. Ibid., 54.

25. Ibid., 55.

26. Yarrow, *Quaker Experiences*, 221

27. Interview with Cookey.

28. Interview with Allison Ayida, former permanent secretary, Ministry of Economic Development, Lagos, July 30, 1991. Gowon comes from the ethnically and religiously mixed Middle Belt region of the North. His father was an evangelist with the Christian Missionary Society for a time in the 1930s, and Gowon himself speaks appreciatively of the kindness of the missionaries and the quality of the primary school education he received at the mission school. A devout Christian, Gowon tells of being guided by prayer in his choice of a career. As head of state he composed a prayer that hung in the council hall of the Supreme Military Council. It asked for God's guidance in the council's deliberations, so that whatever decisions were taken would be motivated by love, rather than hatred and enmity, and would be in the interest of Nigeria and mankind (interview with Gowon; also interview with Sir David Hunt, British high commissioner to Nigeria during the early part of the civil war, Lindfield, West Sussex, U.K., July 4, 1991).

29. Telephone interview with John Volkmar, November 13, 1991.

30. Telephone interview with Haldore Hanson, December 13, 1991. A Lagos-based program officer with the Ford Foundation, Hanson financed most of the Quaker travel for the Nigerian mission with allocations from his discretionary fund. "Of all the discretionary grants I gave," he recalls, "this one I had more sentiment about."

31. See Stremlau, *International Politics of the Nigerian Civil War*, for the most thorough treatment of the many peacemaking efforts. See also Arnold Smith's personal documents and diaries, Leeds University Library Archives, Leeds, U.K.; Arnold Smith with Clyde Sanger, *Stitches in Time: The Commonwealth in World Politics* (Don Mills, Ontario: General Publishing, 1981), 76–105; and Yarrow, *Quaker Experiences*. The list of intermediary efforts compiled from these sources (though not necessarily exhaustive) includes the following. *African leaders*: President Ahmadou Ahidjo of Cameroon; Ghanaian Head of State General Joseph Ankrah; Prime Minister Kofi Busia of Ghana; President Hamani Diori of Niger; President Gnassingbe Eyadema of Togo; President Houphouet-Boigny of Côte d'Ivoire; President Kenneth Kaunda of Zambia; President Jomo Kenyatta of Kenya; President Joseph Mobutu of Congo/Zaire; President Julius Nyerere of Tanzania; President Milton Obote of Uganda; Emperor Haile Selassie of Ethiopia; President Leopold Senghor of Senegal; Prime Minister Siaka Stevens of Sierra Leone; President William Tubman of Liberia; and Foreign Minister Emile Zinsou of Dahomey/Benin. *British and American officials*: British Undersecretary of State Maurice Foley; Malcolm MacDonald, British roving ambassador in Africa; Minister of State Lord Malcolm Shepherd, British Commonwealth Office; British Prime Minister Harold Wilson; New York Senator Charles Goodell; and U.S. Representative Charles Diggs. *International, regional, and subregional organizations*: the Commonwealth, Conseil de l'Entente, East African Community, Organisation Commune Africaine et Malagache, Organization of African Unity, and United Nations. *Religious figures and organizations*, in addition to the Quakers:

E. L. Johnson, secretary for overseas missions, Presbyterian Church of Canada; Pope Paul; Vatican envoys Monsignors Conway and Rochau; and the World Council of Churches. *Academics*: Oxford historian and Africanist Dame Margery Perham and Harvard Professor Roger Fisher.

32. See Smith, *Stitches in Time*, 76-105. Smith colleagues who were active in the secretariat's efforts included Assistant Secretary-General Hugh Springer; Assistant Secretary-General Yaw Adu; Special Assistant Emeka Anyaoku; Assistant Under-Secretary Eric Norris; and staff member Gerald Hensley. Together with Smith or independently they participated in meetings with the parties and traveled to the region on Commonwealth business or on "scouting missions," as in the case of trips made by Adu, a Ghanaian, to Ghana and Lagos before the war, and Anyaoku, an Ibo from Eastern Nigeria, to meet with Ojukwu as tensions were mounting prior to secession.

33. Reports to Smith from Assistant Secretary-General Yaw Adu, dated March 30, 1967, and April 17, 1967, Leeds University Library archives.

34. Smith diary entry dated April 2, 1967, Leeds University Library archives.

35. Smith, *Stitches in Time*, 83–85.

36. Ibid., 87–88.

37. Ibid., 87–88.

38. Ibid., 88.

39. Yarrow, *Quaker Experiences*, 204.

40. This point, suggested in ibid., was confirmed by Ignatius Kogbara, London representative for Biafra, who said that the Quakers' greatest contribution "was persuading us to go to the peace conferences" (interview with Ignatius Kogbara, Port Harcourt, Nigeria, July 23, 1991).

41. Letter from the secretary, International Affairs Division, May 23, 1968, American Friends Service Committee archives, as quoted in Yarrow, *Quaker Experiences*, 204–5.

42. Letter from Kampala, June 1, 1968, American Friends Service Committee archives, as quoted in ibid., 256.

43. Smith, *Stitches in Time*, 99.

44. Ibid.

45. Stremlau, *International Politics of the Nigerian Civil War*, 146. In arriving at this conclusion, Stremlau cites two documents: Republic of Biafra, "Commonwealth Peace Moves," a confidential memorandum prepared by the Directorate of Propaganda, March 1968; and an authoritative analysis by Adamu Ciroma, "Arnold Smith and Prospects for Peace in Nigeria," *New Nigerian* (February 17, 1968). Curle also was of the impression that Smith was never completely trusted by the Biafrans. He notes that Smith made the mistake in Kampala of staying in the same hotel as the Nigerians. Curle and his wife stayed in a hotel where there were no delegations (personal communication, November 1, 1991).

46. See Stremlau, *International Politics of the Nigerian Civil War*, 184–213.

47. Stremlau (ibid., 201) points out that Ojukwu's speech contained "no hint of compromise on the basic issue of secession." A preliminary assessment of the talks made by a member of the Nigerian delegation in a cable to Lagos indicated that Ojukwu's speech was taken as evidence that the Biafran leader continued to believe that foreign intervention would save his regime. It described the conference as "virtually over."

48. Yarrow, *Quaker Experiences*, 208.

49. Ibid., 209.

50. Ibid., 209–10.

51. Ibid., 210–11.

52. Interview with Ahmadu. He recalls that "any religious person who came before me in those days – particularly somebody who was a religious person but was prepared to listen – I was prepared to talk to, to knock down the myth."

53. In any case, except for the Commonwealth-sponsored talks at Kampala, the federal government generally insisted that any negotiations occur within the OAU framework affirming the territorial integrity of Nigeria, rather than experimenting with free-lance efforts. Such was the case, for example, when Pope Paul sought to mediate the conflict in August 1969 (see Stremlau, *International Politics of the Nigerian Civil War*, 343–45).

54. Yarrow, *Quaker Experiences*, 251-2.

55. See de St. Jorre, *Nigerian Civil War*, 284-87.

56. Stremlau, *International Politics of the Nigerian Civil War*, 296, 367. The International Observer Team of Nigeria was composed of representatives from Canada, Sweden, Poland, and the United Kingdom. Created by the federal government in August 1968, it served in the Ibo-populated areas for 16 months and filed numerous reports on its investigations.

57. See Stremlau, *International Politics of the Nigerian Civil War*, 292-300. The government of British Prime Minister Harold Wilson, for example, endured intense public hostility to its outright sale of arms and ammunition to Nigeria. The five Nordic countries – Norway, Sweden, Denmark, Finland, and Iceland – resisted public pressures for political action but gave strong support for humanitarian activities. The Low Countries – Belgium, Luxemburg, and the Netherlands – resisted pressures for recognition of Biafra, although, for a time during summer 1968, the Belgian and Dutch governments suspended arms shipments to Nigeria. The governments of Italy, Switzerland, and Germany had refrained from selling arms to either side from the beginning of the war. The United States also opted for humanitarian aid in lieu of political action. Many of these countries eventually voiced support for the OAU as the appropriate forum for finding a solution to the Nigerian problem.

58. On July 31, 1968, French President Charles de Gaulle issued a statement that the Biafrans had "demonstrated their will to assert themselves as a people" and that the conflict "must be resolved on the basis of the right of peoples to self-determination" (*Le Monde*, August 1, 1968, as quoted in Stremlau, *International Politics of the Nigerian Civil War*, 227). This was acknowledged later by the French government to be "a certain recognition," if not a full diplomatic recognition of Biafra.

59. The African recognitions, which came in the five weeks prior to the first set of formal peace talks in Kampala, were primarily intended to strengthen Biafra's bargaining position in the interest of hastening a cease-fire and a negotiated end to the war (see Smith, *Stitches in Time*, 100). The reasons for French support were more complex and are discussed at length in Stremlau, *International Politics of the Nigerian Civil War*, 224-33. Ultimately, according to Stremlau's analysis, de Gaulle appears to have "inclined to the argument that France's long-term interests and those of her former West African colonies would be best served if Biafra were allowed to sustain a war of attrition long enough to force a political settlement. Such a compromise solution would, conceivably, reduce the likelihood that the new Nigeria would enjoy the internal strength necessary if she ever wished to dominate West Africa" (ibid., 229). Stremlau cites Stanley Diamond (*New York Review of Books*, February 26, 1970) as claiming that in the last year of the war, French arms rose from only 10 percent of the arms received from abroad to about half of the foreign total.

60. Interview with Gowon.

61. Stremlau, *International Politics of the Nigerian Civil War*, 360.

62. Ibid., 142.

63. Ibid., 142–43.

64. Ibid., 143–44.

65. Ibid., 144.

66. Ibid., 364.

67. Interview with Ogbu.

68. Smith, *Stitches in Time*, 79.

69. Ibid., 100. Smith writes that Dr. Michael Okpara, a former top political adviser to Ojukwu, confirmed Azikiwe's analysis of Ojukwu's character during a visit with Smith in England after the war (1972). Okpara said that Ojukwu was essentially an "all or nothing" man who would instinctively shift away from any compromise settlement.

70. Stremlau, *International Politics of the Nigerian Civil War*, 361. Another prominent Biafran who renounced his support for secession was Raph Uwechue, the Biafran representative in Paris. In September 1968, Uwechue told John Volkmar that he and several other Biafran leaders living abroad had recommended to Ojukwu that he give up secession in exchange for terms that would guarantee the security of the Ibo people. Ordered back to Biafra by Ojukwu, Uwechue telexed his refusal and said, in essence, that Ojukwu was immoral in continuing the war. Uwechue resigned his Paris post and subsequently published a book proposing peace terms (Yarrow, *Quaker Experiences*, 218).

71. Telephone interview with Gowon, January 14, 1992.

72. Interview with Ahmadu.

73. MEA, Summary Record of the Plenary Debate of the Nigeria Question During the Sixth Ordinary Session of the OAU Assembly of Heads of State and Government, September 10, 1969, as recounted in Stremlau, *International Politics of the Nigerian Civil War*, 353–54.

74. Interview with Joseph Iyalla, Lagos, July 18, 1991.

75. Ibid.

76. Interview with Gowon.

77. Interview with Ahmadu. Ahmadu had developed a particularly close rapport with John Volkmar. He described how Volkmar "used to come to my home in the night—he'd knock on the door—not at the office very often." The last round of Quaker conciliation activity in the war, from September to November 1969, was prompted by Ahmadu in a meeting with Quaker relief official Kale Williams, whom he told: "If John thinks it would be useful to sample the political climate on both sides, we would be glad to talk with him." Nine days later, Volkmar and Curle were back in Lagos and preparing for a meeting with Gowon (Yarrow, *Quaker Experiences*, 231).

78. Interview with Ojukwu.

79. Ibid.

80. Interview with Ahmadu. Sir David Hunt, British high commissioner to Nigeria during the early part of the civil war, also stressed this aspect of the Quaker approach: "They were not looking for kudos for themselves. Instead they would oil the wheels, get something going, and then slip out without claiming the credit" (interview with Hunt). Both sides had been stung by undue publicity given to third-party efforts. Perhaps the most striking example was the case of Lord Shepherd, the British minister of state. Shepherd made three trips to Nigeria during the war, principally to seek federal concessions that would alleviate public opposition to the Labour government's Nigeria policy. In September 1968, Shepherd was approached by Biafran leaders in Europe who sought negotiations in the context of "one Nigeria." Shepherd went public with the announcement that Biafra was ready to talk of surrender, a move that infuriated the Biafrans and ended the peace overture (Yarrow, *Quaker Experiences*, 217).

81. Interview with Gowon.

82. Interview with Ayida.

83. Air travel into Biafra became quite harrowing after the coastal city of Port Harcourt, with its airport, was taken by federal forces in May 1968. A trip made by Curle and Martin into the rebel enclave in September 1968 is illustrative. Their first flight out of the then-Portuguese territory of São Tome was turned back because of engine trouble. The second flight managed to get up to 18,000 feet to avoid antiaircraft fire; it then descended by a steep spiral to land on the Uli airstrip, an enlarged roadbed, which was only lighted briefly for the final seconds of the landing (Yarrow, *Quaker Experiences*, 213).

84. At a March 1968 meeting with Curle and Martin, Gowon said "he was deeply touched by their willingness to risk their lives and by their diligence in coming back to see him, something other mediating groups had failed to do" (ibid., 200).

85. In one instance, a World Council of Churches delegation, which was sent to Biafra on an ecclesiastical mission, was surprised at being received as "official guests" of the Biafran government. They reported that they were "embarrassed by the amount of press publicity that attended our visit" and that they had been "dragooned" into a television interview that generated press reports "distorted beyond recognition" (report of the Reverend B. T. Molander and Mr. Geoffrey Murray as a delegation from the World Council of Churches to the Christian Council in Biafra, March 22–29, 1968, as quoted in Stremlau, *International Politics of the Nigerian Civil War*, 124).

86. Yarrow, *Quaker Experiences*, 200.

87. Interview with Ojukwu.

88. Telephone interview with Arnold Smith, November 13, 1991. One person who advocated a more hard-line approach to the defeated Biafrans was Joseph Garba, former commander of the Brigade of Guards in the Nigerian Army. Garba felt the top Biafran leaders should have been tried and punished: "We needed to demonstrate to our country people that it doesn't pay to pick up arms against one's brothers" (interview with Jospeh Garba, Jos, Nigeria, August 3, 1991).

89. Telephone interview with Volkmar.

90. Telephone interview with Smith.

91. Interview with Kogbara.

92, Ibid.

93. Interview with Ayida.

94. Interview with Kogbara.

95. Telephone interview with Smith.

96. Yarrow, *Quaker Experiences*, 180.

97. The third member of the Nigeria conciliation team, Walter Martin, is deceased.

98. Interviews, respectively, with Kogbara, Gowon, Ojukwu, and Smith.

99. Personal communication from Curle, October 10, 1990.

100. In addition to the interviews already cited, other individuals interviewed for this study (with titles from the civil war period) were the following. *Federal Republic of Nigeria*: Ukpabi Asika, administrator, East Central State. *Republic of Biafra*: N.U. Akpan, chief secretary to the military government; Okoi Arikpo, commissioner of external affairs; Matthew Mbu, foreign minister; Okokon Ndem, "voice" of Radio Biafra; Godwin S. Onyegbula, joint secretary to the government and permanent secretary, Ministry of Foreign Affairs. It is regrettable that four of the Biafran officials who had the most frequent and closest contact with the Quakers are now deceased. They are Kenneth Dike, head of the Biafran mission in Abidjan; Sir Louis Mbanefo, chief justice and head of the Biafran delegation to the Kampala talks; Eni Njoku, former vice chancellor of the University of

Nigeria at Nsukka and head of the Biafran delegation to the Addis Ababa talks; and Michael Okpara, former premier of the Eastern Region and political adviser to the head of state. A fifth former Biafran official who would likely have been able to comment on the Quaker role was the late C. C. Mojekwu, commissioner of home affairs and a top adviser to Ojukwu. The sons of two of these men, Emeka Dike and Louis Mbanefo, Jr., were consulted, but they were unaware of the Quaker involvement. Also interviewed was J. Isawa Elaigwu, author of *Gowon: The Biography of a Soldier-Statesman* (Ibadan, Nigeria: West Books, 1986).

7 ▪

At the Front Lines of the Revolution: East Germany's Churches Give Sanctuary and Succor to the Purveyors of Change

DAVID STEELE

The Berlin Wall was intended to cement the division of Germany into East and West. Throughout the Cold War, as East Germany struggled to maintain a separate identity, its citizens watched their brethren across the wall develop one of the world's premier democracies. The advent of Mikhail Gorbachev's policies of *glasnost* and *perestroika* in the mid-1980s, however, raised hopes that the freedom and prosperity of the West might one day be replicated in the East. Theoretically, atheism, as a major tenet of communism, should have rendered religion obsolete in the Eastern bloc. Instead, the churches in East Germany not only flourished in their own right but were positioned to play a critical role in the revolution to come.

On Monday, October 9, 1989, stores closed at noon and school teachers advised children to stay away from Leipzig city center. Fears of a Tiananmen-like massacre spread, as doctors and hospitals were told to prepare for a large number of casualties. Leipzig was like an occupied city: army units gathered on its outskirts, and several thousand armed police took up positions outside downtown churches, especially around *Nikolaikirche* ("St. Nicholas' Church"), which was occupied by several hundred members of the Socialist Unity Party (SED, communist), commissioned by the Stasi (state security forces). The numbers of SED were soon overwhelmed, however, by the 10,000 people who gathered for weekly prayer services in the five churches holding worship and protest events that evening in the city center.[1]

Inside the churches a spirit of prayer pervaded, according to Pastor Ulrich Seidel. The beatitudes were read, protest songs were sung (including some from the American civil rights movement), and sermons were preached calling for nonviolent resistance and renunciation of any use of force by all sides.[2] When all the churches emptied and the people joined those waiting outside, candles symbolizing nonviolence and leaflets advocating it were distributed among a crowd that swelled to 70,000 by the end of the evening.[3] The only disruptive incident occurred when provocateurs, who were lower echelon Stasi, tried to incite violence by attempting to storm Stasi headquarters on the way to city hall. They were stopped by various opposition groups, including many church people, who successfully separated the agitators from the other demonstrators and formed a protective cordon around the Stasi building.[4]

Earlier that day, representatives of these same opposition groups had met with Stasi officials to show they would no longer be intimidated by fear of the secret police and to share suggestions on how to prevent violence. Most of these proposals were accepted by the local Stasi leadership, who recognized that the growth of the protest movement was irreversible, according to one of the participants in this discussion, Martin Kind, a pastor to students at the church-run Leipzig Theological Seminary and one of the leaders of the newly formed New Forum opposition group. The fact that this agreement was either not communicated to, or not accepted by, the Stasi rank and file indicates the level of chaos and confusion that prevailed even within the secret police.[5]

Meanwhile, leading officials from the Evangelische Kirche, including the bishop of Saxony-Dresden and the superintendents of two Leipzig districts, had met on October 4 with government authorities in the Leipzig District Council to discuss how to defuse the explosive situation. Even the communists initiated a dialogue process by seeking out three civic leaders, including Peter Zimmermann, a lecturer in theology at the state-run theological faculty at the University of Leipzig, to meet with three party secretaries in a group—which began to be called the "Leipzig six." Meeting two hours before the beginning of the peace prayers, the Leipzig six negotiated with each other and drew up an appeal for calm that was aimed at both police and demonstrators and was broadcast over radio and loudspeaker. They also spoke repeatedly with the authorities in Berlin to appeal for a nonviolent response.[6] Days later, some members of the SED phoned local pastors and spoke of being deeply moved by the prayer services and by the behavior of the church people during the nonviolent demonstration. These communist functionaries had realized for the first time that the church was working for peaceful change instead of violent revolution.[7]

Using a combination of protest and mediation, the Evangelische Kirche (a combination of Lutheran and Reformed churches) in the former German Democratic Republic (Deutsche Demokratische Republik, or DDR) played a critical role in the revolution during the autumn of 1989 and during the subsequent period of transition to democracy in early 1990. From the beginning of the 1980s, the church[8] had provided protection for the growing protest movement, which included both church and nonchurch people, and helped to formulate the issues that fostered the revolution: emigration, ecology, economy, and human rights. In October 1989, this protest movement climaxed—with the peace prayers at Nikolaikirche in Leipzig serving as a nonviolent model for other churches and communities. At the same time, the church's demonstrated ability to serve as a channel of dialogue grew out of years of necessary contact between church and governmental hierarchies. This function culminated in church moderation of round tables throughout the DDR from December 1989 to March 1990. These forums of

conversation, under the leadership of the church, functioned as interim governments and were largely responsible for the peaceful transition to free elections on
March 18, 1990.

BACKGROUND

The major role played by the church in the 1989 revolution was not an isolated
incident. To be understood, the events of *die Wende* ("the turnaround") must be set
within the context of church-state relations during the 40-year history of the DDR.

A Honeymoon with the Communists: 1945–49

During the period of de-Nazification and transition to two German states,[9] there was
a relatively mild attitude toward religion on the part of the Soviet authorities and the
emerging DDR government. In large part, this was due to the influence of the
Confessing Church, a society within the church that consisted of several hundred
thousand members. This had been one of the few movements outside the Communist party that had organized resistance to the Nazis. In fact, there was a considerable
history of association between German communists and the Confessing Church.

After the war, recognition of the Confessing Church's opposition to Hitler,
together with certain personal relationships that had been forged during imprisonment, created a "honeymoon" period between members of the Confessing Church
and the communists. The Confessing Church soon grew to prominence within the
East German church. The hierarchy of the traditional Volkskirche—the leadership
of the state church to which everyone belonged and which had either collaborated
with the Nazis or remained silent—quickly abdicated their positions and were
replaced by Confessing Church leaders at reconstituted provincial synods. This new
church leadership, along with many local pastors from the Confessing Church,
confessed the church's collective guilt for its participation in Nazism and offered
modest support and cooperation to the communist authorities. Unlike most other
members of the educated class, the clergy decided not to emigrate to the West,
believing it had a responsibility to the people of the East.[10] Yet the new church
leadership also brought with it a different understanding of church-state relations.
The church would no longer be the compliant partner of any state, subjecting itself to
governmental control.[11] This changed sense of church identity began, in some
places, even before the Nazis were defeated. In fact, a foreshadowing of the kinds of
protest and mediation roles played in 1989–90 could be seen in 1945 when leaders
from the Confessing Church, along with some Catholic representatives, approached
the commander of the Nazi forces in Breslau (now named Wroclaw and located in
southwestern Poland) and convinced him to surrender to Soviet forces.

The Winter of Stalinization: 1949–58

Church leaders were determined not to repeat the sin of silence to which they had
succumbed during the fascist era. So, with the formation in 1949 of a DDR

government that needed to assert its authority, and with the advent of the period of Stalinist transformation throughout Eastern Europe in the early 1950s,[12] it was inevitable that the early church-state accord would be severely tested. With periods of lesser and greater intensity during most of the 1950s, both church and society experienced an attack on human rights, including some rights that had been guaranteed in the DDR constitution.[13]

The nature of the church's response included both protest activities and negotiation and mediation efforts. On numerous occasions the church leadership wrote letters of protest to government officials, and church synods made declarations on government policy. An annual *Kirchentag* ("church day") rally was instituted in 1949 to address the major social issues of the day. Opposition statements often echoed the words of the anti-Nazi Barmen Declaration of the Confessing Church and sometimes challenged both East and West German governments.[14]

In addition to protest activities, the church response included many meetings between church and state officials during this period. Church officials made a few attempts to act in a mediatory capacity, primarily between the East and West German governments.[15] Most of the church-state meetings, however, were held for the purpose of negotiating the church-state relationship, the nature of which became very important during *die Wende*. An agreement on the relationship, reached in 1958, protected the church from gross state-sponsored discrimination and persecution, but at the price of its previously united protest against social injustice. At least part of the church had settled for an *Überwinterungshaltung* ("a position to survive the winter").[16]

Acquiescing to State Control: 1958–69

The 1958 agreement ushered in a new phase in church-state relations.[17] Protest played a decreasing role, as the main issue of dispute changed from curtailment of rights to severing ties with the West German church and determining who would speak for the East German church.

At the beginning of the decade, the church still engaged in more extensive protest than by the end. The primary issue in the early 1960s was conscientious objection, for which there was no provision in the DDR.[18] Later in the decade, protest was increasingly less unified, as exemplified by the varied responses of different regional churches and their hierarchies.[19]

During this time, the state sought to select the church leaders with whom it would deal. It refused to relate directly to the Evangelische Kirche in Deutschland (EKD), the pan-German expression of the Evangelische Kirche that still existed at this time. Instead, the communist party (SED) emphasized its willingness to talk to those who recognized "the common humanistic responsibility" of Marxists and Christians. The Lutheran tendency to make decisions independently of its own institutional hierarchy made it at times beneficial and at times difficult for the SED who were able to choose their dialogue partners but who also wanted the consequent decisions to be more binding than church polity allowed.[20]

The church, on the other hand, became less clear in its response to the communist state. In 1964 some prominent leaders, in like manner to those of the Nazi era, began to interpret the traditional Lutheran doctrine of the two kingdoms as justifying the state. Others claimed that totalitarianism could never be blessed in any form. Most in the church took positions somewhere in the middle as the church attempted to redefine its role in the midst of a growing identity crisis.

But power was passing increasingly into the hands of the SED, giving it an upper hand in the relationship and forcing internal changes in the church. With the building of the Berlin Wall in 1961, the SED had severely limited any regular contact with the West. A new constitution adopted in 1968 made it illegal for any organization to transcend the borders of the DDR.[21] In order to remain a legally constituted body, therefore, the DDR churches established the Federation of Protestant Churches in the DDR, or the *Kirchenbund*, in June 1969. This body was under the leadership of another prominent Confessing Church member, Bishop Albrecht Schönherr, who was head of Berlin-Brandenburg's Eastern Region (see Figure 7.1). This body was to have great influence in future church-state relations, especially through the mediating figure of Schönherr, the first chairman of its executive board, and Manfred Stolpe, its first general secretary.[22]

A Church Identity Within Socialism: 1969–78

Both church and state hierarchies pursued policies of growing, but cautious, cooperation in the early 1970s.[23] The state gradually accepted the formation of the Kirchenbund and formally recognized it in 1971.

The church, for its part, continued to struggle with the formation of an identity to replace that of the all-German Volkskirche. Among various alternatives, it officially adopted the formulation of the "church *within* socialism" at its 1971 federal synod in Eisenach.[24] This statement emphasized the desire to be a church neither alongside of nor against socialism. It was a rejection of both ghettoization and a position as an opposition movement. The formula was intended instead to, first, affirm the church's existence within the society in which it was located and, second, imply participation in the problems and achievements of society by contributing to its development.[25]

One area of growing cooperation was support given by the Kirchenbund leadership to the anti-imperialistic peacemaking efforts of the DDR. A manifestation of this sentiment by the Kirchenbund was its close affiliation with the Lutheran World Federation and the World Council of Churches, including Kirchenbund support of the anti-Western, pro-Third World stances of those bodies. In addition, the Kirchenbund reflected the concern of the whole East German church over the growing friend-enemy dichotomy and insisted that true peace involved eliminating stereotypes of the West as hostile.[26] Furthermore, the DDR church continued to follow the lead of the international bodies when, in the mid-1970s, they began to address human rights in the East bloc. This issue of human rights within the DDR was to assume a very great role in church-state

Figure 7.1. The German Democratic Republic

relations in the future, especially through the provision of moral foundation, information, and safe forum for the independent peace movement in the DDR.

At the same time, many old issues continued to produce tension, including discrimination in education, military service, restrictions on church meetings and publications, and mandatory inclusion of Marxist ideology and military training in theological education.[27] Yet the church hierarchy's method of confrontation was largely conciliatory in nature, appealing to legal rights or to principles that the state itself officially recognized.[28]

Operating out of the Schönherr approach of dialogue with the state, agreements were reached on many issues by church and SED hierarchies in 1974–75. But there was increasing tension at the grass-roots level of the church. A rift developed between the rapprochement and accommodation approach of the Kirchenbund leadership and the ideological tension experienced by many local pastors. Due to the basic democratic structure of the church, this discontent was able to be transmitted upward, threatening the leadership's policy of accommodation and forcing a more critical line vis-à-vis the state.[29] The church had come face to face with its own schizophrenia: its ability to make institutional gains for itself, but its inability to protect even its own people from state oppression.

This tension culminated in a church-state summit in March 1978 between Head of State Erich Honecker and the executive committee of the Kirchenbund. At that meeting the church achieved de facto legitimation of its role as an independent institution with its own set of responsibilities within the society.[30] The meeting also confirmed the "trusting, discrete discussion" approach advocated by Schönherr.

A Tightrope Between Opposition and Conciliation: 1978–87

The modus vivendi between church and state was severely tested during the 1980s[31] with the steady rise of political dissent both within and outside the church. This time the issues were definitely societal and political in nature: peace and disarmament, human rights, environment, economics, and gay and women's rights. In this new context of disaffection, the church increasingly walked a tightrope between being a channel for the expression of opposition views, on the one hand, and interceding between government and opposition, on the other.

The most significant of these movements of dissent was the independent peace movement, an unstructured, grass-roots association of individuals and groups that began in 1981. The peace movement depended on the church for "space," both in terms of a meeting place and protection from harassment—and it gained much of its support, including its membership, from the church.[32] The official church hierarchy responded cautiously, however, to this new development and became more reactive than proactive on peace issues. In some cases, it embraced the criticisms of the peace groups; in other cases, it attempted to discipline or mute the dissenters within the groups seeking safe haven under the umbrella of the church. As a result, the tensions that existed between the hierarchical and grass-roots levels of the church in the 1970s increasingly appeared in relations between the church hierarchy and opposition movements in the 1980s.

One early example of the tightrope walked by the church became apparent in conjunction with its development in 1980 of an annual "Ten Days for Peace" (or Peace Decade) program held each November. In 1981, this peace education program developed a logo combining Soviet art with the biblical phrase, "swords into plowshares." This symbol was printed on badges and circulated among youth within the church-based peace movements. By April 1982, the SED decided to suppress the movement and sent police to confiscate badges and arrest people. The church responded by indicating that it was not in a position to protect those wearing the symbol and decided to no longer distribute the badges at peace forums. In response to criticism from local clergy and youth, however, the church hierarchy resolved to retain swords into plowshares as a slogan for its peace work and to use it at the annual peace program in November 1982. At its federal synod in Halle that September, the church officially announced its decisions, while still defending the use of the symbol. Leaders stated that their faith called them to continue to participate in the struggle for disarmament, even within the DDR.[33] Caught between the state and the grass-roots, the church leadership assumed the position that would characterize its stance for the next five years: that of limited confrontation with the state and limited support for the peace movements.

One result of effectively walking this tightrope was SED relaxation of emigration in 1983. Since the SED wanted neither to offend the church nor to encourage the opposition movement, it decided to let the dissidents leave. By April 1984, however, the church was appealing to Christians to remain in the DDR and calling on the state to create the conditions under which people would choose to stay. One reason was that the emigration was costing the church some of its most active members. Of the more than 20,000 emigrés, 52 percent were church members, including many pastors. This issue of emigration was to become one of the explosive issues that finally brought down the Honecker regime in 1989.

With the onset of Soviet *perestroika* ("restructuring"), the SED initially adopted an even more relaxed attitude toward the church. In fact, during 1985–86, church and state reached some consensus on peace and environmental concerns, and the Kirchenbund softened some previous stands. This development was also a result of growing concern not to alienate conservative parishioners who viewed the independent peace groups with suspicion. These parishioners believed that the groups were trying to undermine traditional church norms, and they suspected that members of the groups had tenuous connections with the Christian faith. Consequently, there was an increasing distance in the relationship between the church hierarchy and the independent groups. In fact, the church began to openly profess its intention to domesticate and discipline these groups, explicitly defining itself as playing a "critical stabilizing" role within society.

But the church's stabilizing role was overtaken by the counterreaction of the Honecker regime to Gorbachev's reforms. This turn toward reactionary politics accomplished two things that made the changes of 1989–90 inevitable: (a) the economy, which had been steadily improving, took a drastic turn for the worse, which alienated even more of the population, and (b) the state cracked down on the church, which had the initial effect of influencing the church to curtail the activities of the independent groups, but ultimately pushed it closer to the position of those groups.

The curtailment of activities was demonstrated most clearly during the 1987 Kirchentag in Berlin. Without consulting the groups, the Berlin-Brandenburg church canceled the peace workshop that had been part of this annual event since 1982. The peace groups charged church leadership with sacrificing the workshop in exchange for state approval to hold the Kirchentag. Church leaders, finding it hard to justify the workshop as "church activity," charged the groups with irresponsible behavior. The groups began referring to themselves as the Church from Below and, finally, pressured the institutional church to allow them a concurrent forum separate from the conference. In this context, a new and specifically church-related leadership began to emerge from the grass roots in the peace movement.[34]

Shepherding the Opposition: 1987–89

In late 1987, events happened that signaled the end of the "church within socialism" and began to move the church toward greater solidarity with the independent groups.[35] In November and December, the secret service raided the ecology library on the premises of Zionskirche in East Berlin, arresting people, confiscating documents and equipment, and accusing them of printing papers against the government. In response, church and independent groups protested the action by holding remembrance and prayer services, and the Berlin-Brandenburg church leadership succeeded in negotiating the release of some of those arrested.[36]

This event was followed by a series of protests and arrests that lasted into early 1988. Since many of those incarcerated had some association with the church, including Vera Wollenberger, the most prominent leader of the Church from Below, the church began to take a much more public role by late January. First, prayer meetings were held in Berlin, Leipzig, Dresden, and a dozen other cities throughout the DDR with thousands of people attempting to express solidarity. Second, the church established advice and counseling centers throughout the DDR as part of a campaign for human rights and freedom of emigration. Third, church leaders actively supported, even represented in court, many of those arrested, and they managed to negotiate the release of some.[37] The significance of this period is that the church demonstrated its concern for change in the system and developed many of the skills that it would later use in 1989–90.

The Evangelische Kirche continued to register its protest at conferences and synods during the summer and autumn of 1988. With the full authority of the church in Saxony-Magdeburg, "Twenty Theses for the Renewal of Society" were read at the regional church conference in Halle; these called for a revised justice system based on the rule of law, limits on state authority, democratic elections, free media, price reforms, energy conservation, and environmental protection legislation. At the same time, similar demands were made by another group calling itself the Church in Solidarity.[38] Although the Kirchenbund leaders did not go this far, at the federal synod of September even they called for an end to the "irresponsible and degrading treatment of people who want to leave," for "personal and public discussions [which] . . . may not exclude any areas of life," and for freedom to attend church meetings and worship services without harassment.[39]

Another series of formative events took place in the form of three ecumenical assemblies, which met in Dresden (February 1988), Magdeburg (October 1988), and Dresden (April 1989). The underlying content for this "conciliar process" (known also as the Ecumenical Movement for Justice, Peace, and the Integrity of Creation) originated with the World Council of Churches. This forum gave the church the opportunity to discuss DDR concerns in the context of an international focus on the same issues: peace and disarmament, human rights, environment, economy, and the structures of justice within society. The conciliar process also involved DDR Roman Catholics for the first time in the discussion of political issues. According to Superintendent Christof Ziemer of Saxony-Dresden, delegates to the assemblies, freed from any church restraints on their criticism of the state, proceeded to write the "Magna Carta" for the revolution of 1989. The constituencies of and the topics raised by these assemblies became the core of both the personnel and message of the formal opposition groups that finally came into existence in autumn 1989.[40]

The fateful year of 1989 began with church-state relations at one of the chilliest points since the summit of 1978. Church leaders were denied any meaningful contact with state officials and were chided or patronized when they tried to foster it. The church hierarchy concluded that dialogue with the state had become impossible.[41] Simultaneously, local churches expressed their protest in the form of worship services.[42] They challenged government policies in economics, ecology, and freedom of speech and travel, and they called attention to election fraud.

The issue of election fraud and manipulation in May 1989 galvanized the growing opposition. Church-based groups, which had organized to monitor local elections throughout the DDR, found significant discrepancies between their own data and the official election results, particularly with respect to "no" votes and percentage of voter participation. The ensuing public outrage led to the arrest of hundreds of people. The groups responded by sending their own data to each elected official, pointing to the fraud, calling for resignations, and demanding that free and secret elections replace the process of voting for or against a single list of SED candidates. The official church, through several of its publications, as well as voiced objections by leaders (e.g., Bishop Johannes Hempel of Saxony-Dresden), also called attention to the corruption and asked for voting changes. One church-based group (the predecessor to the opposition group, Democracy Now) even called for the creation of a "round table" of church and state representatives to discuss the problem. But the response of the head of the Election Commission, Egon Krenz, was to deny the accusations and to refuse any kind of investigation.[43]

In spite of the obvious manipulation of these elections, *die Wende* of 1989 would probably not have happened without the massive exodus of DDR citizens to the West and the growing protests surrounding this issue.[44] These events caused the weekly Leipzig prayer meetings to swell in numbers, brought calls for increasingly radical change from Protestant church leaders, provoked the beginnings of public dissent from the Roman Catholic hierarchy, and led in September to the formation of opposition groups, such as New Forum, Democracy Now, and Democratic Awakening. Though these new groups were more independent from the church than their predecessors, they too were comprised more of church than of nonchurch people. The opposition, both within and outside the church, supported the decisions of those wishing to leave the country. At the same time, they reaffirmed their call to the population to remain in the DDR and struggle together for internal change.[45]

DIE WENDE: "THE TURNAROUND" OF 1989–90

Culmination of the Protest Movement

The transition from mass exodus to mass demonstration for political reform began in Leipzig at the weekly Monday night prayer services. When these prayers reconvened on September 4, 1989, after a month's hiatus, dissidents, as well as those desiring emigration out of the DDR, went out into the streets after the service. The familiar chant, "we want out," was answered by another group at the edge of the crowd with the declaration, "we're staying here." Even though the total number of demonstrators was small, about 70 people all together, they were met with greater force than usual. Leipzig theologian, Peter Zimmermann captured the import of the moment when, having observed the beatings and incarceration of those committed to staying, he reached the conclusion that the authorities "could get along far better with those who simply wanted to leave than with those who wanted to engage themselves for change." Yet despite the harassment, the "we're staying here" slogan dominated future prayer service demonstrations.[46]

The Kirchenbund responded to this development with an open letter, read from church pulpits on September 10. In it the church leadership addressed Honecker (asking him to institute a process of far-reaching political change) and its own membership (asking them to remain in the DDR). A week later, four Protestant members of the Christian Democratic Union (CDU) broke ranks and proposed 30 "steps on the way to a democratic socialism," including calls for election and media reform, as well as humane treatment of individuals. At the same time, the Evangelische Kirche prepared to continue its own internal debate at the federal synod in Eisenach on September 15–20. At this synod, the Church in Solidarity group proposed specific reforms that reflected widespread opinion within the church. These recommendations included calls for democratic elections, state authority based on law, an independent judiciary, freedom of information, and economic reforms.[47] Even though much of this agenda did not receive official endorsement, the synod did call for economic reforms, a free press, free travel, and free elections within a multiparty system. Bishop Leich, the chair of the Kirchenbund, stated the prevailing mood of the church, saying, "We need clear indications now that the necessary changes are beginning." The communist newspaper *Neues Deutschland* responded with the sharpest attack on the church in two decades.[48]

Meanwhile, at the peace prayers on September 19 at Nikolaikirche in Leipzig, Pastor Wonneberger called for nonviolent resistance to the state, modeled after the

American civil rights movement. He cautioned against carrying anything that could be used as a weapon and counseled against resisting arrest. After the prayers, the police, finding themselves surrounded again, resorted to force. The next day, New Forum was formed, and thousands of East Germans joined.[49] On September 25, when 5,000–6,000 gathered at Nikolaikirche, Pastor Wonneberger again called for nonviolence, preaching from the text, "He who takes up the sword, will die by the sword." This time, the police responded by blocking off traffic as ever larger numbers of onlookers gathered. Nonetheless, state newspapers accused Wonneberger of instigating violence and referred to demonstrators as "rowdies."[50]

The first nine days of October 1989 proved to be the critical turning point for *die Wende*. On October 2, some 20,000 people marched with the worshipers outside Nikolaikirche. Wonneberger, who by this time was receiving death threats, continued to advocate nonviolence and to give practical suggestions on how to avoid provoking a violent response. Nevertheless, the police, alarmed at the increasingly large numbers of demonstrators, resorted to violence. Pastor Hans-Jürgen Sievers reported that people were beaten 50 meters from his Reformed Church, even as they tried to leave the demonstration. Doctors in hospitals confirmed that many of the injuries were serious.[51]

Demonstrations escalated throughout the following week, in Leipzig and elsewhere, and were met with more police violence. Gorbachev's expected arrival the following weekend to celebrate the fortieth anniversary of the DDR appears to have prompted the SED to crack down on the opposition movement. On October 3, visa-free travel to Czechoslovakia was terminated. On October 5, East Berlin Superintendent Werner Krätschell, on a BBC broadcast to East Germany, reported that he had been warned by an SED official that the "Chinese solution" would be used if socialism continued to be questioned. Markus Wolf, retired head of DDR foreign espionage, has since confirmed that "there was a written order from Honecker for a Chinese solution. It would have been worse than Beijing." Coffins and body bags began to arrive in the city, along with army and additional police units. The Stasi made plans for a concentration camp, one of many throughout the DDR, and drew up lists of prospective inmates, including all prominent clergy. Finally, according to Bishop Leich, the crackdown was rehearsed on October 7 when demonstrators were arrested and interrogated while leaving Bachkirche in Arnstadt. In light of the gravity of the situation, Bishop Johannes Hempel (Saxony-Dresden) appealed by radio for nonviolence on both sides to avoid a Tiananmen-like bloodbath. He urged the churches to open their doors so that people could gather in them and then enter the demonstration in a spirit of peace and calm rather than fear and anger, and so that people might have a place of sanctuary from violence if necessary.[52] At the same time that the church was preparing for a crackdown, another significant event took place during the first week in October: the Soviet embassy in East Berlin signaled that it would not intervene to put down the unrest.[53]

It is in this context that the people of Leipzig prepared for the peace prayers and demonstration of October 9, and dialogue initiatives were made by three separate parties. First, the independent groups, in which church people played significant roles, sought out discussions with the feared Stasi. The idea originated within New

Forum where three of the seven designated spokespersons were pastors or theologians and a fourth was a theological student. They suggested to the Stasi that loudspeakers be used to address the crowd and that, instead of police, members of the fire brigade, wearing signs saying "no violence," be placed in front of Stasi headquarters. Along with members of Democratic Awakening, Democracy Now, the Social Democratic Party (SDP), and the Initiative for Peace and Human Rights (IFM), they told the Stasi that they would also work to protect the secret police from violence.[54]

Second, the Evangelische Kirche hierarchy (namely Bishop Johannes Hempel and Superintendents Friedrich Magirius and Johannes Richter) followed up their October 4 meeting with leading SED officials in the Leipzig District Council. On the morning of October 9 they met with Roman Catholic Dean Günter Hanisch to discuss ways to defuse the situation. In addition, Bishop Hempel attended four of the five churches holding peace prayers on October 9 and encouraged people to act calmly. Superintendent Johannes Richter preached in Thomaskirche that evening on Proverbs 25:15 ("With patience a ruler will be persuaded, and a soft tongue will break a bone"). Later he would claim that a few thousand Christians had made all the difference in keeping the demonstration nonviolent.[55]

Third, the Leipzig six (composed of three SED party secretaries plus theologian Peter Zimmermann, entertainer Bernd-Lutz Lange, and Director Kurt Masur of the Leipzig Gewandhaus Orchestra) met with the mayor of Leipzig two hours before the peace prayers to discuss ways to defuse the situation. The group broadcast appeals for calm and signed a declaration promoting more dialogue. This meeting turned out to be the first of 20 sessions that finally concluded on November 13. The group invited church and opposition groups to share their concerns for the reform and reconstruction of society, concluding the month with a written report. Through this process the Leipzig six not only contributed to nonviolence on October 9 but also created an ongoing structure for informing local authorities regarding the wishes of the people.[56]

Meanwhile, in Berlin, where Gorbachev was making it plain that Soviet troops would not be used to quell dissent in the DDR, Gethsemanekirche and Bishop Gottfried Forck of Berlin-Brandenburg also figured prominently in protest and conciliation efforts. On October 7, a spontaneous demonstration sought refuge in Gethsemanekirche, where opposition groups had long functioned. Police then sealed off this church where, since October 2, there had been round-the-clock vigils on behalf of previously detained persons. After hundreds had been arrested and about 100 injured, Bishop Forck negotiated with the police colonel to let the remainder of the people go. The next day (a Sunday), Pastor Bernd Albani led 3,000 people in a service of remembrance for those arrested and in prison, and he called for nonviolent defiance of the state.[57]

By this time, dissent had spread throughout the DDR. Another particularly important focus for both protest and conciliation activity was the city of Dresden. Here the dramatic phase started on October 3, the day the Czech border was closed and many people attempted to board the trains taking East German emigrés from Prague to West Germany. Demonstrations and violence, on the part of both police and demonstrators, continued until, by October 8, about 1,500 people had been arrested. After nearly a week of confrontation, the demonstrators, under the leadership of two Catholic chaplains, sat down on the street. Twenty people were selected and a catalogue of demands was drawn up. At the same time, Bishop Hempel and Superintendent Christof Ziemer were having discussions with the lord mayor at city hall. As a result of both of these independent processes, an official dialogue was held between the group of 20 and the lord mayor in a session moderated by Hempel and Ziemer. On the evening of October 8, Ziemer went back to the demonstration and announced that there would be a series of meetings between the two. At his request, the police opened the chains that had contained the crowd and allowed it to disperse. Four of the major churches in the city then invited in the masses for the purpose of informing them of the decisions and announcing the dialogue.[58]

On October 9, public meetings were held in numerous Dresden churches under the leadership of the group of 20. These sessions had the character of little town meetings, with attenders making demands or raising questions to be included in future dialogues. The result was the first peaceful demonstration in Dresden, held that evening. Regular meetings between the group of 20 and the lord mayor also began on October 9. They met every Monday for three weeks, then less frequently, with the sessions finally ending in January 1990. Within one week after the first meeting, and at the suggestion of the lord mayor, they formed working groups to discuss all aspects of life in the DDR.[59]

Initially, Ziemer moderated the sessions because of his long experience in dealing with the lord mayor. In this capacity, Ziemer clearly functioned as an intermediary. Yet he also consistently protected the group of 20 from attacks, which were especially strong until the Honecker regime was replaced on October 18. One incident occurred when the Stasi opened files on the group of 20 shortly after it had been established. Ziemer responded by informing the lord mayor and putting this question on the dialogue agenda. One week later, he updated the public on the issue through a press conference, at which he insisted that dialogue could only take place if people were free from investigation. Much of the press conference was subsequently printed in the newspaper, but without Ziemer's insistence on investigatory freedom. The next day, however, the editors overrode the objections of the printers and a full report appeared. A second incident occurred in the context of an attempt by the group of 20 to expose, and to seek justice for, the ill treatment of people who had been imprisoned. Two of the initial actions of the group of 20 had been to establish a place for individuals to seek advice and then to ask them to write about their experience. The group quickly submitted a public report containing the collected evidence, which Ziemer then used to address the Dresden City Council at the end of October. He handed out three volumes of documentation on the imprisonments to councillors who did not want to believe it. A third incident occurred at the end of the first week when the government moved to control the dialogue. The SED and the Stasi proposed that the conversations be between state and church rather than between state and the people. Ziemer insisted, however, that the church would only act to facilitate the needed dialogue with the people. In most places in the DDR, this was the response of church officials to similar proposals made at the local level.[60]

Although this conviction that state-church relations should not replace state-people interaction was strongly held, it did not prevent the church from talking with government officials. As described in each of the cities mentioned above, church officials interceded with SED functionaries on behalf of protesters. At the national level, however, Kirchenbund head Bishop Leich had refused all such overtures from the state since February 1989. Nevertheless, given the momentous events of the previous month, the Kirchenbund decided to accept an invitation for mid-October. The decision was based on the need for dialogue at this time, SED willingness to enter into such a process, and the government's apparent ability to trust the church as a more established and predictable institution than the new opposition groups.[61]

Before this meeting took place, the Honecker regime had fallen and was replaced on October 18 by the leadership of Egon Krenz as general secretary of the SED. One of Krenz' first acts was to meet with Leich, Stolpe, and Martin Ziegler, Secretary of the Kirchenbund, on October 19. At this meeting Leich urged Krenz to "give quick and clear signals of a new beginning," starting with "open dialogue with the people." He listed all the points that he had presented to Honecker in February. This time they were not rejected and Leich left more hopeful, though still skeptical. Both Leich and Krenz could at least agree that it was in their common interest to promote the reform upon which survival of the DDR depended.[62]

Another mood prevailed on the local level, however. When, also on October 19, Pastor Walter Bindemann raised the question in Gethsemanekirche of whether Krenz was a "real" change, his remark was met with thunderous applause. Even parts of the church hierarchy soon began to challenge the legitimacy of the SED. Three days later, Bishop Hempel told a church synod in Saxony-Dresden about the allegations of police brutality in that city, requested a state apology, and called for an independent commission to investigate the affair. Other voices joined Hempel. Bishop Forck called on DDR Prime Minister Willi Stoph to condemn the "brutal actions of the security organs." The Youth Ministry Office in East Berlin collected eyewitness accounts that were alleged to demonstrate a widespread and centrally controlled pattern of violence during the demonstration of October 7 in the capital. The ultimate reversal of stance by the church, however, came during the Saxony-Dresden Synod with Hempel's rejection of the designation "church within socialism" and his statement that the SED must reclaim their right to leadership and back it up with trust. By the end of October, even the church did not give Krenz much of a chance to turn the SED or DDR around. Prayer services at Nikolaikirche had swelled to 300,000, while churches throughout the country began organizing for a major transition in the political system.[63]

Moderation of the Round Tables

After the government of Hans Modrow replaced the Krenz government on November 8, and the Berlin Wall opened on November 9, the way was opened for extensive dialogue on the future of the DDR and its entire political system. At this point, the ongoing dialogue process in Dresden between the local authorities and the group of 20 was by far the most developed of any within the DDR. It had become the first fully functioning round table, with its working groups developing into advisory and then investigatory groups. It eventually became the legislative arm of the local government, as happened in more than 350 localities across the DDR. In fact, it soon became the model, not only for other local communities but also for the national political process. This model was then used in all major cities to deal with local issues, such as party property and the secret police legacy. In most cases, local church leaders were invited to preside as moderators.[64]

The one case where the church as an institution took a special part in the initiative was on the national level. The idea came out of discussions that Bishop Forck had with various Berlin opposition groups (Democracy Now, New Forum, and others). After a discussion between Martin Ziegler, secretary of the Kirchen- bund, and Wolfgang Ullmann, church historian and member of Democracy Now, it was agreed that the initiative should come from the Kirchenbund Secretariat. So Ziegler, representing the church hierarchy, officially called for a national round table forum to which representatives of the government and all major opposition groups were invited. The stated purpose was to form agreement on procedures for holding new elections and establishing a new parliament.[65]

In late November, the Modrow government agreed to participate in a forum in which there would be an equal number of government and opposition participants— a firm condition set by the opposition groups for their participation. At first, seven (later 19) opposition groups participated, along with the SED and the other small political parties that had been represented in the parliament since the beginning of the DDR. The church was asked by both sides to act as moderator. Due to the growing ecumenical cooperation resulting from the conciliar process, it was decided to have three rotating moderators—Ziegler of the Evangelische Kirche, Catholic Monsignor Karl-Heinz Ducke, and Methodist Pastor Martin Lange. In addition to these official church representatives, six other pastors participated in various capaci- ties in the planning meetings for the central round table.[66]

The first session of the central round table took place on December 7 on "neutral ground," at a church office building in East Berlin, in the context of increasing suspicion of government actions among the populace and erosion of the state's ability to control citizen activism. On the same day, with the encouragement of opposition groups, citizens had occupied Stasi buildings in various cities throughout the DDR in order to prevent the destruction or relocation of files. This led to an extremely chaotic beginning to the round table, with thousands of demonstrators gathering outside the building. There was much distrust expressed, as the opposition groups demanded that the Stasi be disbanded and that they themselves be given authority to review all new legislation. According to both Ziegler and Lange, the central round table almost floundered that first evening. Even so, it was agreed in that session to hold free elections in the spring and to set up a commission to prepare constitutional changes. By the time of the second session, held on December 18, the demonstrators had begun to call for German unification. On this issue both government and opposition could disagree with the masses. In the interest of maintaining their own respective identities, the two sides rejected the calls for unity, instead passing a resolution for bilateral economic cooperation with the Federal Republic of Germany (FRG). Although this was out of step with the mood of the general populace, it did serve to facilitate a sense of urgency for cooperation in the round table endeavor.[67]

During its early phase, the central round table did not have very great power to make changes. The government sent only lower level representatives and still made its decisions separate from the round table proceedings. Despite this fact, the combination of public protest and round table investigation brought an end to the Stasi by mid-January 1990. This precipitated a crisis of credibility for the last conceivable SED government. With a power vacuum developing in late January, Hans Modrow himself joined the central round table, bringing with him a much higher level delegation. Additional opposition groups also joined at this point. Thus, from this point until the elections on March 18, the round table functioned as the effective parliamentary arm of government. Nothing happened without its consent.[68]

The role of the church moderators was critical in establishing a working accord in such a potentially contentious group. The SED explicitly encouraged them to play an independent role. Nonetheless, there were pressures from both sides. Especially at the beginning, the opposition groups tried to control many of the conditions for dialogue and to issue demands, to the extent that Ziegler complained of being ordered about. The SED, on the other hand, verbalized the need to uncover the truth but then did everything it could to hinder its revelation. The moderators deliberately tried to avoid getting involved in political discussions. Rather than set out "the position of the church," they attempted to facilitate constructive dialogue and parliamentary process. According to Lange, the task was to make sure that each party had an opportunity to say what it wanted, and to help people listen to one another. Sometimes this involved making contact with government officials or opposition group members between sessions. But the purpose of such encounters was to build bridges and facilitate understanding, not to coerce opinion or give a "church solution." After the proposals and suggestions were aired, the moderator would bring a given issue to a vote. This procedure simply followed the same democratic process that had long been in use in synods of the Evangelische Kirche.[69]

In the eyes of the church, the round table was a process of reconciliation. Referring to this process, Bishop Leich declared, "Only the spirit of reconciliation can free us to solve the problems of the present courageously." In the same statement, issued the day after the start of the central round table, he traced this spirit of reconciliation from the peace prayers, to the nonviolent demonstrations, and now to the round table.[70] According to Lange, the success of this conciliation approach was borne out by the fact that the voting often did not conform to party affiliation and that large amounts of heretofore classified information became available to the public.[71] Ziegler adds that the lack of violence during this potentially chaotic period is a tribute to the success of the round table in bringing a sense of stability and in prolonging the life of the DDR.[72]

Not everyone viewed the process so favorably, however. One of the New Forum participants, Rolf Henrich, grants that the church tried to help the opposition groups fulfill their program. He believes, however, that the church's efforts at conciliation actually hindered the process of renovating the old system. The presence of the church in the third-party role ensured that change would not be radical.[73] Uwe Thaysen, a West German observer at the round table, shares this assessment. According to him, during the later phase, beginning the end of January, the church tried to calm those seeking revenge and forced people from opposition groups to apologize for being too rough on the old regime. For him, the crowning stroke came in March 1990 when Ziegler failed, in his concluding speech, to "name what the regime was all about." On the eve of the parliamentary elections for the first freely elected DDR government, Ziegler had only praise for SED cooperation instead of condemnation of SED oppression. Moreover, he was silent about the courage and accomplishments of New Forum. Thaysen contrasts this with the concluding speech of Pastor Georg Kazorke at the Prenzlauer Berg (a district within East Berlin) Round Table in May 1990. Kazorke, who had himself been terrorized by the Stasi, spoke of what the regime had done to the souls of people. He acted as an effective mediator throughout the process. Yet he did not retreat from speaking the truth, nor yield to the fear that the process might break down and result in bloodshed, as many of the church leadership feared would happen.[74] In response to such critics, Lange and Ziegler continue to stress the significance of a peaceful transition of power. In addition, they point to the high degree of consensus reached by the participants during the final session of the central round table.[75] Furthermore, other church leaders, like Christof Ziemer, claim that any break on the revolution was the result of the movement toward reunification on the part of the masses. The church never brought an agenda of its own, but instead responded to the changing demands of the people.[76]

The question of how to treat the old regime, especially those guilty of massive injustices, was a question with which the church struggled at the end of *die Wende*. Bishop Hempel, while admitting the church's complicity, spoke of the need to help in the difficult task of distinguishing between justice and revenge.[77] The church's own struggle with this issue could be seen in the tension between its involvement in various investigatory commissions and its pastoral care offered to individuals from the old regime. Bishop Forck, for example, was part of a three-man commission that investigated the National People's Army. Other church representatives were involved in commissions investigating issues related to ecology, youth, education, and the army. Yet the church also began to shield former communist officials from the people's wrath. Ziegler helped the Honeckers find shelter in the home of Pastor Uwe Holmer, whose own children had been deprived of higher education due to the policies of Honecker and his wife, the former minister of education. For some in the church such shielding of communist officials from people's wrath was the response called for in the gospel. Eventually, however, this sanctuary was terminated due to pressure from within and outside the church, and the Honeckers were moved into Soviet custody.[78]

At the conclusion of *die Wende*, there was generally an affirmative response to the church. The immense popular support for it and many of its leaders was illustrated in the results of the March 18 elections. Nineteen pastors and numerous church lay persons were elected to the new parliament. The variety of party affiliations represented by them (eight social democrats, three centrists, and eight conservatives) reflected the diversity of views within the church. What's more, Lothar de Maiziere, vice president of the synod of the Evangelische Kirche, became the new prime minister. Pastor Markus Meckel, leader of the SDP, became foreign minister. Pastor Rainer Eppelmann, leader of Democratic Awakening, became minister for defense and disarmament. Pastor Hans-Wilhelm Ebeling, founder of the German Social Union, became minister for developmental aid. Bishop Forck was offered the presidency of the DDR, but declined. This overwhelming affirmation of the role of the church overall in *die Wende* has only been slightly tarnished by the subsequent allegations of Stasi collaboration among church people in both party leadership and elected office.[79] It has not been at all diminished by the brief duration of the last government of the DDR before reunification. A number of those same religious leaders now serve in the government of the Federal Republic of Germany.

ANALYSIS

The critical questions which now must be addressed are (a) How can one categorize the various roles played by religious actors in this case? and (b) What influence does the spiritual nature of the church have in determining how these roles are played, and what effect do they have on the process?

Roles Played by Religious Actors

Die Wende can easily be divided into two distinct phases: (a) development and protection of the protest movement and (b) creating a new order after the collapse of the former system. Some have attempted to argue that these two phases also called for two separate church roles: before the institution of the round table, the primary church role was to facilitate the protest; afterward, it was to facilitate conciliation. There is a bit of truth in this categorization in that mass protests did diminish. Many others, however, have pointed out the fallacies of this dichotomy. Professors Wolfgang Ratzmann and Jürgen Ziemer of Leipzig Theological Seminary, together with Pastor Harald Wagner of Holzhausen, state that what matters most is which individuals one is attempting to describe. They argue that the same group that began the protests was still speaking for justice after the beginning of the round table. Likewise, those leading the conciliation attempt at the round table had always placed their emphasis on mediation efforts.[80] Again, this is accurate as long as one does not identify all the church hierarchy with conciliation efforts alone. Markus Meckel rightly points out that some of the church hierarchy (he names Bishop Christoph Demke of Magdeburg) were more supportive of protest than others.[81]

The efforts of Superintendent Christof Ziemer of Dresden also demonstrate a complex relationship between advocacy and conciliation efforts well before the national round table was instituted. Although Ziemer's predominant style seems to fit more the conciliation than the advocacy mode, an assessment with which he would readily agree, it is a style of mediation in which he takes great care to empower the weak. Examples include his protection of the group of 20 from Stasi interference and his appearance before the Dresden City Council with volumes of written protest against the regime. It is protest in the midst of conciliation. To some he would be seen as getting his hands too dirty in politics; a good church superintendent should be more concerned about the care of the pastors and churches within his jurisdiction. To others, he would seem to have protested too little too late. However, Ziemer himself argues that reconciliation can be interpreted as a kind of prophetic expression. "In a monolithic society, making peace between groups is prophetic," in his view.[82]

It would appear that open dialogue presented the regime with the greatest challenge it could have faced. No doubt there were some who failed to force the issues energetically enough, and thereby delayed needed confrontation. In such an unstructured process involving so many actors, that is bound to be the case.[83] In this multiplayer mass revolution, however, there were numerous examples of a creative and courageous mixing of the conciliation and advocacy roles. One example (of many that could be cited) is that of Roland Adolf, rector of a training center for church-related hospitals. Adolf brought his training and concern for pastoral care with him when he served on a commission to investigate the Stasi in Dresden. He took a firm stand to prevent three representatives from the Modrow government from reestablishing the Stasi in Dresden; yet he also expressed great concern for the reintegration of Stasi personnel into society, a stand based on his convictions about confession, forgiveness, and redemption.[84]

In what some have called this moment of *kairos* ("crisis"), it became possible for these roles to be intertwined, albeit with some parts of the church emphasizing one or the other. In fact, General Superintendent Günter Krusche of Berlin claims that to expect anything different at a moment such as this is to overestimate the role that the church could conceivably play. Such is his response to the claim of New Forum leader Bärbel Bohley that the church made peace with the state too early. With the advent of the round tables, when the church assumed a role of official mediation, as well as that of teacher of democratic process, it would have been very difficult to have taken a significantly more confrontational stance. The church would have risked losing the gains that it had accomplished if it had made all the demands that have since been voiced.[85]

Yet the independent peace groups also played their part in moving the church hierarchy to this point of balance between conciliation and advocacy. Bishop Leich admitted their important role when he addressed the federal synod in Berlin in February 1990, saying, "The groups have, with their disturbing and uncomfortable behavior, strengthened the opposition against the pressure of adaptation."[86]

The church in the DDR had always been faced with this identity crisis of accommodation versus opposition, the two extreme expressions of the conciliation/

advocacy tension. It inherited all the baggage of the Nazi era, while it was immediately thrust into the context of another totalitarian regime. In this context, it was easy for the church to try to gain its identity on one extreme or the other. Yet creative tensions have been formulated throughout the history of the DDR. Though Dietrich Bonhoeffer's theology of "a church for others," with its call to speak on behalf of the suffering and the marginalized, formed one of the bases of DDR theology, the church frequently presented itself as a mediator between the state and the oppressed in order to fulfill this calling.[87]

A recent attempt to formulate a creative identity for the church has been proposed by Superintedent Richter of Leipzig, who uses a soccer metaphor to capture the essence of the conciliation/advocacy tension. The "Standbein-Spielbein dialectic" is used to describe how the human body stands, usually resting on one leg (*Standbein*), while the other leg is at ease and can move around (*Spielbein*). The Standbein is the anchor, while the Spielbein provides flexibility. When one can move the latter leg about freely, one can avoid the traps of either accommodation or opposition because one's balance does not entirely depend on the place to which one is stepping. When the church has a healthy identity, it will be rooted, according to Richter, in its faith tradition, its Standbein. It will then be able to move its Spielbein in and around the structures of any state within which it exists. In an unstable state system it can have the independent stability with which to undermine the system and give support to the players at the same time. It is free from the extremes of having to put all its weight on one side of that tension. For Richter this Standbein-Spielbein dialectic is but a metaphor of Luther's doctrine of the two kingdoms. With one foot standing firmly in the kingdom of God, the other can find its way with confidence in the kingdom of the world.[88] Hence, Standbein-Spielbein points to the inherently spiritual nature of the church's self-understanding as it attempts to find the right balance between accommodation and opposition, or conciliation and advocacy. To understand how the church effectively midwifed *die Wende*, it will be important to understand the Standbein from which it acted, and how this affected its Spielbein, as well as the consequent changes in the world within which it stepped.

Influence of the Spiritual

As already indicated, the church struggled extensively with its political identity, its relation to the state. Yet it still represented the primary ideological alternative to the SED, simply by virtue of its existence as the only major institution that the state was never able to control completely. Consequently, the values and theology, as well as the symbols and ritual, of the church had impact beyond their immediate reaches within the society. The important questions, then, are (a) What were these foundations of religious identity in the Evangelische Kirche? (b) How did they, in turn, affect the political identity of the church and culture surrounding it, most particularly the independent peace groups? There are three foundations of religious identity that had particular import for the whole society. The church became the provider of (a) space for expression, (b) empowerment for action, and (c) a model for strategic commitment to nonviolence.

Despite its ever-decreasing percentage of the population, the church remained both a physical and ideological "space" within a state that would wish to be "Big Brother." It offered both a safe place to meet and freedom of expression. Some East German theologians argue that this was simply an extension of values that are at the heart of the gospel—that is, reconciliation, dialogue, participation, and community. These values were in marked contrast to a those of a Marxist state that expected conformity to its communiqués and collusion with its "culture of silence."[89] Not only was there a natural affinity to the church, therefore, on the part of the alienated, but also the values found there continued to form and nourish the dissident spirit. In addition, as they grew in this direction, the value orientation of these individuals became increasingly distant from the observable value system of the SED. According to Klaus Gysi, former state secretary for religious affairs in the DDR, the party leadership had become completely isolated from its own party rank and file, to say nothing of the general populace. Honecker would not even believe the information he got from his own ministers. This was the exact opposite of community as preached by, and experienced in, the church. Gysi's final conclusion about the communist state was that it had lost its moral and ethical norms because "the society (perhaps state would be more accurate) was empty. Nobody believed in it anymore."[90] Given the "lostness" of the SED, even its members were more open to expressions of community than had been the case previously. Therefore, a message of reconciliation could fall on receptive ears. Furthermore, the credibility of the church was such that all parties could entrust it with the task of official mediation.

Second, the church empowered both its own laity and many nonchurch members of opposition groups to overcome fear of oppression and to develop expertise in the social issues confronting the DDR. Bishop Leich stated clearly the call to overcome fear of oppression in a pastoral letter in mid-October 1989. Although he was addressing church members, he sounded a death knell to the old regime when he wrote, "Do not let yourselves be intimidated any longer by the thought that speaking the truth could bring you trouble. . . . God has given us the spirit of strength, . . . and of endurance." According to University of Leipzig church historian Helmar Junghans, there is no question but that a consciousness of God's presence and God's will empowered the people to overcome their fear.[91]

The church also offered a different set of themes that helped the opposition groups to develop and articulate a powerful social vision. Ehrhart Neubert, an East German sociologist of religion, argues that state efforts at indoctrination were only partially successful. When individuals experienced the state ideology as closed and alienating, they tended to withdraw into a private sphere. In the face of the resulting social apathy, two things tended to happen. First, the state had to rehabilitate certain aspects of the cultural, and often religious, past. An example of this is the SED's rehabilitation of Martin Luther on the occasion of his 500th birthday. Second, individuals, feeling threatened by arbitrariness and unpredictability, looked for powerful symbols that visualized their experience and represented unquestionable truths. In the case of the independent groups under the roof of the church, Neubert claims that the themes of "peace," "justice," and "integrity of creation" (taken directly from the church's conciliar process) became sacred, transcendent ideals. Neubert argues that, as a consequence, these groups had a very definite "religious" function that was largely informed by the Lutheran tradition, despite the fact that many of the participants did not attend church. Such an explanation would have explained the potential effect of prayer services on a largely "irreligious crowd" (meaning simply, "not formally trained in religious belief systems"). The power of the vision of the "alternate culture"—that is, the one which had grown up under the safe haven and the influence of the church, would have been enough to both mobilize the crowd and incline it to conform with the behavior implied in the themes of peace, justice, and integrity of creation.[92]

One indication of the power of this vision and its theological themes is the similarity of vocabulary and argumentation used by both church and opposition groups. The groups were more radical in their immediate demands. But their demands were still based largely on the social agenda articulated by German theologians out of the Confessing Church tradition. Their language was often biblical (e.g., the swords into plowshares patches worn during the 1982 peace decade). The Sermon on the Mount was especially important to the groups (e.g., the peace prayers often used this scripture and the initiative group against "delimitation" appealed to Jesus' love of enemies). Some groups even called for change using the terms "conversion" and "repentance." Finally, the groups frequently appropriated religious activities (e.g., worship services, vigils, "solidarity services," pilgrimages, and even Holy Communion).[93]

Third, and most important, the church's strategic commitment to nonviolence had a direct impact on the peaceful nature of the protest. In the course of over 40 interviews conducted by this author in the former DDR, not one person denied that the church's commitment to nonviolence had at least some effect on the relatively peaceful outcome. Most people, including former State Secretary for Religious Affairs Klaus Gysi, credited the church with being one of the primary factors.[94] The strategic nature of the church's commitment to nonviolence could be seen in the willingness to apply it in such a way as to minimize the threat even to one's enemy. It was nonpragmatic and nontactical; it was a baseline commitment to do all one could to avoid violence of any kind to anyone. Strategic nonviolence is inherently corrosive to violence-based systems like the former DDR. According to Zimmermann, when the Stasi and other SED implants in Nikolaikirche on October 9, 1989, realized that the church wanted peaceful change, even they found the will to act with nonviolence.[95] The moral authority of the church counted for more than did all the government troops surrounding the city. This event was undoubtedly one of the crucial factors in the transfer of power to the dissident movement. As DDR writer Rolf Schneider concluded, "The Sermon on the Mount got the better of city hall and finally won the victory over city hall itself: gently, peacefully, in a gesture of forgiveness."[96]

At the same time, the church's strategic commitment to nonviolence influenced the independent groups and the crowds that gathered for the demonstrations.

According to numerous participants in the Leipzig demonstrations, the people outside the church waited for those inside to set the tone. The clear message from the church was always "no violence," a standard accepted as an unspoken agreement.[97] The negative motivation of fear, common to all the demonstrators, was infused with a positive message of the value of nonviolence based on the Sermon on the Mount and the teachings and practice of Mahatma Gandhi and Martin Luther King, Jr.[98] Religious symbols communicated this message even when words were not spoken (e.g., singing "We Shall Overcome" and "Dona Nobis Pacem," wearing sashes saying "no violence," and holding lighted candles).[99] In addition, the church reminded people that they could not scapegoat the state and that they must examine their own behavior. This spirit of self-examination and confession countered a tendency toward intolerance, self-righteousness, and violent fanaticism on the part of some demonstrators.[100]

The spirit of tolerance, the roots of which are found in the strategic commitment to nonviolence, also surrounded the round table process. As already noted, Bishop Leich traced the spirit of reconciliation from the peace prayers to the nonviolent demonstrations to the round tables. Also, moderator Ziegler attributed the lack of violence during this time to an atmosphere of stability that resulted from the democratically organized round table. Two additional round table participants specifically linked the theology of peace to the way in which the moderators developed their conciliation process, saying that the peaceful mood is what made it possible for participants to learn the necessary democratic process. Thus, at least in part because of its strategic commitment to nonviolence, the church was able to use its unique intermediary position to give birth to democracy.[101]

Another somewhat more controversial theological basis for this strategic nonviolence was Martin Luther's doctrine of the two kingdoms, which had been extensively revised. The perversion of this doctrine in the nineteenth and early twentieth centuries had resulted in a theology of submission to the state, to which was given unquestionable authority to establish order. This subservience to authority had led to church passivity under Hitler. The doctrine was therefore severely criticized following World War II. Franz Lau, a Leipzig theologian writing in the 1950s, was a key figure in rehabilitating this doctrine. Lau insisted that one must not rise up against the ruler in defense of one's own interests; he also taught, however, that Luther advocated almost foolhardy opposition against all governmental injustice. Being true to Luther, then, did not always mean subservience to the political authorities. In fact, Luther equated resistance with "bearing the cross." It was not resistance but armed insurrection that he opposed. According to this "rediscovery" of the original Luther, the father of the Evangelische Kirche saw violence as justified in only the most extreme of situations. This perspective on Lutheran church-state relations continued to be affirmed through the 1980s within DDR theology. Leipzig church historian Helmar Junghans demonstrates this by his claim that, at different times, Luther called for both criticism of and support for the state. Furthermore, according to another Leipzig theologian, Ernst Koch, recent assessments of Lutheran tradition have rediscovered a broad stream of opposition to the state on the part of pastors and theologians over the centuries prior to the mid-1900s. This opposition stance then lay dormant until it was once again affirmed in Bonhoeffer's theology, informed by the theologian's experience as part of the resistance to Hitler. It is this understanding of the doctrine with which Richter interprets his use of the Standbein-Spielbein metaphor.[102]

When this dynamic understanding of two-kingdoms doctrine is coupled with the teachings of three of this century's most renowned religious martyrs (Bonhoeffer, King, and Gandhi), and this, in turn, is added to empowering symbols of peace, justice, and integrity of creation, together with the opportunity for greater freedom of expression than is available anywhere else, then one has a Standbein strong enough to balance conciliation and protest. The kind of principled behavior engendered by such a Standbein should be able to generate considerable trust, as indeed we see to be the case in the church in the DDR. Even though the church is an actor in the same society as everyone else in the DDR, it is the agent approached as protector and selected as conflict resolver. Indigenous actors are able to act as both advocates and conciliators due to the trust with which they are bestowed. However, *die Wende* in East Germany included a great many actors. This case represents a quantum leap from the role of spirituality in the lives of individual mediators to the role of the spiritual on an institutional level where there is no possibility of a conscious coordination of efforts. The fact that it was successful was demonstrated by a banner hung across a Leipzig street late in 1989. Placed there by nonchurch people, it read, *Wir danken Dir, Kirche* ("We thank you, Church").

Notes

1. John P. Burgess, "Church in East Germany Helps Create *die Wende*," *Christian Century* (December 6, 1989), 1141; Lance Dickie, "Keepers of the Faith," *Seattle Times*, November 4, 1990, A21; Uwe Siemon-Netto, "Luther versus Lenin," *Lutheran Quarterly* (Winter 1991), 403–5; interview with Hans-Jürgen Sievers, pastor of the Reformed Church in Leipzig and one of the moderators of that city's round table, Leipzig, June 17, 1991; and Martin Steinhäuser, research student of theology at Leipzig Theological Seminary, personal communication, February 1, 1993.

2. Niels C. Nielsen, *Revolutions in Eastern Europe: The Religious Roots* (Maryknoll, N.Y.: Orbis Books, 1991), 27; and Ulrich Seidel, pastor of Stephanuskirche in Leipzig, unpublished lecture given at University of Edinburgh, Scotland, December 4, 1990.

3. Burgess, "Church in East Germany Helps Create *die Wende*," 1141; Kent R. Hill, *"And the Wall Came Tumbling Down!" The Role of Religion in the East German Revolution: 1989–1990* (Washington: Institute on Religion and Democracy, 1991), 6; Kenneth Snyder, "Learning Democracy from East German Church: Living in Faith amid Political and Social Change," *World Peacemaker Quarterly* (February 1990), 18; and Steinhäuser, personal communication.

4. Siemon-Netto, "Luther versus Lenin," 404–7; and interview with Christoph Wielepp, with interpretation by Bernd Wesuls, Leipzig, June 15, 1991. Wielepp is the son of a pastor and was a participant in the Leipzig demonstration.

5. Interview with Martin Kind, with interpretation by Martin Steinhäuser, Leipzig, June 13, 1991.

6. Nielsen, *Revolutions in Eastern Europe*, 27; Snyder, "Learning Democracy from East German Church," 18; Frederick O. Bonkovsky, "Sources of East German Revolution and German Unification," *Occasional Papers on Religion in Eastern Europe*, 11, no. 3 (1991), 36; Johannes Richter, superintendent of Thomaskirche District in Leipzig, undated personal communication (received March 1993); and interview with Peter Zimmermann, Leipzig, June 17, 1991.

7. Burgess, "Church in East Germany Helps Create *die Wende*, 1141; Hill, *"And the Wall Came Tumbling Down!"*, 6; and Snyder, "Learning Democracy from East German Church," 18.

8. "The church" as used here (and elsewhere unless otherwise indicated) refers to the East German church in a generic sense. This includes primarily the Evangelische Kirche, but is not exclusive to it.

9. Sources relied on for the historical background of this period were Robert F. Goeckel, *The Lutheran Church and the East German State: Political Conflict and Change Under Ulbricht and Honecker* (Ithaca and London: Cornell University Press, 1990), 31, 41–44; and Richard W. Solberg, *God and Caesar in East Germany: The Conflicts of Church and State in East Germany Since 1945* (New York: Macmillan, 1961) 10–11, 19–24, 29–32, 58–60, 104.

10. Barbara Green, "Looking Back on a Closing Chapter: The Experience of the East German Churches," *Theology and Public Policy* 3, no. 1 (1991), 51–52; and Uwe Siemon-Netto, "East Germany: Luther vs. Lenin," *First Things* (June/July 1990), 51.

11. For example, in 1948, when pastors were requested by the authorities to support political measures, all the bishops of the East Zone churches wrote a letter to the chairman of the Soviet Military Administration informing him that the church reserved the right to criticize the civil authorities.

12. Sources relied on for this period were Goeckel, *Lutheran Church and the East German State*, 44–55; and Solberg, *God and Caesar in East Germany*, 84–294.

13. The church represented one of the greatest threats to the communist intention to inculcate a new ideological perspective, especially among the youth, and was one of the predominant institutions that questioned state policy. As a result of this frontal assault, church membership began to shrink, creating a minority church for the first time in German history. Alongside this institutional decline, however, an interdenominational structure of house churches began to function within and outside the traditional church structures. These events accelerated the reevaluation of the Volkskirche, the institution that heretofore had provided the societal rites of passage. Reassessment of the state church concept as a valid form of ecclesial identity further enabled the church, in its broadest sense, to play a less traditional role (Green, "Looking Back on a Closing Chapter," 53; and Siemon-Netto, "East Germany: Luther vs. Lenin," 51).

14. In the Declaration of the Synod of Weißensee in 1950, the church refused to align itself with the "National Front," the peace program of the SED. Later, while they convened in Berlin in April 1953, the bishops stated that the judgment of God would rest upon those who misuse civil authority. The church protest also moved beyond words, as when the church decided to hold its annual youth rally in Lübbenau in June 1952, despite government attempts to prohibit it. The Free German Youth (FDJ), under the leadership of Erich Honecker tried to disrupt the event. The church response, again foreshadowing the demonstrations of 1989, consisted of pastors calling for the youth to practice discipline, nonviolence, and respect for the police, as well as asking them to form a peaceful cordon to keep the FDJ out of the rally.

15. The church was concerned to set forth a rationale for negotiation and mediation and attempted to implement this approach. One noteworthy example, again presaging the role played by the church in the round tables of 1990, occurred in 1951 in the context of a dispute over relations between the two new German states. Bishop Dibelius offered the "good offices" of the church to the prime ministers of both East and West Germany, inviting Grotewohl and Adenauer to his home. Though the meeting did not take place, tensions nonetheless eased (Solberg, *God and Caesar in East Germany*, 108–9).

16. Reinhard Henkys, "Evangelische Kirche," in *Kirche und Gessellschaft in beiden deutschen Staaten*, ed. Gisela Helwig and Detlef Urban (Cologne: Verlag Wissenschaft und Politik, 1987), 69. The two most significant meetings were called for the explicit purpose of negotiating the church-state relationship. A few days prior to the workers' uprising in 1953, the government held a crucial summit with East German church leaders, where the state retracted its previous positions and pledged to "guarantee the church's existence" in accord with the constitution. The church promised to "avoid unconstitutional attacks and influences on the political and economic life." But this relaxation of tension proved to be temporary, necessitating a church stance of continued protest, culminating in the second series of church-state discussions in June 1958.

17. The primary source relied on for this period was Goeckel, *Lutheran Church and the East German State*, 56–85, 112–13.

18. As a result of church pressure, the state formed a special army construction unit in September 1964, as a non-weapons-carrying form of military service. The church also advocated a nonuniformed alternative service outside of military control, which was not acceptable to the SED (Joyce Marie Mushaben, "Swords to Plowshares: The Church, The State and the East German Peace Movement," *Studies in Comparative Communism* 17, no. 2 [1984], 125).

19. For example, after the Warsaw Pact invasion of Czechoslovakia in 1968, there was protest from Bishop Hans-Joachim Fränkel of the Silesian Church who was one of the most outspoken critics of the regime (Siemon-Netto, "Luther versus Lenin," 410–13). There was also condemnation of the invasion in the Chancel Declaration by the Berlin-Brandenburg church leadership. Though this was accompanied by numerous arrests in these *Landes-kirchen* ("regional churches"), it was greeted with silence from most of the other Land-eskirchen and even endorsement of the invasion by Bishop Mitzenheim of the Thuringian Church.

20. Pedro Ramet, "Church and Peace in the GDR," *Problems of Communism* 33 (July–August 1984), 45.

21. Otto Luchterhandt, *Die Gegenwartslage der Evangelischen Kirchen in der DDR* (Tübingen: J.B.C. Mohr, 1982), 24–25.

22. The Kirchenbund enjoyed significant influence because Schönherr was a politically engaged churchman who had membership in some groups considered "progressive" by the SED, yet was able to join in circumspect protest. Stolpe, Schönherr's protegé, had even closer relations with the SED.

23. The primary source relied on for this period was Goeckel, *Lutheran Church and the East German State*, 114–18, 123–26, 132–47, 172–200, 206–20, 235–46.

24. Alternative formulations of church identity included the following: the CDU, on behalf of the SED, advocated a "church *for* socialism." Conservatives wished to reaffirm the old Lutheran understanding of the "separation of two kingdoms," with its implications of political abstinence. Long-time critics continued to conceive of the church as a "guardian office," a voice of conscience against abuse of power by the state. Many of those influenced by the theology of Confessing Church martyr Dietrich Bonhoeffer recommended the

"church for others," focusing on support to disenfranchised individuals. The most popular challenge to the proposed accord with the SED was Professor Heino Falcke's call to be in "critical solidarity" with the state. This "critical solidarity" position was particularly criticized by the state for its contention that socialism could be improved.

25. Green, "Looking Back on a Closing Chapter," 54. The weakness of this formulation was that it could be interpreted in so many different ways, including ideological acceptance of the state system.

26. In fact, Bishop Werner Krusche of Magdeburg claimed that when the church became only a tool to amplify the foreign policy of the state, it would lose its potential for conflict resolution and peacemaking (Luchterhandt, *Die Gegenwartslage der Evangelischen Kirchen in der DDR*, 79–81).

27. One important result of the attempt to influence theological education was an enrollment shift from the state university faculties of theology, controlled by the government, to the theological colleges run by the church. A growing split consequently occurred between people affiliated with these two divergent contexts for theological education. This contributed significantly to the development, by the 1980s, of two groups of clergy—one schooled in the perspective and tactics of the opposition, and the other trained to be conciliators.

28. Stephen P. Hoffman, "East Germany," in *Three Worlds of Christian-Marxist Encounters*, ed. Nicholas Piediscalzi and Robert G. Thobaben (Philadelphia: Fortress Press, 1985), 104.

29. As a result, the church synod in Halle in September 1976 even called into question the Schönherr formula for church identity, referring instead to the "church in the current situation." The contrast between this democratic ambiance of church life and the authoritarian control within the SED greatly influenced the different roles played by church and state and the different degrees of trust they engendered during the events of 1989–90.

30. The resulting agreements, which represented significant concessions by the state, benefited the church as an institution and also had implications for the larger society. Among other things, this resulted in state approval of the 500th anniversary celebration of the birth of Martin Luther and agreement to expand discussion on economic and environmental problems (Mushaben, "Swords to Plowshares," 128).

31. Sources relied on for this period were Goeckel, *Lutheran Church and the East German State*, 248–68; Ramet, "Church and Peace in the GDR," 50–57; and Green, "Looking Back on a Closing Chapter," 56–60.

32. Church support for the groups was especially strong throughout Saxony, especially in Leipzig, where all groups were composed of church people. Such was not the case in Berlin (interview with Wielepp; and interview with Werner Krusche, former head of the Kirchenbund and former Bishop of Magdeburg, Magdeburg, Germany, June 3, 1991). One illustration of a strong relationship is the beginning of peace prayer services alongside meetings of independent groups at Nikolaikirche in Leipzig in 1981. These were the same prayer services that by 1989 became a fulcrum of dissent and antiregime demonstrations (interview with Johannes Richter, superintendent at Leipzig's Thomaskirche, Leipzig, June 13, 1991; and Seidel lecture).

33. This development was accompanied by a theological rediscovery of the Sermon on the Mount, a reclaiming of the relevance of this biblical passage for the current political situation. In particular, "loving one's enemies" and "praying for those who persecute you" became the subject of a number of new biblical commentaries and worship meditations. The notion of loving one's enemies was interpreted as discovering certain actions and symbols, recognizable to the enemy, which would lessen hostility.

34. Arvan Gordon, "The Church and Change in the GDR," *Religion in Communist Lands* 18, no. 2 (1990), 151–52. The record is not complete, however, without some indication of the peace stands still being taken by the church and the questions being raised about the "church within socialism." At the 1987 Kirchentag, the official church did not completely avoid sensitive political issues. The Kirchentag ended with calls for a neutral and disarmed Germany, for "New Thinking" as in the Soviet Union, an end to militarization in the schools, and the cessation of government limitation on contacts with the west (Matthias Hartmann, "Signale vom Evangelischen Kirchentag," *Deutsches Archiv* [August 1987], 838–39).

35. Primary sources relied on for this period were Goeckel, *Lutheran Church and the East German State*, 254, 266–73; Green, "Looking Back on a Closing Chapter," 60–62; Daniel Hamilton, *After the Revolution: The New Political Landscape in East Germany*, German Issues no. 7 (Washington, D.C.: American Institute for Contemporary German Studies, 1990), 5–8; and Bonkovsky, "Sources of East German Revolution and German Unification," 22–36.

36. Interview with Hans Simon, pastor of Zionskirche, with interpretation by Jana Zalewski, Berlin, Germany, June 10, 1991; Gordon, "Church and Change in the GDR," 152; and Barbara Donovan, "East German Churches Demand Justice," *RAD Background Report*, Radio Free Europe Research (May 10, 1989), 2, 5. In response to events like this, State Secretary for Religious Affairs Klaus Gysi reports that Honecker became so concerned about the direction of the church-related groups that he began to handle church relations himself. This was to counter the influence of Gysi who advocated greater democratization and gave a listening ear to a church that he believed often spoke for the greater population. Gysi was restricted from access to Honecker after 1985 and, in 1988, was replaced by ideologue Kurt Löffler who, it was thought, could rein in the church and its groups (interview with Klaus Gysi, Berlin, June 20, 1991).

37. One of the principal church negotiators with the state, Manfred Stolpe, joined with Pastor Hans Simon in negotiating the release of those arrested in the raids on the ecology library at Zionskirche (interview with Simon). It was again Stolpe who functioned as chief negotiator on behalf of those arrested in early 1988, while other church leaders fulfilled complementary roles: Bishop Forck attended the trial of Wollenberger, while another member of the church leadership, Manfred Becker, challenged the court's interpretation of the criminal code with respect to her case (Gordon, "Church and Change in the GDR," 152). One price the church paid, however, for the release of the imprisoned was an agreement to discontinue the prayer services and advice centers and to affirm the state's control over emigration policy. Another price was increased state harassment of church press and allegations of church violation of the principle of separation of church and state.

38. "Church in Solidarity" took its name from Falcke's "critical solidarity" position articulated in the early 1970s. See note 26; Gordon, "Church and Change in the GDR," 152; Susan Sanders, "The Independent Reform Debate in the GDR," *RAD Background Report*, Radio Free Europe Research (August 3, 1989), 2–3; and Barbara Donovan, "Church Groups Call for Democratic Reforms," *RAD Background Report*, Radio Free Europe Research (June 10, 1988), 1.

39. Joachim Garstecki, "Ökumenische Versammlung in der DDR," *Deutsches Archiv* (April 1989), 425. The state was so concerned about the effects of these church conferences and synods that it attempted to prohibit publication of the reports it deemed most offensive (Gordon, "Church and Change in the GDR," 152). Furthermore, out of concern that the federal synod in September 1988 might be "misused" to criticize the DDR, State Secretary for Religious Affairs Löffler met with church leaders in advance (Barbara Donovan, "East German Synod: Church Refuses to Curtail Criticism," *RAD Background Report*, Radio

Free Europe Research [September 22, 1988], 2–4). The degree of state consternation can be seen in its attacks on rather conservative church leaders like Bishop Leich when he defended church-based dialogue over social issues.

40. Interview with Christof Ziemer, with interpretation by Bernd Wesuls, Dresden, June 19, 1991.

41. The resulting freeze in church-state relations, and increase in church protest, can be illustrated by a few events in early 1989. In January, Werner Jarowinsky (the Politburo member responsible for church relations) simply read a statement, allowing no time for response, to Bishop Leich and Secretary of the Kirchenbund, Manfred Ziegler, at a meeting purported to be for discussion. The next month, when Honecker invited Leich for a conversation, Leich prepared a paper in advance, with the cooperation of the other bishops, on issues of free speech, travel, and economics. When they met, however, Honecker refused to discuss Leich's points (interview with Hans Schäfer, assistant to Bishop Leich, Weimar, June 17, 1991).

42. In January, on the anniversary of the 1988 march in memory of Rosa Luxemburg and Karl Liebknecht, people were detained in a demonstration for free speech, assembly, and organization. Church services were held to pray and petition for their release. In February, another service was held in Berlin for members of the group Justice and Peace, who had been detained for reasons of making illegal contacts, transmitting information, and demeaning of state organs. In April, 50 people were detained in Leipzig for protesting the conditions of the polluted Pleisse River. Protest services were held at two churches, which worked to plan the events in conjunction with the first organized opposition group. The Initiative für Frieden und Menschenrechte ("Initiative for Peace and Human Rights") had been formed in October 1988 (interview with Karsten Speck, member of Democracy Now and former Baptist pastor, and Matthias Sädewitz, member of Initiative for Peace and Human Rights, with interpretation by Karsten Speck, Leipzig, June 12, 1991).

43. June Carolyn Erlick, "Questions for the East German Church," *Christian Century* 106 (August 30–September 6, 1989), 79; and interview with Gotthard Fuhrmann, pastor of Friedenskirche in Dresden, with interpretation by Bernd Wesuls, Dresden, June 19, 1991.

44. Pressure was also put on the DDR government by other East European governments, especially by Hungary and Czechoslovakia, which were confronted with increasing numbers of East Germans seeking asylum through West German embassies.

45. Roman Catholic dissent began with Bishop Braun of Magdeburg and Bishop Sterzinsky of East Berlin. At the same time, there was extensive involvement of church people in the formation of formal opposition groups. Speaking at a prayer service in East Berlin's Gedächtniskirche, Hans-Jürgen Fishbeck, representing the group Renunciation of the Principle and Practice of Delimitation, called for the founding of a DDR-wide opposition movement. On September 12, this group, with the help of Stolpe, printed an appeal which, later that month, was presented to the federal church synod of the Evangelische Kirche in Eisenach. Though there was no formal decision to endorse this idea, there was considerable grass-roots church support. Many pastors joined the Democracy Now group that grew out of the process. Instead of one organization, however, three groups emerged. The second, Democratic Awakening, though not officially endorsed by the church, remained dominated by Protestant clergy and was seen by many as a "Protestant voice" until its demise in December 1989. The best known of the groups, New Forum, was the most secular, though a few pastors and many lay people did join. Church persons comprised a greater percentage of the membership in Leipzig than in Berlin, resulting in very close cooperation in planning of the worship and protest events that sparked *die Wende*. Many of New Forum's Berlin-based leadership, however, were frustrated by the constraints they often felt were imposed by the

church hierarchy (interview with Hans-Jürgen Fishbeck, founding member of Democracy Now, with interpretation by Jana Zalewski, Berlin, June 11, 1991; interview with Krusche; and interview with Wielepp).

46. Hill, *"And the Wall Came Tumbling Down!"*, 5.

47. Goeckel, *Lutheran Church and the East German State*, 272.

48. Hill, *"And the Wall Came Tumbling Down!"*, 5; "Pleas from GDR Churches," *Christian Century* (October 11, 1989), 905; William Downey, "Communist Party Paper Denounces East German Church Proposals," *Religious News Service* (September 22, 1989), 9; and "DDR: Church Synod Discusses Emigration," *Ecumenical Press Service*, no. 89.10.18 (October 8–10, 1989).

49. Burgess, "Church in East Germany Helps Create *die Wende*," 1140.

50. Ibid.; and interview with Sievers.

51. Interview with Sievers; Hill, *"And the Wall Came Tumbling Down!"*, 6; and Burgess, "Church in East Germany Helps Create *die Wende*," 1140–41.

52. Siemon-Netto, "Luther versus Lenin," 403–7; "Police Arrest Hundreds in East Germany: Demonstrations in 5 Cities Are the Largest Since 1953," *International Herald Tribune*, October 9, 1989, 1; "East Berlin's Party Ends," *Sunday Times* (London), October 8, 1989, 1–2; Hill, *"And the Wall Came Tumbling Down!"*, 6; and Burgess, "Church in East Germany Helps Create *die Wende*," 1140–42.

53. "Too Late to Find an East German Gorbachev," *Independent* (London), October 10, 1989, 12; and interview with Sievers.

54. Much of the support for these groups came from the faculty, students, and alumni of the Leipzig Theological Seminary. Many of these people had been denied participation within state-supported higher education prior to entering the seminary. Therefore, they had been inclined, from the beginning of the decade, to take leadership roles in the peace prayers at Nikolaikirche and the independent groups that formed under the roof of the church (Nielsen, *Revolution in Eastern Europe*, 29; and interview with Kind).

55. Interview with Steinhäuser, Leipzig, June 13, 1991; Richter, undated personal communication; interview with Zimmermann; and Siemon-Netto, "Luther versus Lenin," 403–7, 414–17.

56. Zimmermann reports that he was approached by members of the SED to be the representative of the church in this process. He, in turn, informed Superintendent Friedrich Magirius of the Nikolaikirche District and Bishop Hempel of the invitation and requested the freedom to act in this capacity. Zimmermann teaches at the formerly state-run theology faculty of Karl Marx University (now the University of Leipzig). This faculty had many more ties with the regime. However, some of its students also participated in the peace prayers and opposition groups. Opinion among Leipzigers is mixed as to the significance of the activities of the Leipzig six. Some perceive both Zimmermann and Masur as having been government loyalists. But Masur, in particular, had gained the confidence of many through a West German television interview on October 2, when he had confessed his sense of shame at the violent crackdown on demonstrators (interview with Zimmermann; Nielsen, *Revolutions in Eastern Europe*, 30; Jill Smolowe, "Lending an Ear," *Time Magazine* [October 23, 1989], 11; Snyder, "Learning Democracy from East German Church," 18; interview with Sievers; and interview with Wielepp).

57. At the service of remembrance, the congregation applauded as Albani compared Christ's defiance of the Pharisees with the demonstrators' defiance of the state. Yet the pastor again urged them to follow Christ's way of nonviolence. Some days later, the Gethsemanekirche vigil issued a statement saying that the crisis would only become worse unless the police-state methods were changed (Edward Steen, "East Berlin Prays in the

Shadow of the Night," *Independent* [London], October 9, 1989, 10; "Police Arrest Hundreds in East Germany," 1; "Round-the-Clock Vigil for DDR Peace Activists," *Ecumenical Press Service*, no. 89.10.66 [October 15–21, 1989]; and interview with Gottfried Forck, Bishop of Berlin-Brandenburg, Berlin, June 10, 1991).

58. Interview with Christof Ziemer.

59. Ibid.; Monika Zimmermann, "Wach Auf, Du Deutsches Land, blasen die Posaunen in der Kirche," *Frankfurter Allgemeine*, October 11, 1989, 3; "Vorschläge des Dresdner Oberbürgermeisters," ibid., October 18, 1989, 2; and "Botschaftsflüchtlinge aus Warschau per Flugzeug in den Westen," ibid., October 18, 1989, 1.

60. Interview with Christof Ziemer.

61. Interview with Schäfer; and "Kirche und Opposition in der DDR zwischen Zuversicht und Argwohn," *Frankfurter Allgemeine*, October 13, 1989, 1–2.

62. Stephen Brown, "Church Calls for DDR Reform," *Ecumenical Press Service*, no. 89.11.46 (November 1–10, 1989); and interview with Schäfer.

63. Brown, "Church Calls for DDR Reform"; Monika Zimmermann, "Von Erich Honecker ist nirgends mehr die Rede," *Frankfurter Allgemeine*, October 20, 1989, 3; "Hempel verurteilt brutalis Vorgehen," ibid., October 23, 1989, 2; Günter Bannas, "Die Kerze brutal aus der Hand geschlagen," ibid., October 26, 1989, 5; and "Krenz macht keinen Lenz," *Der Spiegel* 43 (October 30, 1989), 18–28.

64. Interview with Christof Ziemer; interview with Uwe Thaysen, observer at the central round table in Berlin, Hamburg, June 8, 1991; and Green, "Looking Back on a Closing Chapter," 63. One example, as early as November 1989, was in Holzhausen where Harald Wagner, research student at Leipzig Theological Seminary and pastor to the parish in Holzhausen, was asked by both the government and the demonstrators to mediate between the mayor and the opposition (interview with Harald Wagner, with interpretation by Martin Steinhäuser, Holzhausen, Germany, June 12, 1991).

65. Interview conducted by Ewald Rose with Martin Ziegler and Martin Lange, "Blutvergießen konnte vermieden werden (Bloodshed Could Have Been Avoided)," (unpublished translation by Malcolm Clark) in *Vom Runden Tisch zum Parlament*, ed. Helmut Herles and Ewald Rose (Bonn: Buvier Verlag, 1990), 330; and Green, "Looking Back on a Closing Chapter," 63.

66. Monika Zimmermann, "Ein Adventsstern leuchtet über dem runden Tisch," *Frankfurter Allgemeine*, December 8, 1989, 3; Hill, *"And the Wall Came Tumbling Down!"*, 7; Green, "Looking Back on a Closing Chapter," 63; and Rose, "Blutvergießen konnte vermieden werden," (Ziegler) 331.

67. William Downey, "New Role for Church in DDR," *Ecumenical Press Service*, no. 90.01.78 (January 6–15, 1990); Jackson Diehl, "As Crowds Rove, East German Security Chief Warns of Chaos," *International Herald Tribune*, December 8, 1989, 1, 8; Patricia Clough, "East German Secret Police to be Disbanded," *Independent* (London), December 15, 1989, 1; Patricia Clough, "Cheerful Call for a United Germany," ibid., December 19, 1989, 1; and Rose, "Blutvergießen konnte vermieden werden," (Ziegler and Lange) 331, 337–38.

68. Interview with Heiko Leitz, former pastor and representative of New Forum at the central round table, with interpretation by Jana Zalewski, Güstrow, Germany, June 5, 1991.

69. Interview with Martin Lange, Berlin, June 11, 1991; Rose, "Blutvergießen konnte vermieden werden," (Lange) 335; interview with Thaysen; interview with Rolf Henrich, representative of New Forum on the central round table, with interpretation by Jana Zalewski, Eisenhüttenstadt, Germany, June 7, 1991; and Martin Ziegler, interviewed in

"Zwanzig Jahre waren nicht nur ein Zwischenfall," (unpublished translation by Eva Bayer) *Übergänge* 16, no. 5 (1990), 179.

70. Werner Leich, English translation of statement released by the Conference of Evangelical Church Leaders in the DDR, December 8, 1989, "Statement by East German Church Leaders," *Ecumenical Press Service*, no. 90.01.76 (January 6–15, 1990).

71. Interview with Lange; and Rose, "Blutvergießen konnte vermieden werden," (Lange) 335–36.

72. Rose, "Blutvergießen konnte vermieden werden," (Ziegler) 335.

73. Interview with Henrich.

74. Interview with Thaysen. Hans Jürgen Röder, from the Evangelische Press Service, maintains that one of the moderators of the central round table was critical of the old regime. Furthermore, due to long-standing relationships with opposition groups, he states that it was quite common throughout the DDR for the pastor/moderators of regional round tables to express their views more forcefully than did their counterparts in the central round table (interview with Hans-Jürgen Röder, with interpretation by Jana Zalewski, Berlin, June 7, 1991). The greater caution on the part of the latter may well have been due to the fact that the central round table had the potential for a much greater impact on public opinion and political stability throughout the DDR. It was, for example, the only round table with TV coverage (interview with Leitz; and interview with Martin Kramer, chair of the Kirchenbund's Commission for Church and Society and a pastor in Magdeburg, Berlin, June 6, 1991).

75. Interview with Lange; and Rose, "Blutvergießen konnte vermieden werden," (Ziegler and Lange) 335, 338.

76. Interview with Christof Ziemer.

77. Johannes Hempel, as cited in *Ecumenical Press Service*, no. 90.04.01 (April 1–5, 1990).

78. Siemon-Netto, "East Germany: Luther vs. Lenin," 50; interview with Forck; and Rose, "Blutvergießen konnte vermieden werden," (Ziegler and Lange) 336–37.

79. Hill, *"And the Wall Came Tumbling Down!"*, 7–8; interview with Forck; Hamilton, *After the Revolution*, 16–38; and Siemon-Netto, "East Germany: Luther vs. Lenin," 50–52.

80. Interview with Wolfgang Ratzmann, Jürgen Ziemer, and Harald Wagner, with interpretation by Martin Steinhäuser, Holzhausen, Germany, June 12, 1991.

81. Interview with Markus Meckel, Loccum, Germany, June 2, 1991.

82. Interview with Christof Ziemer.

83. For example, some pastors broadcast messages using the Sermon on the Mount to try to convince people in Leipzig not to join in the demonstrations (interview with Jürgen Ziemer).

84. Interview with Roland Adolf, with interpretation by Bernd Wesuls, Moritzburg, Germany, June 19, 1991.

85. Interview with Günter Krusche, general superintendent of the Evangelische Kirche in Berlin, Berlin, June 11, 1991.

86. Werner Leich, "Bericht des Vorsitzenden der Konferenz der Kirchenleitungen, Landesbischof Dr. Werner Leich (Report of the Chairman of the Church Leaders' Conference, Provincial Bishop Werner Leich)," (unpublished translation by Britta Weiß) *Synoden Rückschau*, 6th Synod, First Conference, Berlin-Weißensee, February 23–26, 1990 (Berlin: Bund der Evangelishen Kirchen in der DDR, n.d.), 5.

87. Dietrich Bonhoeffer, *Letters and Papers From Prison*, ed. Eberhard Bethge, trans. Reginald H. Fuller (New York: Macmillan, 1953), 239–40.

88. Interview with Richter; and Siemon-Netto, "Luther versus Lenin," 411–15.

89. John P. Burgess, "Church-State Relations in East Germany: The Church as a 'Religious' and 'Political' Force," *Journal of Church and State*, 32, no. 1 (1990), 24, 34; and Walter Bindemann, "Die Kirche und das Volk," *Bündnis 2000: Forum für Demokratie, Ökologie und Menschenrechte*, 1. no. 8 (March 22, 1991), 5.

90. Interview with Gysi.

91. Werner Leich, "Pastoral Letter from DDR Bishop Werner Leich," *Ecumenical Press Service*, no. 89.11.88 (November 21–30, 1989); interview with Helmar Junghans, with interpretation by Martin Steinhäuser, Leipzig, June 14, 1991; and Bindemann, "Die Kirche und das Volk," 5.

92. Ehrhart Neubert, "Religion in der DDR Gesellschaft," *Kirche im Sozialismus* 11 (June 1985), 47–74.

93. John P. Burgess, "Preparing for the Fall of 1989: Religion and Democratization in East Germany," *Soundings* 74, no. 1–2 (1991), 54–57.

94. Interview with Gysi.

95. Interview with Zimmermann.

96. Jens Langer, "Get with It!: The Ability of Systems and Their Components to Operate and Cooperate," *Journal of Peace and Justice Studies* 2, no. 2 (1990), 6, quoting Rolf Schneider in the *Vienna Weekly Press* (November 17, 1989).

97. Interview with Kind; interview with Zimmermann; and interview with Steinhäuser.

98. Interview with Rolf-Dieter Günter, press secretary for the Kirchenbund, with interpretation by Jana Zalewski, Berlin, June 10, 1991; interview with Werner Krätschell, superintendent of Berlin-Pankow, Berlin, June 11, 1991; Seidel lecture; J. Martin Bailey, *The Spring of Nations: Churches in the Rebirth of Central and Eastern Europe* (New York: Friendship Press, 1991), 86; Leich, "Pastoral Letter"; interview with Werner Krusche; interview with Jürgen Ziemer; and interview with Gerlinda Haker, church laywoman and protester, Schwerin, Germany, June 5, 1991.

99. Bindemann, "Die Kirche und das Volk," 4; Langer, "Get with It!," 6; Bailey, *Spring of Nations*, 86; interview with Kramer; and interview with Haker.

100. "Bundessynode 1989: Was nötig ist," in *Die Opposition in der DDR: Entwürfe für einen anderen Sozialismus*, ed. Gerhard Rein (Berlin: Wichern Verlag, 1989), 214–17; and Heino Falcke, "Die Kirchen sind jetzt die Politik nicht los," in ibid., 218–19.

101. Leich, "Statement by East German Church Leaders"; Rose, "Blutvergießen konnte vermieden werden," (Ziegler) 335; interview with Fishbeck, Democracy Now representative to the central round table, June 11, 1991; and interview with Krätschell.

102. Interview with Richter; interview with Junghans; interview with Ernst Koch, professor at Leipzig Theological Seminary, with interpretation by Martin Steinhäuser, Leipzig, June 17, 1991; interview with Werner Krusche; Siemon-Netto, "Luther versus Lenin," 408–15; interview with Uwe Siemon-Netto, Hamburg, June 8, 1991; and Franz Lau, *Luthers Lehre von den beiden Reichen* (Berlin: Evangelische Verlagsanstalt, 1952), 86–96. In addition to the influence of Bonhoeffer and Lau on Lutheran theology, it is important to also note the influence of Reformed theologian Karl Barth. His emphasis on "obeying God more than men" had a tremendous impact on all German theology, especially that coming from those parts of the DDR where Lutheran and Reformed traditions are united. The Confessing Church's Barmen Declaration bears the stamp of Barth's imprint on the traditional two-kingdoms theology. According to Werner Krusche and Hans Schäfer, Barth's theology did not merely influence Lutheranism to return to a place where it could confront the state; it also emphasized the need for nonviolence and a mediation process (interview with Richter; Goeckel, *Lutheran Church and the East German State*, 290–91; interview with Werner Krusche; and interview with Schäfer).

8 ▪

Faith at the Ramparts: The Philippine Catholic Church and the 1986 Revolution

HENRY WOOSTER

Three centuries of Spanish domination of the Philippines were followed by American rule in the first half of the twentieth century, which set the stage for an era of close ties with the United States. Throughout the Cold War, two U.S. military bases there served as key assets and critical links to Asia. But the Philippines was unable to match the economic dynamism of its regional neighbors. The authoritarian rule of Ferdinand Marcos, who came to power in 1965, failed to achieve equitable economic growth and political stability. Population growth, poverty, and the lack of land reform, together with a communist insurgency, produced massive social discontent that by the mid-1980s made Marcos's hold on power increasingly tenuous.

The Roman Catholic Church in the Philippines (hereafter the Church) was instrumental in ousting the regime of President Ferdinand Marcos in February 1986. The Church did this by coalescing the religious opposition to the regime after the imposition of martial law in September 1972 and then, increasingly through the 1980s, by providing support, resources, and leadership to the political parties in opposition to Marcos.

Ferment rose within the Catholic Church as martial law prohibited religious leaders from working with labor and peasant groups. Human rights violations escalated, causing clergy, who had previously understood their role as restricted to service inside the Church community, to reconsider their position.

By the early 1980s, the corruption that had run rampant among Marcos's cronies was ruining the economy and had alienated the Philippines from the international financial community. Incomes fell, unemployment rose, rural poverty worsened, and the communist insurgency gained ground. The mounting discontent triggered the concern of Cardinal Jaime Sin, archbishop of Manila, who began making increasingly searing public assessments of the Marcos regime.

But perhaps the event most responsible for precipitating the 1986 "People Power" revolution was the assassination of Benigno "Ninoy" Aquino, former Philippine senator and scion of one of the country's wealthiest families. Returning to the Philippines (see Figure 8.1) after three years of self-exile in the United

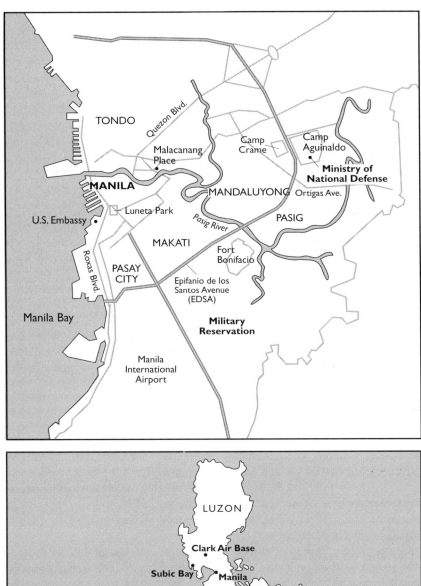

Figure 8.1. Manila and the Philippines

States, Aquino was killed as he left his plane at Manila International Airport on August 21, 1983.[1] This incident set in motion a series of events that would eventually bring about the downfall of President Marcos.

Two and a half years later, during the "snap election" of February 1986, the Catholic Bishops Conference of the Philippines issued a pastoral letter asserting that the Marcos regime had lost its moral legitimacy to govern. This letter from the conservative Church hierarchy sanctioned the expulsion of the president. The Church defended its position on the grounds that the situation had created a moral and religious imperative for the Church—and its faithful—to intervene.

THE CONTENDING FORCES

Six parties held power at the time of the 1986 Revolution: (a) the Marcos regime, including the executive, legislative, and judiciary branches of the civil government; (b) the armed forces of the Philippines; (c) the Catholic Church; (d) the mainline Protestant churches; (e) the evangelical Protestant sect, Iglesia Ni Kristo; and (f) the Communist party of the Philippines.[2] In addition to these institutions, the business community, labor groups, and the media each held some degree of authority in Philippine society. Outside the Philippines, the most influential party was the United States government.[3]

Before Aquino's assassination in 1983, most political groups—with the exception of the Communist party—were either aligned with Marcos, neutral, or divided. Marcos counted as his allies the civil government, the top echelon of the military, the Iglesia Ni Kristo, the mainstream Philippine media, and the U.S. government. The business community was largely passive. The non-Communist political opposition parties were all but powerless. The United Nationalist Democratic Opposition (UNIDO), the party from which the future vice-president, Salvador Laurel, would emerge, had not yet developed as a distinct identity.

The balance changed, however, after the Aquino assassination. The Church, the business community, and the middle class became aligned with the political opposition. In the United States, the State Department and Congress began to withdraw support from Marcos. In the meantime, disgruntled military officers in the Philippines established a reform movement,[4] while others began plotting a coup.[5]

Marcos

Eliminating the Communist party of the Philippines was a continuing military goal, and Marcos had a plan of his own to remove the economic and social injustices in the Philippines. His plan called for a New Society. In practice, however, this New Society took a back seat to Marcos's primary purpose, which was to stay in power.

The Philippines, he argued, needed a strong leader who could get past the various political interests thwarting the country's development: a recalcitrant landed oligarchy, nationalists in the private sector, and an array of both rural- and urban-based leftist movements. As he stated on numerous occasions to the U.S. diplomatic community, the Philippines was not yet ready for "American-style democracy," so out of political expedience the New Society would have to wait. The options, he warned, would not be good without him in charge, thus evoking the threat of communist insurgents who were eager to turn the Philippines into another Chinese or Soviet satellite.[6]

During his first years in office, however, Marcos's promises of a New Society had appeared legitimate. Some land reform was accomplished, and exports increased. But these efforts were ultimately stymied by the traditional power structure, cronyism, and a culture suffused with patron-client relationships.

Cory Aquino and the Opposition Parties

Beyond ousting Marcos from power, goals within the political opposition ranged from transforming Philippine society along various lines (as opposed to the more radical "restructuring" advocated by the communists) to simply replacing Marcos with an opposition candidate. Those who favored the latter option are referred to in the Philippines as *trapos*, short for traditional politicians or other powerful people for whom politics is merely another instrument of influence to which they are entitled.[7]

It was against this backdrop that the candidacy of Ninoy Aquino's widow, Cory, was launched to unite the moderate, centrist forces in their fight against Marcos, to provide an alternative to a military coup, and to thwart the far Left. Notwithstanding the fact that she and her late husband came from two of the Philippines' wealthiest families, Cory Aquino stood out from Marcos and the trapos.

The Left

The Left included three organizations: (a) the Communist Party of the Philippines (CPP), (b) the CPP's military wing, the New People's Army (NPA), and (c) the CPP's front organization, the National Democratic Front (NDF). All three groups adhered to Marxist-Leninist-Maoist ideology and saw armed struggle as the principle strategy for gaining power. The revolutionary Left's plan called for a restructuring of Philippine society, usually through the consolidation of the ownership of wealth in the state, with the goal of eventually bringing about a classless society.

The parties of the Left saw the replacement of Marcos with Aquino as yet another accommodation to trapo politics, which they considered to be elitist, factional, and class-centered. They were convinced that Aquino's ascension to the presidency would leave many of the same faces in place.

The insurgency, coupled with the armed forces' counterinsurgency campaign, militarized political, social, and economic issues. It created instability, hardened political positions, displaced hundreds of thousands of people, and killed or maimed thousands of others. It also drained the government's coffers.[8]

Thus the Catholic Church was faced with a dilemma. Marcos had made a mockery of democratic principles. At the same time, the CPP dismissed democratic procedures as a bourgeois palliative and continued to respond through insurgency. As Father John Carroll of the Ateneo de Manila University observed:

> There was a time, early in the period of martial law, when it could be said with some semblance of truth that President Marcos, the Communists, and the bishops were in agreement on one basic point. The President argued that 'I am the only alternative to the Communists.' The latter argued: 'We are the only alternative to Marcos.' And the official spokesmen for the Church seemed to be saying, 'Amen, amen.'[9]

But through the 1970s and early 1980s, the events of February 1986 were still unimaginable. Almost no one held out hope for a nonviolent revolution. Most Filipinos thought that they were in for either despotism or communism.

THE CHURCH'S ROLE

By the time of Marcos's downfall during the 1986 People Power revolution, the Church had achieved an elevated moral and political status. But this did not come easily. The Church had been faced with a complex situation: how to insist on social and economic justice and keep the opposition alive without provoking further repression by Marcos.

Competing Spiritual Visions

Divisions within the Church's clergy and laity would never have allowed it to unite during more normal times under a single political banner.[10] Although faith can be a powerful catalyst for sociopolitical involvement, that same faith can also lead to commitments of very different types.

Filipino clergy, religious adherents, and laypeople understood Catholicism and its obligations in different ways, some of which were in direct contradiction to one another. The impediments to a common theological perspective were complex and included diverse theological views held by members of the Church's hierarchy and the influence of theology, history, geography, and social factors on other segments of the Church community.

So-called progressive elements within the Church argued that there had been an insufficient alignment with the poor and that the Church was functioning as a largely conservative force. They argued that the effect of the encyclicals issued during the papacy of Pope John XXIII coupled with the concepts of justice introduced by liberation theology were being quashed by the vested economic interests of the Church, the higher social class backgrounds and education of the clergy, and pressures from the Vatican. They argued further that out of a desire to remain "above" politics—as well as to share in the ownership of land and in political power—the Philippine Church had historically declined to challenge the concentration of power and wealth among a very small element of Filipino society. While acknowledging that Vatican II (the Second Vatican Council, 1962–65; discussed later in this chapter) profoundly affected the Catholic Church by highlighting the Church's renewed commitment to human rights, freedom, and social justice, the progressive elements of the Church hierarchy argued that the Church must address more fully the inequity of the economic "disenfranchisement" of the majority of Filipinos.

Father Ben Moraleda, who runs a parish in one of Manila's impoverished areas and is a member of the progressive camp, criticizes the Church for not going far enough in working to correct social injustice before—or after—the 1986 revolution. He and his like-minded colleagues contend that "faith is not a vertical relationship only; it must be proven and demonstrated through social justice and action." The Church must be an instrument of liberation and, in keeping with the humanist impulses of Marxism, be seen to bring the society of the future—the kingdom of God, in Moraleda's view—into being.[11] Some progressives, including Moraleda, considered the Church hierarchy's links to the Philippine elite to be insidious. "This Church hasn't merely stymied the work of God, they have worked actively against it."[12]

Having taken a strategic view of the Church, the revolutionary Left (CPP) attempted to assign a role to the Church:

> The Catholic Church must realize that with its moral influence and solid but widespread organization it can play a decisive role in persuading the fascist dictator to yield to the people's sovereign will. . . . The Holy Scriptures is [*sic*] one with Marxism-Leninism in upholding the principle of just war against tyranny.[13]

The Left questioned "whether the church would disarm David as he confronts Goliath or condemn him because he used a slingshot."

Many Church members, on the other hand, tolerated state violence as an unfortunate imperative for the attainment of social stability and sociopolitical goals. Church conservatives worried about preserving the Church as an institution, its liturgical and educational functions, and the financial base needed to support these activities. From a theological perspective, many conservatives were still uncomfortable with the fallout from Vatican II and the increasing popularity of liberation theology and Marxist structural analysis, especially among the younger priests and religious brethren.[14] These shifts in theological orientation—as manifest in the the Church's approach to social justice—were seen as trading on the assumption that traditional beliefs, scriptures, and liturgies cannot be the essence of religion. Relevance had become the new theological criterion. In this context, the conservatives feared that any amount of tinkering would be permitted so long as it was vindicated by gains in moral or political growth. Regime support, they concluded, offered the best available way to maintain the integrity of the gospel, the Roman Catholic faith, and the Roman Catholic Church.

Cardinal Jaime Sin was emphatic in his condemnation of the alleged leftist influence in the Church. He accused Filipino leftists of using the Church and its lay organizations to solicit foreign funding for the NPA. He also issued several directives warning priests against joining or supporting political organizations or movements that advocated class struggle or violence as a means for social change.

Cardinal Sin led the moderate clergy who, though occupying the middle range between the progressives and conservatives, were adamant about the protection of Church institutions. At the same time, as archbishop of the most important archdiocese in the Philippines, the cardinal understood that his position required flexibility and that popular identification of the Church with Marcos could damage its legitimacy and his own. Preservation of the Church would require a united clergy.[15] Therefore, to preserve the Church, Sin had to maneuver skillfully across the spectrum of Church divisions.

From this vortex of sometimes starkly divergent theological and political perspectives, Cardinal Sin's leadership in the period leading up to and during the revolution forged a working consensus in the Church on matters relating to peace and justice, which, while often contentious, were broadly accepted within the Church as worthy spiritual and political goals.

Pastoral Letters

Through its various organs, the Church frequently issued pastoral letters focusing on sociopolitical matters and making concrete suggestions and demands. The themes they sounded were the need for truth-telling, protection of human rights, and respect for human dignity. They also spoke of the need for a conversion of the heart, social justice, and the rejection of violence as a means of attaining a new society. When the cardinal or the bishops issued a pastoral letter to the Philippine Church, they were targeting 2,000 parishes in virtually every corner of the country.

The Church began a series of increasingly direct attacks on the Marcos regime in February 1983, with "A Dialogue for Peace," a critical pastoral letter from the Bishops Conference that charged the regime with repression, corruption, and economic mismanagement. It also warned that tensions were likely to increase without fundamental reforms that recognized "a certain pluralism of positions in the way . . . people strive for justice according to their faith."[16] "Over the past half year," the bishops wrote, "a number of priests, sisters and layworkers have been arrested, or put on the arrest list, on charges of rebellion and subversion."[17]

On November 27, 1983, the Catholic Bishops Conference issued a statement titled "Reconciliation Today," which was read in all of the churches of the country on the birthday of the late Senator Ninoy Aquino. In light of the August 1983 assassination of Aquino and subsequent events, this statement shifted the emphasis to reconciliation as an alternative to continuing injustice and revolutionary violence. The bishops explained that reconciliation would require "truth, sincerity, freedom, and justice" and emphasized that the love proclaimed in the gospel had the power to transform people and society. Finally, they called for "the social transformation required by authentic reconciliation with God and one another" and suggested that the chief means to bring about social transformation was a conversion of hearts among the powerful.[18]

Less than a year after Aquino's assassination, in July 1984, the Bishops Conference issued another pastoral letter, "Let There Be Life":

> The murder shocked us all as no other killing has in recent history, and for many of us it was the one, single event that shook us out of our lethargy and forced us to face squarely the violence that has through the years been building up and becoming practically an ordinary facet of our life as a nation. . . . For years now we have been, for all intents and purposes, in a state of war. . . . This is the hard reality we are faced with now.[19]

In spite of this austere assessment, in the same letter the bishops repeated their call for conversion and reconciliation, pointing out the resources within the Catholic faith for achieving social transformation in a peaceful manner.

In July 1985, the Bishops Conference issued "Message to the People of God," which denounced specific activities of the regime. "The increasing use of force to dominate people," it warned, "is a frightening reality which we as pastors cannot ignore."[20]

Before the presidential election that was hastily called by Marcos to throw the opposition off balance — what came to be known as the *snap election* — Cardinal Sin and his colleagues issued two strong pastoral letters that could leave no doubt in parishioners' minds about exactly whom the Church hierarchy supported. The first, on December 28, 1985, from the cardinal and his auxiliary bishops, emphasized their belief that religion and politics were not opposed and that voting was a Christian duty. The letter also sketched out what qualified as a clean election; it pledged the Church's cooperation with NAMFREL (the National Citizens' Movement for Free Elections[21]); it stated that "to cheat or make others cheat" was "a seriously immoral and un-Christian act"; and it decried cheating and violence in elections as "sins that cry to heaven for vengeance." Although the letter advised against selling one's vote, it compromised on the issue by noting that "acceptance of money to vote for a candidate" was not binding, as one was not "obliged to fulfill an evil contract."[22]

On January 19, 1986, the second preelection letter, "A Call to Conscience," was issued by Cardinal Sin, the auxiliary bishops, and the entire Presbytral Council of Manila:

> We already see many signs that show a very sinister plot by some people and groups [meaning the Marcos regime] to frustrate the honest and orderly expression of the people's genuine will. Already money has flowed freely into the hands of teachers, barangay [village] officials and the common people to induce them to support particular candidates in a manner unworthy of free persons. Already we have seen, heard and read lies and black propaganda used by some quarters against opponents who are on the other hand deprived of adequate access to media, and are thus unjustly left defenseless. Already we hear of undue pressure exerted on hapless government employees to make them work [against the law!] for certain candidates.[23]

The letter concluded with a note of inspiration and encouragement: "Make of this election not one more national scandal and offense to God but a new beginning, a giant step in our conversion to the Lord and change in our society."[24]

Less than a week later, on January 25, 1986, the Catholic Bishops Conference issued a letter entitled "We Must Obey God, Rather Than Men," which warned against a "conspiracy of evil" that would require resistance.[25] This letter also exhorted the faithful to high standards of political behavior on the basis of the nation's missionary vocation as the only Christian country in Asia, a point emphasized by Pope John Paul II during his 1981 visit to the Philippines. In Cebu City, Cardinal Ricardo Vidal, long regarded as a member of the Church's conservative camp, published his own preelection letter, as did Bishop Gaudencio Rosales of Malaybalay, Bukidnon; Bishop Antonio Tobias of Pagadian, Zamboanga del Sur; and Bishop Antonio Fortich of Bacolod City.[26]

Presidential candidate Cory Aquino echoed the principles put forth in the Church's pastoral letters when, on February 5, she said:

> While I have done everything humanly possible to bring back power to our oppressed people, there comes a point when God's power has to intervene.
>
> We cannot win this election without God's help. I have no cheating experience. I have no "salvaging" experience. I have no experience in arresting and terrorizing people.
>
> After we have made a vow to be vigilant and to sacrifice even our lives to dismantle the Marcos regime, we can only pray.
>
> We already have our people's overwhelming support. And prayer is all we need right now.[27]

Within days after the February 7 election, the Catholic Bishops Conference, whose members were appalled (though not surprised) by the widespread voting fraud, issued its extraordinary "Post Election Statement," which described the elections as "unparalleled in the fraudulence of their conduct." The statement concluded by asserting that "a government that assumes or retains power through fraudulent means has no moral basis" and that the faithful had an obligation to correct the evil inflicted upon them "by peaceful and nonviolent means in the manner of Christ."[28]

The Church's denunciation of the election, coupled with its declaration that the regime had lost its mandate to govern, was a momentous step. With the exception of a somewhat similar role under similar circumstances in Poland, the Roman Catholic Church has seldom sanctioned the undermining of a government in power, leaving such matters instead to the individual conscience. Thus this action had "an electrifying effect" both on the regime and on the populace of this Catholic nation.[29]

On February 16, a day after the Philippine legislature declared Marcos the winner of the snap election, a "victory of the people" mass was held at the Luneta, a huge park in downtown Manila. Millions attended; the clergy prominently celebrated the mass, and Aquino asked the crowd to join her in prayer. When she spoke, she recounted to her fellow Filipinos how she "could not help but compare the events that transpired from the death of Ninoy to the ousting of Marcos, to the Lenten story."[30] After the prayer, she announced a campaign of civil disobedience to force Marcos to concede defeat. Following this rally, 30 computer technicians at the Commission on Election walked off their jobs in protest of the election fraud and were hidden at the Loyola House of Studies on the campus of the Ateneo de Manila University, where Cardinal Sin visited them.

While clergy preached on political and personal morality, Church members, including nuns, took part in partisan politics. Many were active in NAMFREL, which though officially nonpartisan, was home to a large number of anti-Marcos activists. Radio Veritas, a station owned by the Catholic Bishops Conference and run by the Archdiocese of Manila, whose primary function was to evangelize Asia, had become the voice of the opposition.

In the meantime, the conservative bishops remained uneasy. Discomfited by the notion that political ideology and faith were becoming enmeshed, the conservatives pointed out that Catholic doctrine emphasizes the need to discern between partisan politics and politics that threaten faith and morals.

Cardinal Sin did not agree that these concerns were sufficiently worrisome to disengage the Church from the political arena. Rebutting a police commissioner's remarks about his priests being "dilettantes" in political affairs, the cardinal told a meeting of Rotarians:

> I am reminded . . . of the wise man who said that war was much too important a business to be left exclusively in the hands of generals. Might not the same be said of government, that government is much too important a business to be left in the hands of politicians and political scientists?[31]

REVOLUTION: FEBRUARY 22–25, 1986

The revolution lasted four nights and three days. On the afternoon of February 22, Defense Minister Juan Ponce Enrile and Lieutenant General Fidel Ramos, vice-chief of staff of the armed forces, announced a military rebellion against President Marcos. As a result, Cardinal Sin was confronted with a necessity for decisive action, probably before he had hoped to act. Upon receiving word that troops loyal to Marcos had begun moving toward his stronghold at the Ministry of National Defense building at Manila's Camp Aguinaldo, Enrile moved across Epifanio de los Santos Avenue (EDSA) to Camp Crame, where Ramos was headquartered.

Both Enrile and Ramos had reason to be unhappy. Enrile knew that he had nowhere to turn. A coup he had been plotting with other disgruntled officers had been discovered in the eleventh hour by General Fabian Ver, a staunch Marcos loyalist and relative of the president. Ramos had long resented that General Ver was made chief of staff of the armed forces on the basis of nothing more than his relationship to Marcos. As a West Point–educated professional, Ramos believed that this position should rightfully have been his.

When Enrile arrived at Camp Aguinaldo, he prepared to make a final stand. He called U.S. Ambassador Steven W. Bosworth, who assured him that the embassy would closely monitor developments and maintain contact with Washington. He also called Radio Veritas and Cardinal Sin in the hope that they would urge religious groups to fight alongside him. "Your eminence," said Enrile, himself a

Protestant, "you must help us. We will be dead in an hour if you don't help us." "Are you supporting Aquino?", Sin asked. Enrile replied in the affirmative. The cardinal agreed to help.[32]

The cardinal went into prayer and, upon emerging, received urgent pleas from his bishops to go on Radio Veritas. This he did, broadcasting an appeal to the Filipino people—"to all the children of God," not just Catholics—to protect Minister Enrile and General Ramos, "our idealist friends."[33] Over the next few hours, citizens from metropolitan Manila began to gather at the camps. Later that evening and throughout the revolution, Sin and his auxiliary bishop, Teodoro C. Bacani, encouraged people to go to camps Aguinaldo and Crame on the EDSA. Among the first to respond were nuns and parish priests.

Broadcasts from Radio Veritas kept the people informed, mobilized them into action, and gave them directions, telling them where to go and what to do when they arrived. "Without this constant contact with the multitudes," Father Miguel A. Bernad has written, "the February Revolution would have been impossible."[34]

Radio Veritas continued to broadcast the cardinal's appeal around the clock until its transmitter was destroyed the next morning, February 23, by troops loyal to Marcos.[35] From 6:00 A.M. to 11:00 P.M. that day, Veritas was off the air while its staff searched for an alternate transmitter. Within hours, Father James B. Reuter, an American Jesuit who had served for many years in the Philippines, found two: one that belonged to the Reformed Armed Forces Movement (RAM), station DZRJ, and the other, DZFE, to a Protestant church.[36] Because the RAM transmitter was strategically situated in the heart of Manila, it was chosen, and Veritas continued its broadcasts. From 11:00 P.M. until 11:00 A.M. the next day, February 24, Veritas announcer June Keithley went on the air on DZRJ. Nuns sat on the stairs leading to the broadcast room praying the rosary. As described by Father Carroll:

> The tone set by the station, and also by the Cardinal and other leading churchmen, constituted a moderating influence. It was responsible, serious, sorrowful, but neither inflammatory nor provocative. The nation was kept informed at a time when other media tended only to disinform; and this probably contributed immeasurably to the rapid erosion of the credibility of both the government and the controlled media.[37]

Various media covering the event estimated the crowds at Camp Crame at up to 2 million—a large percentage of whom came in response to the cardinal's call—and including for the first time the Makati businessmen, the most conservative element of the Philippine social milieu. Philippine journalist Felix S. Bautista, who witnessed these events, described the EDSA crowds:

> Most important of all, they came with rosaries in their hands and prayers on their lips. Most of them were scared to death. In the back of their mind they knew that the full force of Marcos' legions—numbering some 250,000 fully armed troops—could be let loose on them. But they came anyway. Their spiritual leader had told them to go.[38]

At about 6:45 P.M., Enrile and Ramos called a press conference. With the statue of the Blessed Virgin conspicuously poised behind them, they declared that

Marcos had cheated in the election and that they believed Cory Aquino was the true president.

One of the most precious assets that the cardinal's intervention had afforded these men was time—time for Ramos to persuade critical military units to defect, and time for the U.S. Department of State to convince U.S. President Ronald Reagan to withdraw support from Marcos. Had time not been on their side, had Cardinal Sin not called the faithful out to EDSA (where the two camps were located across from each other), Marcos could easily have smashed the coup attempt.

Instead, over the next several days people formed into human barricades that confronted Marcos loyalists. Priests and nuns moved amid the crowds, praying and passing out food and water. Numerous images of the Blessed Virgin Mary stood guard above the throngs all along the avenue. Posters, banners, and grafitti with religious messages and statements on nonviolence covered walls and billboards. Huge crucifixes were hoisted in various places, including strategic locations that would impede armored personnel carriers and troops from moving swiftly. In the view of one church-based observer, "So visible was the religious component that for many the end of Marcos could not but be the work of God."[39]

On the third day, when rebel forces had attained a critical mass, the U.S. government, seeking political stability as well as the isolation of far Left forces, strongly urged Marcos to relinquish the presidency. The next day, loyalist military forces withdrew from their positions around Camp Crame and Camp Aguinaldo. Riding the wave of mass euphoria that followed the successful rebellion—and projecting an image of integrity and deep spirituality—Cory Aquino took the oath of office as president, while Marcos fled into exile.

HOW THE CHURCH CAME TO BE INVOLVED

By 1986, the prospects for reconciliation between Marcos and the opposition, or between Marcos and the Church, were nonexistent. From the beginning of his rule in 1965, Marcos instituted "constitutional authoritarianism," a system he claimed would advance the New Society in a manner uniquely fitted to the environment of the Philippines. In 1972 Marcos proclaimed his new and improved version of martial law to be "a smiling martial law." Yet both efforts failed to convince Church authorities.

Vatican II

Vatican II[40] and subsequent papal encyclicals stressed that efforts to eradicate injustice and economic inequality were an integral part of preaching the gospel. As a result, the Roman Catholic Church evolved from acting as a generally conservative force in the political life of countries to a belief that it must "live in the world" and transform it according to the Church's interpretation of the gospel. But for this monumental change over the two preceding decades, the Philippine Church would very likely not have engaged in activist political action on the scale that it did, nor would it as readily have claimed for itself the necessary moral legitimacy to act as a major force for social change. Although certain individual bishops, priests, and nuns would likely have engaged in some level of political activity, the Church as an institution almost certainly would have remained aloof from, if not critical of, the rebellion. The outcome would have been altered accordingly, with an increased likelihood of violent suppression of the rebellious soldiers and the protestors, whose numbers would probably have been fewer.

The "Preferential Option for the Poor"

The idea of the "preferential option for the poor," a tenet found in liberation theology (though with roots in more conventional Catholic social doctrine), was articulated during a Latin American bishops conference held in 1968 in Medellín, Colombia. This conference, which was held to discuss the implementation of Vatican II, issued a report (often referred to as the "Magna Carta for liberation theology") that substantially expanded the definition of sin. The concept of sin was enlarged from the realm of the individual to that of economic and political structures, which were now understood to be prime instruments in the violation of the inherent dignity of human life, proclaimed in the gospels. It thus eliminated the difference between the social and the spiritual and highlighted, instead, what Samuel Huntington has referred to as "the contingent character of social and political structures."[41]

This enlarged understanding of sin prompted the Church to recognize an obligation to aid people in resolving situations in which exploitation took place.[42] In subscribing to this obligation, the Catholic Church in Latin America, in effect, acknowledged its former tacit alliance with economic and political elites and signaled the desire for an adjustment of that relationship.

Liberation Theology

Until the advent of liberation theology in the early 1970s, a common presumption was that poverty was inherent in the human condition. But liberation theology charged priests and other religious adherents with analyzing its causes and finding a cure. Because liberation theology is suffused with Marxist economic and class analysis, many Filipino priests (like their counterparts in Latin America) determined that the cause of Filipino poverty was the exploitation of the masses (the peasant and working classes) by the small upper class. But while the Communist party and its Filipino supporters encouraged the establishment of a Marxist government as an antidote to both Marcos and capitalism, the majority of priests and church members who adhered to liberation theology were not entirely comfortable with this notion and, instead, aligned themselves with the socialists.[43]

Most Philippine bishops had no quibbles with accepting development and justice as ecclesiastical tasks; they feared, however, that if the destruction of social institutions became acceptable, little could be done (by any party) to promote human or Christian values. The bishops, who perceived the far Left as antireligious, nonetheless knew that some in the Church were sympathetic to these forces. They also knew, as did the regime, that the Left would attempt to make use of the Church and the power of religion to motivate and mobilize people to serve leftist ideological purposes.[44]

Radicalization

When Church laity organized meetings in their homes to discuss and pray for the national situation, they frequently asked priests to come to speak.[45] Because these were often anti-Marcos gatherings and took place in private homes, they were periodically monitored by the armed forces or police, which were employed by the regime throughout the country to suppress "subversive activities."[46] In such an atmosphere, over time, the Marcos government attributed revolutionary intentions to even the most innocuous of church activities. Eventually, the harassment, imprisonment, and even killing of church-related workers contributed to the radicalization of some members and created anti-Marcos animosity among many others. Marcos, however, was reluctant to alienate the mass of Filipinos by attacking priests within the archdiocese of Manila.

A Vacuum

Another factor that drew the Church into the revolution was the absence of credible leadership alternatives. When Marcos ordered the arrest of Enrile and Ramos in February 1986, the opposition knew that this meant the start of a crackdown. Cory Aquino and the rest of the opposition leadership went into hiding, and Cardinal Sin stepped in to fill the vacuum. The Church's moral authority, which it asserted through its pastoral letters, enhanced its political influence, particularly because other institutions of the Philippine government—such as the armed forces, the Supreme Court, and, indeed, the constitution itself—had been discredited. As Father Reuter explained, "The church was the strongest institution in the Philippines, and the government the most uncredible [*sic*]," in effect forcing the church into a leadership position.[47]

Throughout much of the country and especially in rural areas, there were no competing (noninsurgent) organizations, and the Church had in place what Huntington refers to as a "latent national political machine"[48]: a widespread organizational, communications, and logistical infrastructure that permitted participation in the political process. Church personnel administered an array of programs ranging from health and education to community organization and development, and from social welfare to relief work.

"A Mass Media Vehicle"

With the Manila-based hierarchy, parishes throughout the country, and Church-supported radio stations and newspapers, the Church's infrastructure represented a formidable communications and support network. "In the Marcos era," said Corazon Calub, an Aquino activist at the time, "the Church was a mass media vehicle." Sermons from the pulpit, newspapers, pastoral letters, Radio Veritas, and various Bible and religiously oriented discussion groups were all employed in the Church's campaign.[49]

The Church produced or assisted with the publication of bulletins that challenged the Marcos-controlled media. Church-related newspapers featured editorials that were widely credited with keeping the people both informed and calm. Tracts attesting to Christian duties in the face of adversity were tacked to Church bulletin boards. A network of priests, seminarians, and religious adherents carried messages among members of the opposition when they were in hiding.

During 1985–86, the Church-related Communications Foundation of Asia distributed a video, "Eleven Days in August," documenting the period from the Aquino assassination to the funeral, which evoked the experience again and highlighted its religious overtones. This video was especially effective in the provinces where, for lack of media coverage, people knew little of the events being documented.

Throughout the 1980s, the Association of Major Religious Superiors published a newspaper, *Philippine Signs*, which made a practice of challenging the regime's press accounts. A group of Makati businessmen published *Veritas*, a news magazine sponsored by Cardinal Sin, which took a similar stand. Other Church-related publications, such as *Philippine Concerns* of the Communications Foundation of Asia, contributed to the national political awakening with articles critical of the repression of human and civil rights under the regime and likewise of its economic policies that were increasingly seen as having disastrous consequences for the nation.[50]

But the Church's most authoritative communicator remained Cardinal Sin. Sin has popularly characterized his relationship to Marcos in the waning years of the regime as one of "critical collaboration." The cardinal agreed to meet with, listen to, and minister to Marcos so long as Marcos conformed to certain publicly delineated standards set forth by the cardinal. At the same time, Cardinal Sin reserved the right to be critical of Marcos when he violated those boundaries.[51]

The Archbishop of Manila

To understand Cardinal Sin's approach to the mounting tensions, it is essential to examine his record as archbishop of Manila. At his installation in 1974, Sin delivered an address entitled, "A Revolution of Love." "We need a revolution," he said, "there is no doubt about that. But what we need is a revolution of the heart, a revolution of love." At the 1983 International Synod of Bishops in Rome, striking a seemingly contradictory note, Sin declared that a priest who wishes to be a "minister of reconciliation must first be a prophet of denunciation." In his dealings with the Marcos regime, Cardinal Sin adhered to both convictions. He regarded reconciliation as an act of Christian love between equals. But "if a man runs roughshod over you," he told his priests, "violating your rights and not respecting your dignity as a human being, you cannot ask for a reconciliation. You must first have the courage to denounce what he is doing. . . . That way you can earn his respect."[52]

Thus "reconciliation" was understood in the Philippines in a variety of ways: for Marcos, it meant "let's forget the past and work together to face the economic crisis"; for the radical opposition it meant "resign"; and for Cardinal Sin, it meant "repent."[53]

More than five months before the Aquino assassination in 1983, Cardinal Sin addressed a meeting of the Bishops and Businessmen's Conference for Human Development at which a number of prominent government officials were in attendance.[54] He used the occasion to articulate his vision of the proper roles of the Church, state, and people in the promotion of human development. He identified the national problem as between the state and the people, and he insisted on identifying the Church with the people in the face of state oppression. To his thinking, this was the source of tension between the Church and state.[55] Next, Sin outlined the basic values around which a Philippine political order could be developed, and he sharply criticized the regime for its failure to promote these values. He ended with an appeal for the creation of a "council of national reconciliation" composed of representatives of the Church, the government, and the private sector for the formulation of policy proposals based on consensus to be presented to the president.

Later, in his homily at Aquino's funeral, Cardinal Sin spoke of how "all of us can be instruments of national peace and reconciliation." In his "National Prayer for Peace," read over Radio Veritas on August 31, 1983, he made clear his view that true conciliation must be based on a willingness to admit and, as far as possible, to right past wrongs.

In a speech delivered on December 6, 1983, the cardinal was again critical of the government's performance as it adversely affected the welfare of the people. The core of this problem, he asserted, was neither political nor economic but, rather, moral. He described national reconciliation as moral in essence, based on the "solidarity that results from a shared meal and which is preeminently symbolized by the sacrament of God's covenant of love."[56] The government's isolation from its citizens had been exacerbated by its unwillingness to begin the process of reconciliation—to the point where its legitimacy as a government was in question.

INTERPRETATION AND ANALYSIS

Denouncing the abuses of power is not so radical a step as denying its legitimacy. The Roman Catholic Church of the Philippines evolved from the former position to the latter, once it began speaking out on Philippine politics in 1983. The Church was undeniably a social and political force, and it knew how and when to operate as one. But what distinguished the Church's actions on the political stage—and what has become the Church's proud legacy—was its powerful Christian witness and truth-telling. The Church acted as the nation's moral conscience: speaking out against the regime, denouncing repression, defending human rights, and pushing for a transition to democracy. The Church never championed the option of a violent revolution. Instead, throughout its campaign against the Marcos regime, the Church upheld the goals of reform and reconciliation.

The events of February 1986 marked a significant departure from the Philippine Church's previous pattern of political participation, from dependency on the state and dominant classes into a more activist, autonomous role. An array of influences, which encouraged social transformation, contributed to the Church's change over the years, beginning with the reforms of Vatican II. What created friction within the Church was the process of defining the proper boundaries of its involvement in the political realm. While it was clear, for example, that Marcos would not allow an effective political opposition to function, it was not clear to what extent the Church should participate by providing for and supporting such opposition.[57] In a Catholic nation such as the Philippines, the state was tied directly to the Church for its moral authority. In turn, the Church understood itself as dependent on voluntary adherence to its authority. (It had no civil incentive mechanism, only spiritual.)

The Spiritual Dimension

The Catholic Church, and in particular Cardinal Sin, introduced an uncommon dimension to the February 1986 revolution. The cardinal operated with the conviction that he was doing his duty as a Christian leader, instructing the faithful on matters of faith and morals. Extending Church pronouncements into the political and social spheres conformed with the legacy of Vatican II. What was extraordinary was the degree to which the Philippine Church exercised its moral authority in concrete actions.

It is not uncommon to hear Filipinos depict the events of February as "religious" in accounts laced with the imagery of the passion of Jesus Christ. Biblical metaphors easily assumed sociopolitical connotations: the regime was popularly portrayed as evil, and parallels were often drawn between the struggles of the Filipino masses and the persecuted followers of Christ. Religion — in the form of clergy or a crucifix — provided comfort and structure to the thousands gathered at EDSA on both sides of the confrontation. "The revolution of February 22 was preceded, accompanied, and followed by prayer on the part of millions," writes Bernad.[58] "The soldiers were overwhelmed by love," recounts Calub. "This was an appeal to brotherhood and the love of Jesus Christ. Without this [appeal], there would have been carnage."[59] Emmanuel Pelaez, former vice-president of the Philippines and currently ambassador to the United States, maintains that "the christology of the masses was crucial; it enabled the pastoral letters of the bishops to have impact."[60] For these three observers, this triumph was not so much one of the strength of a political grouping but of the power of prayer. "They feel," attests Calub, "that they have been part of a miracle."[61]

Recalling those days in 1986, Araceli Lorayes, a former *Asian Wall Street Journal* correspondent, remembers: "One had only to reflect on how desperate the situation of the mutineers was, on how utterly powerless we all were — both the opposition who were in hiding and the crowd at EDSA—to realize that ultimately we were all in the hands of God."[62] To Lorayes, the foreign journalists who focused on the fiesta-like atmosphere missed the point:

> Coming from secular societies, not speaking our language and only superficially acquainted with our culture, they failed to realize that [the revolution's] inner life, its motivating force, was prayer; the gaiety was a coping mechanism to control and mask real dread. I am a very rational Christian, not easily given to supernatural explanations for ordinary events, but I am convinced that [the revolution] was, if not a miracle in the classic sense (i.e., an event in which the laws of nature are suspended) certainly an extraordinary manifestation of divine power, wisdom and mercy. I believe that [the revolution] was the gift of the Holy Spirit—working through very imperfect human beings as his instruments (we later learned that major players had murky motives). . . . He nevertheless brought about the deliverance of the Filipino nation from almost certain disaster.[63]

But this view is not universally held. Some Filipinos today recall the revolution as an aberration in an otherwise violent and corrupt political past. Others fear that an affirmation of the events of February 1986 as "religious" could open the door to ecclesiastical supervision of political life.

A Reordering of Values or a Momentary Attitudinal Shift?

Traditional spiritual values were reaffirmed—faith in God and in the power of prayer, Christian hope, nonviolence, peace, and unity—and a dramatic reversal in attitudes toward the notion of armed conflict occurred during the events surrounding the 1986 revolution. The CPP stayed away from EDSA, dramatically miscalculating the will of the people to respond without its assistance and viewing the whole encounter as no more than a conflict within factions of the elite. Had the People Power revolution not occurred, it is likely that the frustrations of a substantial portion of the moderate segment of Filipino society would have led it to form a strategic alliance—albeit temporary—with the CPP. The CPP also misread the degree to which Marcos would be able to rally the armed forces to his defense.

It has been said that it is the transition from romance to routine that kills a relationship. From a political and economic perspective, the revolution proved a disappointment; it did not result in a new dispensation or spectacular changes. Filipinos today bemoan that they are back to the same old ways. "We thought," lamented one priest, "that EDSA was what Exodus was to the Jews, but it wasn't. We're back to normal."[64] The events of 1986 failed to produce a genuine ethic of reconciliation in the Philippine government or national life, and political wounds remain to be healed. President Aquino was able to achieve only feeble progress on land reform and in bringing a halt to the insurgencies; the country's foreign debt liability is enormous; and progress toward social equity has been nominal. Reconciliation and the restoration of democracy are long-term processes, and there remains a chasm between the winners and the losers. The revolutionary Left continues to wage its insurgency.

Notwithstanding this, many Catholics continue to recall with mythic overtones the episodes that united them as believers, demonstrating to them that God still has the power to perform miracles provided that the cause is righteous. They recall, for instance, how 500,000 NAMFREL volunteers, most of them church-related, united, putting themselves and their families at risk to protect the integrity of the ballot boxes.

Moreover, while it is possible only to speculate on what might have occurred had the Church not been involved, it is likely that the Enrile-Ramos revolt—and the subsequent capitulation of the military to the opposition—would have progressed differently had the Church not exercised its considerable moral and political authority in support of the rebels. Marcos relied on military backing to retain his office. Because of its impressive administrative and institutional resources, as well as its command of the moral high ground, the Church was instrumental in coalescing the opposition. Had it not done so, the military would have been faced with a bleak alternative to the overthrow of Marcos—probably an eventual showdown between it and the Communist party.

The Church's opposition to the Marcos regime, culminating in the events of February 1986, marked a significant departure from its previous pattern of political participation. Where the Church had before granted the state control over virtually all temporal matters—especially those clearly political in nature—it had now moved to a more autonomous posture. By criticizing those in power, by offering alternative goals and the means by which to reach them, and, finally, by mobilizing and supporting people to articulate those alternatives, the Church also precluded extremist elements on both sides from escalating the issues at hand into out-and-out violence. Given the Church's position in Philippine society as the only institution vested with significant moral legitimacy, no other actor—Filipino or foreign—could likely have played a comparable role.

Although true national reconciliation has yet to be achieved—Christian social teaching has never promised an earthly paradise—by first inculcating the majority of Filipinos with religious values and then by exercising spiritual leadership of the faithful, the Catholic Church had a singularly powerful and unique influence during the 1986 election and the People Power revolution.[65]

Notes

1. John J. Carroll, S.J., "The Church: A Political Force?", Human Society Booklet (Manila: Human Development Research and Documentation, 1985), 1.

2. An estimated 4 million Filipinos belong to Iglesia Ni Kristo, a church that has achieved political influence in the Philippines through its ability to deliver the votes of its members in a block. The Roman Catholic Church in the Philippines, by contrast, cannot claim this hold on the voting preferences of its members. Detractors claim that the Iglesia uses its ability to deliver the vote as leverage to acquire power and money.

3. Throughout most of Marcos's rule, U.S. foreign and defense policies had favored maintaining him in power. Thus, as his election campaign progressed in late 1985, and he began to be challenged on a number of issues by U.S. government officials, the waning of U.S. support must have struck him as sort of an eleventh-hour betrayal. A number of

influential U.S. government officials had previously held the belief that martial law was necessary for political stability and for ensuring a climate hospitable to foreign investment and the maintenance of key military facilities at Subic Bay and Clark Air Base. U.S. backing—official and unofficial—had also helped the Philippines secure large loans from international lenders. Robert Youngblood has argued that the ability to obtain large foreign loans allowed Marcos to deflect criticism of the economy by maintaining that his economic policy had a "seal of approval" from the International Monetary Fund and the World Bank (Robert L. Youngblood, *Marcos Against the Church* [Ithaca, N.Y.: Cornell University Press, 1990]).

4. The Reform Armed Forces of the Philippines Movement (RAM), begun in March 1985, was increasingly making its presence felt. Several promising junior officers, most of whom were graduates of the Philippine Military Academy, resigned their commissions, alleging that the senior ranks of the officer corps were corrupted. A good number, however, remained on duty, some of whom began planning an assault on the Presidential Palace to force Marcos to resign. They intended to establish an interim ruling council to govern the Philippines for six months until a new constitution could be drafted and elections held. In January 1986, the RAM launched Kamalayan '86, a series of prayer rallies and "consciousness-raising seminars" to promote honest and clean elections.

5. The criterion for promotion in the upper ranks of the officer corps was loyalty to Marcos, a policy that horizontally divided the armed forces. As a result, during the revolution, senior officers were forced to make a choice between their loyalty to Marcos or to the constitution (interview with General Luis Villa-Real, Manila, April 4, 1991).

6. David Wurfel notes that "the worries of the American business community were clearly communicated to the U.S. Embassy, so that Marcos found support for retaining power while restricting participation" (David Wurfel, *Filipino Politics: Development and Decay* [Ithaca, N.Y.: Cornell University Press, 1988], 329).

7. In an analysis of political development and the indigenous causes of internal wars, William E. Odom writes of the Philippine political system:

> Patron-client relations . . . created a vertically integrated political system. Political parties . . . had no horizontal aggregating role across groups and provinces. They [had] not become modern institutions for accommodating expanding political participation. Rather they . . . remained loose election umbrellas for a political process played out among a narrow circle of wealthy elites, cliques connected more effectively by family and kinship ties than by party loyalties. . . . the party system was essentially an institutional veneer over the traditional oligarchy of privileged families (William E. Odom, *On Internal War* [Durham, N.C.: Duke University Press, 1992]).

8. The drain on resources continued even after the revolution, and most estimates of the amount of the Philippines' budget allocated to counterinsurgency do not take into account the millions expended by the CPP/NPA.

9. John J. Carroll, S.J., "The Philippine Bishops: Pastors or Politicos?" Human Society Booklet no. 37 (*Manila: Human Development Research and Documentation*, 1987), 14–15.

10. This is in marked contrast to the Protestant sect, Iglesia Ni Kristo, which does impose political discipline on its members. To their thinking, this corporate discipline is a strength that symbolizes their unity of thought and action.

11. Interview with Father Ben Moraleda, Manila, March 29, 1991. In reference to the post-Marcos period, Moraleda lamented that "people were too tired of violence, and they went back to God."

12. Ibid.

13. As quoted in Carroll, "The Church: A Political Force?", 18–19, from a document distributed by the NDF, "On the Possibility of Restoring Democracy." According to Carroll, evidence strongly suggests that the author is CPP leader José M. Sison, who is in exile in the Netherlands, headquarters of the NDF's international office.

14. *Structural analysis* refers to theological activity that analyzes social structures to discern their congruence in both economic and political terms with a theological notion of justice.

15. The Philippines has one of the lowest ratios of clergy to parishoners of any Catholic country.

16. As quoted in Youngblood, *Marcos Against the Church*, 197. Clerical political commentary was not a new phenomenon. Philippine clergy had made numerous statements, formal and informal, assessing the political climate well before 1983.

17. *The Philippine Bishops Speak*, as quoted in Teodoro C. Bacani, *The Church and Politics* (Quezon City, P.I.: Claretian Publications), 49.

18. Carroll, "The Church: A Political Force?", 11.

19. As quoted in Bacani, *Church and Politics*, 50–51.

20. As quoted in Bacani, ibid., 51.

21. Before National Assembly elections held in 1984, a group of citizens organized NAMFREL to oversee the polling and canvasing of ballots. The Church strongly supported NAMFREL and encouraged priests and laity to join.

22. Paraphrase of Youngblood, *Marcos Against the Church*, 199.

23. As quoted in ibid.

24. As quoted in Bacani, *Church and Politics*, 78.

25. "We Must Obey God, Rather Than Men," Catholic Bishops Conference of the Philippines, January 25, 1986. In *Dictatorship and Revolution: Roots of People's Power*, eds. Aurora Javata-De Dios, Petronilo Bn. Daroy, and Lorna Kalaw-Tirol (Quezon City, Philippines: Conspectus Foundation Incorporated, 1988), 709–12.

26. Some of these letters appeared in newspapers as paid advertisements.

27. As quoted in Francisco S. Tatad, *People Power: The Philippine Revolution of 1986* (Manila: James B. Reuter, S.J., Foundation, 1986), 8, 56.

28. "The People Have Spoken," Post-Election Statement of the Catholic Bishops Conference of the Philippines, Manila, February 13, 1986. In *Dictatorship and Revolution*, 738–40.

29. Araceli Lorayes, correspondent with the *Asian Wall Street Journal*, personal communication dated March 25, 1991.

30. Conrado de Quiros, "'People Power' and the Paradigm of Salvation," in *The February Revolution: Three Views*, ed. Conrado de Quiros (Quezon City, P.I.; Karrel, 1987), 16.

31. As quoted in Felix B. Bautista, *Cardinal Sin and the Miracle of Asia* (Manila: Vera-Reyes, 1987), 57.

32. "Butch" Aquino, Cory's brother-in-law, was one of the first to arrive at Camp Aguinaldo. He and Joaquin "Chino" Roces, former publisher of the *Manila Times*, also called Cardinal Sin and other opposition leaders, asking them to support the revolution declared by Enrile and Ramos.

33. As quoted in Bautista, *Cardinal Sin and the Miracle of Asia*, 5; also, interview with Bishop Francisco Claver, Manila, March 23, 1991.

34. Miguel A. Bernad, "The Philippine Revolution of February 1986: Reflections from the Sidelines," *Kinaadman (Wisdom): A Journal of the Southern Philippines* 9 (1987), 4.

35. Radio Veritas is also credited with being one of the U.S. Embassy's principal sources of information.

36. Stanley Karnow writes that "providence was assisted by clandestine American intervention. . . . On Sunday morning when Marcos' troops smashed the Radio Veritas transmitter, CIA specialists provided an alternative system. Usually posing as reporters, CIA men assisted the mutineers in a disinformation campaign to spread phony news about Marcos' intentions" (Stanley Karnow, *In Our Image: America's Empire in the Philippines* [New York: Ballantine Books, 1990], 417).

37. Carroll, "The Church: A Political Force?", 7.

38. Bautista, *Cardinal Sin and the Miracle of Asia*, 5.

39. Ponciano Bennagen, "Goals, Rules, and Procedures: The Dynamics of People's Power," *TUGON* [National Council of Churches in the Philippines, Manila] 6, no. 2 (1987), 95.

40. The Second Vatican Council, which was convened in October 1962, at St. Peter's Basilica in Rome, was the twenty-first ecumenical council of the Roman Catholic Church. The council, opened by Pope John XXIII and continued by his successor, Pope Paul VI, was held to discuss the role of the Church in the modern world and to promote Christian unity. It was attended by approximately 2,500 Roman Catholic bishops and nearly 50 observer-delegates from other Christian denominations.

41. Samuel P. Huntington, "Religion and the Third Wave," *National Interest* 24 (Summer 1991), 31. On a separate but related note, Youngblood points to the significant intellectual debt that Marcos owed to Huntington. Evidently Marcos "justified the need for greater executive powers" during his New Society campaign by referring to Huntington's *Political Order in Changing Societies* (New Haven: Yale University Press, 1968) (Youngblood, *Marcos Against the Church*, 14, 28, 35).

42. Phillip Barryman, *Liberation Theology: The Essential Facts About the Revolutionary Movement in Latin America and Beyond* (New York: Pantheon Books, 1987), 22–23.

43. Thousands of priests belonged to Christians for National Liberation (CNL), a CPP-led legal revolutionary movement. Most joined out of disappointment with their ability to coalesce significant mainstream (middle- and upper-class) support for social and economic reforms. CNL members provided the logistical support necessary for developing and sustaining the CPP's underground arm in the countryside and in the cities. See also Gregg R. Jones, *Revolution: Inside the Philippine Guerrilla Movement* (Boulder, Colo.: Westview Press, 1989). It is important to distinguish between liberation theology as a sort of diluted Marxism, used primarily by the CPP for indoctrination purposes, and the more mainstream form of liberation theology, whose aim it is to draw out the social implications of faith.

44. The temptation to counter violence with violence was becoming increasingly powerful for many clergy throughout the Third World. Pope John Paul II (Karol Wojtyla) recognized this and made it clear that the sanctioning of revolution (tacit or otherwise) would not be tolerated by Rome:

> The overthrow by means of revolutionary violence of structures which generate violence is not *ipso facto* the beginning of a just regime. A major fact of our time ought to evoke the reflection of all those who would sincerely work for true liberation of their brothers: Millions of our own contemporaries legitimately yearn to recover those basic freedoms of which they were deprived by totalitarian and atheistic regimes which came to power by violent and revolutionary means, precisely in the name of the liberation of the people. This shame of our time cannot be ignored: While claiming to bring them freedom, these regimes keep whole nations in conditions of servitude which are unworthy of mankind. Those who, perhaps inadvertently, make them-

selves accomplices of similar enslavements betray the very poor they mean to help (Congregation for the Doctrine of the Faith, "Instruction on Certain Aspects of Liberation Theology," *Origins* [September 13, 1984]).

Catholic moral theology does not, however, rule out the use of force under certain, specified conditions: (a) that there is a manifest, long-standing tyranny that would do great damage to human rights and dangerous harm to the common good of the country; (b) that there is legitimate hope of success; (c) that the good to be obtained is proportionate to the evil that will have to be inflicted and suffered; and (d) that the use of force is the last resort.

45. Interview with Dr. Epimaco Densing, director, Provincial Program Development Office, Tulay Sa Pag-Unlad, Inc., Manila, March 31, 1991. Dr. Densing drew a distinction between the anti-Marcos nature of these laity-organized meetings and those organized by the CPP, which were antigovernment in nature.

46. One aspect of the NPA's strategy was to increase its presence in urban areas through one of its front organizations, the National Democratic Front, and by organizing labor unions. The labor union efforts brought the NPA and Church laity into close contact, albeit unwittingly.

47. Interview with Father James B. Reuter, Manila, March 25, 1991.

48. Huntington, "Religion and the Third Wave," 29–42.

49. Interview with Corazon Calub, Washington, D.C., January 28, 1991. Calub is currently an attaché at the Philippine Embassy in Washington, D.C.

50. See Youngblood, *Marcos Against the Church*, for a thorough discussion of the effect of these economic policies and their relevance to the Philippine Church's social justice activities.

51. *Critical collaboration* is explained in "Statements and Interviews by Jaime L. Cardinal Sin of Manila," IDOC Bulletin, nos. 8, 9, 10 (August, September, October 1980), 5.

52. Bautista, *Cardinal Sin and the Miracle of Asia*, 55–56.

53. Paraphrase of Carroll, "Philippine Bishops: Pastors or Politicos?", 8.

54. The conference is a gathering of professionals who strive to implement the doctrine of Roman Catholic social encyclicals. Although it has no official position within the Philippine Church, its members are influential, and the Church supports their activities.

55. Carroll, "Philippine Bishops: Pastors or Politicos?", 8.

56. Carroll, "The Church: A Political Force?", 9.

57. *Gaudium at Spes*, the 1965 Vatican II Pastoral Constitution on the Church in the Modern World, declared that "Christ did not bequeath to the Church a mission in the political, economic, or social order." Catholic social and political thinking, supported by natural law, holds that the political order constantly progresses toward wholeness and healing, rather than possessing an unrelenting tendency toward disintegration. Political institutions exist to perform the work of restraining sin. People may change their alignments, but the state should remain constant. Society is essential for providing all that people need to come to full humanity.

58. Bernad, "Philippine Revolution of February 1986," 4.

59. Interview with Calub.

60. Interview with Emmanuel Pelaez, Washington, D.C., January 28, 1991.

61. Interview with Calub.

62. Lorayes, personal communication.

63. Ibid.

64. Interview with a priest who requested anonymity, Manila, April 2, 1991.

65. In addition to the interviews and personal communications already cited, other individuals interviewed for this study were Justice Nestor B. Alampay, Sr., director and

corporate secretary, United Coconut Planters Bank; William G. Applegate, director, International Catholic Migration Commission, and president, American Chamber Foundation of Philippines, Inc., Manila; Father John Carroll, S.J., director, Human Development Institute, Loyola School of Theology, Ateneo de Manila University; Cecilio L. Chan, deputy executive director, Philippine Council for Foreign Relations, Inc., Manila; Amando Doronila, editor-in-chief, *Manila Chronicle*; Richard Fisher, policy analyst, Heritage Foundation, Washington, D.C.; Brother Andrew Gonzalez, Brothers of Christian Schools, professor, De La Salle University System, Manila; Father Thomas Greene, S.J., professor, Loyola School of Theology, Ateneo de Manila University, Manila; Father Romeo J. Intengan, S.J., M.D., professor, Loyola School of Theology, Ateneo de Manila University; Dr. Carl Lande, professor, University of Kansas, and visiting fellow, Heritage Foundation, Washington, D.C. (1990–91); Father Donlan O'Hanlon, Missionary Society of St. Columban, Manila; Norberto "Boy" C. Nazareno, president, Citicorp Vickers Philippine, Inc., Manila; Minister Bienvenido Santiago, Iglesia Ni Kristo; Florante B. Solomon, director of research, Citicorp Vickers Philippine, Inc., Manila; Monsignor Antonio B. Unson, Saints Peter and Paul Church, Manila; and Dr. Bernardo Villegas, chief economist and senior vice-president, Center for Research and Communication, Manila.

9 ▪

The Churches and Apartheid in South Africa

DOUGLAS JOHNSTON

The origin of South Africa's race-based policy of apartheid stems, in large measure, from three centuries of Dutch and British colonial presence. Attracted by its strategic position and rich diamond and mineral reserves, white South Africans exploited black labor to develop a world-class economy and, with it, an unparalleled system of racial discrimination and domination. In the formulation and institution of apartheid, the ruling National party relied heavily on the Dutch Reformed church for the theological underpinnings of a social system that contained the seeds of its own destruction.

"It doesn't often happen that in one generation a nation gets the opportunity to rise above itself." So said South African President F. W. de Klerk immediately following the March 21, 1992, referendum on apartheid. "The white electorate has risen above itself in this referendum."[1]

In some respects, this episode marked the beginning of the end of a broad-based national and international movement to abolish apartheid in South Africa and move toward a multiracial democratic form of government. The results of the referendum, which exceeded even de Klerk's expectations, were as impressive as they were unexpected.

After a vote in which 85 percent of the electorate participated and 68 percent of the voters supported continued negotiations on a new constitution, a black population that had historically been indifferent to white elections showed genuine excitement at the prospect of achieving political representation for the first time. In one brief moment in time, South Africa had finally turned the corner on apartheid and reached a major watershed in its rebirth as a nation.

Critical among the factors contributing to political change in South Africa was the failure of the economy. While the country enjoyed impressive economic growth from 1950 through 1975, averaging about 5 percent a year, it slowed considerably thereafter until it actually reached a zero-to-negative rate during the 1980s. With the population growing by 2.5 percent each year, it became increasingly clear that major change would be required to turn the country around.[2]

In 1985 then-President P. W. Botha gave a milestone speech that was extremely reactionary in tone, confounding widespread expectations that he was about to

177

present a liberal program of reform. As a result, Chase Manhattan Bank withdrew its loans, seeing South Africa as a poor risk. Other banks shortly followed suit, after which governments also intervened by imposing economic sanctions. According to Zach de Beer, leader of the Democratic party in South Africa, with the single exception of the cutoff of military arms, the governmental sanctions proved largely irrelevant. However, shortage of capital became an Achilles heel, as the financial community's lack of confidence took its toll.[3]

Within this context, the stage was set for a process of genuine reform. It is no small irony that selected church leaders played an important role in this process after decades in which the most influential denomination, the Dutch Reformed church,[4] had provided the theological justification for apartheid. In some respects, the history of the churches' role in apartheid is the history of South Africa itself. To appreciate fully what was required to abolish apartheid, it is necessary to understand first the dynamics of its establishment and the part played by the churches in that process.

EVOLUTION OF APARTHEID

The Early Years

The first permanent white settlement in southern Africa was established as a stopover station at the site of present-day Cape Town (see Figure 9.1) by the Dutch East India Company in 1652. At that time, southern Africa was inhabited by Bantu-speaking farmers in the east and the Khoisan peoples in the west, who for the most part were either cattle and sheep ranchers or nomadic hunter-gatherers. For a century, European ships had stopped intermittently at the Cape, and a network of trade had developed that stretched deep into the interior.[5]

In 1657 nine former Dutch East India Company employees were given land and allowed to establish themselves as free burghers, raising crops and cattle to be sold to the company. This small, but growing, contingent of whites was buttressed with an influx of about 150 French Huguenots who migrated via the Netherlands to escape religious persecution.[6]

Almost immediately, a pattern of farming began to develop that depended on the exploitation of nonwhite labor, as the Dutch came to rely on indigenous inhabitants and imported slaves (mainly from the East Indies and Madagascar). The whites grew to despise manual labor and to equate inferior status with inferior talent—and both with race.[7] As they expanded their holdings, the colonists either absorbed the indigenous peoples as farm workers or drove them further inland. A subordinated working class evolved and, with it, the stratification of South African society along racial lines. By the end of the century, the status distinctions of color had come to be regarded by many whites as a social absolute, with any suggestion of equality between the races considered a threat to the white way of life.

Figure 9.1. South Africa

British Rule

Great Britain seized control of the Cape Colony in 1806. Like the Dutch, the British were interested in using it as a link in their trade with India. Unlike the Dutch, however, the British became enmeshed in the internal dynamics of the evolving multiracial society. Evangelical missionaries, backed by powerful groups in Britain, condemned the whites' unjust treatment of the enslaved non-white working class and exerted pressure on the early Cape governors to remedy the injustices.[8] Some discriminatory ordinances were lifted, and the slaves were emancipated in 1834. But the reforms antagonized the Afrikaners[9] and contributed to a resentment toward the English that lingers to this day.[10]

During this period, a large number of Zulu chiefdoms were consolidated into a centralized, militarist kingdom with a large standing army. This triggered a chain of migrations by Dutch *trekboers* (semi-nomadic pastoral farmers), who vacated large areas of the Natal, Orange Free State (OFS), and Transvaal. Facing resistance by the Bantu-speaking peoples in the east and British interference in their social structure, many trekboers sought their independence in the north. This Great Boer Trek of

1835–43 led to settlements in the upper Natal and the plateaus along the Vaal River in the eastern part of southern Africa, areas that became points of departure for further white expansion at the expense of the Bantu-speaking peoples.

The British subsequently annexed these new white areas and vacillated between maintaining peace on the one hand and leaving the Boers[11] and Africans to fight it out on the other. In the 1850s, in a move to reduce their commitments in South Africa, the British withdrew from the Transvaal and Orange Free State and recognized them as independent Boer republics. But the annexation of the Natal was not reversed, and as former trekboers left that colony in protest, they were replaced by English settlers. These settlers adopted the racial ideas of the trekboers and then proceeded to apply them even more systematically.[12] Further complicating the racial mixture, Indian workers were imported in 1860 to provide labor for the developing sugar plantations.

South Africa's strategic relevance was transformed in the second half of the nineteenth century as the opening of the Suez Canal in 1869 dramatically decreased the significance of Cape Town along the European-Indian trade route. The discovery of diamonds two years earlier, however, gave South Africa new prominence, as mining displaced agriculture as the key sector of the economy.

Diamond mining required the employment of large numbers of migrant workers from areas that were still exclusively black. Despite fierce resistance, these areas were brought under white control by the end of the nineteenth century. The wealth created from diamond mining exacerbated the economic polarization between indigenous Africans and those of European descent, while it further cemented the tradition of white reliance on black labor.

The Afrikaner-British rift intensified in the last quarter of the nineteenth century when the British attempted to form a confederation, centered in the Cape, which included annexation of the Transvaal Republic. To win the support of the Afrikaner Transvaalers, the British sought to capitalize on their latent feelings of insecurity by provoking a conflict with the Zulus. After an initial and somewhat disastrous defeat for the British, the Zulus were defeated and their land was parceled out to the white settlers. Despite the victory, the British government's confidence in its South African policy was clearly shaken.[13] Later, when Transvaal farmers rebelled and defeated British forces, Britain withdrew and restored the state's independence. The Transvaalers' successful freedom struggle marked the beginning of a nationwide Afrikaner nationalist movement.

With the discovery of gold in the Witwatersrand Reef in 1886, the Transvaal displaced the Cape as most powerful state in the region. It also became a magnet for foreign investment. The British, fearing that an independent Transvaal might draw other South African states into its political and economic orbit, pressured the Transvaal for concessions that would have undermined the republic's independence. Seeing no recourse, the Transvaal and the Orange Free State (the two Boer republics, which were joined in a military alliance) declared war and invaded the British colonies in October 1899. After a fierce struggle, the Boers surrendered in 1902; the Boer republics ceased to exist, and the whole of South Africa was brought under British sovereignty.

After the Boer war, the British sought to anglicize the Afrikaans-speaking population by imposing English as the language of instruction and settling thousands of English speakers in the Transvaal. These efforts only served to revitalize a discouraged Afrikaner nationalist movement; private schools were established, and Afrikaner national sentiment was fostered among the rising generation.

British efforts at economic revival led to the importation of Chinese laborers to work in the Transvaal mines. In time, the immigrants' wretched working conditions evoked an outrage in Britain that led to a change of government and a radical reversal of policy toward the former Boer republics. The new British government granted greater independence to the Transvaal in 1906 and to the Orange Free State in 1907, thus paving the way for eventual South African unification.[14]

Union of South Africa

The Union of South Africa was formed in 1910 as a British Dominion under the monarchy with the previously separate colonies assuming status as provinces with limited local powers. In some respects, this union reflected a political desire to resolve Afrikaner-British differences and to begin anew on the basis of white equality. A short-lived African rebellion in 1906 had led many to think that union was essential for white security. There were compelling economic imperatives as well, for without union, the divergent material interests of the four colonies were bound to undermine their interdependent economies. The resulting constitution gave virtually total political authority to the white minority.

In 1913 James Hertzog, leader of the Afrikaner nationalists in the Orange Free State, formed the National party. The Natives Land Act was also enacted that year, effectively consolidating white control by making it illegal for blacks to own land outside of the African Reserves. (The Reserves comprised only 13 percent of South Africa's territory and lacked any major urban centers, known mineral reserves, or significant ports.) As a consequence, independent African farmers, sharecroppers, and rent-paying tenants on white-owned lands were forcibly relocated.

During World War I, South African forces fought on the side of the British and, among other achievements, conquered the German colony of South-West Africa. Despite the obvious benefits of this acquisition (as a mandate under the League of Nations), many Afrikaners who had opposed South Africa's participation in the war appealed to the fears of British influence as they fanned the flames of Afrikaner nationalism.

Afrikaner Nationalism

Afrikaner nationalism took firm hold in the first half of the twentieth century as a result of the economic and racist fears of a disparate, largely farm-based population. It became "a civil religion based on a doctrine of creation, history, culture, and calling, designed to uphold the Afrikaner people in their struggle for identity, survival, and power, against all odds."[15]

An immediate post–World War I boom was followed by a severe economic depression during which thousands of poor, inefficient white farmers were forced to seek employment in the urban areas. This Afrikaans-speaking rural population was ill-equipped for urban life, but with strong help from the *Broederbond* ("League of Brothers," a secret society of male Calvinist Afrikaners established in 1918[16]) and the Dutch Reformed church (through its extensive local parishes), a network was established for the creation of jobs, and the Afrikaners eventually acquired a degree of economic security. In the process, a spirit of nationalism was forged around the Afrikaans language and culture.

In 1924 a "populist" alliance of the National and the Labour parties gained a parliamentary majority and Hertzog became prime minister (1924–39). It was an alliance of mutual interest: the farmers sought to keep cheap black labor available for farming, and white workers sought to preserve the established racial hierarchy in the mines.[17] During his first 10 years in power, Hertzog achieved his principal goals of reinstating Afrikaner pride and establishing South African control over its own affairs, even though it officially continued as a British Dominion.

A further realignment of South Africa's political parties in the 1930s produced a splintering of the National party with a contingent of devout Afrikaner nationalists, led by Daniel Malan, forming the Purified Nationalist party (Malanites), precursor to the present-day National party that has ruled since 1948. The Malanites were able to use the 1938 centennial celebration of the Great Trek to reignite Afrikaner nationalist sentiment.

A rift over the role that South Africa should play in World War II caused yet another political realignment. Although Prime Minister Jan Smuts (1921–24 and 1939–48) succeeded in gaining sufficient support in Parliament to enter the war on the side of the allies, the decision to fight in a war that did not directly threaten South Africa's national security gave further credence to Afrikaner arguments that the long-standing ties to Britain should be severed. At the same time, inadequate measures by the Smuts government to address problems of racial policy in the face of an increasingly restless black population were also generating concern. Thus, the stage was set for the 1948 election that brought the National party to power.

Apartheid

Apartheid is a philosophy that evolved from a combination of traditional South African practice, a belief in the racial superiority of whites, and Afrikaner neo-Calvinist theology. The word itself means *separateness*. According to this doctrine, every race has its own unique destiny and cultural contribution to make to the world. Different races should therefore be kept separate and allowed to develop along their own lines. Some proponents take the case a step further in arguing that each ethnic African sect should be kept separate, as should Afrikaners from English-speaking whites.

As might be expected, there were different views on apartheid among whites; but ironically, these were manifested more by geographic locality than by ethnicity. In Cape Town, for example, there was considerable racial desegregation, especially between whites and the large coloured (mixed race) population. By the same token, strict segregation was observed in the "British" Natal and in the Afrikaner farm regions. In short, Afrikaners and English speakers who lived in the same area tended to have similar racial attitudes and to adopt broadly similar practices.[18]

From the birth of the union in 1910 until 1948, the groundwork for an apartheid-based system was laid as successive governments systematically enacted policies designed to (a) provide whites with cheap black labor, (b) ensure white dominance over blacks, both politically and economically, and (c) confine extraneous African labor to the African Reserves.[19] In the election of 1948, the National party was able to capture an upset victory over the United party by framing the debate as a choice between apartheid and the vague racial policies of the United party, policies that could be interpreted as moving in a desegregationist direction.

Once the Nationalists were in power, apartheid policies keyed to white fears of the African majority, with tough government seen as inevitable and necessary. The increasing strength of the governing party between 1948 and 1970 was matched by a corresponding decline in opposition to this hard-line approach within the white community.

The foundation of apartheid was one of explicit racism. It was set forth in the enactment of a series of major laws under the stewardship of Prime Minister Daniel Malan from 1948 to 1954.[20]

- The *Population Registration Act of 1950* classified individuals into one of three racial categories: white, coloured, or African. Subsequent laws subdivided coloureds into Indian and "other coloured." Considered the cornerstone of apartheid, the racial classification determined a person's political, civil, economic, and social rights.
- The *Prohibition of Mixed Marriages Act of 1949* outlawed marriage between "Europeans and non-Europeans."
- The *Immorality Act of 1950* (revised in 1957) extended the existing ban on sexual relations between whites and blacks to include relations between whites and coloureds.
- The *Black Abolition of Passes and Coordination of Documents Act of 1952* formally institutionalized a "pass system," dating back to 1809, which controlled the movement of Africans. It also extended the pass requirements to women. Failure of an African to produce his or her pass upon request could result in a fine and a jail term.
- The *Group Areas Act of 1950* (revised in 1957 and 1966) placed restrictions on movement, place of residence, and place of business. It established separate "racial areas" for whites, coloureds, and Asians to live and work. It mandated the relocation of those who were in areas designated for another racial group.
- The *Reservation of Separate Amenities Act of 1953* established as lawful "separate and unequal" status for different races in all public spheres. Known as petty apartheid, its effects permeated all walks of daily life.

- The *Bantu Education Act of 1953* placed control of African education in the Native Affairs Department, thereby empowering the government to control the quality of African education.
- Other acts restricted civil liberties: *The Suppression of Communism Act of 1950* was a first step toward eventual police-state controls. Under this act the definition of communist was continually broadened to serve the government's purpose. The *Internal Security Act of 1976* further increased the spectrum of those who could be persecuted. Its implementation, in combination with the *Sabotage Act of 1962* and the *Terrorism Act of 1967*, gave the government license to extinguish any opposition to apartheid that might arise.

Malan's resignation as prime minister in 1954 was followed by the successive ascension to power of two ultra-hard-liner separatists: J. G. Strijdom (1954–1958) and Hendrik Verwoerd (1958–1966). During Verwoerd's tenure, enactment of the full range of apartheid legislation was completed, with the addition of certain elements that reflected an even harder line.

A policy of separate development (or "homelands") was announced in 1959 with the Promotion of Bantu Self-Government bill. (This initiative sought to establish independent self-governing regimes for different African tribes in reserves designated by the Natives Land Acts of 1913 and 1936. Under its provisions, blacks were to be permanently segregated from whites by revoking their citizenship and forcing them to become citizens of "independent" homelands. Massive population shifts occurred, as more than 1.5 million blacks were uprooted during the 1960s. Government investment in the homelands focused on the creation of housing to support labor reservoirs for whites, rather than industrializing the territories to facilitate true separate development.

The Legitimating Role of the Church

Religious beliefs, movements, and leaders played a central role in the development of apartheid and subsequent attempts to sustain it. Early Dutch and French settlers of South Africa brought with them a Calvinist orientation that led to the eventual adoption of the Dutch Reformed church (DRC) as the established church in the country.

The master-slave relationship of these early days was complemented by a Christian-heathen differentiation that included a strong element of cultural chauvinism. As in Europe, Christianity was equated with civilization and cultural refinement. With the hardening social stratification, differences in faith gave way to differences in color as the criterion for exclusion (lest the baptism of blacks ultimately undermine the political and social status of whites).[21]

By 1824 the DRC had gained full autonomy from the mother church in Holland, making it the first truly independent church in South Africa. Although some of the early DRC clerics had liberal leanings, the evangelical wing of the church combined with those who interpreted Calvinism as "an all-embracing philosophy and lifestyle"[22] in providing a religious legitimization of Afrikaner nationalism. The degree to which Calvinism actually weighed in the balance, however, is a topic of some debate. Doubters suspect that the claims of Calvinist influence have been no more than ex post facto attempts by Afrikaner historians to justify the present through making the past meaningful. As noted philosopher André du Toit points out, the only theological tenet that can be characterized as distinctly Calvinistic is that of predestination. He then notes the absence of any evidence to suggest that early colonial settlers ever held such a belief.[23] Taking it a step further, he concludes:

> The theory of an authentic Calvinist tradition going back to a primitive Calvinism nurtured in the isolated trekboer society . . . is an historical myth. And to the extent that we do find Calvinist notions among leading Afrikaners at the end of the nineteenth century . . . this Calvinism was not particularly representative of, or influential in, contemporary political thinking.[24]

Many theologians who supported apartheid developed their theses on the basis of ideas set forth by the renowned Dutch theologian and statesman Abraham Kuyper (1838–1920). As Angus Gunn, professor emeritus at the University of British Columbia, describes Kuyper's theology:

> Kuyper maintained that God exercised direct control over every detail of natural phenomena and human affairs. Furthermore, in so doing, the Creator recognised certain spheres of human activity that had identities and intrinsic organic orders that set them apart. These spheres, or creation ordinances as Kuyper called them, had a sovereignty of their own. They were supposed to evolve harmoniously and independently under the direct government of God.[25]

Calvinist influence is also claimed in the Old Testament notions of "the called" and "the chosen" used by nineteenth-century Afrikaners to justify white supremacy. As expressed in a speech by M. W. Pretorius in 1871, "fathers of Israel chosen by the Lord, who like the Israelites trekked out of Egypt to escape the yoke of Pharaoh, also trekked from the Cape Colony to escape the yoke of the hated British Government."[26] F. A. van Jaarsveld took this thinking a step further:

> The Great Trek established the thinking of the nineteenth century Afrikaner: The blacks were the descendants of Ham [the Son of Noah] and the Canaanites; the British Government, Pharaoh, who suppressed them in colonial Egypt; and their departure from the country a movement towards the Promised Land, Canaan.[27]

Because Noah cursed Ham's descendants to become "the lowest of slaves,"[28] this analogy effectively relegated blacks to a permanent status as servants.

In response to du Toit's expressed concern about the lack of evidence in colonial times, Allister Sparks suggests that the early Dutch settlers were influenced by the "chosen people" mentality that existed in Holland during its war with Spain, which ended in 1648. "Spain was seen as the antichrist from which William of

Orange had delivered his people by leading them through ordeal and exodus to a national rebirth in their promised land."[29] Sparks maintains that the absence of early references to this tenet is understandable because "the notion of being a chosen people is not the sort of thing that would have been much spoken about or considered appropriate for public record"; nevertheless, "all the circumstantial evidence suggests that this is something the early Afrikaners brought from Holland."[30]

On the other hand, Dr. Beyers Naudé, a respected figure within the Nedervitse Gereformeerde Kerk (NAK), the main branch of the DRC,[31] who forsook his position to join the struggle against apartheid, sides with du Toit:

> Prof. du Toit's viewpoint that Calvinism played a relatively minor role in the formation of the apartheid policy is correct. An important root of the later apartheid policy can be traced to the so-called native policy of the British colony of Natal with the concept of separate development and the reserve policy initiated by the native commissioner, Theophilus Shepstone, the son of an English missionary. This has nothing to do with Calvinism. Certain elements of the Calvinist tradition were later isolated from their original context and used for the legitimation of the apartheid policy. I suggest that the same applies to Kuyper's theology. It had a completely different root and function in the Dutch context.[32]

On a related note, Naudé suggests that it is important to take into account that

> the different Trekker and Voortrekker groups who left the Cape Colony and moved into the interior of South Africa did not from the outset regard themselves as one people or as a nation. The awareness of belonging together as a nation only arose later as a result of British pressure on these groups, which had the effect of uniting them and standing together. Even if the different Voortrekker groups penetrating into the interior of South Africa compared their situation with that of the people of Israel traveling into an unknown territory, this comparison pertained initially to the individual group, not to the Boer people as a whole.[33]

However one comes out on these arguments, there is ample evidence to suggest that the Dutch Reformed church carefully manipulated biblical references in serving its political interests and providing the early underpinnings for apartheid.

Beyond their own discriminatory practices in the Natal and elsewhere, the British played a significant, albeit indirect, role in the evolution of Afrikaner-sponsored apartheid. By introducing the notion of equality in the Cape Colony (through granting the right to vote to coloureds in 1853), the British evoked a strong protest from the Afrikaners. Indeed, it has been argued by one author that the Great Trek grew out of these British efforts to put "coloureds on a par with whites."[34] Yet another author saw the British initiative as "contrary to the laws of God and the natural divisions of descent and faith."[35] This same right to vote was specifically denied all nonwhites in the constitutions of the Boer republics. Moreover, in the Transvaal, blacks were seen as "barbarians" and fundamentally "incompetent" to assume the responsibilities of a civilized life.[36]

As early as 1857, an important synod of the Dutch Reformed church called for separate services for whites and blacks. This facilitated a division of the church along racial lines and was later used to justify a policy of separate development as being "the will of God."[37] Although the British churches were originally more liberal than the Dutch, they, too, eventually adopted a policy of separate churches for the blacks.

The mid-to-late nineteenth century was characterized by a number of splits on this issue among various clerics, leading to the departure from the DRC of one of the more prominent theological leaders of the time, the Reverend S. J. du Toit, who formed his own church and became a founding father of Afrikaner nationalism. The twentieth century saw an even more assertive Dutch Reformed church as it effectively prepared the way for implementation of specific apartheid-related dogma. In 1942, for example, a Federal Mission Council was established from among DRC members to pursue policies of segregation not merely within the church but in other aspects of life as well.[38]

Theologians expounded on Kuyper's views to argue for the continued separation of South Africa's ethnic groups. In addition, Kuyper's view of a church incorporating people of "like minds" was a perfect model for those seeking to justify apartheid on theological grounds. Arguments supporting the purity of separate entities as envisioned in their divine form were expounded to justify the benefits for all—black and white—of keeping distinct ethnicities separated from one another. The biblical story of the tower of Babel (Genesis 11:1–9) was used to reinforce this concept and became a cardinal tenet of apartheid theology. In the DRC's view, the Babel experience made the separation of the world's races and peoples a God-decreed principle. As pointed out by one critic, however, commonly accepted scholarship suggests that it was human frailty and arrogance that led directly to the building of the tower and, in turn, to God's punishment for aspiring to His own supreme creativity. It thus becomes difficult to see how God's punishment of human arrogance logically implies that humans should follow that same course as a commandment.[39]

In 1950 a Dutch Reformed missionary conference recommended the establishment of "territorial apartheid." This was the foundation upon which the segregationist Group Areas Act was made law and from which later sprang the official policy of separate development.[40]

It should come as no surprise that the church and the government functioned in tandem in this fashion. According to the 1980 census, 77 percent of the total South African population belong to a Christian church or movement. More than 90 percent of Afrikaans speakers profess to have a church affiliation, with 70 percent of those belonging to the DRC.[41] Thus, the highly religious orientation of Afrikaner society all but required a theological basis to rationalize apartheid. The DRC not only provided that theology, it essentially provided the policy itself. As noted by Michael Cassidy, the founder of Africa Enterprise, a multiracial African evangelistic association:

It was the white Dutch Reformed Church that, from 1932 on, sent delegation after delegation to the government to support proposals for racial legislation. It worked hard to devise practical policies of apartheid that could be implemented by the government, while formulating theological constructs to justify the policy. It was these plans the church finally presented to the Nationalist Party in 1947. The Nationalist Party accepted them and the programme won at the polls in 1948.[42]

Since its ascension to power, the National party has been closely linked with the Dutch Reformed church. Indeed, the DRC has often been referred to as "the National party at prayer." This influence is consistent with the fact that every prime minister and president since the establishment of the union in 1910 has belonged to one of the sister churches of the DRC.[43]

The Indigenous Church Movement

The consolidation of white power over time created considerable dissatisfaction on the part of many blacks. An early manifestation of this dissatisfaction took place in the 1880s when a number of blacks left the white-controlled mission churches to form what are now known as the African independent churches (AICs) in an indigenous church movement. This movement soon developed a dynamic and momentum of its own. By 1913 about 30 separate churches had formed, and it is now estimated that one out of every three South African blacks belongs to this movement. Collectively, today's 4,000 or so independent churches have a combined membership of more than 7 million, making it the largest religious grouping in the country.[44]

The Zionist Christian church (ZCC) of Moria[45] is representative of the indigenous church movement, particularly with respect to its political orientation. The single largest church in southern Africa, it has approximately 4 million adherents scattered throughout South Africa, Malawi, Botswana, Zimbabwe, Swaziland, Lesotho, and Namibia. Like most other AICs, the ZCC has an all-black membership and little or no contact with white religious groups. Throughout its history, the ZCC has sought to maintain an apolitical stance toward the social order, preaching that political activity is not a church matter. A strong leadership and discipline in the ZCC binds its membership to the virtues of law and order and the recognition of governmental authority. Thus, the ZCC has generally represented a conservative, stabilizing force in South African politics, even during the apartheid era.

APARTHEID OPPOSED

African Nationalism

A number of modern African political groups trace their roots to these initial breakaway churches. One such group, the African National Congress of South Africa (ANC), was formed in 1912 as the South African Native National Congress. The first permanent (and longest lived) African political organization, it initially sought only to gain social and political acceptance for the African elite within a white-dominated structure.

Enactment of the major apartheid laws in the early 1950s, however, sparked a wave of political activism. In 1955 the Freedom Charter, a blueprint for a nonracial South Africa, was developed by members of the ANC, the Indian National Congress, the Coloured People's Organization, and the white Congress of Democrats. The government subsequently arrested 156 members of this Freedom Charter movement, and their trials dragged on until 1961 when all were acquitted. Meanwhile, some ANC members became dissatisfied with working with other races and broke away to form the all-black Pan-African Congress (PAC).

During this period, there were numerous localized boycotts and political protests. In 1960 a PAC protest against the pass laws turned into a massacre when the Sharpeville police fired on an unarmed crowd. The South African government declared a state of emergency, banned the ANC and PAC, and arrested their leaders. Recognizing the futility of peaceful protests, the ANC abandoned its policy of nonviolence and formed a militant wing, Spear of the Nation, which began to sabotage white property. At about this same time, the government also declared South Africa a republic and withdrew from the British Commonwealth, thus achieving its long-sought independence from Britain.

In 1969 South African student leader Steve Biko launched a "black consciousness" movement that sought to coordinate Africans, Indians, and coloureds in opposition to white domination. Although its impact was not immediate, black consciousness greatly infuenced the thinking of future black leaders. Together with "black theology," which was (and is) widely preached in the black churches (including the African branch of the DRC), black consciousness promoted self-awareness and the positive value of being black as a reaction to socio-political oppression and the dehumanizing nature of white rule in South Africa.

Similarly, black theology seeks to conceptualize the meaning of the central tenets of Christianity for black Christians on the basis of the black experience. In certain respects, it parallels the Calvinist teachings of the DRC in that it aims to reclaim and nourish a racial identity.[46] But while the DRC supported Afrikaner nationalism, black theology stands apart from black nationalism. Desmond Tutu, Allan Boesak, and other prominent black theologians have all stressed that black theology seeks to humanize both blacks and whites. As Tutu stated in 1976: "We are involved in the black liberation struggle because we are also deeply concerned for white liberation. The white man will never be free until the black man is wholly free."[47]

In 1976 a protest by black students in Soweto against a new government requirement that Afrikaans be spoken in high schools escalated into widespread rioting of unprecedented proportions. The violence spread to other townships in the Cape and continued for more than a year. The entire episode made Soweto a symbol for antiapartheid activism and ushered in a generation of militant black youths.

By mid-1987 the ANC had acquired growing support among white, coloured, and Indian antiapartheid activists and achieved the highest profile of the various groups opposed to apartheid. Ever since, it has enjoyed a unique leverage in negotiating change with the government.

Although a measured retreat by the government from its more extreme racist policies created a right-wing reaction among militant Afrikaners, white opinion in South Africa during the 1980s generally shifted toward negotiation and compromise as the preferred approach for resolving the apartheid issue. The role of the church in this process was significant and telling.

Early Church Opposition: 1940s–1950s

When apartheid policies were formally adopted in 1948 with the support of the Dutch Reformed church, they were not uniformly endorsed by the other white churches. Indeed, many churches were adamantly opposed to apartheid; even some members of the DRC repudiated their own church's role in the matter. In 1949 at the Rosettenville Conference, the first ecumenical gathering following the National party's victory, the English-speaking churches came out in clear opposition to apartheid. For most white DRC parishioners, however, the transition from supporting apartheid to questioning its validity to opposing it outright took years to unfold.

The historic role of the South African churches in the antiapartheid movement can be characterized as a struggle for organizational influence and voice. As other organizations and individuals opposed to apartheid were effectively nullified through banning orders and arrests, the churches gradually assumed a frontline position in the defense of human rights. Government attempts to restrict church activity were opposed by all churches, including the DRC (which, despite its support of apartheid philosophy, wanted no part of state intervention in religious affairs). For example, a 1958 law prohibiting black attendance at designated "whites only" churches was rejected by the DRC. Until the 1980s, however, the decade of the 1950s was the last period in which the government tolerated significant criticism of apartheid.

The churches were virtually the only "space" where antiapartheid activists could meet for political discussion, but attending such meetings was not without its risks. Church gatherings were often used to facilitate the organization of peaceful protests, and there were numerous incidents of attacks by South African police on people gathered in or outside of church buildings.[48]

Suppression: 1960s–1970s

Although the 1960s and 1970s could generally be characterized as years in which the government essentially suppressed all dissent, a number of church-related interventions provided a foundation for more effective opposition later. In 1960, for example, the World Council of Churches (WCC) sponsored the Cottesloe Consultation in Australia in response to the Sharpeville episode. This was the first ecumenical conference specifically protesting apartheid and the last in which the Dutch Reformed church participated. The congress adopted 17 resolutions, among them that no one should be excluded from any church based on color or race, that there is no biblical justification for the prohibition of mixed marriages, and that all people should have the right to own land and participate in the government where they live. The DRC delegates initially accepted these resolutions, but later repudiated them under pressure from the government. Shortly thereafter, the DRC withdrew from the WCC.[49]

In 1963, after continuous and unsuccessful efforts to force the DRC to reexamine its proapartheid position from within, Dr. Beyers Naudé, respected DRC minister and church elder, became chairman of the Christian Institute (CI), an ecumenical organization dedicated to nonracial Christianity and the training of black theologians. The CI became an influential adversary and thorn in the side of the DRC and the government. In connection with his protest, Naudé also renounced his membership in the Broederbond.[50]

Naudé's resistance to apartheid is particularly significant in that he was well situated to assume highly influential positions within the DRC. In his own words:

> I was told that if I handled my career wisely I would become the moderator of, first, the regional synod and then of the national synod. . . . . It is important to realize at that stage, the moderator of the NGK was the second most powerful position in the country [after the prime minister].[51]

In similar fashion, the South African Council of Churches (SACC)[52] was also resisting National party policies. In 1968 the SACC stirred public debate when it published its "Message to the People of South Africa," a six-page document supported by more than 600 ministers that outlined the incongruity between the teachings of Christianity and the concepts of apartheid and separate development.

The message evoked a strong reaction from Prime Minister John Vorster, who warned against people "who wish to disrupt the order in South Africa under the cloak of religion."[53] The press published a series of conflicting letters between the SACC and the government, with each side accusing the other of using religion in a political context. While the editorial boards of the English newspapers generally supported the document, the Afrikaans papers resoundingly denounced it.

In parallel with these efforts of the Christian Institute and the South African Council of Churches, external pressures were building as well. In 1968 at its Fourth Assembly in Uppsala, Sweden, the World Council of Churches formally inaugurated the Program to Combat Racism (PCR), which involved an activist approach to fighting racism in the religious, political, social, and economic spheres. In 1970 the WCC (at the request of the PCR) agreed to provide humanitarian support to the liberation movements opposing the South African government. Prime Minister Vorster responded by threatening government action against the remaining South African churches in the WCC unless they withdrew from the council. Although there was some support among their church members for withdrawal, the four major English-speaking churches found a middle ground: they rejected and condemned the WCC decision, while retaining their membership despite its implied support for violence. The government responded by making it illegal for any funds to be transferred from South Africa to the World Council of Churches and by making it extraordinarily difficult for WCC representatives to visit the country.[54]

During these years, the most definitive statement of the Dutch Reformed church was issued as a document entitled *Human Relations and the South African Scene in the Light of Scripture*. Adopted by the General Synod in 1974, this document rejected racial injustice and discrimination in principle but accepted a policy of separate racial development in practice as being consistent with the scriptures. In contrast, a number of the English-speaking churches spoke out against the apartheid policies of the national government. Such pronouncements, however, were in direct contradiction with the fact that many church members continued to practice what came to be known as "social apartheid."[55]

The Watershed Years: 1980s–1990s

The courageous activities of Naudé and others were crucial in paving the way for bold acts of opposition on the part of a number of church leaders during the 1980s. A few of these acts stand out as particularly significant.

At its 1982 conference in Ottawa, the World Alliance of Reformed Churches (WARC), an international grouping of about 150 churches of the Reformed, Presbyterian, and Congregational traditions, declared that apartheid was a "heresy" and suspended the two proapartheid Afrikaans-language churches, the NGK and NHK (Nederuitse Hervormde Kerk).[56] It also elected Allan Boesak, the leader of the Dutch Reformed Mission church (NGSK, the coloured branch of the South African Reformed church), as its new president.

Later that same year and prior to the convening of the DRC synod, the Mission church issued what became known as the Belhar Confession in which apartheid was declared a heresy. In effect, the Mission church threatened to withdraw from the DRC unless it unequivocally revoked its theological support of apartheid. Moreover, it indicated that the other two "daughter" churches of the DRC representing Africans and Indians were likely to follow suit. This attack on the legitimacy of apartheid came as a great and unexpected shock to the white DRC, primarily because it came from within the "family," but also because the daughter churches were almost totally dependent on the white "mother" church for their financial support.[57]

Rather than revising its position on apartheid, the DRC General Synod deferred the matter by forming a commission on race policy that was to report to the next synod four years later. It also passed a resolution rejecting racism but without equating it to apartheid. As for the ultimatum of the Mission church, the synod claimed the statement had been submitted too late to be properly considered. It did, however, send a message to the Mission church, promising to consult the Bible in a search for answers to "the various stumbling blocks" in the relationship between the mother and daughter churches. It urged the Mission church to undertake the same pursuit.[58] In response to its suspension by the World Alliance of Reformed Churches, the DRC deferred a decision on its WARC membership by stating that it would resign in four years if the WARC did not end the suspension by that time.

One year later, the DRC Cape Province Synod declared that apartheid could not be justified biblically, and it disassociated itself from attempts to rationalize separate development on that basis. Apartheid was declared to be sinful if in practice it took the form of racism. The Cape Province Synod also rejected the Prohibition of Mixed Marriages Act and opened its religious services to all races in the western cape.[59] These events served to deepen the debate in South Africa on the role of the church in a politicized society. In addressing this issue, three general groupings emerged among the churches: (a) the *conservatives*, consisting of the orthodox DRC and some English-speaking church elements, which characteristically avoided confrontations with the government; (b) the *progressives*, consisting of the "protest churches" aligned within the South African Council of Churches (SACC), which took strong and sometimes confrontational stances against the government; and (c) the *evangelicals*, consisting of the more moderate churches—some with links to the SACC—which took a more qualified critical stance. The conservatives did not regard South Africa's political or social system as illegitimate on biblical grounds but did allow for criticism of certain aspects. The progressives viewed the system as irredeemably evil and advocated complete structural transformation. The evangelicals, on the other hand, supported systemic change in order to facilitate personal transformation.[60]

In July 1985 President Botha declared a state of emergency to cope with the increasing violence in the black townships. The declaration itself legalized detention without trial and certain other controversial practices. A number of churches protested this development and called for a national strike on October 9. Before the deadline, however, 153 predominantly black church leaders and theologians issued the Kairos ("moment of truth") Document, a theological critique of the South African situation calling for decisive action in confronting apartheid. This call to action was supported primarily by the younger Christian leaders who were dissatisfied with the seeming passivity of the established churches. According to Naudé, who was also a signatory:

> The Document was intended to draw the attention of the church leaders to a theological interpretation of the South African situation that prevailed widely at the grass-roots level of the black church constituency. It assumed that the church leaders of the so called antiapartheid churches were possibly unaware of this theological interpretation of the South African situation.[61]

The Kairos Document addressed three types of theology: (a) *state theology*, which was described as upholding the status quo of the state, an obvious reference to the theology of the DRC; (b) *church theology*, which was portrayed as colluding with the state in subtler ways, such as placing greater emphasis on reconciliation than on justice (many of the liberal English-speaking churches were considered to fall into this category); and (c) *prophetic theology*, which argued that if "a particular regime is tyrannical, it forfeits the moral right to govern; and the people acquire the right to resist and to find the means to protect their own interests against injustice and oppression."[62]

The Kairos Document also contained a chapter entitled "Challenge to Action," which advocated that

> The Church should not only pray for a change of government, it should also mobilize its members in every parish to begin to think and work and plan for a change of government in South Africa. . . . The Church will have to be involved at times in civil disobedience. A Church that takes its responsibilities seriously in these circumstances will sometimes have to confront and to disobey the State in order to obey God.[63]

Critics of the Kairos Document called attention to its suggestion that civil disobedience by blacks be treated with understanding. The seemingly strident tone of the document implied a tacit acceptance of confrontation against an oppressor, much like that associated with the concept of liberation theology.[64]

This radical statement from the progressives elicited a complementary response from the more moderate evangelicals. Whereas the Kairos Document attacked the social structure, it said almost nothing about the need for individual reconciliation. The document of the evangelicals addressed both of these themes, seeing each as being necessary to effective change.[65]

The instrumental role that a number of the South African churches were playing in promoting change was well recognized internationally. For example, a conference sponsored by the U.S. Department of State in Washington, D.C., in June 1986, had as its theme "The Church as a Force for Peaceful Change in South Africa." At this conference U.S. Secretary of State George Shultz stated:

> South Africa's churches, many of them affiliated with U.S. counterparts, represent a major asset to help all those who wish to build rather than destroy their country. They represent voices of conciliation, decency, dialogue, and community service in the interest of the common humanity of all South Africans.[66]

Three months later Desmond Tutu was named Anglican archbishop of Cape Town, making him leader of more than 1.6 million parishioners. Foremost among the clerical opponents to apartheid, Tutu had championed nonviolent resistance to apartheid for more than a decade (for which he received the Nobel Prize in 1984), always walking a tightrope between white Christians who found him too extreme in his stance against the government and younger militant blacks who viewed him as too moderate. Among blacks, Tutu always argued strongly against violence, particularly that aimed at other blacks. But, Tutu himself has bluntly stated, "If I were younger, I would have rejected Bishop Tutu long ago."[67]

Through his activities abroad, Tutu raised the consciousness of millions around the world about the plight of blacks in South Africa. Further, he consistently criticized the government's policies on religious and moral grounds. In a celebrated letter in April 1988, for example, he responded to then-President P. W. Botha's charges that he was a communist with the following:

> I want to state the obvious — that I am a Christian religious leader. By definition that surely means I reject communism and Marxism as atheistic and materialistic. I work for God's Kingdom. For whose kingdom do you work? I pray for you, as I do for your ministerial colleagues, every day by name. God bless you.[68]

At its quadrennial general synod in 1986, the DRC finally faced up to the earlier challenge by the Mission church. After heated debate, it issued a document entitled "Church and Society" in which it submitted that apartheid could not be justified on Christian ethical grounds. It proclaimed that "the forced segregation and separation of groups is not biblical and any attempt to justify this from the Bible would be recognized as a fault."[69] While the DRC stopped short of declaring apartheid a "heresy," referring to it instead as "Scriptural error,"[70] the document nevertheless sent shock waves through the Afrikaner community and the government. Although carefully formulated and qualified, the document effectively rejected apartheid as a legitimate ideology.

On other issues, the DRC found that, theoretically, civil disobedience as a last resort against injustice could not be rejected. But because it frequently ended in violence, it should not be supported. Opposition to mixed marriages by the DRC was also withdrawn, although the synod warned of the "serious tensions" that could arise in such unions. Finally, the DRC stated that withholding political rights from blacks was a "serious attack" on human dignity.[71]

The statement also called for the church to be open to all races, but it fell conspicuously short of calling for unification with its three daughter churches. As long as the white DRC, the DRC in Africa (black), the Dutch Reformed Mission church (coloured), and the Reformed church in Africa (Indian) remained separate, opening the white churches to all would have very little effect. The DRC justified the continuation of separate church branches on the basis of differences in "ministerial needs" (i.e., language and culture).[72]

The "Church and Society" statement led to a crisis within the DRC in which some 2 percent of its members broke off to form a new, extremely conservative, and racially exclusive church called the Afrikaans Reformed church (APK).[73] The statement also contributed to a moral soul-searching that had already begun within certain segments of the Afrikaner community, some of whom left the National party in 1987 to form the Independence Movement, a movement motivated by strong biblical and moral objections to apartheid.

These various attacks on the morality of apartheid were complemented by pragmatic efforts to support international sanctions against the government. Tutu was the most visible leader in this regard, seeing sanctions as the only nonviolent path to eliminating apartheid. Although this issue became a source of deep division within the South African churches, with opponents maintaining that sanctions would hurt the black population the most, the advocates ultimately prevailed.

In December 1985 the World Council of Churches had held an emergency meeting in Harare, Zimbabwe, at which it issued the Harare Declaration calling for WCC members to press for immediate and comprehensive sanctions against South Africa. The general secretary for the conference, Dr. Emilio Castro, stressed that the Harare Declaration represented an appeal for the nonviolent resolution of South Africa's problem.[74]

That same year President Ronald Reagan signed an executive order imposing limited U.S. trade and financial sanctions against South Africa.[75] By 1986 massive

U.S. disinvestment in South Africa was beginning to take hold, and the U.S. Congress enacted the Comprehensive Anti-Apartheid Act (CAAA).[76]

Pope John Paul II added his voice in September 1988 by indicating his approval of strict sanctions. In 1989 the Vatican again condemned apartheid, calling it "the most marked and systematic form of racism in the world."[77] Although it is difficult to determine the precise impact of the sanctions on Pretoria's willingness to change its policies, it is reasonable to conclude that they contributed to white South Africa's feeling of isolation and helped set the stage for the dramatic changes that followed.[78]

At no point along the way did the South African churches officially endorse the use of violence to overthrow the system. Calls for civil disobedience and for understanding why violence was taking place were as far as they went. Many of the progressives, however, supported the African National Congress. As Archbishop Denis Hurley of the Roman Catholic church stated in early 1986, "We have to relate to the liberation movements."[79]

The debate that took place surrounding the issue of violence focused more on the legitimacy of the state than on the specific ideology of apartheid. The South African state was seen as not having legitimate or moral grounds for its existence. It was without a mandate from the majority of South Africans and served the interests of only a small minority, often using violence to do so.

Among other things, this debate contributed to the "dedemonizing" of the ANC.[80] As the government came under increased criticism for its use of violence, the reputation of the ANC as a terrorist organization moderated accordingly. In May 1987 a conference organized by the World Council of Churches was held in Lusaka, Zambia, and was attended by members of both the ANC and the SACC. It subsequently became fashionable for church leaders to travel to Lusaka for talks with exiled leaders of the ANC. This activity was part of a deliberate strategy by the ANC to develop closer links with some of the South African churches and their leaders. Although the ANC's motives were undoubtedly mixed, the strategy was a direct acknowledgment of the important role that the churches were playing. The government's banning of most black political organizations had effectively left the field to the churches and the trade unions to carry "the flag of freedom and liberation."[81]

The Final Crescendo

In September 1989 de Klerk succeeded Botha as president under the banner of "Fairness, Firmness, Peace." De Klerk told reporters, "South Africa must develop into a country where all the people . . . will have a share in the say in all decisions affecting their lives. Our vision of the future is that in the new South Africa no one group should dominate another."[82] This was the most important statement undermining the legitimacy of apartheid ever expressed by a white South African political leader.

In late 1989 de Klerk ordered the release of Walter Sisulu, former secretary-general of the African National Congress, along with seven other prominent political prisoners who had been active in the antiapartheid movement. Then, in February 1990, Nelson Mandela, worldwide symbol of the struggle against apartheid, was released after serving 27 years in prison. A month later de Klerk went further than anyone expected and announced that all remaining apartheid laws would be repealed. That was followed by a gradual, but total, lifting of the state of emergency that had been in existence since 1985.

Unlike his predecessor, de Klerk moved ahead forcefully by not looking back over his right shoulder. In effect, he "marginalized" the hard-liners and largely eliminated them as a major obstacle to progress. An important ingredient in de Klerk's strategy was enlisting the support of the key religious denominations, not a small factor in a country in which three-quarters of the population are active church-goers.[83] The influence of the church on de Klerk himself is thought by some to have been substantial.[84] In his own self-description, de Klerk lists his religion first: "I'm a Christian, I'm a South African, an Afrikaner, a lawyer."[85]

Willem de Klerk, the president's brother and biographer, has noted that in the Gereformeerde Kerk (GK),[86] to which President de Klerk belongs, "pragmatism coexists with Calvinist piety. [F. W.] de Klerk's calculated risks are governed more by deliberation than recklessness."[87] The president himself has said:

> If you read my brother's book, you will find him probing [for] a Damascus experience. And the answer is no. The fundamental moment of change for me and all my colleagues in the National Party was in 1986 when we changed our policy from separate development to power sharing.[88]

This change of policy was the first move toward power sharing with the blacks, although the government had already extended limited powers to coloureds and Indians two years earlier when it instituted a tricameral Parliament. The change was upheld in "whites-only" municipal elections the following year, and it was with this perceived mandate that de Klerk was sworn in as president in 1989. Thus, on the basis of his own statement, it is likely that, while de Klerk's actions may have been informed by his religious convictions, his commitment to reform was not motivated by them in any immediate sense.[89]

A Spiritual Dimension

In his Christmas message to the nation in 1989, however, de Klerk said, "I need the churches to speak to me."[90] The response from the churches was overwhelming, but the views expressed were disparate to the point of not being helpful.[91] Wanting a coordinated input, de Klerk contacted Dr. Louw Alberts in January 1990 to organize a meeting of church leaders in order to achieve a consensus viewpoint. A loyal Afrikaner and a person with seemingly impeccable credentials (noted physicist, philosopher, professor, and preacher; a past director general of Mineral and Energy Affairs; and chairman of the Council for Scientific and Industrial Research), Alberts was nevertheless a strong advocate for change. Indeed, his reformist convictions and interdenominational approach had led some leaders of his home church, the NGK, to treat him as persona non grata in earlier years.[92]

Responding to de Klerk's challenge, Alberts developed a set of criteria for targeting the more than 20,000 churches in South Africa. He sought to capture the major streams of Christian thought (Pentecostal, Charismatic, and others) by inviting 12 to 15 representatives from a range of churches and organizations to form a steering committee. But because the idea of the conference itself was a presidential initiative, it was opposed by the South African Council of Churches. Participating in a conference on church matters under the sponsorship of the very entity that represented apartheid would have been politically impossible for the SACC, which had consistently opposed apartheid.[93]

After a period of negotiation between de Klerk and the SACC, de Klerk agreed in June to withdraw as convener of the conference. Soon thereafter, Frank Chikane, secretary-general of the SACC, called a meeting at SACC headquarters to discuss the possibility of convening a church-sponsored conference. Of the 20 participants invited to the meeting, five were from Alberts's original steering committee.[94] The group decided that for such a conference to be useful, it should last at least five days. To distance itself from the governmental initiative, which was to have focused largely on social issues such as health, housing, and AIDS, the original steering committee and agenda were scrapped and plans were made to start anew. Alberts and Chikane were selected to be cochairmen, and the focus was limited specifically to the church's role in the future South Africa. Two months later, in November 1990, the largest representation of black and white churches in South Africa's history was assembled to determine ecumenical guidelines for the post-apartheid era. The conference attracted approximately 230 church leaders from 80 denominations and 40 para-church organizations, including two of the three white branches of the DRC.

Shortly after the conference began, Professor Willie Jonker, a Dutch Reformed theologian who had been invited to speak on "Understanding the Church Situation and Obstacles to Christian Witness in South Africa," made a dramatic and unexpected announcement:

> I confess before you and before the Lord not only my own sin and guilt, and my personal responsibility for the political, social, economical and structural wrongs that have been done to many of you and the results of which you and our whole community are still suffering from, but vicariously I dare also to do that in the name of the DRC of which I am a member, and for the Afrikaans people as a whole.[95]

Jonker's confession, which echoed a similar declaration by the General Synod of the DRC two weeks earlier,[96] created a ripple effect in which others present confessed guilt as well, either for their past tacit acceptance of apartheid or for their attitudes of bitterness. Consistent with the Anglican tradition, Desmond Tutu responded spontaneously to Jonker, "When that confession is made, then those of us who have been wronged must say, 'We forgive you,' so that together we may move to the reconstruction of our land."[97]Others quickly followed suit and an atmosphere was created in which no one felt comfortable in pointing an accusatory finger.[98] Although Professor Jonker had not consulted with the DRC delegates prior to making his confession,[99] DRC moderator Pieter Potgieter indicated support later in the conference: "The delegates of the DRC want to state unambiguously that we fully identify ourselves with the statement made by Professor Jonker on the position of this Church."[100]

The document issued by the conference, the Rustenburg Declaration, was endorsed by representatives from 97 denominations and 40 organizations. It confessed general responsibility for having perpetuated and benefited from apartheid and proclaimed that the churches had been guilty of "a colonial arrogance toward black culture." It further stated that "by our opinions we have encouraged a fragmented and intolerant society. Most of all, we have been unwilling to suffer, loving our comfort more than God's justice and clinging to our privilege rather than binding ourselves to the poor and oppressed of our land."[101]

Post-Rustenburg

Rustenburg left in its wake a sense of urgency among participating church leaders about the need to reach their grass-roots constituencies on a similar basis. Because fewer than 5 percent of the South African churches had refused to participate in the conference, it was hoped that the spirit captured in the Rustenburg Declaration could be conveyed by individual churches operating at the local level. The fact that the conference had been cochaired by the black leader of the South African Council of Churches and an Afrikaner grounded in the Dutch Reformed church (Chikane and Alberts, both of whom were widely respected) was also viewed as having grass-roots appeal. Steps were subsequently taken to implement this grass-roots strategy, although their full impact could not be determined at the time of this writing.

As might be expected, the conference also generated a degree of criticism. Conservative party leader Andries Treurnicht and former President Botha led the way in expressing anger among conservative whites over the Rustenburg Declaration, with some DRC leaders expressing fears of a possible exodus of church members to the more conservative NHK or the right-wing breakaway APK.[102]

Unanticipated, though, were the criticisms from the black and coloured branches of the DRC, especially from among those who did not participate in the conference. Typically, these critics characterized what took place as no more than a ploy on the part of white church leaders to manipulate the process of change. Further, they criticized the forgiveness expressed by Tutu and others as "cheap grace," and even accused Frank Chikane as having "sold out."[103] Although this dampened the spirit of unity, the churches continued to play a mediating role between the government and the ANC, most recently in addressing the violence in the townships. In addition, ecumenical groups sprang up to facilitate negotiation and mediation at the local level.[104]

Whatever the negatives, in the cosmic scheme of history, Rustenburg may one day be viewed as the coup de grace for apartheid. In important respects, the struggle to abolish apartheid has been a struggle to abolish its theology. With the overwhelming number of church denominations having at last denounced apartheid, its delegitimization is virtually complete. Absent its theological prop, apartheid will fall of its own weight.

ANALYSIS AND CONCLUSION

This case demonstrates the full range of roles that religious institutions can play in a process of social change. First, they can be an active force for change as demonstrated by the actions of various international ecumenical bodies and of selected bishops and other senior churchmen from the South African Council of Churches. Second, they can provide political "space" for dissidents to convene and express their views. For a considerable time, the churches were the only such venue not shut down by the South African authorities. This function, while more passive than the first, was crucial in sustaining the momentum for change.

By the same token, religious institutions can be totally acquiescent to the status quo. Indeed, they may go so far as to undergird the forces of oppression, as did the Dutch Reformed church in its attempts to justify apartheid from the beginning. In such a context, resistance from within is generally not tolerated. As individual DRC spokesmen arose to oppose apartheid, they were ostracized and rejected by fellow church members. Beyers Naudé and Louw Alberts, though of dissimilar backgrounds and theological persuasion, were two cases in point.

Perhaps the most interesting aspect of this case is the process of change within the Dutch Reformed church itself, as successive layers were stripped from the onion of deniability—from its proactive support for apartheid, to its acknowledgment that racism was bad but apartheid was acceptable, to its final declaration that apartheid was not only wrong but sinful. This was a tortuous transition in which a few courageous church leaders stepped forward to plant the seeds of doubt and then persevered over time to bring the church body around. In view of the fact that many of the DRC hierarchy were prominent members of the National party with a great deal at stake in maintaining the status quo, this was no small challenge.

This evolutionary change gathered force in 1982 when the Dutch Reformed church issued the Belhar Confession, which broke the National party's chokehold on church doctrine. It gathered further steam with the call to action by young black church leaders and theologians in the Kairos Document of 1985 and in the later response of the DRC to the Mission church's challenge when it acknowledged apartheid to be a "scriptural error." In November 1990, the process culminated at Rustenburg with the delegitimation of apartheid theology.

In tracing this evolution, it becomes increasingly clear that, in most instances, churches are captives of their congregations. While there were a number of courageous acts by individuals from within the DRC, the DRC as an organized religious institution was a significant force in resisting change. To a lesser extent, the same was also true for the English-speaking churches. Although certain of these church leaders also acted courageously, their leverage on the domestic political process was marginal until they were able to bring their congregations along. In other important respects, however, these same leaders had a major influence on the process of change. For example, Desmond Tutu's efforts to sensitize the rest of the world to the fundamental injustices of the apartheid system and to encourage international sanctions were instrumental factors in squeezing the South African economy to a point where the need to institute reforms became irresistable.

The impact of other prominent forces in abolishing apartheid in South Africa should also be recognized: the efforts of the ANC and other political parties, the pressures exerted by the trade unions, and the effect of the sports boycotts.[105] Even so, the role of the churches was critical, perhaps central. Without their influence, the process of change would have either taken longer to gain momentum or would have degenerated into a race war.

History offers few parallels to the experience of South Africa, where a centuries-old system of racial oppression is being transformed from within by relatively peaceful means. If this achievement stands, it will be due in large measure to the facilitating role of the South African churches.

Notes

1. Christopher S. Wren, "South African Whites Ratify de Klerk's Move to Negotiate with Blacks on a New Order," *New York Times*, March 19, 1992, A14.

2. The 1976 Soweto uprisings gave rise to massive capital flight. In 1977 alone, long-term foreign capital investment dropped from $2.3 billion to $7 million (Hermann Giliomee, *The Parting of the Ways: South African Politics 1976–1982* [Cape Town, S. Afr.: David Philip Publishers, 1982], 51).

3. Interview with Zach de Beer, Cape Town, February 11, 1991.

4. The *Dutch Reformed church* is a generic label that encompasses three Afrikaans Calvinist sister churches: the Nedervitse Gereformeerde Kerk (NGK), the church to which most Afrikaners belong; the Nederuitse Hervormde Kerk (NHK), historically the most avid proponent of apartheid; and the Gereformeerde Kerk (GK), the smallest in size and the most liberal politically. While the term *DRC* as used in this chapter is meant to include all three churches, it is used with the understanding that the GK divorced itself theologically from the concept of apartheid a full 20 years before the NGK did so at Rustenburg in 1990.

5. The principal references used for the history of South Africa as a country were the *Encyclopedia Britannica* (Chicago: William Benton, 1966); T. R. H. Davenport, *South Africa: A Modern History* (London and Toronto: University of Toronto Press, 1978); Richard Elphick and Hermann Giliomee, eds., *The Shaping of South African Society 1652-1980* (London: Longman, 1979); Study Commission on U.S. Policy Toward Southern Africa, *South Africa: Time Running Out* (Berkeley and Los Angeles: University of California Press and the Foreign Policy Study Foundation, 1981); and William Minter, *King Solomon's Mines Revisited: Western Interests and the Burdened History of South Africa* (New York: Basic Books, 1986).

6. In 1685 King Louis XIV of France revoked the Edict of Nantes, a law signed by Henry IV in 1598, which granted religious liberties and civil rights to his Protestant subjects, the Huguenots.

7. Study Commission, *South Africa: Time Running Out*, 33.

8. The evangelical missionaries were largely from a nonconformist background and, as such, did not enjoy the same rights as members of the established Anglican church. Victims of discrimination themselves, they tended to sympathize with oppressed peoples in the British colonies. By the same token, their recorded statements reflect a strong feeling of European superiority (personal communication from Beyers Naudé, chairman of the

Christian Institute, September 7, 1992). This view is consistent with the opinion of Charles Villa-Vicencio, a respected member and critic of the English-speaking churches:

> On occasions they [the missionaries] intervened on behalf of the indigenous population and often found themselves in confrontation with the white settler churches as well as the colonial government, and yet they never doubted the superiority of English cultural values over those of the African people whom they sought to proselytize.

(Charles Villa-Vicencio, *Trapped in Apartheid* [Maryknoll, New York: Orbis Books, 1988], 18).

9. *Afrikaner* was the name assumed by the early Dutch settlers to show allegiance to their new country.

10. It would be misleading to suggest that the British were totally reform-minded in their treatment of Africans. As pointed out by former Minister for State Affairs G. Van N. Viljoen:

> It is a matter of historical record that many of the discriminatory practices still in force in South Africa until comparatively recently were, in fact, inherited from the British colonial era. Pass laws and influx control measures which were to later become some of the most discredited and maligned 'pillars of apartheid' were, for example, first introduced at the Cape under the British colonial administration of Lord Charles Somerset.

(Personal communication from Viljoen, November 23, 1992)

11. The term *Boer* derives from the Dutch word for farmer (*gheboer*) and is used to mean a Dutch colonist or descendant of a Dutch colonist in South Africa.

12. Study Commission, *South Africa: Time Running Out*, 34.

13. British Governor Theophilus Shepstone initially supported the claims of Zulu King Cetshwayo against the government of the Boer Republic in the Transvaal. Later, after having occupied that republic, Shepstone opposed the Zulu claims, thus provoking war (personal communication from Naudé; and Villa-Vicencio, *Trapped in Apartheid*, 50).

14. This "self-government" for the Transvaal and Orange Free State did not include the participation of Africans who constituted the majority of the people and who consequently felt betrayed by the policy of the British government following the Anglo-Boer war (personal communication from Naudé).

15. John W. de Gruchy, *The Church Struggle in South Africa* (Grand Rapids, Mich.: William B. Eerdmans, 1979), 32.

16. The Afrikaner Broederbond, formed to promote the interests of Afrikaners, was composed of influential Afrikaners from across the social spectrum: politicians, clergy, civil servants, teachers, and others. From its founding, the Broederbond's two most important goals were to gain full independence for South Africa and to overcome the Afrikaner's sense of inferiority (Newell M. Stultz, *The Nationalists in Opposition 1934–1948* [Cape Town and Pretoria: Human and Rousseau, 1974], 35–36). The Broederbond presently numbers about 12,000 members.

17. In 1921 the South African Chamber of Mines, in reaction to rising costs and a fall in the price of gold, moved to organize the industry more rationally by moving blacks into semiskilled positions. White workers revolted, and the attempted reorganization was thwarted, although 230 of them lost their lives in the process.

18. Study Commission, *South Africa: Time Running Out*, 38.

19. Ibid., 39.

20. Ibid., 48–79.

21. W. P. Esterhuyse, *Apartheid Must Die* (Cape Town: Tafelberg Publishers, 1981), 26–27.

22. de Gruchy, *Church Struggle in South Africa*, 6.

23. André du Toit, "Puritans in Africa? Afrikaner 'Calvinism' and Kuyperian Neo-Calvinism in Late Nineteenth-Century South Africa," *Comparative Studies in Society and History*, vol. 27 (London: Cambridge University Press, 1985), 213.

24. Ibid., 234.

25. Angus M. Gunn, "From Assent to Dissent—Apartheid and the Dutch Reformed Church," *South Africa International* (July 1991), 29.

26. As quoted in Esterhuyse, *Apartheid Must Die*, 29.

27. As quoted in Esterhuyse, *Apartheid Must Die*, 29.

28. Genesis 9:25, *The Holy Bible*, New International Version (Grand Rapids, Mich.: Zondervan, 1978), 8.

29. Allister Sparks, *The Mind of South Africa* (New York: Alfred A. Knopf, 1990), 25.

30. Ibid., 30.

31. In 1990 the NGK numbered 4,299,000 members or 87.7 percent of the total DRC population (*South Africa 1991/92 Official Yearbook*, 17th ed. [Pretoria: South African Communications Service, 1991]), 217 (first English edition in new, shortened version).

32. Naudé, personal communication.

33. Ibid.

34. Karel Tregardt, as quoted in Esterhuyse, *Apartheid Must Die*, 27.

35. Anna Steenkamp, as quoted in ibid.

36. Ibid., 29.

37. Ibid., 34.

38. Colleen Ryan, *Beyers Naudé: Pilgrimage of Faith* (Claremont, S. Afr.: David Philip Publishers, 1990), 34.

39. Douglas Bax, "The Bible and Apartheid 2," in *Apartheid is a Heresy*, eds. John W. de Gruchy and Charles Villa-Vicencio (Grand Rapids, Mich.: William B. Eerdmans, 1983), 117.

40. de Gruchy, *Church Struggle in South Africa*, 32–33.

41. G. C. Oosthuizen, "Christianity's Impact on Race Relations in South Africa," in *Christianity Amidst Apartheid*, ed. Martin Prozesky (New York: St. Martin's Press, 1990), 113.

42. As quoted in Allan Boesak, *Black and Reformed: Apartheid, Liberation, and the Calvinist Tradition* (Maryknoll, N. Y.: Orbis Books, 1984), 112.

43. J. A. Loader, "Church, Theology and Change in South Africa," in *South Africa: A Plural Society in Transition*, ed. D. J. van Vuuren et al. (Durban, S. Afr.: Butterworth, 1985), 288.

44. *South Africa 1991/92 Official Yearbook*, 215.

45. The African Zionist church has no connection to Jewish Zionism. Its origins stem from a small U.S. revivalist movement, the Christian Catholic Apostolic church in Zion, founded in 1896 by John A. Dowie in Zion City, Illinois.

46. de Gruchy, *Church Struggle in South Africa*, 166.

47. As quoted in ibid., 186.

48. According to Bruce A. McKenney, a research assistant at the Center for Strategic and International Studies, who attended a number of church meetings in and around Cape Town during 1989 and 1991, community leaders often collected information from attendees at these meetings for the use of human rights lawyers in the event of arrest or detention. Moreover, attendees were required by police to exit the church in groups of fewer than 10 or face arrest for an illegal gathering. Everyone leaving the church was also

recorded on film. Despite these strained circumstances, attendance at such meetings was always quite high.

49. Gunn, "From Assent to Dissent," 32.

50. Zolile Mbali, *The Churches and Racism* (London: SCM Press, 1987), 43–44.

51. Ryan, *Beyers Naudé*, 43. Another indicator of Naudé's prospects within the DRC is the fact that the Broederbond was established in his father's home in 1918.

52. The South African Council of Churches (SACC), known as the Christian Council from 1937–1968, is an alliance of English-speaking churches that was formed to facilitate interchurch cooperation. The Anglicans, Methodists, Presbyterians, and United Congregationalists are the largest of its member churches. Although widely recognized for its antiapartheid positions, the SACC has also been deeply involved in a range of nonpolitical community-based projects throughout South Africa.

53. *Pseudo-Gospels in South Africa*, report published in Johannesburg, 1968, as quoted in de Gruchy, *Church Struggle in South Africa*, 118.

54. Ibid., 128–30.

55. W. P. Esterhuyse, *Brothers—But Not in Earshot Distance. The Split Among South African Churches* (Cape Town: Tafelberg Publishers, 1989), chapter 3.

56. In 1990 the NHK had 357,000 members or 7.4 percent of the total DRC population (*South Africa 1991/92 Official Yearbook*, 217).

57. Interview with W. P. Esterhuyse, Washington, D.C., April 28, 1992.

58. Allister Sparks, "South African Church Faces Breakup," *Washington Post*, October 27, 1982, A25.

59. Brian Stuart, "NGK in W. Cape Opens Doors to All," *Argus* (South Africa), October 31, 1983, 3.

60. Interview with Esterhuyse.

61. Naudé, personal communication.

62. *The Kairos Document: Challenge to the Church* (Braamfontein, S. Afr.: Skotaville Publishers, 1986), 22.

63. Ibid., 29–30.

64. Many theologians, including Tutu and Boesak, view black theology as a type of liberation theology. Black theology recognizes liberation as the primary message of the Old Testament. Because reconciliation is only possible between equals, liberation is a necessary precondition. Liberation theology is a call for action that interprets the scriptures on a class-based axis of oppressor and oppressed, arguing that Christians must side with the poor and oppressed.

65. Concerned Evangelicals, *Evangelical Witness in South Africa: A Critique of Evangelical Theology and Practice by South African Evangelicals* (Grand Rapids, Mich.: William B. Eerdmans, 1986), 26–32, 37.

66. George Shultz, "The Church as a Force for Peaceful Change in South Africa" (Washington, D.C.: United States Department of State, Bureau of Public Affairs, 1986), Current Policy No. 841, p. 2.

67. As quoted in Serge Schmemann, "Archbishop Rites Honor Tutu Today," *New York Times*, September 7, 1986, I21; and subsequently confirmed in personal communication from John Allen, media secretary, Office of the Archbishop of Cape Town, October 12, 1992.

68. Letter from Tutu to P. W. Botha, April 8, 1988, as reprinted in "Botha's Bible—and Mine," *Harper's Magazine* (July 1988), 26.

69. "Dutch Reformed Church Drops Apartheid," *Southern Africa Report* (October 24, 1986), 2.

70. Ibid.

71. Ibid.

72. Ibid.

73. Allister Sparks, "Key Church Splits in South Africa," *Washington Post*, June 28, 1987, A25.

74. Jan Raath, "Churches to Urge Tough Sanctions on S. Africa," *London Times*, December 7, 1985, 40.

75. By this time the Reagan administration's hand had been forced by intense congressional pressure. In 1981 President Reagan had departed from the policies of the Carter years when he stated that the United States would back Pretoria while it worked out its own problems. Early in 1982, an earlier ban on the sale of nonmilitary items to South African police and military forces was lifted; and in 1983 the United States formally endorsed the new South African constitution as a step in the right direction. A few weeks prior to the imposition of sanctions, President Reagan also established a Working Group on South and Southern Africa in the State Department to communicate U.S. goals and objectives to domestic and foreign audiences and to promote private-sector cooperation that could facilitate constructive change toward a postapartheid system. Many viewed this initiative as a belated quest by the administration for greater support of its controversial policy of "constructive engagement" (interview with Ambassador J. Douglas Holladay, first and only Director of the Working Group on South and Southern Africa, Washington, D.C., July 20, 1992).

76. The Comprehensive Anti-Apartheid Act (CAAA), passed by the U.S. Congress over President Reagan's veto on October 2, 1986, levied economic sanctions against South Africa prohibiting new investments, imports, and air travel. It stated that the goal of U.S. policy would be "to seek international agreements with the other industrialized democracies to bring about the complete dismantling of apartheid." It required that five conditions be met for the lifting of sanctions: (a) scrapping of the apartheid laws, (b) release of political prisoners, (c) elimination of the Group Areas Act, (d) elimination of the Population Registration Act, and (e) legalization of black political entities such as the ANC. In summer 1991, President Bush repealed the CAAA in response to progress toward meeting the above conditions.

77. John Wyles, "Vatican Condemns Racism in South Africa," *Financial Times*, February 11, 1989, 2.

78. In response to a question posed to F. W. de Klerk, in June 1990, concerning the impact of sanctions, the president replied:

> Their economic impact is that while we've learned to live with them and while they didn't succeed to bring us to our knees, they did and do impede the sort of growth rate we need to address, in all spheres, the challenges we face in South Africa. Social and economic and human development, housing, education, all require a growth rate in the vicinity of 5 percent per year. Sanctions without question prevented us from meeting these urgent needs. So sanctions have hurt us and are hurting each and every citizen.

("Q&A: de Klerk Insists 'New Reality' Has Arrived," *Washington Times*, June 14, 1990, B6).

79. As quoted in Esterhuyse, *Brothers—But Not in Earshot Distance*, chapter 6.

80. Ibid.

81. Ibid.

82. Television interview, BBC, September 25, 1989.

83. President de Klerk has reviewed the manuscript for this chapter, including those passages dealing with his motives and activities, and found it "overall, to be a fair and

balanced chronicle of South African events" (personal communication from G. Van N. Viljoen, minister for state affairs, office of the president, November 23, 1992).

84. Interview with de Beer.

85. "White Domination Must End, South Africa Leader Says," *Christian Science Monitor*, June 5, 1989, 6.

86. The GK is known for its adherence to a rather narrow interpretation of the scriptures. The GK, which numbers between 165,000 and 200,000 members, is thought by many to be the most conservative branch of the DRC, both theologically and socially. Politically, however, and in contrast to the NGK, the GK treats theology and politics more flexibly, thus freeing the politicians in its ranks from any theological obligation to apartheid. In point of fact, two decades before the NGK admitted that apartheid was a mistake, the GK had formally declared apartheid to be a sin and without grounding in scripture (Scott Kraft, "De Klerk's Tightrope in South Africa," *Los Angeles Times*, January 4, 1990, A1).

87. As quoted in Christopher S. Wren, "Practical, Not a Gambler, De Klerk Tells His Story," *New York Times*, March 26, 1992, A6.

88. As quoted in Stephen Glover and Cal McCrystal, "Convert on the Long Trek," *Independent* (UK), April 28, 1991, 25.

89. According to Beyers Naudé, personal communication:

Many . . . would regard Mr. de Klerk as an astute politician, whose main concern is to protect the interests of the white constituency which brought him to power in a situation in which it is no longer possible to control the black majority by the police force or the army and in which it has become inevitable to give them some share in political decision making.

90. Interview with Dennis House, executive director of Mission South Africa and a coordinator of the Rustenburg Conference, Bedfordview, South Africa, February 4, 1991.

91. Interview with Louw Alberts, Washington, D.C., February 1, 1991.

92. Interview with House.

93. Telephone interview with Frank Chikane, December 9, 1992. A preliminary meeting did take place between those churches that had either directly or tacitly supported apartheid—that is, the NGK and the NHK, the evangelical Pentecostal churches, and the Zion Christian church. Not only had they never previously met with the SACC, but they had never met with one another. They thus saw a need to prepare collectively for what lay ahead.

94. Interview with House.

95. Louw Alberts and Frank Chikane, *The Road to Rustenburg: The Church Looking Forward to a New South Africa* (Cape Town: Struik Christian Books, 1991), 92.

96. The resolutions of the General Synod are usually published only in Afrikaans. Because very few of the attendees either spoke or read Afrikaans, neither the existence nor the content of the resolutions was widely known. The resolutions themselves acknowledged that the Dutch Reformed church had misjudged the policy of apartheid by not anticipating its negative impact. They concluded by indicating that apartheid may be sinful (telephone interview with Willie Jonker, November 16, 1992).

97. Alberts and Chikane, *Road to Rustenburg*, 99.

98. Ibid., 9.

99. Jonker's statement, which was a last-minute addition to the text of his address, was motivated by his sensing an attitude of distrust on the part of many fellow participants toward the DRC. At the same time, there was a general expectation that somehow the churches could find one another. Because one of the principal points of his talk had to do with the different attitudes that various churches had toward apartheid, Jonker felt led to speak out as he did. His status as an invited speaker (but not a delegate) gave him a certain

freedom to do so; had he been a delegate, he would have had to get permission from higher DRC authority (telephone interview with Jonker).

100. David Beresford, "Churchmen Atone for Sins," *Guardian*, November 8, 1990, 11; and confirmed in telephone interview with Jonker.

101. National Council of Churches in South Africa, *Rustenburg Declaration* (Pretoria, S. Afr.: National Initiative for Reconciliation, 1990), 2.

102. Interview with Robert A. Evans, executive director, Plowshares Institute, Washington, D.C., April 27, 1992.

103. Ibid.

104. Prominent among these groups is the Empowering for Justice and Reconciliation Project, a cross-cultural Christian partnership formed in 1991 to train priests and lay leaders from the various religious communities in South Africa in techniques of negotiation and mediation.

105. The strong "yes" vote in the March 21, 1992, national referendum appears to have been influenced in part by the fact that South Africa's cricket team, which had just reached the semifinals of the World Cup tournament in Australia, would have had to abandon the competition in the event of a negative vote. South Africans, who are an extraordinarily sports-minded people, were particularly inspired by their team's progress in the aftermath of a ban that had excluded them from international sports competition for an extended period of time (interview with Helga Liebenberg, director of the South African Forum, Washington, D.C., March 23, 1992).

10 ▪

Transition From Rhodesia to Zimbabwe: The Role of Religious Actors

RON KRAYBILL

As African states, one by one, broke free from the shackles of colonialism, black Rhodesia's quest for self-rule encountered an entrenched white establishment. Ian Smith, the stubborn and resourceful leader of the heavily outnumbered whites, unilaterally declared Rhodesia independent of Britain in 1965, effectively tightening the grip of white control. Sanctions by Britain and the United Nations followed, while internally a guerrilla campaign was waged against the government by competing African nationalist factions. The struggle left the nation with a war-ravaged infrastructure, a fragmented opposition, and little hope for a peaceful solution.

Rhodesia[1] in 1979 was a nightmare. By the estimates of some, 20,000 people, many of them civilians, had already died in a costly war for liberation now frozen in a deadly stalemate.[2] The issue, at first glance at any rate, was simple. Black Africans, numbering nearly 90 percent of the population, wanted majority rule from a government clinging at all cost to white control and privilege.

The future, without a doubt, belonged to Africa. Old-style colonialism teetered on the brink of its own grave; England, formally Rhodesia's ruler,[3] chafed to complete the painful process begun more than 20 years earlier of shedding its ill-acquired African colonies. Neighboring Zambia had been independent since 1964, Botswana since 1966. Two other regional neighbors, Angola and Mozambique, had just gained their independence from Portugal in 1975 (see Figure 10.1). Rhodesia was the obvious next candidate to bear the torch of African nationalism. Oddly enough, even South Africa, long a backer of Salisbury's war efforts, had in 1976 begun withdrawing financial support and pressuring for reform.[4]

Within Rhodesia, the forces of liberation held the upper hand, as well. After 14 years of warfare, guerrilla troops now roamed large areas of the country and maintained a steady barrage of attacks on white farms, government offices, and outlying security establishments. The economy lay in ruins from heavy military expenditures and 13 years of economic sanctions by the outside world. Emotionally, whites were exhausted by the war. Not only had they lost sons in the fighting, they

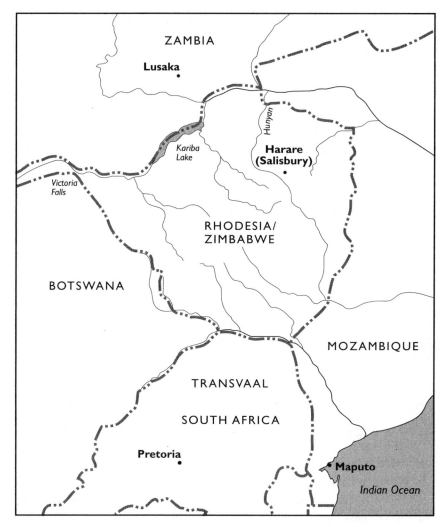

Figure 10.1. Rhodesia/Zimbabwe

had lost faith in their future. Thousands had already fled to South Africa and elsewhere; many more contemplated leaving as well. The question in 1979 was not *if* black Africans would gain their rightful place in the nation, but *when.*

The discouraging part for the majority of Rhodesians was that the experience of the last decade suggested the moment of true African rule might still be a long and costly way off. Salisbury was on the defensive militarily, economically, and politically, but it still possessed a deadly modern military machine and the will, evidently, to use it for a long time to come. Not only had Prime Minister Ian Smith earned a reputation for being bull-headed, he had proven cunning at political maneuvering in the ancient method of "salami-style" negotiation. When stonewall and steel failed to contain the forces seeking to snatch the prize he held, Smith more than once yielded. It was a stingy slice of political power he offered to Bishop Abel Muzorewa and two other blacks in the 1978 Internal Settlement, but it gave what he doubtless sought: deep division in the camp of African nationalists and a black leader willing to go to Washington and London in defense of a government still controlled by whites.[5]

Meanwhile, as usual in war, it was the civilians who suffered the most. One in six black Rhodesians had been displaced by the war; one in 10 lived in forced government resettlement camps where they were vulnerable not only to diseases but also to harassment by hostile government forces.[6] Many thousands more lived in refugee camps in the bordering states of Mozambique, Botswana, and Zambia.[7] Agriculture proved difficult and in many places impossible, leading to widespread hunger and impoverishment. Even worse for many was the calamity of getting caught in the crossfire of a vicious war. As control of territory changes constantly in guerrilla warfare, "neutrality" on the part of civilians offers the only means of survival. But as thousands of unfortunate victims discovered, neutrality is a difficult act to maintain. Killings, torture, rape, and pillage became commonplace for villagers.

If Rhodesia was a nightmare for its citizens, it was also a graveyard of failed peace initiatives. Between 1966 and the end of 1978, some 20 efforts had been launched, most involving governments outside Rhodesia in a brokering role. Some of the world's best-known politicians and mediators were involved. British Prime Minister Harold Wilson and his adviser, Lord Goodman, British Foreign Secretary David Owen, U. S. secretaries of state Henry Kissinger and Cyrus Vance, U.S. Ambassador Andrew Young, and Zambian President Kenneth Kaunda—all invested substantial efforts to secure peace in Rhodesia, and all failed.

But in September 1979, following a pivotal Commonwealth conference held two months earlier in Lusaka, Zambia, the impossible happened. Meeting in London at Lancaster House with the British Foreign Secretary Lord Peter Carrington as mediator, the warring parties negotiated for 13 weeks without a pause. Returning home just before Christmas, they carried to Salisbury the welcome news of a cease-fire, agreements on a transitional government, and settlement on a new constitution. For many Rhodesians, the possibility of genuine peace seemed incredible. Many thought whichever side lost in the elections slated for early in the new year would take to the battlefields again. General Peter Walls, commander of the Rhodesian Security Forces, was said to have a coup prepared in the event that the election turned against the white minority. The guerrilla forces of the Patriotic Front, led by nationalist leaders Robert Mugabe of ZANU and Joshua Nkomo of ZAPU,[8] were rumored to have kept men and weapons in reserve as well, outside the gathering points where the liberation armies were supposed to convene and lay down arms to a Commonwealth Monitoring Force of 1,500 men.

In February 1980, an independently monitored election was held, and ZANU leader Robert Mugabe won a clear majority. This was the outcome whites dreaded the most. Misled by the propaganda of Smith and Muzorewa, most had thought a Mugabe win highly unlikely; just in case he did win, however, many had packed their cars in readiness to leave the country immediately.[9] Their fears were understandable—their government had long portrayed Mugabe as a bloodthirsty, atheistic communist. ZANU's actions had not helped, either. Just over a year previously, a "death list" had circulated from ZANU headquarters in Maputo, naming individuals with government connections for execution.[10] Though surely a minority, some young militants confided in later years that as the brutal war drew to a close, they were waiting with "pangas in hand to kill every white in sight" if the word were given.[11]

What the citizens of Rhodesia, soon to become Zimbabwe, experienced on Tuesday, March 4, 1980, shocked people in all camps. Lord Christopher Soames, the British representative charged with governing the country during the transition period, announced on Tuesday morning that Mugabe had won. Soon thereafter, Ian Smith made a public announcement indicating that he accepted the election results. What is more, he had met personally with Mugabe and found him to be a "reasonable man." Smith added that he intended to stay in the country and recommended that others do so as well.[12] That evening Mugabe, Grim Reaper of the guerrilla war, addressed the nation. Zimbabweans, he said, must now "beat their swords into plow shares . . . I urge you," he said, "whether you are black or white to join me in a new phase to forget our grave past. Forgive others and forget. Join hands in a new amity and work together, Zimbabweans."[13]

Arriving in London with duties completed several months later, Lord Soames groped for words to explain what was taking place in Zimbabwe. "Every time we thought the thing would explode in our faces, some miracle came about," he reflected. "When we went out there I was not one who believed in miracles. I think I am reversing my position now."[14]

Without a doubt, something remarkable took place in 1979–80. Although there were tragic exceptions in later years, a generally peaceful outcome was attained in a situation that looked dismal.[15] What is more, religious influence was pervasive, not only in the historical development of the country—Jesuits played a key role in the early colonizing efforts of the British in the late 1800s, and the Roman Catholic Church provided moral blessing for the status quo until well into the 1950s—but also during this period, including in the personal lives of many key leaders in the conflict.[16] At the grass-roots level, liberation fighters turned in large numbers to spirit mediums for guidance and protection during the war,[17] while thousands of Christians participated in special days of prayer during the time of the Lancaster House talks and subsequent elections.[18]

Not only were religious influences explicitly present at all levels in the Rhodesia/Zimbabwe struggle, to an unusual degree religiously based peacemakers—virtually all Christian in orientation—were at work as well. Most prominent of these was the Catholic Commission for Justice and Peace, which, beginning in 1972, played an active role both within Rhodesia and internationally. Initially it functioned almost exclusively in the role of advocate, attacking the Salisbury regime for its abuses. But in 1978, as the war escalated and the suffering of civilians became intolerable, the commission, along with other Catholic agencies, mounted a global campaign to get the parties to the negotiating table.

Moral Re-Armament (MRA), a worldwide network of individuals committed to the concept of social and political change through personal transformation (see Chapter 4), was also extensively involved in the Rhodesia/Zimbabwe conflict from 1975 through 1980. MRA workers, in fact, arranged a final-hour, face-to-face meeting between Robert Mugabe and Ian Smith a day before the remarkable speeches of March 4, 1980. The spirit of reconciliation that astonished the world on that day is evidence, MRA workers believe, of the power of a spiritually-based approach to bring change.

Operating quietly from a London base, the Quakers were also deeply involved in negotiation efforts, plying skills grounded in a 300-year-old tradition of Christian pacifism and radical equality, and well-honed by several decades of nongovernmental peacemaking efforts. Like MRA, the Quakers had a team of workers present both at unsuccessful peace talks held in Geneva in 1976 and the 1979 Lancaster House negotiations. In between, Quaker teams made several trips to Africa, visiting government leaders in Salisbury, liberation leaders in Maputo and Lusaka, and leaders of the Frontline States,[19] seeking to get negotiations started.

THE ROLE OF THE CATHOLIC CHURCH

Largest, longest, and most complex of any religious response to the Rhodesia/Zimbabwe conflict was that of the Roman Catholic Church (hereafter the Church). There is good reason for this: Jesuit missionaries were among the first white settlers in the 1890s, and in the first half of the twentieth century Catholics erected most of the country's infrastructure of schools and hospitals. By the time the liberation struggle had begun, the Catholic Church claimed the allegiance of nearly 10 percent of the populace, in a nation in which 25 percent of the people are reckoned as Christian.

Until the 1950s, the Church assumed an uncritical role as sanctifier of the white-dominated status quo. Archbishop Aston Chichester, who headed the Church from 1931 till the mid-1950s, captured the spirit of the era in his consecration speech, expressing appreciation for "the fine relationship that existed between the Church and the civil authorities, for both were striving for the welfare of the same people." At public functions, the archbishop was accorded a special seat next to the British governor-general.

The 1950s brought the African nationalist movement, and for the first time Catholic leaders were confronted with an articulate challenge from their own laity. In 1959 came the first major reaction by the Rhodesian state against the nationalist movement: the government declared a state of emergency, banned the fledgling African National Congress, and detained 500 of its members.

But it was white right-wingers who in the end shook the Catholic Church out of its lethargic role as cosmic umbrella for the white government. Ian Smith's Rhodesia Front came to power in 1962, and in 1965 they announced a Unilateral Declaration of Independence from Britain. One motivation for this was perhaps garden-variety aspiration to self-rule. But Smith was open about another goal: he would save whites from the horrors of Kenya and the Congo by halting any advance toward majority rule by Africans. As Smith implemented one piece of racist legislation after another, the Catholic bishops reacted, issuing a series of pastoral letters that publicly confronted Rhodesian Front policies.

The year 1969 marked the beginning of a new era for the Catholic Church in Rhodesia, and the entry point for this study, for in that year Smith sought powers to impose the absolute separation of races on all church institutions. The Catholic Church, along with some Protestant counterparts, openly disobeyed, threatening to close its vast network of schools and hospitals.[20] Church and state compromised in the end: the state agreed not to enforce the act, and the churches agreed to withdraw their opposition. But from this point onward the Catholic Church became a persistent and aggressive critic of the Salisbury government.

Truth-Telling to the Nation and the World

The primary role of the Catholic Church was that of "truth-telling"—conveying the reality of what was happening in Rhodesia to the nation and the world. The context was a battle the Salisbury government was fighting, not only in the field but also in the media. "The government propaganda machine was advertising, publicizing the atrocities of the guerrillas wholesale and never admitting any of their own atrocities or [that they were] doing anything wrong at all," recalls one Catholic worker.[21] Central in the Catholic response was a long-distance liaison between two Catholic institutions—the Commission for Justice and Peace (JPC), based in Salisbury, and the Catholic Institute for International Relations (CIIR), based in London.

The bishops of Rhodesia established the Commission for Justice and Peace in 1972 to institutionalize their commitment to racial justice.[22] Initially dominated by whites and perceived as an extension of the Church hierarchy, the JPC soon established a reputation in its own right that ultimately overshadowed all other institutions in the large network of Catholic hierarchies, orders, and missions active in the country.

Listening to Victims. The foundation of JPC activities, especially in its early years, was listening to the victims of the war. As news of the commission filtered out through the townships to the Tribal Trust Lands in the early 1970s, writes one Catholic historian, "Africans grew to see in it a major means at their disposal to speak of their oppression." Villagers trekked long distances to Salisbury to tell the commission of their plight. "Often there was no thought of redress, simply the quest for someone who would listen, see the wounds, and understand what was happening in the guerrilla war. It was strangely not so much a quest for justice and peace as a quest for truth. And it was ultimately truth, rather than justice and peace, that the Commission achieved and will be remembered for."[23]

Many rural Catholic missionaries throughout the war were intimately connected to the agony of the communities they served, as much and more so than members of the JPC staff and board who were mostly Salisbury-based. Priests and sisters were increasingly radicalized by the stories brought to them daily by parishioners, and numbers of them openly sided with the liberation movements. The JPC relied heavily on this well-grounded and far-reaching "listening Church" (as it came to be known in contrast to the "teaching Church" based in traditional hierarchy) for access to the experiences of Africans in the townships and rural areas.

Confronting the State. Emboldened by the stories it was hearing, the JPC sent a Catholic delegation in March 1973 to Prime Minister Smith to "express concern over certain methods allegedly used by the Security Forces and the possible deterioration of race relations."[24] For a year the commission delayed further action, waiting for Smith and the minister of justice to act on the complaints of Security Force atrocities. When a second meeting with Smith in 1974 yielded no results, the commission began aggressively pursuing measures to bring the experiences of the people to whom they were listening into the public eye.

The JPC initially reached for domestic attention. In 1974 it provided documentation to a member of Parliament who called for an independent commission of inquiry into the conduct of the Security Forces. The JPC ran a large advertisement in the *Rhodesia Herald* supporting this call. It also compiled a dossier of Security Forces atrocities, which in an interdenominational "Appeal to Conscience" was sent to 500 prominent Rhodesians. The Catholic hierarchy backed up the appeal with a statement of its own.[25] Finally despairing of results at home, the JPC staff turned in 1975 to the outside world.

The London-Salisbury Connection. The JPC chose as its ally the London-based Catholic Institute for International Relations (CIIR). The fate of Rhodesia, after all, was subject to decisions in England, the legal ruler of the colony.[26] Thus, informing the British public and decisionmakers about the realities of Rhodesia became a critical aspect of the Catholic struggle against a racist regime. CIIR involvement on behalf of Rhodesia had begun in 1972, when it led an ecumenical justice for Rhodesia campaign. Over the next several years, the connection forged between Rhodesian Catholics and British policymakers via the JPC and CIIR proved pivotal, bringing events in Rhodesia "home to Whitehall, and the world, with a rapidity and accuracy that was acutely damaging to the image of the Rhodesian Front."[27]

In 1974 Smith escalated the war against the liberation armies. An aggressive counterinsurgency campaign moved villagers out of their home areas and sequestered them in centralized "protected villages." By the end of the year, 36 such camps existed, holding 70,000 people. These forced removals imposed enormous suffering on villagers. Occupants in many of the camps lived without water or sewage facilities and were unable to cultivate food. Catholics and Protestants organized relief—blankets, clothing, milk, and medical treatment.[28]

Publications. But the Catholics went beyond their Protestant counterparts. They published far and wide the ills they were treating. In May 1975, the CIIR published in London on behalf of the JPC *The Man in the Middle*, which described the plight of Rhodesian "protected" villagers. It also documented torture and indiscriminate killing of villagers by the Rhodesian Security Forces. These accounts were widely published in British daily newspapers and stirred great controversy in Salisbury.[29] In November 1976, again through the CIIR, the JPC published *Civil War in Rhodesia*, a further dossier of brutalities by the Defence Forces. Even more than the earlier book, this work received extensive press coverage in Europe and Canada.[30]

With an eye to influencing an Anglo-American peace initiative under way at the time, in 1977 the JPC published *Rhodesia: The Propaganda War*. This paper further detailed the devastating impact of the protected villages, as well as the widespread use of torture by Rhodesian Security Forces and the misuse of security legislation by the Salisbury government. "We prepared the papers because we felt that when Andrew Young and David Owen met with the government they would only hear one side," recalls Sister Janice McLaughlin, a Catholic nun deeply involved in writing the document. "We knew we weren't being balanced. We were only giving one side very deliberately because the other side was quite well presented and distorted by the government."[31]

Efforts by the Salisbury government to counter the truth-telling efforts of the JPC and CIIR only increased the pressure. For several years the JPC had pursued the minister of law and order in court for conduct of the war. With procedural delays exhausted, the state in September 1975 enacted the Indemnity and Compensation Act, sheltering government employees from liability for actions committed in the war.[32] This amounted to a virtual carte blanche from the Rhodesian Front to its military personnel regarding conduct in the field. Given the widespread and well-documented abuses already taking place, this desperate response only underscored the moral vacuity of the Salisbury government. The measure was met with increased pressure from domestic and overseas critics.

Following the Internal Settlement in 1978, an ill-fated alliance between a desperate Ian Smith and a compromising Abel Muzorewa,[33] press censorship in Rhodesia tightened even further. The country was isolated from more than superficial scrutiny by the outside world. "Reliable information about life in the war zones and protected villages now came almost exclusively through Church channels, often deported missionaries and Church workers."[34]

Once again the link to London via the CIIR proved decisive. "We had something the press didn't have," recalls the director of the CIIR in London at the time. Through the JPC and the Catholic network in Rhodesia, CIIR had "access to the situation on the ground that was denied the media."[35] Several London newspapers reprinted information provided by the CIIR from Rhodesian sources. The JPC and CIIR also jointly published several documents critically assessing the Internal Settlement.[36] These reports circulated widely and succeeded in influencing many British members of Parliament and strengthening the hand of British Foreign Secretary David Owen and American U.N. Ambassador Andrew Young in their opposition to the Internal Settlement.

Joint International Lobbying Efforts. The JPC and CIIR cooperated in lobbying efforts as well. As early as April 1972, the CIIR arranged a meeting between

Rhodesian Bishop Donal Lamont, prominent scourge of the Salisbury regime,[37] and British politicians. These included Prime Minister Wilson, Foreign Minister James Callaghan, and several members of Parliament.[38] Between 1975 and 1979, there was a steady stream of Catholic delegations to London and other capitals. On a second trip in 1975, Lamont visited London, France, and Germany, where he met statesmen and lectured to large audiences. In the same year, the JPC hosted a visit to Rhodesia by the secretary-general of the International Commission of Jurists.[39] In 1978 and again in 1979, Catholic delegations traveled to London and Washington to caution against acceptance of the Internal Settlement and lifting of sanctions.[40] Additionally, the JPC mobilized a major international lobbying effort in 1979 (see p. 218) to pressure all parties to engage in negotiations.

Voice of Moral Conscience. The Church also sought to serve as a voice of moral conscience for the country. The Catholic bishops, often assisted by the JPC, released 10 pastoral statements between 1961 and 1980 calling for racial justice and, as the war escalated, for principled behavior on the part of the combatants.[41]

The thrust of the bishops' statements, as well as the JPC truth-telling campaign, was largely directed against the Rhodesian state, which did not take kindly to criticism from its most powerful religious constituent. The Catholic Church was a frequent target of attack in the press and Parliament, and Catholic workers were often harassed by the Security Forces. In February 1977, Salisbury deported the fiery Bishop Lamont, long the most outspoken of his brethren.[42] Between 1976 and 1980, 17 other Catholics were also deported.[43]

But Catholic structures addressed the liberation forces as well. In December 1976, the bishops publicly deplored guerrilla atrocities, and in the same month, during the Geneva talks, the JPC sent a private memorandum "To all the African Nationalist Leaders in Geneva." The letter expressed "grave concern about the apparently growing incidence of guerrilla atrocities," noting as an example that burial had been denied certain victims. The letter was received "with cold hostility" by members of the two liberation armies in Geneva.[44]

Later, during mediation efforts in 1978, the Catholic delegation again raised the issue with Mugabe and Nkomo of atrocities committed by liberation forces, and urged that special measures be undertaken to avoid harm to civilians.[45] On this occasion Mugabe admitted the occurrence of atrocities due to the difficulties of maintaining discipline over remote groups of guerrillas, stated his regret, and requested that the Church bring any future cases that arose to his attention.[46]

Advocate of Negotiations

Awareness of the massive scale of human suffering prompted a shift in emphasis in 1977 within the Commission for Justice and Peace, a shift that placed the JPC and the Catholic hierarchy in the new role of actively advocating for negotiations. "We decided that because the suffering was so great in the country, the suffering of all people, black and white, whether they deserved it or not . . . , our direction must now be toward actively searching for peace," recalls then-JPC Secretary Michael Auret.[47]

In December 1977, JPC staff sought to arrange a meeting involving representatives of the bishops and the JPC with the liberation organizations. The archbishop of Maputo and the apostolic delegate in Lusaka were contacted to explore such a meeting, but the initiative became mired in Church protocol.[48] In 1978 the JPC called upon the CIIR in London to initiate contacts with the two liberation movements. In July the bishops publicly added their weight to the effort by calling for all-party talks and offering their services "to do whatever we can to assist in the process of reconciliation." After weeks of effort, arrangements were finally made for a delegation to meet ZANU and ZAPU in their respective headquarters.

On August 13, 1978, a six-person delegation traveled to Lusaka, where they met with Nkomo and visited with Zambian President Kaunda.[49] Accompanied by Nkomo, they also visited Zimbabwe House, a resource center for exiles from Rhodesia, and refugee camps of black Rhodesians who had fled the war. A few days later the delegation met with Mugabe, who was traveling through Lusaka from talks in Nigeria.[50] With both leaders the delegation focused on the extent of the suffering in the country, and the primary message was "we must move toward peace."[51] The delegation made it clear that they would be conveying the same message to the internal leaders as well.

One result of these meetings was "to reinforce the commitment of the Commission to act as a force for reconciliation."[52] A series of meetings followed in quick succession. The delegation met in Salisbury with three leaders of the Internal Settlement government—Ndabaningi Sithole, Abel Muzorewa, and Chief J. S. Chirau—to explore the possibility of an all-party conference. The fourth leader, Ian Smith, refused to meet and sent instead Deputy Prime Minister David Smith.[53] They met as well with two top army commanders, Peter Walls and Sandy McLean, stressing the desperateness of the situation and urging that they use their influence with the government to end the war. In September 1978, two Catholic representatives traveled to London and met with Foreign Secretary Owen "to underline the gravity of the situation."[54]

In addition, as requested by the Patriotic Front leadership, the Church devoted greater attention "to the growing problem of refugees outside the country in camps in Mozambique, Botswana, and Zambia."[55] Mike Traber, a priest with many close friendships in top ZANU circles, went to Maputo and helped set up the Zimbabwe Project, which responded to the needs of Rhodesians fleeing the violence in their homeland. Traber also secured Mugabe's permission to place a Catholic worker in the camps of the ZANU forces.

But in the weeks after the meetings with the political leaders, the possibility of negotiations appeared more remote than ever. The Executive Committee of ZANU, whose army accounted for 85 percent of the guerrillas operating inside Rhodesia, refused to meet with Smith unless the British foreign secretary, legally the representative for Rhodesia, was also present.[56] What is more, long-simmering tensions between ZANU and ZAPU flared into the open at a meeting of the Frontline States in September. To make matters worse, while the Frontline States were still in session, Nkomo's forces shot down a commercial Air Rhodesia Viscount aircraft and then slaughtered 10 of the 18 survivors on the ground. Government troops had in the past visited massacres on a far larger scale on Africans, of course. But the white reaction in Rhodesia and abroad was visceral horror.

The war continued to escalate. In October Rhodesian forces raided Nkomo's camps in Zambia, killing 1,500 people.[57] In addition to the government forces, there now roamed, virtually at will, private armies established by Muzorewa, Chirau, and Sithole. In some areas, five different sets of African militias fought for control.[58] As a direct result of the war, for the first time in recent memory, Rhodesians began dying from famine.

Meeting with the Pope. Despairing of results from efforts to work directly with the political leaders involved, the JPC shifted course and moved once again to the world stage in a truth-telling role. The goal: "to alert world opinion to the tragedy of an anarchic collapse into famine and increased bloodshed."[59]

Circumventing protocols that normally required six weeks' advance contact, staff at the Vatican arranged an urgent meeting with Pope John Paul II on a few days' notice in early April 1979.[60] Two Rhodesian bishops and a JPC staff member urged the prelate to use Vatican influence to pressure all parties to enter negotiations. The pope responded vigorously to their plea. Before the three left Rome, he had contacted diplomats in Italy, the United States, Britain, France, and Germany[61] and called in the British representative to the Vatican to urge British intervention in Rhodesia. Individuals from the trio followed up with personal visits to diplomats in Germany, Britain, and the United States and found in each case that the pope's contact had left a mark. The message to Western diplomats was the same as to parties themselves: the suffering must end. The goal of the lobbying was "pressure, more pressure on Smith, more pressure on the guerrilla forces to negotiate."[62]

In August 1979, the breakthrough came. At the Commonwealth Conference in Lusaka, British Prime Minister Margaret Thatcher encountered virtually unanimous opposition from the Commonwealth Nations to her oft-reiterated position of support for the Muzorewa government. Bowing to a consensus forged by the joint efforts of President Julius Nyerere of Tanzania and Prime Minister Malcolm Fraser of Australia, Thatcher agreed to reject the Internal Settlement government and to convene a constitutional convention under British auspices as soon as possible.

Lancaster House and the Transition Period. Catholics were in the background at Lancaster House and sought no direct role in the negotiations. But staff from the CIIR picked up their previous role as truth-teller and published five public briefing documents on key issues.[63] For their part the Bishops Conference issued a public appeal to all leaders "to put the good of the whole nation before personal or party interests, for the sake of the people's suffering."[64]

During the transition period between the Lancaster House settlement and the elections, the JPC and observers sent from CIIR in London used their intimate knowledge of the country and access to key leaders to support the tenuous peace. Lord Soames, sent from England to serve as governor of the country until the election, held the unenviable task of maintaining order in a political tinderbox with a small Commonwealth Monitoring Force. Several bombings, multiple assassination attempts on the life of Mugabe, roving bands of armed men, and ceaseless rumors threatened to plunge the country at any moment into warfare. Soames relied in part on the corps of international observers present to inform his decisions. Lord Chitness and Eileen Sudworth, British observers sent by the CIIR, drew extensively on Church knowledge and resources in assisting other observers, providing transportation, arranging for observers to meet key people, and writing reports for the press.[65]

There were persistent reports of misconduct by armed men in the northern and eastern regions of Rhodesia. Soames had been told that Mugabe's army was responsible, and he threatened several times to take action against them. But from their extensive networks, Catholic observers knew that the perpetrators were not Mugabe's forces, but rather the auxiliary forces of Muzorewa. In what was perhaps the most assertive Catholic intervention, Archbishop Chakaipa took this information to Soames, who accepted it as credible and ended his criticism of Mugabe's army.[66]

Partisan and Victim Roles. At no time was it official Church policy to support the war effort of either side, but in reality large amounts of Catholic resources contributed to the support of both sides. Individuals and in some instances groups of Catholic workers actively supported the guerrilla cause. Some of the rural Catholic missions provided medicine, food, clothing, money, and rest to the guerrillas.[67] Notable here were the Burgos Fathers, a Spanish-based order still radicalized by their experience with the fascists in Spain, and with an emphasis on living simply in close connection to the people they served. Many in this order "actively supported the guerrillas and were positively hostile to the Security Forces."[68] One Catholic worker interviewed six amputees at random at a Red Cross unit in Maputo and discovered that all six ZANU-affiliated soldiers owed their lives to Catholic missionaries, each in a different incident.[69]

A minority of Catholic workers, on the other hand, openly supported the government. A substantial number of the Marianhill missionaries and some of the German Jesuits "saw the war as a struggle between the State and terrorism" and maintained friendly contacts with the Security Forces.[70] What is more, decades of coziness between church and state had established conventions of cooperation that the Church never challenged. The Catholic Church provided chaplains for the Security Forces throughout the war and never reciprocated with the guerrilla forces.[71] Though Lamont denounced the legitimacy of the state, neither he nor others in the hierarchy ever called for a boycott of payment of taxes. Catholic laypeople thus were a large and compliant source of funding of the war efforts of the Salisbury government throughout.[72]

Combatants on both sides of the conflict perceived the Church as partisan, and consequently Church workers and institutions suffered severely. The national network of Catholic schools, missions, and hospitals put Catholic workers at great risk. Between December 1976 and February 1980, a total of 25 Catholic expatriate missionaries were killed, and 18 were deported.[73] Nineteen Catholic-run secondary schools and an even larger number of primary schools were closed as a result of harassment by guerrilla forces.[74] The Rhodesian Security Forces, of course, had been hostile from the early stages of Catholic opposition. Putting a gun behind one African priest's ear, a member of the Security Forces gave a command that seemed to capture a common attitude: "You black bastard, speak up. One dead missionary is better than one hundred dead terrorists."[75]

Summary. When it came to conversation with top-level leaders, the role that most frequently characterized Catholic responses was the voice of morality. Church representatives either stressed the immense scale of human suffering or they appealed for more humane conduct of the war by the fighting forces. Even the major effort in mid-1978 to get talks started was pitched at the level of moral concern. A delegation of six was sent, which in itself implied an intent to register a message with the parties rather than to attempt the more facilitative tasks of practical negotiation where one or two are quite enough to accomplish the purpose of the meeting. No effort was made to convey messages between parties or to draw the parties into the practical issues of "getting to the table." Similarly, in the 1979 effort, the JPC staff members made no effort to work through the parties. They went directly to outside pressure groups. In short, Catholics were lobbyists on behalf of moral concerns, not mediators.

Assessment of Catholic Involvement

Because the target audience of Catholic involvements was so vast—the entire public sphere in Rhodesia and concerned countries abroad—it would be impossible to measure the full impact of the Catholic efforts. But leaders in present-day Zimbabwe credit the Catholic Church for a major contribution. In 1980 President Robert Mugabe commented:

> I think the Catholic Church played a very significant role in the liberation struggle. Not that they fought with arms as we did, but they opposed racialism, and refused to be made an agent of the Government implementing racial policies. We valued the support which the Church gave us as it helped to internationalize our grievances and helped to mobilize international support for us. Within the country it gave us a broader base than the one which we ourselves, acting entirely on our own, could have created.[76]

Canaan Banana, the former president and preeminent historian of the Rhodesia/Zimbabwe struggle, concluded in a 1989 essay that the JPC "played an invaluable role of publicising and condemning the excesses of the Rhodesian army in its conduct of the war. In this way atrocities of the Rhodesian security forces were effectively disclosed and the psychological warfare counteracted."[77]

For the scholar of conflict resolution, the Catholic involvements are a remarkable study in the potential and limitations of a religious organization to contribute to the resolution of a national conflict. The Church's roles as truth-teller, voice of moral conscience, and advocate of negotiations depended on each of several key attributes.

At the heart of the Catholic contribution lay a value system in which survival and power were not the ultimate goal, but rather faithfulness to transcendent values that included justice, truthfulness, and service to others. These values led Catholic workers to enter into engagement with victims of the war, and only as a result of this engagement were Catholic workers able to see and act on the issues destroying the people of Rhodesia. But Catholics did not merely see the issues; their far-flung church system provided an unparalleled information-gathering network, making it possible to compile information essential for mobilizing domestic and world opinion. When it came to influencing decisionmakers, the Catholic efforts depended on an international structure for collecting, analyzing, and disseminating information and ready entrée to political figures and media channels, domestically and abroad.

With the possible exception of the first, none of these attributes is "religious" per se, but in Rhodesia, the Catholic Church was the only institution that embodied all of them. In this regard, the case study illustrates the Church at her best potential for peacemaking.

A fundamental part of the problem in the Rhodesia/Zimbabwe struggle was the apathy of the white ruling elite to the injustices of their own government. Like ruling elites elsewhere, they believed their own government's propaganda. Rhodesia thus demonstrated a generic problem: the opiate of patriotism makes it harder for citizens to see the moral issues at stake in national conflicts with the clarity available to those at a distance. The Catholic Church, like other white-led churches and institutions in Rhodesia, was for many years lethargic in the face of massive injustice. But two fundamental differences set Catholics apart from other churches:

1. Catholic ecclesiology supports a global rather than a national orientation by placing final fiscal, theological, and organizational authority in an extranational agency, the Vatican.
2. The worldwide Catholic Church was in the midst of a major renewal at every level in the aftermath of Vatican II, and one result of the renewal was an unprecedented commitment to supporting efforts to achieve structural justice. (See the Philippines case study, Chapter 8 in this volume.)

Consequently, the individuals within Rhodesian Catholic structures who challenged the injustice of their political system had access to a massive global structure that "leveraged" their efforts, even though they were a minority in their country and, initially at least, within their own church. At the individual level, Bishop Lamont and priests more radical than he were buoyed by the trends of the global Catholic Church in confronting the many in Catholic structures who supported Salisbury. At the institutional level, the Commission for Justice and Peace found a ready and powerful ally in the London-based Catholic Institute for International Relations long before many Rhodesian Catholics supported a position that, to blind patriots, looked subversive. To the extent, then, that injustice imposed by ruling elites is part of a conflict—and surely it is in many national conflicts—the Catholic Church in Rhodesia demonstrates the potential of religious organizations to cut through the lethargy of blind patriotism to a genuinely moral basis of analysis and action.

On the other hand, the case also demonstrates the limits of a massive, institution-bound religious structure as a base of response to conflict. In Rhodesia the Church had for decades cultivated a cozy alliance with the state. In providing a "cosmic umbrella" for an unjust social and political structure, the Church stood culpable as a contributing cause of the war. As individuals and agencies within the Church finally began awakening to reality, they faced debilitating resistance from within the Church itself to confronting the actions of the state. Though the Church found her way in the end to outspoken resistance to white privilege, one must ask why it took so long. African nationalism was already rocking the Catholic boat in the early 1950s, but it was not until 1969 that the Catholic bishops disengaged themselves from the embrace of the state, and it was not until 1972 that they established the Commission for Justice and Peace as a structure for responding to the racial injustices that undergirded the society. Even then, these actions came only after much anguished debate, arousing enormous ambivalence among the bishops and great resistance within the Church.

Thus, if the global orientation and networking capacity of international Catholic structures proved an enormous asset in mobilizing a response to the Rhodesian conflict, the institutional inertia and patriotic bent of domestic Catholics nearly paralyzed the initial responses. It took many years for the Church to come to a point of sufficient clarity about its own moral position that it could begin mobilizing its far-flung resources effectively.

As will be seen in the case of the Quakers, the roles undertaken by the Catholic Church could perhaps have been undertaken by another actor. But no organization without a spiritual identity could have had an impact comparable to that of the Catholic Church. The point here is that it may not be the roles and responses per se that are the key to understanding what religiously based actors do. The key may lie instead in the *identity* of the religious actors and their resulting credibility in the eyes of the parties, as well as, in this case, in the power that the Catholic Church wielded to influence public opinion at home and abroad.

MORAL RE-ARMAMENT

Salisbury in February 1980 crackled with tension. Lancaster House had yielded a peace plan two months previously, but the real test of the settlement was now at hand. Elections had just taken place and, after several days of vote counting, the results were about to be announced. Rumors swirled about what each group planned to do if it lost. Whites were counting on Muzorewa to win the election and finally gain the recognition denied him in 1978 under the abortive Internal Settlement. But it was widely known that General Peter Walls of the Security

Forces had a coup prepared to intervene in the event that the election turned out differently than expected.

On the other hand, many had also heard, and believed, reports that Mugabe's guerrilla fighters were no longer in the agreed holding zones. The word was that they were quietly moving out in preparation for battle and were being replaced by *mujibas*, young, less-experienced guerrillas.[78] Cuban troops were said to be just over the border in Beira, Mozambique, with tanks and weapons, and the Nigerians allegedly had 19,000 troops waiting at airstrips in the event of a white takeover or South African intervention. At the request of the Rhodesians, South Africa had placed a small army unit on the Rhodesian side of Beitbridge. "Everybody had their contingency plans," recalls one Moral Re-Armament worker. "It appeared to us that whoever won the election, we were back into confrontation."[79]

A sober group of MRA workers—the Cabinet of Conscience, as they had come to call themselves—gathered on Saturday morning at the end of election week to assess the situation. The moment of truth was nearing, for on Tuesday the election results would be announced. The fate of the country, not to mention the lives and future of their families, seemed to hang in the balance. After lengthy discussion yielded no way forward, Joram Kucherera, a member of the group with personal and family connections to ZANU, stood and said he knew what must happen. "Two people have to meet—Smith and Mugabe. There's no other way."[80] Others doubted the possibility of such an event, but agreed it wouldn't hurt to try.

Kucherera, who had been laying the groundwork for such a meeting, contacted a cousin who was a senior aide to Mugabe. To his surprise, the response was positive. Kucherera then rang Alec Smith, son of the prime minister and key member of the MRA group. Over the last several years Alec had arranged numerous meetings between his father and individual nationalists, so the invitation to meet with Mugabe could hardly have come as a complete shock to the elder Smith.

Both sides were interested in a meeting, but wary.[81] The elder Smith insisted on meeting personally with Kucherera and sought clarification from the Mugabe side about the agenda before agreeing to the meeting. For their part, Mugabe and his top aides undertook a quick series of consultations with their allies: Mugabe flew to Dar es Salaam to consult with President Nyerere, and Kucherera himself was asked to meet at Mugabe's house with a representative of Mozambican President Samora Machel to gain that country's support.[82]

Though frightened by the thought that his bold venture to get the two leaders together could easily end in the loss of his own life, Kucherera felt he was undertaking a divine mission and made no secret of what he saw as the source of his inspiration. Told in an exploratory session that the idea of a meeting was a "thought from God," a skeptical Emmerson Munangagwa, Mugabe's head of security, shot back, "You think God fixes things like this? A meeting with Ian Smith?" But Mugabe himself saw no need to challenge Kucherera's assertion that "this country needs a miracle."[83] What Kucherera offered was something the Mugabe camp keenly sought—low-visibility access to Ian Smith via Kucherera's trusted friend, Alec. After several days of almost round-the-clock meetings, both sides gave their approval.

Two and a half days after the MRA group had met, the man who had squandered the lives of thousands and the economy of his nation to destroy Mugabe and his fellow African nationalists was driven by Kucherera in an aging Morris Minor automobile to ZANU headquarters. Accompanied only by Kucherera, Smith walked past 50 tense and heavily armed guards into the house. "Let's get rid of him now," shouted a brash young guerrilla, raising his rifle. A senior commander of the ZANU forces turned, and with the butt of his own weapon, sent the young man sprawling. Inside the house, Mugabe invited Smith to sit next to him on a couch, and for the next several hours, the two men talked about the future of the nation.

Both had been tipped off regarding the expected outcome of the election, so they entered the meeting aware that in less than 24 hours Mugabe would be announced the winner. In the meeting, Mugabe indicated that, as a civilian leader, he would approach things differently than he had as leader of a liberation army, and he outlined policies he intended to pursue. He stressed his eagerness to retain the confidence of whites and inquired from Smith what measures would be necessary to do so. Mugabe also put an offer on the table: Smith would be welcome to nominate two white ministers to serve in Mugabe's cabinet.

The following morning, Tuesday, March 4, came the public announcement of the election results followed by Smith's astonishingly positive response, encouraging fellow whites to stay. That evening Mugabe made his famous "reconciliation speech."[84] A few weeks later, with the political transition process nearing its completion, Prime Minister Mugabe reiterated the theme: "If yesterday I fought you as an enemy, today I have become a friend and ally. If yesterday you hated me, today you cannot avoid the love that binds you to me and me to you."[85]

MRA Beliefs

MRA has no creed or dogmas. God is assumed to exist and to be actively involved in implementing a just and loving masterplan for the world.[86] Beyond these fundamental assumptions, MRA workers and literature reflect little interest in prescribing "correct belief." The closest the organization comes to doctrine is a belief in "four absolute standards": honesty, purity, unselfishness, and love. To the extent that individuals apply these standards to their life, it is believed, they will find themselves and their relationships transformed. To the extent that leaders apply these standards to their personal and public lives, society will be transformed.

But what, specifically, does "absolute love" demand? Where ethicists write books in answer, MRA leaves the problem to the individual. Such a response could appear to be sheer abandonment, but MRA points to some assistance: the traditions of various religious faiths, the insights of others, and divine guidance. Recurrent in MRA literature is the call to "listen to God." God is in charge of the world, and any individual who listens will find that God speaks, giving guidance about what needs to be done. Active MRA workers and supporters typically spend at least 20 minutes each day alone in "quiet time," "listening" for "thoughts" about what to do. Often these thoughts are about individual actions to set aright one's own life and relationships, which MRA stresses as the place where genuine change of any kind must begin. But as one's own life comes aright, God will also prompt the individual with thoughts about actions needed to effect God's purposes in the world. The Mugabe-Smith meeting and the Reader-Chavunduka partnership (described later) are examples MRA workers would cite here.

MRA in Rhodesia

MRA was active in southern Africa from 1928 onward,[87] holding conferences and workshops in South Africa and Rhodesia. MRA workers in the 1970s were surprised to discover that numerous liberation front leaders, including Nkomo and Mugabe, already knew about the organization. Nkomo, like many black Africans, held positive views from his encounters with MRA in the 1950s, for MRA had already then challenged individual whites to change their racist attitudes. Mugabe had seen MRA films as a student and told an MRA worker in 1976 he respected the organization's concept of beginning with mending one's own ways as the key to healing relationships. But he held serious reservations. The idea "works in the family, and also in society," he said, but "it doesn't work in politics . . . They are the oppressors and we are the oppressed. If we change our attitude, nothing happens. We've tried it."[88]

After influencing the lives of thousands of young people in southern Africa in the 1940s and 1950s, MRA faded. By 1970 activities in Rhodesia had dwindled to personal visits by a handful of retirees. "My first contact with MRA was at a quaint old house in Salisbury and nobody in the room was under 75 years old," recalls Alec Smith, a key figure in the revival of MRA in Rhodesia. But as Smith soon discovered, the MRA people possessed a major asset: they had "built up a network of friendships across society that laid the basis for everything [that followed]."[89]

Smith's involvement with the small and aging group of pensioners began in 1974 and led in a remarkably short time to the reactivation of MRA in Rhodesia. He was on the rebound himself from a decade of vintage 1960s-style rebellion. Alcohol and other drugs, partying, and dismissal from Rhodes University in South Africa all figured in a past of which Smith had now wearied. A few months prior to encountering MRA, he had experienced a profound personal religious conversion. Awakened for the first time to the painful realities of war-torn Rhodesia, he was convinced that God was able to bring about great change in the lives of human beings, and he was filled with a burning desire to carry this message to his own countryfolk. An MRA film about Dr. William Nkomo from Pretoria, the first president of the African National Congress Youth League in South Africa, had deeply impressed Smith. Nkomo was a committed MRA supporter who had overcome bitterness through his own experience of God, and who traveled widely in Europe and Africa, challenging audiences with fundamental MRA concepts: to begin living by absolute moral standards, to hand over control of their lives to God, and to listen to Him for guidance.[90]

Impressed by the Nkomo account and the MRA vision for rebuilding broken societies through individual renewal, Alec Smith took up an active role in MRA. Others were becoming active at the same time, including Sir Cyril Hatty, a former government cabinet member, and Dr. Elliot Gabellah, vice-president of Rhodesia's African National Congress. Meeting regularly and groping for a way to reach their countrymen with a message they felt offered the only possibility of a peaceful future, the group decided to convene an international MRA conference in Salisbury.

The event, held in June 1975, drew more than 1,000 participants and laid the groundwork for MRA work in Rhodesia for the next five years. Among those present were four cabinet members from the Smith government, as well as a delegation from the opposition United African National Congress (UANC), whose leader, Bishop Muzorewa, was out of the country at the time but sent a message of support.[91] Several individuals who later numbered among MRA's most active workers encountered the organization for the first time at this conference.

One key relationship that resulted was a close friendship between Alec Smith and Arthur Kanodereka, an African nationalist. At the conference Smith spoke with deep feeling about fellow Rhodesians being driven in desperation to fight in the bush for liberation. "It's people like me who have sent them there," confessed the son of the prime minister before the whole assembly. "For my part, I am deeply sorry for the thoughtlessness of my past life and I have now committed myself to finding a solution for our country, to building bridges of reconciliation, and to showing the rest of Africa that black and white can live together. That, under God, there is an answer."[92]

Alec's speech stirred a response in Kanodereka, a Methodist minister who, deeply embittered by his experiences with whites, was now a recruiter of young men into the guerrilla forces. Kanodereka was touched by Smith's words and invited him to come to his church to speak. A friendship resulted, and the two began addressing audiences together on a regular basis. Kanodereka also began holding weekly meetings in his congregation to enable blacks and whites to dialogue together. On occasion, as many as 800 people attended at a time.

Smith and Kanodereka traveled widely in Rhodesia and to South Africa as well, offering, in classic MRA style, first-person accounts of their own experiences of the power of God to bring change and reconciliation. They challenged listeners to set aright their own lives in accordance with the four absolute standards as a first step toward finding God's plan for themselves and the nation. Until Kanodereka's assassination in December 1978,[93] the pair were by far the most visible in MRA activities in Rhodesia.

But a larger nucleus stood just behind them. At the heart of MRA activities between 1975 and 1980 was the group that came to be known as the Cabinet of Conscience. Meeting eight to 10 times a year for much of this period, the "Cabinet" served partly as a central strategy-planning group, partly as a place of encounter and dialogue for people of diverse backgrounds, and partly as a forum for confronting individuals with the call to change their own lives according to the four absolute standards.

The core group was small—less than a dozen.[94] They were also poorly balanced: they were more white than black, more reliably connected to government than to black nationalist circles, and better connected to Muzorewa and other

Internal Settlement leaders willing to strike a compromise with the Smith regime than to the leaders of ZANU and ZAPU.[95] But they were ambitious and deeply committed. They carried a message of reconciliation both challenging and hopeful at a time when the nation was weary of war. Perhaps most important, on a continent where personal relationships often transcend politics and ideology, they were tireless in cultivating friendships across the political spectrum.

As a result of all these factors, Moral Re-Armament was on the scene of most of the critical political events affecting Rhodesia between 1976 and 1980, and MRA workers interacted with many of the key players on the political stage over this time, in several cases at substantial depth. During this period, from four to eight people, more than half of them volunteers from England and Scotland, worked full-time for MRA in a variety of activities.[96]

Promoting Reconciliation Between Key Individuals. MRA teaches that individual change is the key to social change. Thus bringing individuals of diverse backgrounds together for face-to-face encounters formed the heart of MRA activities. MRA strategies to accomplish this were diverse and creative.

Providing the foundation for many of MRA's activities in Rhodesia was the MRA conference, an event refined through long MRA experience elsewhere to a unique blend of inspiration, admonition, and confession, all conveyed in the genre of the personal narrative. It was to such an event, the gathering described above, that Alec Smith and others turned in 1974 to put MRA "on the map." MRA workers in Rhodesia also took advantage of the large international MRA conferences, held every year in Caux, Switzerland, for bridge-building purposes of their own. Over the critical period 1975–79, MRA took delegations of 10 to 20 Rhodesians every year to Caux. In 1979, one such group spent a week in Caux before continuing on to London for the Lancaster House talks.

In addition to the large Caux gatherings, Rhodesians attended a shorter regional conference that took place every year in southern Africa. MRA workers held small workshops every few months in Rhodesia as well, seeking to apply MRA principles to family life, education, industrial relations, and so on.

Another innovative strategy for interpersonal encounter was dinner parties. Desmond Reader, a senior academic at the University of Rhodesia, was prompted during a morning "quiet time" to apologize to an African colleague for underestimating his abilities and underemploying him. Gordon Chavunduka, the man in question, responded warmly; his work and the relationship were transformed as a result. This experience brought the two men into deeper conversation, and they began working together on a series of lunches and dinner parties to bring together people who were, in Reader's words, "extreme opposites." Chavunduka was secretary-general of the African National Congress and thus had access to a variety of internal nationalist leaders. A dozen dinners or so were held in 1975–76, each involving perhaps 20 people. Among the guests were several members of Ian Smith's Cabinet and prominent African National Congress leaders.[97]

MRA also set up several one-on-one encounters among key leaders with the intent of destroying stereotypes and fostering new attitudes. The high-stakes, eleventh-hour meeting between Mugabe and Smith, which opens this section, provides the most dramatic example of MRA's use of interpersonal encounters. But there were others, among them the following:

- Every six to eight months over a several-year period, MRA workers took people connected to political rivals of Ian Smith to visit the prime minister.[98] Usually these were arranged by Alec Smith. On two occasions, Alec Smith took his friend and MRA co-worker, Arthur Kanodereka, to have tea with his parents. These meetings, Alec felt, were a precedent for the elder Smith, who had previously never invited blacks on a social basis into his home. On the first occasion, after Kanodereka and his wife had departed, the prime minister thanked his son and commented: "If all black nationalists were like him, I'd have no trouble turning over the country tomorrow."[99]
- Kanodereka had a similar impact on Minister of Law and Order Hilary Squires. MRA arranged a meeting between the two in early 1976 in which Kanodereka, then treasurer of the UANC and thus a key leader in the internal nationalist camp, recounted his personal struggle with bitterness against whites. Squires was visibly impressed. "I've never seen such a change in a man's attitude in my life," recalls Tom Glenn, the MRA worker who arranged the meeting. Later that year during the Geneva Conference, Squires and Kanodereka held several additional meetings. From that point on, Kanodereka was able to secure permission for public meetings of the UANC with a mere phone call to Squires.[100]
- A few weeks prior to the Mugabe-Smith meeting, an MRA team went to visit officials at Mugabe's headquarters. One member of the group, a former secretary of foreign affairs under Smith, broke the ice after a tense beginning by sharing his struggle with the near-loss of a son injured in the war. A top ZANU official, the man who was instrumental in setting up the meeting a few weeks later between Mugabe and Smith, was deeply touched and responded by sharing his own experience of picking the body of his brother out of the trenches after a battle between Rhodesian Security Forces and ZANU.
- At the Geneva Conference in 1976, MRA was present and set up several meetings—albeit of no apparent consequence—between members of Smith's delegation and leaders of the UANC.[101]
- Aware that Ian Smith harbored bitterness toward the British for what he regarded as dishonesty and broken promises regarding Rhodesian independence, MRA workers arranged a meeting between Smith and several senior British diplomats who in their personal capacity apologized for British actions.[102]

Moral Discourse with Public Figures. The second major category into which MRA activities fell was efforts to inject moral principles into the decision-making process of key political leaders and, to a limited extent, of the public as well. "In order to build a new society, you must have people who are willing to begin with themselves," was the way Alec Smith summarized a key MRA assumption.[103] Henry Macnicol, described by some as the central strategist of MRA activities in Rhodesia, believes "you can change the system all you like but unless you change the hearts of men, you're changing nothing."[104] Yet another MRA worker put it this way: "If you change the attitude of one person, he begins to change society if he's a prominent person."[105]

Thus MRA hoped to support social change, but sought to do so by way of individual change. Whether engaging in private prayer sessions with Abel Muzorewa, meeting with aides of Joshua Nkomo, or arranging a one-on-one encounter between Robert Mugabe and Ian Smith, MRA workers maintained a clear, if often unspoken, agenda.[106] Their task was to enable individuals to listen to God. This would lead to a change of heart and to clarity about the "right" thing to do. And if leaders would get themselves oriented in the right direction, society must follow. MRA strategies for engaging leaders were several and varied, as discussed in the following paragraphs.

1. Dedicated pursuit of personal friendships formed the heart of MRA activities. Alec Smith, of course, related to his father extensively throughout the period and had many conversations with him about the issues he faced as prime minister.[107]

Another significant relationship was with Bishop Muzorewa, with whom several MRA workers met from the early 1970s onward. Senior MRA worker Henry Macnicol recalls accompanying Arthur Kanodereka in 1978 to visit Muzorewa after an embittering incident with the British. Muzorewa had been left out of a meeting with the liberation front leaders because, he was told by the British, he had no army. Concerned about the obvious temptation this offered for Muzorewa to establish his own army,[108] Macnicol and an accompanying MRA worker visited at some length with Muzorewa. At the end of the visit the three knelt and prayed and Muzorewa "thanked God for these men who have come to call me to my Christian faith."[109]

At Lancaster House in 1979, Macnicol and Hugh Elliott, a London-based MRA worker who knew Muzorewa from visits to Rhodesia, again met with Muzorewa. Elliott shared a "word from God" he felt that he had received specially for the bishop in "quiet time" that day. "Bishop," he told Muzorewa, "you just fight this election [the upcoming campaign in February 1980] as the man the people trust to be a man of God, and on the basis of love but not hate."[110]

MRA teams were present at both the failed Geneva Conference as well as Lancaster House and actively sought opportunities to interact with the negotiators in these critical meetings. At Geneva, Macnicol and Kanodereka (at that time still on the Executive Committee of the UANC) had breakfast several times with UANC leaders to discuss the negotiations. The king and queen of Romania joined one of these breakfasts to share insights from their personal struggle with bitterness in the aftermath of exile from fascist and communist governments.[111]

At Lancaster House, members of the eight-person MRA delegation had numerous late-night conversations with members of the negotiating teams.[112] A common theme was the concern of the MRA workers that a settlement be reached. These meetings often took place without an explicit MRA identification. For example, the head of the African Farmers' Union stayed at the Moral Re-Armament House and, due to extensive prior relationships, MRA workers viewed him as part of the MRA "team." He arranged a meeting with Mugabe in his role as head of the Farmers' Union, not as a representative of MRA. Mugabe responded with great surprise and concern to the accounts of personal suffering among villagers offered to him.[113]

But it would be misleading to suggest that MRA workers established friend-ships with an agenda restricted to moral concern. MRA team members sought, particularly at the time of the Geneva and Lancaster House conferences, to support individual members of the negotiating teams on a personal basis.

Ian Smith, for example, was invited to the MRA guest house in London during the Lancaster House process and came, commenting later to son Alec that "it was such a change to come to that house." The MRA workers sought to create an atmosphere where the senior Smith "could relax like he was amongst friends."[114] Concerned about Smith's status as a pariah in London—other politicians on the scene were so reluctant about being in the same photograph with him that they refused to go near when the press were around—the MRA staff rang an old friend of Smith, a well-known retired European leader, and asked him to come to London to provide personal support for Smith.[115]

Similarly, MRA workers took members of Mugabe's team away to the country to relax on several weekends during Lancaster House.[116] Henry Macnicol sought to provide moral support to his old friend, Bishop Muzorewa, whose willingness to support new elections was essential and hung in the balance for much of the conference.[117]

2. Sharing a personal struggle or confessing wrong as a means of breaking barriers was an approach MRA workers used frequently with remarkable effect. Examples include Alec Smith's confession at the 1974 MRA conference in Salisbury; the meeting, described above, between MRA staff and Mugabe aides at which the ice was broken by an exchange, initiated by an MRA member, of intimate stories of personal struggle and tragedy; and the fruitful Reader-Chavunduka liaison in sponsoring dinner parties, begun as a result of Reader's confession to Chavunduka.

"It's a key MRA concept," reflects Alec Smith, "to be honest about yourself." Others may then "drop their guard" and respond with similar scrutiny of them-selves. Politicians in particular are accustomed and resistant to being told what they ought to do, believes Smith. Often the only way to engage in dialogue at the level MRA sought was for MRA workers to take the first step toward personal vulnerability.[118]

3. Inviting carefully chosen outside visitors to Rhodesia was another fre-quently used approach. A group of about 20 MRA workers as far scattered as London, Washington, Caux (Switzerland), and Salisbury communicated regu-larly through letters and phone calls to identify candidates for these visits.[119] Several individuals with extensive previous experience in the British Foreign

Office were part of the British team and helped to ensure that the group did not commit political blunders. "We would constantly be trying to figure out who has the experience anywhere on the globe that is relevant to what is going on with these people at the center of these negotiations," recalls one of the participating MRA strategists.[120] From 1976 to 1979, MRA workers arranged two or three group tours and up to a dozen individual visits a year with visitors. In addition to the exiled king and queen of Romania, these included a minister of education from Australia, a West Indian cricket star, religious figures, business people, educators, and politicians. Some of these foreign visitors had 50 or more meetings, most of them private encounters with individuals or small groups, but some involving groups of 100 people or more.[121] The goal of these meetings was to encourage Rhodesian leaders to engage in moral reflection. The visitors did not preach; rather they shared personal experiences of transformation, reconciliation, and healing as a way of opening dialogue.

4. To exert moral influence on the larger society, MRA pursued a strategy of outreach to the public via publications, newspaper ads, and open meetings. Over the war years, MRA ran several full-page newspaper ads putting forward MRA concepts at key moments. Ten days before the 1980 elections, for example, MRA took out an ad in the leading newspapers of Salisbury, Gweru, and Bulawayo. It was a manifesto calling for "God-led unity" and urging Rhodesians to "rise above our conflicts and sufferings and launch the new Zimbabwe in unity and peace." "What is right, not who is right" is the key to the future, the manifesto proclaimed. Rhodesians should do three things: forgive others and ask forgiveness; live "with standards of absolute honesty, unselfishness, clear morals and care for one another"; and "help our leaders to do the same." Signatories included Chief Chirau, one of the participants in the Internal Settlement, and Cabinet of Conscience members Joram Kucherera, Alec Smith, and Stan O'Donnell, a former government cabinet member under Smith, along with 11 other Rhodesians from various walks of life.

MRA also held regular showings of MRA films[122] and circulated tens of thousands of copies of a pamphlet calling readers to set their own lives in order as a part of rebuilding the nation. Perhaps the greatest impact in the public arena was from the many dozens of meetings held throughout the country by Alec Smith and Arthur Kanodereka, who shared their experience of personal reconciliation and the principles through which they had found it.

Assessment of MRA Involvement

Moral Re-Armament is simultaneously the easiest and the hardest to assess of the three major groups in this case study. The Mugabe-Smith meeting without a doubt altered the history of the nation. It is certain that white Rhodesians would have fled the country in far greater numbers had it not been for the conciliatory mood between Mugabe and Smith resulting from this MRA-arranged meeting. Even if Mugabe had been planning a policy of reconciliation before this meeting, it is doubtful that jittery whites would have believed him—or cooperated so readily in the critical early months of the transition—had Smith not led the way for them. Then, too, it is possible, if not probable, that the coup-in-waiting by General Walls would have been executed.

Beyond this verifiable success, MRA activities resist evaluation. Its goals and modus operandi were the most narrowly and self-consciously "spiritual" of the three groups. What mortal can judge whether the targets of MRA activities "listened to God" and acted accordingly, which is at the root of all that MRA sought to accomplish? Similarly, it is almost impossible to determine whether targeted public figures acted with greater moral conscience as a result of the promptings of MRA friends or associates or, if so, what the impact of their behavior might have been.

At its best, the MRA experience in Rhodesia offers inspiring insights about attitudinal and value changes unparalleled in either the Catholic or Quaker involvements (although the Catholic Church itself underwent an historic transformation in its relationship to the state). Underlying MRA encounters with the political actors was a radical sense of individual responsibility and openness to a transcending purpose. "How you respond could transform the entire situation" was implied in virtually every MRA encounter. Further implied was this: "Be prepared for the possibility that you will be guided, in the interests of reconciliation, in a direction that may be difficult and unpopular." It is difficult to imagine Joram Kucherera risking his life by setting up a meeting between two bitter enemies unless motivated by such values. Alec Smith, Arthur Kanodereka, Desmond Reader, Gordon Chavunduka, to mention only the more obvious examples, all experienced profound personal transformations through their encounter with MRA and undertook risky reconciliation efforts as a consequence.

MRA's genius lay in part in the way it communicated these values to others. Sharing a story with an inescapable moral or theological implication was at the heart of most MRA activities. This parable-telling approach enabled MRA workers to communicate values of individual responsibility and commitment to larger purpose without prescribing or preaching. Almost always the stories contained a central note of confession or error or vulnerability, further reducing defensiveness and inviting similar vulnerability from others.

MRA's emphasis on individual change demarcates it most clearly from the other actors in this study, particularly from the Catholics. Where the Church published dossiers to the world detailing the consequences of an unjust structure, MRA challenged individuals to do what is "right," as defined by general standards of honesty, purity, unselfishness, and love. MRA had been on record for decades in opposing racism—a creditworthy tradition to be sure—but it dealt with a structural evil by individual remedies.

This emphasis on individual change also made MRA workers both more sympathetic toward and attractive to the reformers of Rhodesia than to the revolutionaries. It is not chance that MRA's closest and most reliable affiliations were with Muzorewa and other compromised supporters of the Internal Settlement who in the end proved to be out of touch with the Rhodesian grass-roots. An emphasis on individual change as the avenue to social change, after all, is virtually by definition a gradualist and reformist approach. In a situation that cried out for a sharp break from the structures of the past—the election of Mugabe established that this was surely the verdict of the majority of Zimbabweans—MRA attracted and publicly allied itself with reformers.

But Zimbabwe's revolutionaries must provide the final verdict on the work of Moral Re-Armament in Rhodesia. According to MRA workers, after the war both President Mugabe and one of his top lieutenants, then Security Minister Emmerson Munangagwa, initiated meetings in 1980 with MRA members to acknowledge their work.[123] Additionally, a few months after the elections, Zimbabwean Vice President Simon Muzenda summoned Alec Smith and Joram Kucherera to his office and thanked them for their role in the struggle for a new nation.[124] While these acknowledgments appear to have responded primarily to the Smith-Mugabe meeting, in 1982, Speaker of the House Didymus Mutasa addressed an MRA conference in Harare and spoke with enthusiasm of the importance of MRA's work and principles.[125] If in principle, then, MRA is vulnerable to criticism as individualist and reformist in approach, there is no denying the perceptions of those at the forefront of the struggle for structural change: the organization contributed in significant ways to the creation of a new Zimbabwe.

THE QUAKERS

Though both the Catholics and Moral Re-Armament played key roles in the Rhodesia/Zimbabwe conflict from their bases in Salisbury, in the end it was a London-based group of Quakers that became the most strategically involved in negotiation efforts to end the war. Between 1972 and 1980, Quakers conducted four missions to Africa in the interest of peaceful change in Rhodesia, and they sent delegations to both the Geneva and Lancaster House conferences. The trips to Africa formed the heart of the Quaker contribution, but London was the scene of other activities as well. On numerous occasions the Quakers met with leaders from the liberation movements visiting in London, and they met with staff from the British Foreign and Commonwealth Office (FCO) frequently.

Quaker Characteristics and Goals

Establishing Human Solidarity with All Parties. More than either the Catholics or Moral Re-Armament, the Quakers engaged the combatants in substantive discussion about the war and how to end it. This is paradoxical for, of the three groups, the Quakers consistently brought the simplest agenda to their meetings with the parties: establishing human solidarity with everyone involved. They engaged the parties at other levels, to be sure, as will become clear later. But, whether meeting Mugabe in Maputo, Nkomo in Lusaka, Muzorewa in Salisbury, or the heads of Frontline States, the Quakers' subordinated even the most ambitious tasks to their primary agenda: engaging the parties as human beings suffering from a ghastly war and struggling to find their way out. In a situation where everyone else was lobbying for something, the Quakers were a unique phenomenon: a traveling reservoir of unconditional and uncomplicated good will.

Several points deserve particular attention: For one, the amount of time and effort a small group like the Quakers was prepared to devote to such an apparently innocuous activity is extraordinary. For another, the breadth of their connections was remarkable. They were best connected to black Rhodesians, notably the leaders of the external liberation fronts, Joshua Nkomo and Robert Mugabe, and to Abel Muzorewa. Though they never succeeded in meeting with Ian Smith, they met regularly with several top white government officials, including an under secretary and a permanent secretary in the Ministry of Foreign Affairs, and they regularly visited with business and church leaders in Salisbury.

But their connections extended well beyond the combatants. Keenly aware of the larger forces at work in the Rhodesia/Zimbabwe conflict, the Quakers maintained active personal ties to a network of leaders outside Rhodesia. In their missions they met with President Julius Nyerere of Tanzania, President Kenneth Kaunda of Zambia, and President Seretse Khama of Botswana. They also met with top officials in the capitals of each of these countries on several occasions, as well as with officials from Mozambique, South Africa, and Nigeria.

In addition, they met regularly with British and Commonwealth policymakers. These included a meeting with British Foreign Secretary Owen and many other meetings with officials from the Foreign and Commonwealth Office (FCO). On numerous occasions they met with individual members of Parliament. They also maintained close ties with officials at the Commonwealth Secretariat, including Emeka Anyaoku, then deputy secretary-general.

This broad range of active relationships proved fundamental to the Quaker contribution. With the possible exception of British and American diplomats, who were inescapably perceived as bearing heavy agendas for their own governments, no other individuals or organizations maintained active communication with so broad a network of actors in the web of political influence at work in the conflict.

Seeking solidarity with others as an end in itself is an act of altruism, and altruism, even at its best, elicits skepticism in today's world. But the Quakers practiced their art with such transparent fidelity that expressions of compassion alone not only provided a consistent theme guiding their actions throughout the conflict but also served as their primary means of access.

Their primary agenda, for example, in their first several trips to Rhodesia and the Frontline States, in 1977 and 1978, was to express their concern about the suffering of the people of Rhodesia. This humble concern proved quite adequate to open doors. "Without exception we were warmly and sympathetically received and almost universally encouraged to remain in touch with the parties," recalled one team member later.[126] The same theme shaped Quaker involvements throughout. At a later stage, for example, when their role was well established and they were exploring the possibility of informal, off-the-record talks under Quaker auspices, concern for the ever-mounting suffering caused by the war continued to serve as their rationale for such an encounter.

It would be misleading, however, to highlight the effectiveness of a modest agenda as a means of entry without noting the context. The Quakers benefited enormously from their own history in solving the "entry problem." In addition to a reputation within the broader circles of diplomacy for a quiet, principled approach to peacemaking, the team operating in Rhodesia profited from a recent history of involvements in Rhodesia and elsewhere in Africa.

An American Quaker couple living in Salisbury, for example, had openly supported the African nationalist cause in the 1950s and 1960s, before the outbreak of violence, and the wife, Margaret Moore, had served as secretary of two political parties started by Joshua Nkomo. A British Quaker couple had worked extensively with families of political detainees held by the Smith government in the mid-1960s, developed a friendship with Sally Mugabe, the activist wife of Robert Mugabe, and also made acquaintance with nationalists Robert Mugabe, Joshua Nkomo, and Josiah Chinamano. Another Quaker couple had worked extensively with political prisoners in the 1960s and 1970s, and, backed by funds from British Quakers, they founded a well-known rural training center at Hlekweni. The husband, Roy Henson, was the only white member of the African National Council, a broadly based coalition of African nationalists, at its founding in 1971, the heyday of its credibility in the African nationalist community.[127]

Old connections also assisted the Quakers in gaining entry into the extraordinary range of governments influencing the evolution of the Rhodesia/Zimbabwe conflict. The British high commissioner in Botswana was himself a Quaker and arranged meetings there with President Khama. In Mozambique, the Quaker team met a warm welcome from President Joachim Chissano because of assistance American Quakers had given to gaining United Nations recognition for Frelimo.[128] In Zambia, President Kaunda had known Quakers for many years.[129]

Thus when the Quaker team initiated a role in the Rhodesia/Zimbabwe conflict by sending a team to the Geneva Conference in 1976, they were pleased to discover that many of the delegates, particularly the nationalists, were already personally acquainted with one or more of their team members. This provided ready access to many delegates, particularly for private meetings in hotel rooms.[130] One key member of the team felt in retrospect that later mediation efforts would have been far more difficult had it not been for this "pioneering" work of other Quakers in the country and region.[131]

Access to white Rhodesian government officials was deficient throughout the Quaker effort, but the two best Quaker contacts also resulted from Quaker history. The under secretary of foreign affairs had years earlier participated in a Quaker conference for diplomats as well as in the Quaker-sponsored London Diplomats Group and had been deeply impressed with Quaker commitments. As a result, he met with Quaker delegates regularly in their visits to Salisbury and commented later that Walter Martin had "changed his life" with his low-key but persistent emphasis on compassion, reconciliation, and justice.[132] The permanent secretary of foreign affairs was a personal friend of a Quaker family in Salisbury. This introduction led to a request by the permanent secretary that the Quakers seek the release of a dozen white Rhodesians who had been abducted into Mozambique by guerrilla forces.[133]

But the team of peacemakers benefited from more than Quaker history; they also demonstrated the genuineness of their compassion by calling a network of Quaker relief organizations into play in the conflict. The war created many refugees; the most hard-pressed fled the country to Mozambique, Zambia, and Botswana. At the urging of the team of peacemakers, Quaker service agencies or foundations forwarded cash and materials to the Red Cross in Salisbury for refugees within Rhodesia, as well as to U.N. organizations, to the Christian Council of Mozambique for refugees under the care of ZANU, and also directly to ZANU and ZAPU for refugees. The amounts sent were modest, totaling some 10,500 pounds sterling in value at the time, but they reinforced the genuineness of the Quaker concern.

Whatever the advantages offered by Quaker history and charitable activities, the original point still holds: a simple, straightforward agenda of concern for the human beings involved in the conflict was the dominant theme of Quaker involvement and provided their primary tool for entry. Entry, after all, is never a once-and-done challenge; mediators must constantly re-earn the trust that sustains their role. The Quaker team benefited from their past, but they moved far beyond it by their tireless rounds of personal contact with key parties.

Disciplined Listening. If expressing concern for human suffering opened doors for the Quakers, practicing disciplined listening opened hearts. In memos drawn up in preparation for major missions, the desire to hear and support the parties invariably topped the list. The number-one goal chosen by the team that attended the Geneva Conference was typical: "To build up relationships with participants so as to develop a sympathetic understanding of their fears, hopes and intentions and to support and strengthen their efforts at achieving a just settlement in a conciliatory manner."[134] Listening well opened the doors for further conversation, for increasingly the parties became eager to know what the Quakers were hearing from *other* parties.[135] The Quakers were diligent not to betray confidences but found that their own growing knowledge of the situation soon became a resource eagerly sought by the parties. "Very rarely was access a problem," recalls Trevor Jepson, a key member of the team. Thus the Quaker role emerged from the dynamics of the relationships that were formed. "We felt we had been put into the role and must continue."[136]

It would be simplistic, of course, to suggest that the Quakers held no goals in their meetings other than listening. Clearly they sought to influence the parties to function more humanely and to encourage nonviolent means of resolving the conflict. But listening was for the Quakers no mere prelude to serious talk. Listening was itself a genuine contribution to change—a means to support the dignity, credibility, and rationality of the individuals with whom they were interacting. And because the Quakers consulted widely each time they expanded their role, listening was also a manifestation of their political values. Rather than give advice, the Quakers *sought* advice about what they should do and at all times presented themselves as quiet servants of the needs of the parties. Theirs was the politics of transformative listening.

Opening Channels of Communication. As the parties' trust in the Quakers grew, the depth of their discussions expanded and, with it, so did the scope of possible Quaker involvements. The Quakers were open at all times about their contacts with other parties and, as a result, people with whom they were meeting asked them to convey messages to other parties on several occasions, as follows.

In May 1979, President Nyerere requested a "personal, nongovernmental link" with Muzorewa, then prime minister of Rhodesia.[137] Nyerere was deeply concerned about the potential for the conflict to expand into an East-West confrontation and hoped that Muzorewa might assist in moderating the war. In addition to establishing a communication link, he sought from Muzorewa a less bellicose stance toward the Frontline States and toward the Patriotic Front itself. The Quakers carried the request to Muzorewa, who responded positively to the idea of a link. This led to a second round of "shuttle diplomacy" for the Quakers, to explore further the nature and purpose of such a nongovernmental link. In their second meeting, Muzorewa handed to Walter Martin, the Quaker representative, a packet of conciliatory letters to deliver: to Nyerere, Kaunda, Mugabe, and Nkomo.

That same day, however, the Rhodesian Air Force bombed Lusaka in a "preemptive strike" against Nkomo's troops headquartered there, a move later publicly endorsed by Muzorewa. That Muzorewa had a hand in planning this military adventurism was perhaps unlikely. But even the kindest interpretation of his role suggested that Muzorewa was impotent to control his own government, and Nyerere concluded there was now no point in further communication with the prime minister. "Perhaps, after all, the British will help more to solve the Rhodesia problem than the Bishop," he mused to Martin.[138]

A month later, Nyerere played a key role in the move to convene the Lancaster House conference. At the gathering of the Commonwealth states in August in Lusaka, the elder statesman of Africa called for British intervention in Rhodesia and all-party talks among the combatants. In the days that followed, Thatcher, Nyerere, and others in a six-member caucus forged an unprecedented consensus: the recently "elected" Muzorewa/Smith government would remain unrecognized and instead constitutional negotiations would begin as soon as possible under British auspices.

There were other instances of Quaker efforts to open channels of communication.

- Toward the end of 1978, several members of the Quaker team met with David Owen, a key formulator of British policy as head of the Foreign and Commonwealth Office. In response to a comment by the Quakers about the depth of suspicions that existed within the Patriotic Front regarding the motives of the British, Owen expressed a desire for more interaction with Robert Mugabe.

- A few weeks later, in November 1978, the Quakers mentioned this to Mugabe's associates and received their support to work on such a meeting, so long as it could be set up in a way that threatened no damage to the fragile unity of the Patriotic Front. One possibility would be for the Quakers to arrange for Mugabe to address a small group of people at the Quaker House in London, a meeting to which Owen and other FCO officials would also be invited. Personal interaction could follow such a meeting without the implications of a formal, planned encounter. Preliminary signals from both parties were positive, such that the Quakers arranged funding for Mugabe's trip and began making arrangements for meetings. But in the end, other events intervened and the trip never took place.[139]

- The Quakers provided financial support in late 1978 for a peace initiative by three black African nationalist Rhodesians. At their request, the Quakers secured funds for travel enabling further discussion of a proposal to found the Committee for Permanent Indaba in Rhodesia. This initiative looked promising for several months, but fell to pieces when Reverend Arthur Kanodereka, the central figure, was assassinated.[140] Though the Quakers had no role other than providing moral and financial support for the initiative, the incident demonstrates the depth of the Quaker commitment to support any bona fide effort to establish negotiation among the parties.

- In early 1979, after British Prime Minister James Callaghan had explored the prospect of, but then decided against, convening all-party talks, the Quakers actively pursued the possibility of bringing together a small, private, informal gathering of second-level people from all parties.[141] In a series of meetings over a period of several months, the team consulted extensively with officials, many of them at high levels, from the United Nations, Zambia, Tanzania, Nigeria, and England, in addition to top-level representatives from the liberation armies and Smith's government. Responses to the possibility of such a gathering were generally positive. But again, other events overtook the initiative.[142]

- At Lancaster House, the Quakers met informally with numerous delegates, many of whom had by now become old friends. From these conversations arose six different requests to bring individuals or groups who were officially incommunicado together in special meetings. The chairman of one of the Rhodesian internal parties, for example, requested assistance in meeting delegates from ZANU and ZAPU, the much more radical external political fronts, and the Quakers arranged such a meeting.[143] In another instance, the Quakers conveyed to Nkomo and Mugabe a query from the Salisbury government delegation about the possibility of an informal meeting of Muzorewa, Nkomo, and Mugabe.

Supporting Formal Negotiations. The Quakers never viewed their work as more than a footnote to a larger story. There were moments, to be sure, when the footnote nearly leaped into the text. But even in their most ambitious efforts to convene face-to-face meetings between representatives of the parties, the Quakers saw themselves as serving a larger process: formal negotiations that would have to involve the British in a convening role.[144] Most of the activities already described above had the effect of supporting formal negotiations. But there were other activities that also deserve mention, as follows.

- In October 1978, after their second major mission to Africa in which they had met representatives of all the key parties, the Quakers arranged a meeting with British Foreign Secretary Owen. They sent a follow-up letter a few days later, listing 10 concerns and suggestions regarding ways to move the negotiation process forward. They stressed "the need for preparation, yet speed, in convening an All-Party Conference."[145]
- The Quakers usually informed the British Foreign Office before leaving on their trips, and on several occasions they visited with officials from the FCO upon returning.
- The Quakers held a series of interviews in Lusaka, Maputo, and Salisbury with representatives of virtually all the key parties just after the Lusaka Commonwealth Conference in 1979. The external liberation fronts, in particular, were deeply skeptical of British motivations. The Quaker team listened to these objections but still supported the viability of the Lancaster House negotiations as a step to end the war.
- Present at both the failed Geneva Conference as well as Lancaster House, the Quakers interacted with many key delegates and sought to offer low-key suggestions about courses of action and attitudes to adopt that they felt would enhance the likelihood of resolution. At Lancaster House the Quakers wrote personal letters of welcome to all the delegates whom they knew personally and met with many of them privately—in all, over 100 meetings.[146] In these conversations, they tried to interpret the perspectives of each delegation to other delegations.[147] "Our role had become that of a lubricant," reflected Trevor Jepson later, "by identifying sticking points and where appropriate making representation with a view to problems being overcome rather than used as a reason to break off negotiations."[148]
- As it became apparent at Lancaster House that the British would supervise a transitional period, the Quakers directed substantial effort to influencing British policymakers toward strategies that, based on their interactions with all the parties, the Quakers believed were essential to the implementation of the cease-fire and establishment of monitoring forces. They had numerous meetings with officials in the British Foreign and Commonwealth Office, wrote letters to Lord Carrington, and in one instance, to Prime Minister Thatcher.[149]
- At one point the Patriotic Front threatened to walk out of the Lancaster House talks, as did the Salisbury delegation on another occasion. In both instances, the Quakers urged the delegates in private conversations to stay— in the interests of the people of Rhodesia as a whole.
- It was a secret to no one that the Patriotic Front struggled to maintain unity between the parties of Mugabe and Nkomo. Predictably, the Lancaster House talks brought new strains to this relationship that the Quakers sought

to overcome by stressing to both Patriotic Front wings the importance of a unified stand.

- Toward the end of the Lancaster House conference it became apparent that there was poor coordination between the Patriotic Front and the Frontline States and that the British were using this to increase pressure on the Patriotic Front. Concerned that this could lead to misunderstanding and abrogation of agreements later, the Quakers encouraged African diplomats to better coordinate their policies.[150]
- In the months just after Lancaster House, an advisor to Nkomo asked the Quakers to relay a message to a British MP requesting that Carrington be sent to Rhodesia urgently to render an "agreed interpretation of the Lancaster House Agreement." The request was delivered but Carrington remained in England.[151]

Advocating Policies and Actions in Support of Reconciliation. The Rhodesia/Zimbabwe conflict presented the Quaker intermediaries with seemingly conflicting roles. On the one hand, they were mediators, at least potentially, and keen to maintain their impartiality. On the other hand, they were deeply sensitive to questions of justice. They were also British citizens, concerned that their own government handle its role responsibly, and they had access to a variety of key British policymakers, the majority of whom knew far less about the dynamics of the Rhodesia situation than did the Quakers. At several points, therefore, the Quakers shifted from the role of mediator to policy advocate in relationship to their own government. They chose to go to Geneva, for example, in part because the British government was reticent to assist a peaceful transition by being involved in any way in a transitional period. The Quakers felt that it might be necessary to play a role in "informing the UK public and building a sympathetic understanding" for support of agreements reached.[152]

The Quakers harmonized their roles in this complex situation by framing their advocacy in the language of reconciliation. For example:

- They conveyed to several British Members of Parliament their conviction that if sanctions against Rhodesia were lifted too soon, the fighting would escalate and the war would be prolonged.
- In the months prior to the Lusaka decision to call all-party talks, they communicated to British officials the universal rejection among African leaders of the Muzorewa/Smith Internal Settlement government and the concern raised by President Nyerere that if Great Britain and the United States recognized the Salisbury government, a major East-West conflict was likely to result.
- At Lancaster House, as described above, they devoted substantial effort toward helping the British and the Rhodesian government understand the concerns of the Patriotic Front, in order to reduce the likelihood of a walkout or abrogation later of an agreement perceived to be unfair.
- Also at Lancaster House, Quakers participated in writing several briefing papers designed to inform and influence all parties. Mediation team

member Tony Gilpin, for example, assisted the Catholic Institute for International Relations in preparation of a briefing paper regarding cease-fire arrangements.[153]

- In the two-month interim period between the Lancaster House agreement and the elections, a report by Quaker Adam Curle raised concerns in urgent tones about British handling of sensitive governance issues in Rhodesia.
- In the same period, Quakers cooperated with Tim Sheehy of the Catholic Institute for International Relations in writing a letter to Lord Soames suggesting measures to reduce tensions before and after the elections.[154]

In other instances they sought to influence the liberation fronts toward actions they thought would be constructive:

- Following the downing of a civilian aircraft by Nkomo's troops in September 1978, Gilpin and his Quaker colleague, Trevor Jepson, pointed out in a meeting with ZAPU officials the serious damage that had been done to ZAPU's credibility by the incident.
- Throughout their involvement, the Quakers were deeply concerned about the great fear expressed by whites about the liberation fronts, particularly Mugabe's ZANU forces. In a meeting with ZANU officials in October 1978, Jepson and Gilpin noted the amount of thought being given in ZANU to the nature of the new society sought for Zimbabwe: changes were to be made gradually, "avoiding the mistakes made through precipitate action in other African countries."[155] Impressed, the two stressed to the ZANU leadership the importance of conveying this thinking to Rhodesia and the outside world.

Grounded in deep principles of justice and fairness, the Quakers were open at all times about their own values. But they were cautious in advocating specific strategies to be taken by a given party. When they did, however, as in the above instances, they couched their appeals in the language of a higher nonpartisan purpose: reconciliation, fairness, and long-term peace. "Our motivating power is reconciliation, not advocacy" was the way senior team member Walter Martin put it.[156]

Assessment of Quaker Involvement

The Quaker involvements in Rhodesia are, at one level, a study in failure as a fundamental aspect of peacemaking. The Quakers invested substantially in four major efforts to set up meetings among top leaders, all of which failed to materialize: a Nyerere-Muzorewa link in 1979; an Owen-Mugabe meeting in 1978; an effort to convene a meeting of second-level leaders in 1979; and the peace initiative by Kanodereka, Hove, and Chigwida in 1978, which the Quakers funded. What, then, did the Quakers contribute?

Fundamental to a response to this question is an understanding of the nature of the Quaker focus. While MRA focused on individual and attitudinal change, and the Catholics on structural change, the Quakers focused on perceptions and processes that would enable a negotiated settlement. In the end, the parties reached this outcome at Lancaster House, rendering the work of the Quakers almost invisible against the backdrop of larger success. Their work was so interwoven in the complex fabric of influences moving the parties toward a negotiated peace that it is virtually impossible to isolate the Quaker impact from that of other more visible and powerful actors.

But one measure might be the amount of access accorded the Quakers by the parties. Mugabe, Nkomo, and Muzorewa, as well as many of their top aides, met repeatedly with the Quakers throughout their involvement in the conflict. These leaders must have found the meetings useful. The British apparently recognized the significance of the Quaker role as well: when at the start of the Lancaster House talks Lord Carrington invited the incoming delegates to a dinner party, the only person not affiliated with any of the parties was Quaker Walter Martin.

Another measure of the value of the Quaker contribution can be found in subsequent comments made by the parties. A few weeks after Mugabe's election in early 1980, two prominent members of ZANU strongly encouraged the Quakers to maintain a role in Zimbabwe, with a focus on race relations.[157] A leading figure in the Commonwealth Secretariat echoed this sentiment, stressing the need for informal gatherings between whites and blacks.[158] Josiah Chinamano, a leading figure in ZAPU, also encouraged a Quaker role in the post-independence period, adding that "not only we but you have a responsibility in all this."[159] Joseph Msika, another top ZAPU leader endorsed this, adding that a quality he had always appreciated about the Quakers was their optimism: "During our darkest times in Lusaka, we were greatly heartened by visits from Quakers whose faith in the possibility of progress towards peace helped to revive our hopes."[160] President Nyerere wrote a letter thanking the Quakers for their work in Rhodesia/Zimbabwe.[161] A U.N. diplomat commented some years later that it was widely recognized that "the Quakers had played an important part in creating the conditions for a satisfactory settlement."[162]

The personal assistant to Nyerere expressed a similar conviction a few months after Lancaster House. In a letter of "congratulations to you and your colleagues who have been active for peace with justice in Zimbabwe," she expressed to Walter Martin her belief that "the quiet intervention of Quaker Peace and Service personnel may well have had a special importance at different moments in the lead-up to Lusaka, and during the Conference itself."[163]

Then, too, there are times when nothing clarifies like failure. President Nyerere was angry and let down by the Rhodesian air strikes against Lusaka that coincided with the messages the Quakers were conveying between him and Muzorewa. But having failed in his effort to work cooperatively with Muzorewa through the good offices of the Quakers, he was prepared a few weeks later to take leadership in the call for the British to convene the Lancaster House negotiations. It is likely that this Quaker-assisted failure contributed to the evolution of Nyerere's decisive stance.

It is precisely the difficulty of "proving" success or impact that illustrates an important characteristic of many religious peacemakers. The Quakers intentionally operated in such a way that their own contribution to any success would be invisible. They made no effort to hide their role, but they sought to be genuine servants to the interests of others, and they understood that their ability to contribute depended on keeping a Quaker stake in the outcome to a minimum. To paraphrase American sociologist Robert Theobald: you can have social change, or you can have credit for social change, but you can't have both at the same time.[164]

Thus it should come as no surprise that the Quakers would be the least concerned about evidence of "success." Religious peacemakers at their best engage in their work, ultimately, not because they seek success, but rather because they feel "called" by a reality larger than the empirical "facts" in the situation. If this appears at one level to be naive or unrealistic, at another it reflects what is perhaps the fundamental asset of the religious intermediary. War, after all, is a consequence of the loss of hope that talking can yield results. Any peacemaker motivated by "success" as a yardstick would fade quickly in the atmosphere of pessimism that envelops most serious conflicts. A sense of transcendent calling is more sustaining than pragmatic ambition, and the Quakers, faithful to their call, persevered in the face of long odds and major setbacks.

Spiritual Dimensions of the Quaker Approach

ZAPU leader Msika's description of the Quakers was insightful, but, if anything, it understated the truth. Quakers are more than optimistic; they are "cosmically optimistic." God, who is loving and good, is seen to be present everywhere working to bring things aright. The hopefulness, then, that pervades the Quakers' work is not the cocky but ultimately brittle confidence of a clever strategist or a skilled practitioner. Rather, it is the calm assurance of a spiritual thinker who knows that, all appearances to the contrary, in the end a deeper reality will prevail. It is difficult to imagine anyone functioning with the quiet perseverance that characterizes Quaker mediation efforts without such a deeply rooted optimism.

Claims to "trust in God," of course, are as common as the American penny.[165] But Quakers add to it an essential trust in human beings. For centuries they have taught that within the heart of even the tyrant there exists a divine spark. The challenge is to kindle that spark, to "speak to that of God in every person." Thus Quakers are hopeful about the possibility of establishing constructive relationships even in discouraging circumstances with difficult people.

Other traits come closely aligned. If God resides in every person, there is no room for pretense, arrogance, or superficiality in relations with others. Nor is there room for injustice, selfishness, or "looking after our own" at the expense of other people. It was not by chance that the Quakers won trust rapidly with most of the people with whom they met. Though they were "foreigners" to most of their contacts, they operated with such modesty, such transparent openness to and concern for each party, that doors opened relatively quickly for them.

Getting through the door, after all, was the sole prerequisite for the Quakers' role. The situation was not yet ripe for negotiation, either face-to-face or via "shuttle diplomacy." The Quakers focused rather on preparatory efforts at the level of attitudes, understanding, information, and rational analysis—activities that required little more of the parties than to engage in thoughtful discussion with the visiting peacemakers.

The whole Quaker contribution depended, then, on a quality of interpersonal bearing that, more than merely psychological or sociological, is profoundly rooted in faith and theology. Getting "through the door" is no spiritual exercise, of course, but the Quaker example suggests that the right kind of spiritual roots are an enormous asset. An interpersonal bearing that is grounded in a spiritual vision brings consistency, congruency, and simplicity of purpose to the task, and thus heightens the odds of getting through the many doors that await the aspiring peacemaker—and of rapidly building trust once inside. This bearing, reinforced by the Quaker reputation for integrity, nonpartisanship, and work in the field of peace and justice, secured for the team ready and continued access to the parties in the Rhodesia/Zimbabwe conflict. While there was was little in the Quakers' words and actions that appeared "spiritual," then, it is difficult to imagine a comparable effort being conducted without a deeply spiritual base.

OTHER RELIGIOUS EFFORTS

Though less involved in direct conversation with the combatants than the three groups that form the heart of this chapter, the work of the Christian Council of Rhodesia at least deserves mention. From 1964 onward, the council was a focus of ecumenical efforts within Rhodesia to oppose the Smith government and the war it was waging. Though sympathetic to the African nationalist perspective throughout, from 1971 to 1979 the council was often paralyzed in the debate between the moderate nationalism associated with Bishop Muzorewa and the more militant nationalism of the external liberation movements.[166]

In July 1979, the council formed a Christian Council Reconciliation Committee (RC) to initiate involvement in the quest for political solutions. The RC undertook as its primary goal to seek unity among the African nationalist parties, now bitterly divided by the Internal Settlement.[167] Though able to meet Muzorewa, himself a member of the Executive Committee of the Christian Council until 1978, the RC was prevented by logistical problems of travel arrangements and visas from meeting with Mugabe and Nkomo.[168]

Four members of the RC traveled to Lancaster House, with a clear mission: "to impress upon the three main actors on the Zimbabwean scene the need to end the war in Zimbabwe through Political Reconciliation."[169] One of their main concerns was to support unity among the African leaders.[170] The RC made several efforts to get Muzorewa, Mugabe, and Nkomo to meet, but gave up when Nkomo[171] declined. Instead, they met separately with the three leaders and their aides: three times with Mugabe, twice with Muzorewa, and twice with Nkomo. They pleaded moderation with all three, stressing the suffering taking place at home. To the liberation movements they urged that so long as the settlement put full political control in the hands of the majority, including control of the police and security forces, the remaining issues were not urgent enough to block agreement.[172] Muzorewa, for his part, promised he would not "stand in the way of a good deal for Zimbabwe."[173]

In the latter part of the Lancaster House conference, the group sought to support "the credentials of the Patriotic Front to Christian groups in Great Britain and to the international press."[174]

CONCLUSION

The three religious groups in this study present a remarkably broad spectrum of responses to conflict. What is the problem that peacemakers are choosing to address? The question cleaves to the heart of the differences between these three groups. Consider the following spectrum of problem analysis:

$$\text{Persons} \quad \text{Processes} \quad \text{Structures}$$

Microanalysis < -- > Macroanalysis

Moral Re-Armament focused on the personal aspects of the problem: individuals were not living according to high moral standards nor listening to God, and, consequently, conflict and injustice prevailed. Thus MRA devoted almost exclusive attention to reaching individuals and working for attitudinal and moral change. MRA left a mark, willy nilly, on the processes by which the parties communicated with each other and on the structures that emerged as a result of its work with individuals. The Mugabe-Smith meeting, after all, probably altered the destiny of the nation. But these processes and structures were effects, not the targets of MRA activities.

The Catholics, for the most part, defined the problem as *structural*: the political and economic structures were fundamentally unjust and needed to be overhauled. This required mobilizing opinion against the existing structures via publications and lobbying efforts. The Catholics, too, devoted some attention to problems of process. The Catholic appeal to commence negotiations, made directly to the parties a year before Lancaster House and to the international community just prior to the Commonwealth meeting in Lusaka, undoubtedly was one of several important influences that eventually brought the parties to the table. But the Catholics influenced process by structural methods. They were moral lobbyists within the structures of power, not facilitators of negotiation.

The Quakers centered their activities around problems of *process*: the parties were not communicating clearly, and negotiation efforts were bedeviled by misinformation, misinterpretations, and a lack of forums and mechanisms to communicate constructively. The Quakers sought to fill this gap, interpreting each side's concerns to the others, conveying messages, trying to arrange face-to-face meetings, exploring options for resolution with the parties informally at Lancaster House and elsewhere. Far more so than either MRA or the Catholics, the Quakers were involved in discussion of substantive issues with a broad range of leaders, and thus they came the closest to a mediating role.

Although the Quakers devoted the bulk of their attention to problems of process, they were also directly concerned with individuals and with structural problems. Like MRA, they spent a great deal of time with individual leaders in a listening and supportive role. Like the Catholics, they demonstrated a profound awareness of structural imbalances. Though they were careful not to endanger their mediation role through open activism, they interacted quietly with London-based groups, such as CIIR and the British Council of Churches, which sought to highlight injustice in Rhodesia, and they sought to influence the British government to take what they felt would be more enlightened approaches to the situation.

The groups focused on different aspects of the problem because they defined the problem itself differently, and the stategies they employed differed accordingly. But the effect of the three involvements proved to be complementary in nature. The Catholics and the Quakers recognized this and cooperated throughout the war years by keeping each other well informed about their respective activities. Contacts between MRA and the other two groups were minimal, however, and this seems a regrettable gap. Closer cooperation—if only in the sharing of information and insights about the conflict—particularly between the Quakers and MRA might have substantially enhanced the work of both organizations.

The three groups shared a striking similarity: all dealt with the "entry" problem by the use of listening strategies. Individuals from both the Quakers and MRA teams repeatedly emphasized in later interviews the importance of low-key, nonjudgmental listening to the parties as a central part of their work, and both organizations spent enormous amounts of time doing it. The Catholics were less self-conscious about it, but they based their truth-telling on listening nevertheless. The far-flung network of Catholic personnel in Rhodesia and the reports from the thousands of individuals who brought complaints to the Commission for Justice and Peace formed the backbone of Catholic truth-telling efforts in the world arena. If anything sets the work of these three religious organizations apart from that of many other organizations, it is the scope and the quality of the listening in which they engaged.

Did the religious groups make a difference in the outcome of the conflict? This conflict was concluded by formal political negotiations, and the religious groups were only several of the numerous actors on the scene. Clear proof of their impact is hard to come by. Even so, the answer is unequivocally yes.

The evidence is episodic but incontrovertible in the case of MRA where Ian Smith, a key protagonist, confirms that the MRA-brokered meeting altered his subsequent public response to Mugabe before a breathless nation.[175] The evidence is less dramatic in the case of the Catholics, who tirelessly goaded the world to take action on Rhodesia. But the magnitude and scope of the Catholic efforts, particularly at truth-telling, make it virtually certain that the conflict would have been prolonged and the human toll thus substantially higher had the Church not been so deeply involved. With regard to the Quakers, the evidence is neither decisive nor voluminous. Yet the levels of access gained to the disputing parties and to key external policymakers, and those parties' expressions of appreciation afterward suggest that the Quakers played a role that the parties found constructive as they groped their way towards a settlement. It is hard to imagine the Rhodesia/ Zimbabwe conflict becoming "ripe"[176] for resolution and moving into a new dispensation with so little bitterness had it not been for the roles played by these religious actors.

This study suggests that there may not have been a "religious response" per se to the conflict, but rather that there was a multiplicity of responses—conceivably available to anyone—that were undertaken by religious bodies. What sets these religious groups apart was their unique ability to combine elements essential to resolving many conflicts. The values that motivated them, the methods of operation that sprang from those values, the transcendent identity they frequently held in the eyes of the parties and others, and the international support structures that sustained them enabled the religious actors to accomplish essential preparatory tasks that were beyond the reach of any other intervenor.

Notes

1. The guerrilla forces of the Patriotic Front called the country Zimbabwe, and the government of Abel Muzorewa (May–December 1979) called it Zimbabwe-Rhodesia. For simplicity, in this study the name Rhodesia will be used in reference to the period prior to formal independence and the takeover by a bona fide government on April 18, 1980; thereafter its contemporary name, Zimbabwe, will be used. Similarly, the capital city will be referred to as Salisbury prior to formal independence and as Harare thereafter. The conflict itself will be referred to as the Rhodesia/Zimbabwe conflict.

2. Interview with M. Kuchera, Zimbabwe Council of Churches, Harare, August 19, 1992.

3. Unlike other colonies, Rhodesia had been granted status as a "self-governing colony" in 1923, but in an effort to "restrain the racist excesses of the settlers," England still retained a right of veto over aspects of governance, particularly those having to do with black rights (Anthony J. Chennells, "White Rhodesian Nationalism—The Mistaken Years," in *Turmoil and Tenacity: Zimbabwe 1890–1990*, ed. Canaan S. Banana [Harare: College Press, 1989], 123–27).

4. White leaders in Pretoria remained committed, to be sure, to an apartheid system even more comprehensively racist than Rhodesia's. But Vorster and Co. were playing shrewdly to win a long-term game of *realpolitik*. In 1962 South African Prime Minister John Vorster had already counseled Rhodesian Prime Minister Winston Field against a Unilateral Declaration of Independence from England, on the grounds that, unlike South Africa, Rhodesia's African majority was so vast as to rule out the possibility of a white-ruled state. Black rule in Rhodesia, Vorster maintained, was inevitable, and it would be better for Rhodesian whites to move cautiously and cultivate a moderate black leadership (personal communication from journalist Colin Legum, who interviewed Field on this question, dated November 20, 1992). Furthermore, strategists in Pretoria, contemplating the lessons of a Mozambique suddenly gone fanatically Marxist, had concluded that prolonged guerrilla warfare created radical nationalism. Thus white racism to the north increasingly looked destabilizing for the region to Pretoria. Much better to succor instead the emergence of a pliable client state like Malawi. That required not arms for fellow white racists, but black faces in government offices in Salisbury.

5. Bishop Muzorewa was brought into politics in 1971 with foot-dragging reluctance because his nonpolitical background made him acceptable as leader to the several factions

of nationalists seeking to oppose an agreement worked out between the British and Ian Smith. But by 1975, he was thoroughly despised by ZANU and ZAPU, the external liberation fronts, for entering into negotiations with Ian Smith against the wishes of fellow nationalists. Cf. note 8.

6. Ian Linden, *The Catholic Church and the Struggle for Zimbabwe* (London: Longman, 1980), 272.

7. In Zambia one camp alone contained 6,000 boys who had been separated from their parents (interview with Trevor Jepson, a member of the Quaker conciliation team, Wales, July 7, 1991).

8. The Patriotic Front consisted of two liberation movements: the Zimbabwe African National Union (ZANU), headed by Robert Mugabe and based in Maputo, and the Zimbabwe African Peoples' Union (ZAPU), headed by Joshua Nkomo and based in Lusaka. In 1976, at the urging of leaders from surrounding African states, the movements joined forces in an uneasy alliance and formed the Patriotic Front. The two movements had different political orientations, different sponsors, and different instincts about when and on what issues to compromise with the Rhodesian government; both sought preeminence in the eventual new Zimbabwe. The resulting tension constantly threatened their ability to collaborate during the war, at Lancaster House, and after independence.

9. Interview with Ian Robertson, Harare, May 25, 1991. Robertson is a Scottish biologist who moved to Rhodesia in 1977 to assist with MRA activities and has been deeply involved there ever since.

10. ZANU Death List, issued by Dr. Edison Zvobgo, deputy secretary for information and publicity in Maputo, November 13, 1978.

11. Interview with Robertson. A panga is a sword-like traditional African weapon.

12. Interview with Robertson, May 25, 1991, and with Ian Smith, Harare, April 28, 1992.

13. Victor de Waal, *The Politics of Reconciliation* (London: Hurst and Co., 1990), 46.

14. Lord Christopher Soames, speaking on his arrival at Heathrow Airport on April 19, 1980, as quoted in Hugh Elliott, *Dawn in Zimbabwe: Concept for a Nation* (London: Grosvenor Books, 1980), 9.

15. Since 1980 Zimbabwe has experienced crises that belie Mugabe's noble words. The conflict in Matebeleland in the early 1980s was particularly tragic, an African ethnic conflict writ large in a struggle for political power that cost thousands of lives. But given the recent background of a high-stakes and divisive war of liberation, the sense of reconciliation that still characterizes the country is remarkable; equally remarkable are the consistent efforts to restore unity with former opponents after each crisis. Joshua Nkomo, former ZAPU leader and Mugabe's rival during the war for the mantle of chief nationalist, was the instigator of the Matabeleland conflict, but he was later brought back into government as a result of a lengthy series of negotiations mediated by Methodist minister and former President Canaan Banana from 1983 to 1987. Nkomo currently serves as vice-president under President Mugabe. So consistent has the theme of reconciliation been that one author, Victor de Waal, called his study of the first decade of Zimbabwe's history, *The Politics of Reconciliation*.

16. To list just a few examples: Canaan Banana, the first president of Zimbabwe (1980-87), was an ordained Methodist minister. Robert Mugabe, like many other liberation leaders, was educated in Catholic mission schools and maintained active communication with Catholic leaders throughout the war. Nationalists Abel Muzorewa and Ndabaningi Sithole, who in the end discredited themselves in a fatal alliance with Smith, were both ordained ministers.

17. See David Lan's fascinating account, *Guns and Rain: Guerrillas and Spirit Mediums in Zimbabwe* (Berkeley and Los Angeles: University of California Press, 1985).

18. Gary Strong, *Keys to Effective Prayer* (Basingstoke, U.K.: Marshalls, 1985), 11–24.

19. The Frontline States consisted of Zambia, Mozambique, Tanzania, Botswana, and Angola, a "closely-knit caucus within the Organization of African States" formed in 1974 to achieve majority rule in southern Africa. Their influence on the Rhodesia/Zimbabwe struggle was critical, particularly because of Zambia and Mozambique, both of which were hosting a Zimbabwean liberation army. For more information, see Colin Legum's encyclopedic work, *The Battlefronts of Southern Africa* (New York: Africana Publishing, 1988), 26ff.

20. Linden, *Catholic Church and the Struggle for Zimbabwe*, 95.

21. Interview with Sister Janice McLaughlin, Harare, May 6, 1991.

22. Linden identifies the establishment of the JPC as a turning point for the Rhodesian Catholic Church, "the first formal structural commitment to social justice made by the hierarchy" (Linden, *Catholic Church and the Struggle for Zimbabwe*, 163).

23. Ibid., 196.

24. Roman Catholic Bishops' Conference, April 25, 1973, quoted in Linden, *Catholic Church and the Struggle for Zimbabwe*, 190.

25. Ibid., 197.

26. Whites had viewed themselves as subjects of the Crown from the time Cecil Rhodes's Pioneer Column arrived from British-ruled South Africa in 1890. Britain had indicated already in the 1950s her intent to offer independence to Rhodesia, but had made clear in 1956 that she would not allow political groups that were racist to come to power. Smith's Unilateral Declaration of Independence in 1965 was thus a brazen tweak of the nose at the British. As Smith rightly calculated, British Prime Minister Harold Wilson chose not to respond militarily. What Smith had not anticipated was that his "independent" Rhodesia would remain economically and politically at the mercy of the British. Wilson imposed selective economic sanctions, and, in 1966, the United Nations followed suit. By 1970 it was apparent that without the blessing of the British—and increasingly that meant the whole Commonwealth as well—Rhodesia was destined to become an isolated and economically handicapped pariah, all but surrounded by hostile African states.

27. Linden, *Catholic Church and the Struggle for Zimbabwe*, 208.

28. Ibid., 207.

29. Ibid., 209.

30. Ibid., 229.

31. Interview with McLaughlin.

32. Linden, *Catholic Church and the Struggle for Zimbabwe*, 210.

33. In March of that year, Muzorewa and Smith entered into the Internal Settlement, an arrangement that replaced Smith with a four-member Executive Council until elections. The council consisted of Smith and Muzorewa plus two other Rhodesia-based black leaders—Ndabaningi Sithole and Chief J. S. Chirau. The Internal Settlement provided for a Parliament to be established at elections to be held within a year, in which 28 seats were to be guaranteed for whites in a body of 100 members. The externally based Patriotic Front, which had not been consulted in this arrangement, immediately rejected this proposal for diluted majority rule, as did the United Nations and the Frontline States. Many parties, including the Catholic bishops, were initially ambivalent. The new leaders were installed, but it soon became apparent to outsiders that the three black "prime ministers" were mere puppets in a quartet controlled by Smith. By June 1978, the Catholic bishops and numerous

other groups had rejected the arrangement. Meanwhile, the war continued to escalate, often with Muzorewa at the forefront in castigating the Patriotic Front. On one occasion he appeared on television brandishing a machine gun, and on another he was quoted as saying that news of the Rhodesian Forces' bombing of Nkomo's forces in Lusaka was a great start to his day. Cf. ibid., 277.

34. Ibid., 264–65.

35. Interview with Mildred Neville, director of the Catholic Institute for International Relations throughout the war years, London, July 8, 1991.

36. The CIIR published "Comment #34," and the JPC published "An Analysis of the Salisbury Agreement." The Rhodesian bishops wavered on whether to support or reject the Internal Settlement and asked the JPC to withhold publication of the latter booklet in April 1978. But after two massacres had taken place, and it became apparent that the Internal Settlement would not end the war, the bishops supported the release of the booklet in July 1978 (interview with Michael Auret, secretary and primary staff person of the JPC from 1974 to present, Harare, May 28, 1991; also Linden, *Catholic Church and the Struggle for Zimbabwe*, 274).

37. The Catholic role in Rhodesia may well have been much different were it not for bishop Lamont, who led the way in establishing the JPC and in bringing often-reluctant fellow Bishops to a position of clear opposition to state policies. Lamont grew increasingly harsh in his criticism of the state and, after eventually denouncing it as "illegitimate," was finally deported to his native Ireland in February 1977.

38. Linden, *Catholic Church and the Struggle for Zimbabwe*, 166, fn.

39. Ibid., 213.

40. Ibid.; also interview with Auret. On the U.S. visit, the JPC was assisted by the Commission on Justice and Peace of the U.S. Catholic Conference of Bishops in opposing the Byrd Amendment, which would have allowed the United States to import strategic minerals from Rhodesia, in contravention of U.N. sanctions.

41. R. H. Randolph, *Dawn in Zimbabwe* (Gweru, Zimbabwe: Mambo Press, 1985), 197-214.

42. Infuriated by an authorization by the minister of defense for his commanders to bomb villages harboring guerrillas, Lamont issued an open letter to the state charging it with being "racist," "oppressive," and not a legitimate government.

43. Randolph, *Dawn in Zimbabwe*, 220.

44. Linden, *Catholic Church and the Struggle for Zimbabwe*, 250.

45. This was done in a prepared speech delivered to both ZANU in Maputo and ZAPU in Lusaka by Archbishop Patrick Chakaipa (report on meetings with the Patriotic Front August 13-21, 1978, quoted in ibid., 278).

46. Interview with Auret. The JPC acted on Mugabe's request shortly after this meeting when guerrillas massacred 16 overseas Pentecostal missionaries, and, according to Auret, it felt satisfied with the ZANU response.

47. Ibid.

48. Linden, *Catholic Church and the Struggle for Zimbabwe*, 275–76.

49. The delegation consisted of Archbishop Patrick Chakaipa, JPC President Monsignor Helmut Reckter, S.J., JPC Secretary Michael Auret, Brother Fidelis Mukonori, Ishmael Muvingi, and Father Bernard Ndlovu.

50. One scholar, Carl Hallencreutz, identifies this meeting as a turning point in church-state relations in Zimbabwe and believes that it laid the groundwork for cooperative relations after the war ("A Council in Crossfire: ZCC 1964–1980," in *Church and State in*

Zimbabwe, ed. Carl Hallencreutz and Ambrose Moyo [Gweru, Zimbabwe: Mambo Press, 1988], 88).

51. Interview with Auret.

52. Linden, *Catholic Church and the Struggle for Zimbabwe*, 280.

53. Interview with Auret.

54. John Deary and Dieter Scholtz, as quoted in Linden, *Catholic Church and the Struggle for Zimbabwe*, 280.

55. In ibid.

56. Ibid.

57. Ibid., 284.

58. Ibid.

59. Ibid.

60. Interview with Auret.

61. Ibid.

62. Ibid.

63. Bishop Lamont, now living in Ireland, met with ZANU and ZAPU leaders, urging them not to outlaw Christianity and not to conduct a Nuremburg-type trial. The Bethlehem Fathers met with the liberation fronts as well to discuss the closing by guerrillas of several schools they ran and to express concern about incidents of guerrilla misconduct. Numerous individuals from the liberation fronts came to CIIR and JPC for personal and logistical needs that arose in the course of the protracted negotiations (interview with McLaughlin; and interview with Neville).

64. Randolph, *Dawn in Zimbabwe*, 36.

65. Interview with McLaughlin.

66. Ibid.

67. In ibid.

68. Linden, *Catholic Church and the Struggle for Zimbabwe*, 270.

69. Sister Janice McLaughlin, October 1978, as reported in ibid.

70. In ibid.

71. However, the Jesuits sent a worker in a chaplaincy-oriented role to work in a ZANU refugee camp in Zambia in early 1979 (interview with Auret).

72. A small number of Catholics did, however, refuse to pay the 5 percent defense surtax to finance the war effort that Salisbury imposed toward the end of the war.

73. Randolph, *Dawn in Zimbabwe*, 220. Randolph gives no indication as to how many native Zimbabwean Catholic workers died in the war.

74. Linden, *Catholic Church and the Struggle for Zimbabwe*, 271.

75. *Daily News* of Tanzania, May 12, 1977, quoted in ibid., 252.

76. Interview on U.K. ITV Religious Programme, broadcast November 30, 1980, as quoted in Randolph, *Dawn in Zimbabwe*, 57–58.

77. Canaan Banana, "The Role of the Church in the Struggle for Liberation in Zimbabwe," in *Turmoil and Tenacity*, ed. Canaan Banana (Harare: College Press, 1989), 205.

78. Interview with Robertson.

79. Ibid.

80. Ibid.

81. The events of the meeting were reconstructed from interviews with former Prime Minister Ian Smith, Harare, April 28, 1992; Emmerson Munangagwa, former head of intelligence and special advisor to Robert Mugabe, Harare, August 17, 1992; and Joram Kucherera, MRA worker, Kwe Kwe, Zimbabwe, August 18, 1992. All three were present at the meeting. Additional information came from interviews with MRA workers who

assisted in arranging the meeting: Alec Smith, Harare, May 27–28, 1991, and by telephone, September 6, 1992; Henry Macnicol, Edinburgh, June 9, 1991; and Robertson.

82. The representative was Machel's young special assistant on Frontline affairs, Fernando Homwano (interview with Kucherera).

83. Ibid.

84. There has been private speculation among some who were aware of the Mugabe-Smith meeting that the speech was a direct result of the encounter. It is possible that the meeting had an impact on the tone and nuances of the speech—Kucherera was present on Tuesday at Mugabe headquarters and witnessed the content being modified in a last-minute rehearsal between Mugabe and top aides in ways he believes to have been a consequence of the meeting (interview with Kucherera). But the evidence is overwhelming that Mugabe and others in the ZANU leadership had been working on unity as a theme of political leadership for months previously. To cite just a few examples: before Lancaster House, the Quakers had noted the topic being discussed by ZANU leaders in Maputo. At Lancaster House, Josiah Tongogara, by no means a moderate among ZANU leaders, spoke at length in an interview on October 29, 1979, about the need to include old enemies in a new government. Throughout his election campaign, Mugabe made clear his intent to create a society with room for everyone. (Cf. de Waal, *Politics of Reconciliation*, 40–47).

85. de Waal, *Politics of Reconciliation*, 49.

86. Although most MRA supporters are theistic, they do not insist on belief in God. They believe that anyone, including atheists, can receive guidance by merely undertaking the discipline of listening to the "inner voice."

87. Frank Buchman, *Remaking the World* (Washington, D.C.: Mackinac Press, n.d. [1948]), xxiv.

88. Interview with Robertson.

89. Interview with Alec Smith by Douglas Johnston and Cynthia Sampson, Falls Church, Va., September 23, 1990.

90. Peter Hannon, *South Africa: What Kind of Change?* (Johannesburg: Grosvenor Books, 1977), 13–18.

91. Henry Macnicol, personal communication dated October 30, 1992. Muzorewa later fell into disrepute within the liberation movement for opting to participate in compromise measures with the Rhodesia Front. But at this time he stood in high esteem as the formal representative of the liberation movement within Rhodesia.

92. Elliott, *Dawn in Zimbabwe*, 63.

93. Kanodereka was an enigmatic figure around whom controversy lingers. He was assassinated by unknown gunmen outside his home after initiating a promising peace effort in 1978 (see Quaker section for more information). Almost a decade later, Ken Flower, the man who for years directed Ian Smith's Central Intelligence Organization, asserted in his memoirs, *Serving Secretly* (Johannesburg: Galago Books, 1987), that Kanodereka was a paid agent of the organization. Flower, now dead, claimed that Kanodereka cooperated in a scheme that recruited many hundreds of young men into the guerrilla forces and then sent them into the bush in poison-doused trousers to die a slow death.

MRA workers dismiss this claim. Says Henry Macnicol, a key MRA worker who worked closely with Kanodereka: "I saw Kanodereka risk his life too many times for the cause of peace to believe such a claim from a man who made his living as a professional deceiver" (interview with Macnicol). Macnicol believes Flower's account is "an elaborate lie, told to discredit [Kanodereka's] life and influence by a man who hated and opposed everything Arthur stood for" (personal communication dated October 30, 1992). According to Alec Smith, the ZANU(PF) leadership went out of its way to provide financial support to the family of Kanodereka in the early 1980s, and over this time Simon Muzenda, Tongogara, and Munangagwa all expressed in strong terms to him or other MRA workers their respect for Kanodereka (telephone interview with Alec Smith).

A verifiable verdict on Kanodereka may never be possible. What can be documented is that he risked his life repeatedly in an ambitious campaign for reconciliation and forgiveness, that he was eloquent and forceful in his many public and private presentations, and that he was unforgettable to all who met him.

94. At the core of the group were a handful of individuals deeply committed to the work of MRA: Alec Smith; Arthur Kanodereka; Ian Robertson; Henry Macnicol, a lifetime MRA worker from Edinburgh, Scotland, who lived in Rhodesia from 1974 to 1984; Steven Sibare, a young Rhodesian who joined MRA as a full-time staff person in 1979; Don Barnett, an accountant; Stan O'Donnell, former secretary of foreign affairs for nine years; Champion Chigwida, a trade unionist; Kevin Hongwe, a student; and Dixon Maremba, a school headmaster. Other sporadic attenders included Sir Cyril Hatty, a former government cabinet minister; Dr. Elliott Gabellah, a member of the Executive Committee of Muzorewa's ANC; Desmond Reader and Gordon Chavunduka, both academics at the University of Rhodesia; Hugh Elliott, a British MRA worker; and Andre Holland, a cabinet member.

95. Individuals in MRA developed friendships with members of ZANU and even more so with ZAPU, and secondary players from both organizations attended MRA conferences on occasion. But no leaders in the external liberation forces publicly identified themselves with MRA in the way that several leaders involved in the Internal Settlement did. Muzorewa, for example, was a close friend of the key MRA strategist Henry Macnicol and attended several MRA gatherings. Chief Chirau, one of Muzorewa's colleagues in the Internal Settlement, was the only politician among a small number of individuals signing a call for unity published by MRA just prior to the elections in 1980.

96. Transcript of presentation by Richard Ruffin, head of MRA activities in the United States, to the Religion and Conflict Resolution Project Steering Group, Center for Strategic and International Studies, Washington, D.C., September 25, 1989.

97. Elliott, *Dawn in Zimbabwe*, 20; Peter Hannon, *Southern Africa: What Kind of Change?* (Johannesburg: Grosvenor Books, 1977), 36–37; and interview with Macnicol.

98. Transcript of Ruffin presentation.

99. Alec Smith, *Now I Call Him Brother* (London: Marshalls, 1984), 85.

100. Interview with Tom Glenn, Harare, April 29, 1992.

101. Interview with Macnicol.

102. Dates of this encounter unknown. Transcript of Ruffin presentation; confirmed in interview with Alec Smith.

103. Interview with Alec Smith.

104. Interview with Macnicol.

105. Interview with Robertson.

106. MRA's intentions are noble, but the reputation of the organization has been mixed due to the earnest agenda MRA workers have brought to their interaction with others. Particularly in South Africa, the author encountered as many people who harshly criticized MRA as a result of personal experience as those who appreciated the group. A common theme is that MRA relationship-building strategies in the 1960s and 1970s, the period when these individuals encountered MRA, were utilitarian and, in the eyes of some, manipulative. For example, one South African described with anger the way in which MRA workers got him to attend what he thought was a social function, but which turned out to be a high-powered call to personal morality. Another individual prominent in the Rhodesian political scene for several decades was scathing in his criticism of MRA visitation strategies: "I

could tell how popular I was from the amount of attention I was getting from MRA. When I was popular, they were interested. When I was not, I didn't hear from them." When they did visit, this politician found the meetings contrived: "They would do anything, absolutely anything, as a pretext to come and talk with me" (interview with Garfield Todd, former prime minister of Rhodesia, Harare, April 30, 1992).

107. The elder Smith claims not to have been aware of any particular moral concerns from his son, nor even of the fact that Kanodereka and other MRA visitors whom Alec took to meet him were affiliated with MRA (interview with Ian Smith).

108. Muzorewa did in fact later yield to this temptation. By the end of the war he had an "auxiliary force" of about 26,000 loyal to his party, the UANC ("The 1980 Rhodesian Election: A Report" [London: Catholic Institute for International Relations, 1980], 10).

109. Interview with Macnicol.

110. Ibid. History again shows that Muzorewa failed to heed the advice of his MRA friends. He conducted an acrimonious, highly personalized election campaign that played heavily on stereotypical fears of Mugabe et al.

111. Ibid.

112. Ibid.

113. Ibid.

114. Interview with Alec Smith by Johnston and Sampson.

115. Interview with Macnicol.

116. Interview with Alec Smith by Johnston and Sampson.

117. Interview with Robertson, Harare, May 1, 1992.

118. Interview with Alec Smith.

119. Transcript of Ruffin presentation.

120. Ibid.

121. Ibid.; also interview with Robertson.

122. One MRA worker estimated that there were three or four showings a week at the MRA house in Salisbury over this time, for groups ranging from two to 20 in size (interview with Robertson).

123. Ibid.; also interview with Alec Smith, Harare, May 1, 1992.

124. Telephone interview with Alec Smith.

125. Ibid.

126. Confidential Quaker report, Quaker Peace and Service, William Penn House, London, 1981.

127. Interview with Jepson.

128. Ibid.

129. "Quaker Experience of Political Mediation," a document resulting from a Quaker consultation, Buckhamshire, England, August 21–24, 1989.

130. Ibid.

131. Interview with Adam Curle, London, July 10, 1991.

132. Interview with Tim Hawkins, Harare, August 17, 1992.

133. The Quakers took up the issue with Mugabe's aides in a later meeting to no immediate avail. But some months later, four abductees were released and the Quakers' contacts in the Salisbury Ministry of Foreign Affairs wrote and thanked them for their contribution to the release, "brought about by the water-dripping-on-a-stone technique of pressing the matter at every opportunity" (the confidential Quaker report cites an undated letter from Tim Hawkins).

134. Confidential Quaker report.

135. Interview with Jepson.

136. Ibid.

137. Although Muzorewa had begun his role in politics as a respected leader of the internal nationalist party, the African Nationalist Congress (ANC), by June 1979, when Nyerere made this overture, Muzorewa was a part of the Internal Settlement government and stood in the ironic role of supporting a war against his old comrades, a task he undertook with all the bombast and rhetoric of his predecessor, Smith.

138. Confidential Quaker report.

139. British Prime Minister James Callaghan sent Cledwyn Hughes on a high-profile mission in November–December 1978 to explore the possibility of all-party talks, an eventuality that would have rendered moot a meeting with Mugabe. After the initiative had dominated the scene for nearly three months, Callaghan announced that the time was not yet ripe for a conference.

140. *Indaba* is a term used widely in southern Africa meaning "palaver." Kanodereka and Byron Hove, a Salisbury lawyer, had recently left Muzorewa's ANC; the third person was Max Chigwida. Kanodereka, of course, was a central figure in MRA from 1975 until his death, and Chigwida, to a lesser extent, was also involved in MRA.

141. Confidential Quaker report.

142. The events included the April 1979 election in Rhodesia; the Quaker-facilitated round of communication between Muzorewa, Nyerere, ZANU, and ZAPU; and, ultimately, the Lusaka Accord, which turned the attention of the parties toward Lancaster House.

143. Of the six requests for meetings, this is the only one that the Quakers knew for certain had taken place (confidential Quaker report).

144. The external liberation fronts were adamant that the British be at the table since, in their view, Rhodesia had yet to become genuinely independent from British rule.

145. Confidential Quaker report.

146. "Quaker Experience of Political Mediation."

147. Although they sought to do this without bias, much of their attention was directed toward helping the Salisbury delegation and the British government understand the position of the Patriotic Front (PF). By all accounts, Carrington played a highly assertive role in mediating the talks. He frequently undertook a strategy of first testing proposals on the Salisbury delegation, and after getting their approval, putting them to the Patriotic Front. On several occasions, when the PF balked, he threatened to go ahead with the proposals anyway and simply work out a bilateral settlement between the British and the Rhodesian governments. A reluctant partner to the talks in the first place, the PF reacted with increasing negativity to these dynamics of the negotiation process. Concerned about the possibility of the whole exercise breaking down, the Quakers sought to reduce the possibility of a walkout by trying to create better understanding, particularly among the British, of PF concerns.

148. "Quaker Experience of Political Mediation."

149. Confidential Quaker report.

150. Ibid.

151. Ibid.

152. Ibid. Throughout this period, the Quakers interacted frequently with the British Council of Churches and thus were able to amplify the impact of their own efforts.

153. Ibid.

154. Ibid.

155. Ibid.

156. Ibid.

157. Nathan Shamuyarira, minister of information and tourism, and Didymus Mutasa, member of the ZANU Executive Committee and later elected speaker of the House of Assembly, made these comments in private meetings with Tony Gilpin (confidential Quaker report).

158. Emeka Anyaoku, then deputy secretary-general of the Commonwealth Secretariat, speaking with Tony Gilpin in March 1980. Anyaoku, of course, was not a party to the conflict but had been at both Lusaka and Lancaster House and was intimately acquainted with the perceptions of all parties (confidential Quaker report).

159. Confidential Quaker report.

160. Ibid.

161. Interview with Curle.

162. Adam Curle, *Tools for Transformation* (Stroud, U. K.: Hawthorn Press, 1990), 85. The comment was made by an American diplomat attached to the United Nations throughout the war to Curle, whom the speaker had no idea was himself a Quaker.

163. Letter from Joan Wicken to Walter Martin, March 27, 1980, as quoted in confidential Quaker report. Wicken had been deeply involved in arranging all of the Quaker meetings with Nyerere.

164. Robert Theobald, *The Rapids of Social Change: Social Entrepreneurship in Turbulent Times* (Indianapolis, Ind.: Knowledge Systems, 1987), 141.

165. Many Americans are oblivious to—and readers from elsewhere may be unaware of—the fact that the American penny is inscribed with the motto "In God We Trust."

166. See Hallencreutz, "Council in Crossfire," 51–101.

167. Interview with Kuchera.

168. Ibid.

169. Hallencreutz, "Council in Crossfire," 98. Presumably this is a quote from council documents.

170. Interview with Kuchera.

171. Right up until the 1980 elections, Nkomo apparently entertained notions of singlehandedly dominating the political future of the country. Cf. Flower, *Serving Secretly*, 264, 268.

172. The Patriotic Front leaders were ambivalent about the churches. On the one hand, their resentment toward Bishop Muzorewa, whom they regarded as a traitor, made them suspicious of churches in general and in particular of members of the delegation thought to favor him. On the other hand, recent grants from the World Council of Churches to the liberation movements had helped restore their faith in the churches, and, additionally, the movements sought the support of the influential council (interview with Kuchera).

173. Quoted by Kuchera during interview.

174. Hallencreutz, "Council in Crossfire," 99, cites a report to this effect by Bishop Shiri, a member of the committee.

175. Interview with Ian Smith.

176. The "ripeness" school of negotiations theory holds that settlement has relatively little to do with the skills and attitudes of the negotiators, and rather is a function of the balance of inputs of internal and external actors involved in the conflict system at any time. When the key parties all decide in a given moment that now is the time most favorable to their own interests to settle, the conflict is "ripe" and settlement becomes likely. So notes Mottie Tamarkin in a thought-provoking paper, "Negotiations or Conflict Resolution in South Africa: Lessons from Zimbabwe" (published in conference proceedings, *Conflicts and Negotiations* [Munich: Herbert Quandt Foundation, 1992], 15–22). Tamarkin draws on Richard Haas's elaboration of ripeness theory to analyze the Rhodesia/Zimbabwe

negotiations. Although this author finds Tamarkin's analysis overly Machiavellian, according to it one could reasonably conclude that the religious actors were several of numerous important influences bringing the situation to a point of "ripeness." To take one instance, Tamarkin believes Margaret Thatcher's about-face in rejecting the Internal Settlement was the key to this conflict becoming "ripe." It is likely that both the Catholics and Quakers contributed to what some called "the education of Maggie Thatcher": the Catholics through their protracted lobbying efforts, and the Quakers through their quiet conversations with British politicians and FCO officials who were part of the complex web of influence at work on Thatcher. Legum (*Battlefronts of Southern Africa*) highlights the influence of the Australians and Mozambicans in Thatcher's change of heart. MRA workers believe that they were influential in tipping Malcolm Fraser, then Australian prime minister, toward challenging Thatcher (interview with MRA worker and senior official in Fraser's administration, Allan Griffith, Washington, D.C., July 19, 1991).

11 ▪

Review of the Findings

DOUGLAS JOHNSTON

Constantly rebuffed, but never discouraged, they
went round from state to state helping people settle
their differences, arguing against wanton attack
and pleading for the suppression of arms, that the
age in which they lived might be saved from its
state of continual war.

Fourth-century B.C. description
of Sun Tzu and his followers

The cases that have been presented demonstrate the important potential for peacemaking represented by religious groups and institutions. This chapter highlights the principles and considerations illustrated in the case studies that might have application in future situations.[1] But first, a few disclaimers are in order.

ANALYTICAL LIMITATIONS

Each case is unique, which creates a problem of comparing dissimilar experiences. Moreover, not all of the cases are about the same aspect of conflict. Three are about nonviolent struggles for political change: East Germany (Chapter 7), the Philippines (Chapter 8), and South Africa (Chapter 9).[2] Three others are about ending wars that were already under way: Nicaragua (Chapter 5), Nigeria (Chapter 6), and Rhodesia/Zimbabwe (Chapter 10). The remaining case is about longer term reconciliation between France and Germany in the aftermath of war (Chapter 4).

Further limitations are imposed by the small sample size of seven case studies, which should be viewed only as a point of departure. There are also limitations of data. Although there is some documentation in the open literature about the role of religious institutions in promoting social change—both violent and nonviolent—there is very little about the intermediary peacemaking role, either on the part of institutions or of other religious actors. The documentation that does exist, usually in the press, is often only fragmentary.

Several reasons explain this gap in coverage. For one thing, some religious actors maintain a very low profile; indeed, confidentiality is often a precondition for their engagement. For another, religious actors have at times been all but invisible to a press that tends to limit its focus to the official activities of government officials and diplomats. That this is changing is evidence of the changing nature of conflict, as well as the increasing involvement of religious figures in peacemaking.

In turn, the limits of the written record have required a heavy emphasis on personal interviews as the principal method of inquiry for the studies included in this volume—an approach that offers both strengths and weaknesses. Perhaps its greatest strength is the fact that the case interviews provide rich new sources of primary data. At the same time, there is a substantial subjective element involved. It is difficult enough to assess after the fact what actually happened in each case situation, but characterizing properly whatever spiritual dimension was at play, with all the intangibles this suggests, is a daunting task. To capture the critical parameters of each of the case studies, a research outline was developed and applied by each of the researchers. This proved useful in reconstructing the historical aspects of the cases (including the political, economic, security, and social context) and the specific activities of the religious actors. Evaluation of the impact of the spiritual dimension has required a more subjective assessment on the part of the individuals interviewed and, ultimately, the researchers.

Beyond the subjective aspects of the analysis, other elements convey a wide and complex array of involvements. Some case studies, for example, suggest that resources from within the local religious community should be tapped (the Philippines, East Germany, Nicaragua, South Africa, and Rhodesia/Zimbabwe). Other cases highlight the value of involving key people from the outside (France/Germany, Nigeria, and, again, Rhodesia/Zimbabwe). In some instances, religious actors worked within the political process (Nicaragua and Nigeria). In others, they remained external to it (France/Germany, the Philippines, and South Africa). In Rhodesia, there was a mix, with the Quakers and, at times, MRA working within the political process, while the Catholic church (and sometimes MRA) exerted influence from the outside. In East Germany, church members operated outside the process during the initial stages of the revolution but later assumed roles integral to the political transition from within.

THE ART OF THE POSSIBLE

The deeper context for all of the cases is the relationship between religion and politics, any treatment of which is bound to carry with it equal dangers of oversimplification and overcomplication. The challenge is to understand the complexities of a given conflict situation and determine the kind of involvement that is needed at any point in time. In making such a determination, however, it is important to remember the critical and often overpowering constraints imposed by the associated political, economic, and security factors. An approximate and favorable congruency on these fronts is often an essential prerequisite to any effective spiritual or religious contribution. In providing an impressionistic survey of the possibilities suggested by the case studies, a distinction will be drawn between those situations in which the churches functioned in their institutional capacity as instruments of change and those in which either church figures or spiritually motivated laypersons engaged in third-party mediation or conciliation.[3]

THE CHURCH AS AN INSTRUMENT OF CHANGE

As suggested earlier in this book, religion as it relates to social conflict is a double-edged sword: it can cause conflict, or it can abate it. Intolerance, divisiveness, and resistance to change have all too often typified the religious contribution. Even in the case studies reported here, one sees the Catholic church supporting an oppressive elite during much of Filipino history and the South African Dutch Reformed church providing the theological justification for apartheid. Yet there is the other side to the coin of religious involvement, the helpful side that comes into play in varying degrees in each of these cases.

In some instances, this positive contribution relates to the evolution of the church's role over time. The Catholic church, for example, underwent a dramatic transformation during the 1960s in which it progressively abandoned its historic role as a supporter of the status quo to become a major force for change. This was a direct result of changes introduced by Pope John XXIII and the Second Vatican Council, stressing the need for social justice.[4] Other denominations have their own histories, with each reflecting a greater or lesser willingness to engage in social action.

The cases demonstrate three forms of church advocacy in promoting nonviolent sociopolitical change:

1. The church can be an active force for change as it was in East Germany and the Philippines.
2. It can serve the same end in a passive capacity by providing a forum for political expression where alternatives do not exist (as the English-speaking churches did in South Africa). In the process, it can assist opposition groups in developing a compelling social vision, much as the churches did in East Germany.
3. It can function as a follower of change, essentially supporting the status quo until such time as secular considerations force a shift in people's expectations. This was best exemplified by the Dutch Reformed church in South Africa. In this mode, the church usually does not accommodate voices of dissent from within, at least not during the early stages.

The church's potential for advancing social change on a nonviolent basis is an important reference point for politicians and foreign policy practitioners alike. This potential can be applied with particular effect where religious values are important to the community or to a key political figure, as they were in the Philippines. Sometimes this opportunity relates to the temporal power of the church within the community. Sometimes it is simply that the church is the only institution having moral legitimacy in the eyes of the populace. At times it is both.

A critical asset in its role as protester is the church's commitment to nonviolence. As demonstrated by the East German churches and the Catholic church in the Philippines, strategic nonviolence is inherently corrosive to a violence-based system. It is also useful in fostering a spirit of self-examination and confession that can mitigate the tendencies toward intolerance and self-righteousness that often lead to violence.

Finally, the church can empower individuals to act by helping them overcome their fear of repression, fear that might otherwise lead to paralysis. In a broader sense, the inculcation of church values can nourish the dissident spirit. This was certainly the case in East Germany and the Philippines. It was also true for the protesting churches in South Africa.

To summarize, the church functions most effectively as an advocate for social change when it possesses and exploits the following attributes:

- institutional stability and moral authority
- a capability for empowering individuals to act
- a commitment to nonviolence.

THE CHURCH AS PEACEMAKER

The church as an institution is often a reflection of the society of which it is a part. Consequently, if a church moves too strongly against forces for social change, it faces the possibility of losing some of its followers. At the same time, as the institutional conscience of society, it is expected to be a voice for justice and peace. Thus, the church is often constrained in the stance that it takes because of its need to balance these sometimes contradictory considerations.

Peacemaking on the part of the church is widely accepted as a humanitarian act consistent with religious belief. Beyond that, and as illustrated by the Rhodesia/Zimbabwe case, the church in some instances enjoys a ready legitimacy based on its respected set of values and the organizational resources to pursue them. When the churches display a general commitment to confession, repentance, and forgiveness, they can also help undermine negative stereotypes and rehumanize relationships (as they did at Rustenburg in South Africa and to a lesser extent in Nicaragua). In this same vein, the practical as well as the spiritual power of prayer should be recognized. Beyond its direct impact on the individuals involved, group prayer offers a means of facing politically awkward ideas—admitting fault, expressing regrets, asking forgiveness, even acknowledging an adversary's humanity.

Another strong attribute that the church can bring to the search for peace in certain situations is a general popular belief that church officials will speak the truth. The influence of the Catholic church in Rhodesia and in the Philippines keyed largely to this presumption. Without truth, there is no trust. With trust, church-sponsored efforts to resolve conflict are likely to be viewed as objective and fair. The same holds true for the feedback that is so essential to the successful conduct of a peace process.

In facilitating conciliation, the church can mobilize community support to reinforce the peace process. Its organization and networks generally give it unique access to most levels of society. And to the extent that it has international connections, it can often generate financial and other forms of assistance from external sources to support the peace process, as was done by the Conciliation Commission in Nicaragua.

Finally, as a community insider, the church is in a strong position to follow through on implemantation of a settlement, addressing future disagreements as they may arise. The role that the South African churches have already played in addressing the violence stemming from political reform provides an excellent example.

Thus, the qualitative assets that contribute to the church's ability to promote peace include:

- an established record for humanitarian care and concern
- a respected set of values, including a reputation for trustworthiness
- unique leverage for promoting reconciliation between conflicting parties
- a capability for mobilizing community, national, and international support for a peace process
- an ability to follow through locally in the wake of a settlement.

OTHER THIRD PARTIES

Another category of intermediary in religious peacemaking is the third party who operates with the extended and often loose sponsorship of a church or ecumenical organization. For example, the Quakers enjoy the financial support of their parent denomination, while Moral Re-Armament is an independently funded network of spiritually motivated individuals without organizational ties to any specific church. Whether church-supported or not, these individuals typically operate with a degree of independence that sets their efforts apart from those of the institutional church. Both the Quakers and MRA, which figure prominently in the case studies, provide good examples for assessing the potential offered by religiously motivated third parties in resolving conflict.

Unlike church-based third parties, independent intermediaries may not be based in the community. This, in turn, limits their long-term ability to monitor and follow through on succeeding developments, a capability that derives from their ongoing connectedness to the parties in conflict.

A number of special attributes come into play when considering the role of spiritually motivated peacemakers acting either apart from or as a loose extension of the church. They often bring a spectrum of capabilities to peacemaking that official-level efforts can seldom assemble. As demonstrated in the Nigeria and Rhodesia/Zimbabwe cases, the Quakers' well-established reputation for pacifism and humanitarian concern greatly enhances their right to be heard and taken seriously. The credibility of this reputation is strengthened even further when there has been an historic involvement in peacemaking within the community, as was the case with both MRA and the Quakers in Rhodesia.

Religious convictions may not enter explicitly into a peacemaker's discourse, but they underlie and inform his or her practice. The Quakers, for example, operate out of a sense of spiritual calling that takes to heart the "blessed are the peacemakers" dictum of Matthew 5:9. As demonstrated in both Nigeria and Rhodesia, this sense of calling enables them to rise above pessimism and the inevitable setbacks that would otherwise discourage and possibly defeat those who operate on a political basis.

These groups are also by nature self-effacing. They recognize that their ability to contribute to a just and lasting solution is often inversely proportional to the credit and recognition that they receive. This quality enabled the Quakers to gain acceptance by both sides in Nigeria where many others had failed.

As illustrated in two of the cases, the Quaker approach to peacemaking involves establishing personal relationships with the individual disputants. This, in turn, facilitates opening lines of communication, taking steps to reduce suspicions on both sides, and pursuing a negotiated settlement of differences.

MRA, for its part, seeks social change through changing the attitudes of individuals, particularly those in positions of influence (on the assumption that morality among an enlightened leadership will ultimately trickle down and affect those below). In so doing, it leans heavily on personal networking and the enlistment of outsiders who are able to offer relevant insights based on past experience. Unlike the Quakers, MRA often incorporates a major public outreach in its approach, as reflected in its numerous newspaper ads leading up to Rhodesia's independence.

In summary, beyond those characteristics that "other third parties" share in common with church actors, additional attributes that they may bring to peacemaking include:

- an historic involvement in peacemaking within the community
- unusual persistence in the face of adversity
- a special ability to influence the attitudes and actions of political leaders.

THE REALITIES OF REALPOLITIK

The political, economic, and security dimensions of most social confrontations usually outweigh the religious, even when the conflict is superficially about religion. In South Africa, for example, the National party's August 1986 decision to move toward power sharing may have been motivated, at least in part, by the Rhodesian experience. The choice would have been either to coopt the reform process while the white government still had the leverage to do so or to let events deteriorate to a point where whites could lose power altogether (as they did in

Rhodesia) or, worse, be plunged into a violent revolution with substantial loss of life. This is not to suggest that the role played by the churches was insignificant. On the contrary, it was a critical ingredient and recognized as such by South African President Frederik de Klerk in his call for the churches to participate in the decision-making process. So, at least in the case of South Africa, religion was not the missing dimension of statecraft. It was recognized and subsumed in a larger and complex whole.

At other times, religious institutions may engage in political activism. As illustrated in South Africa, the Philippines, and East Germany, the church may be the only major institution over which the state has not been able to exercise complete control. The fact that this was so in East Germany is particularly interesting, given that the church was effectively outlawed in most communist regimes. As long as the church is independent, as it eventually was in East Germany, it becomes facto ipso an alternative authority to a corrupt regime that has run its course.

When the church steps in to fill a political vacuum, its contribution becomes all the more credible when it is prepared to extricate itself as quickly as possible—lest it preempt the needed development of viable political institutions. The South African churches attempted to do exactly this once the political process had caught up with the reform movement (Desmond Tutu, for example, reverted to shepherding his flock), but they were subsequently called back to deal with the violence in the townships. Even the best of plans can go awry.

THE POSSIBILITIES

Each of the case studies has presented a situation in which religious or otherwise spiritually motivated actors played a role in promoting nonviolent social change or in preventing, attenuating, or resolving conflict. Clearly, the realpolitik aspects of any given situation always loom large, if not overwhelming; but these studies show that religious factors can also be significant. In all probability, their special contributions could not have been achieved by comparable secular efforts.

Each of the case studies describes a response to the imperatives of a given situation. Where there is no viable "second party" to provide an effective counter to oppressive behavior on the part of a regime, as was the case in East Germany, the Philippines, and South Africa, the church becomes a logical candidate to fill that role.

By the same token, when the need is for a third-party intermediary to reconcile conflicting interests among two or more principals, it becomes important to take into account the institutional base of the prospective third party in terms of its acceptability to the principals. A temporal base, such as that of an established church (which may or may not have a vested interest in the outcome), might be appropriate in one set of circumstances. In others, a distinctly nonpartisan, outside entity such as the Quakers may be more effective.

At times, both roles—second and third party—might be required, and they may in some circumstances be played by the same religious actor, as was the case with certain of the East German churches. In other situations, these roles are better played by multiple actors as in Rhodesia, where MRA, the Quakers, and the Catholic Church all contributed. In this latter scenario, it is interesting to note the potential for genuine synergy across organizational lines, in which the whole truly does become greater than the sum of the individual parts. This, in turn, suggests the desirability of a multiplicity of actors and roles in some settings.

CONCLUSION

The principal contribution that religious actors can bring to secular confrontations is their unique potential for mediating conflict in situations where a mutually debilitating impasse has been reached or where the major political, economic, and security issues have largely been resolved. Without the higher level of trust elicited by their involvement, breakthroughs to settlement would undoubtedly take longer or might not take place at all. By its very nature, any spiritual contribution to conflict resolution will be impossible to isolate and measure. But at least it is possible to determine with some degree of certainty that strictly secular approaches would have had even greater difficulty in achieving similar results. This test would clearly have been met in Nigeria and Nicaragua. It was probably also the case in postwar France and Germany and in Rhodesia during its war of independence.

It is axiomatic that things are never totally as they seem. Just as consideration of the Rhodesian experience may have been a contributing factor to South African reform, so too might the MRA initiative to bring Robert Mugabe and Ian Smith together have saved the lives of countless Rhodesians. One may never know. But one thing is certain: the stakes in the wake of the Cold War are high and getting higher. The central lesson of these case studies is that religion does not always have to be a negative factor in the policymaking equation. Its potential contribution to peacemaking is substantial and worthy of further study.

Notes

1. Many of the observations cited in this chapter flow from the discussions of the case studies by the project's steering group.

2. While South Africa has been plagued with isolated incidents of violence for a number of years, the conflict has not erupted into anything approximating full-scale civil war. It is on this basis that the political change process is characterized as nonviolent.

3. The term *mediation* is commonly applied to the act of resolving substantive differences by acting as an intermediary between two or more conflicting parties. *Conciliation*, on the other hand, applies to those actions taken by an intermediary to improve the attitude of the conflicting parties toward one another (largely by correcting misperceptions, reducing unreasonable fears, and improving communication).

4. Samuel P. Huntington, "Religion and the Third Wave," *National Interest* (Summer 1991), 31.

12 ∎

World Religions and Conflict Resolution

HARVEY COX

with ARVIND SHARMA, MASAO ABE,

ABDULAZIZ SACHEDINA, HARJOT OBEROI, AND MOSHE IDEL

*It is the will of God that we be tolerant of those who
disagree with us about the will of God.*

Richard John Neuhaus

The story is told of the late John Foster Dulles that, during one of the recurrent conflicts between Israel and its Arab neighbors, he invited an Israeli and a Syrian representative—the first a Jew, the second a Muslim—to have a private heart-to-heart conversation with him. When they met, the secretary of state warmly shook hands with each of them, then smiled and asked, "Why can't we all sit down together and work this thing out like Christian gentlemen?"

The story is probably not true, but it does highlight two important considerations about religion and conflict resolution in the contemporary world. The first is that people continue to believe (correctly, it can be argued) that there are important if untapped resources within religious traditions for addressing the conflicts that often divide peoples and nations. The second, however, is that when one thinks of religious values as an aid to conflict resolution, most—and not just Mr. Dulles—tend to draw too exclusively on their own faith traditions, if only because they have so little awareness of the analogous possibilities offered by those of their global neighbors. This chapter suggests both the possibilities and the difficulties involved in drawing on the moral insights of the living religions of the world to help resolve human political and cultural antagonisms.

The role the religions of the world might play in helping members of the human family live together amicably is a particularly critical one today. A century ago, forecasters often predicted the disappearance or increased marginalization of religions in the modern era, but this has hardly turned out to be the case. Those who in the late nineteenth and early twentieth centuries foresaw the triumph of scientific rationality or of various secular and humanistic ideologies did not, it turns out, read the tea leaves very accurately. Instead, the twentieth century has witnessed a phenomenal renaissance of religious traditions in virtually every part of the globe.

It is true that, for understandable reasons, not many people perceive this resurgence of religious sentiment as a resource for conflict resolution. In fact, the revival of religion has often accompanied and even fueled ethnocultural and national rivalries and has more often stoked the fires of discord than contributed to devising solutions for extinguishing them. Thus, when one thinks about the role religions have played in recent world history, one's thoughts jump immediately to the numbing conflicts in Northern Ireland or to Lebanon where Catholics, Protestants, and Muslims seem to fight incessantly—both with each other and among themselves. One might also be tempted to think only of the negative aspects of the resurgent Islam in the twentieth century and the bellicose rhetoric of the Ayatollah Khomeini and others. When one adds the communal riots in India between Hindus and Muslims and between Hindus and Sikhs, the ethnic violence between Sinhalese Buddhists and Tamil Hindus in Sri Lanka, and the Tibetan resistance to the Chinese suppression of Buddhism in their country, once again it is bloody, not peaceable, images that come to mind.

True, on further reflection, these clashes often turn out to be rooted more in culture and class than in religion. Still, religion often seems to add complications. In conflict situations, a particularist and exclusivist religious worldview has often become the source of one group's intolerant behavior toward another within the same country. To be sure, the reasons underlying this intolerant behavior are complex; however, the manipulation of religious beliefs by those in positions of authority, in both matters of religion (imams, priests, rabbis, and others) and politics, is clearly a contributing factor.

But could it go the other way? Could the religions of the world make a valuable contribution to increasing understanding and harmony between conflicting parties rather than exacerbating tensions? Are there resources in these spiritual traditions that could contribute to the healing of human community? The answer is decidedly yes, and this chapter sketches some of the key values of selected religious traditions of the world (exclusive of Christianity, which is well represented in the case studies) that might be drawn upon to facilitate mutual understanding, trust, and dialogue.

Many other religions might have been included in this survey. The spiritual traditions of indigenous peoples such as Native Americans are not addressed, for instance, and nothing is said about Shintoism, the powerful tradition of one of the world's most important nations, Japan. Nor is there a discussion of the amalgam of Confucianism and Buddhist elements that underlies the sometimes seemingly secular society of China. Rather, this chapter surveys three of the largest religious groups—Hinduism, Buddhism, and Islam—and two smaller traditions—Sikhism and Judaism (which although not global in the sense of the first three, are nonetheless important because of their ongoing involvement in major areas of tension).

In each case, the basic themes and stories, the scriptures, and traditional wisdom are briefly explored. An examination is then made of the lives of selected exemplary figures nourished by these traditions, including personalities from historical periods and, in some instances, more recent times. One of the questions addressed to each of these traditions, in turn, is how it views other faiths. This aspect is helpful because a religion's evaluation and definition of other religions can often serve as a valuable clue to its attitude toward human conflict in general and to its specific behavior in any given conflict situation.

HINDUISM

18. *The wise one [i.e., the* Atman, *the Self] is not*
     born, nor dies.
     This one has not come from anywhere, has not
     become anyone.
     Unborn, constant, eternal, primeval, this one
     Is not slain when the body is slain.
19. *If the slayer think to slay,*
     If the slain think himself slain,
     Both these understand not.
     This one slays not, nor is slain.
20. *More minute than the minute, greater than*
     the great,
     Is the Self that is set in the heart of a creature
     here.

Katha Upanishad 16–20

The term applied by Westerners to the religious traditions of the Indian sub-continent—*Hinduism*—sometimes obscures the fact that India is the nurturing mother of a range of metaphysical theories, ritual practices, and devotions that defy reduction to a single system. Hinduism comprises a multiplicity of sects that are more or less closely affiliated with the major Indian religious traditions (Vaishnava and Shaiva) that recognize the priestly status of the Brahmans. Consequently, when one asks about the resources of Hinduism for the resolution of conflict, it is natural that a host of contradictory images should leap to mind. On one side crouches the stereotype of the passive other-worldly yogi, so intent on internal spiritual concerns that nothing in the outside world affects him; on the other lurks the brutal memory of the riots between Hindus and Muslims that erupted following the partition of India and that continue sporadically today. Above all towers the familiar profile of the man in loincloth, sandals, and spectacles who was perhaps the twentieth century's greatest exemplar of religiously inspired conflict resolution. How do these pieces all fit together?

In the primal sources of Hinduism—the tradition of the Vedas (produced from about 1500–500 B.C.E.)—the underlying value is *order*. The Sanskrit term for order, *rita*, means that which is right and proper in the universe and in human society. *Rita* signifies the cosmic design that applies to both men and to gods. It is the all-inclusive and single most important Vedic idea. The social expression of *rita* is the distribution of responsibilities among the various strata and groups in society: priests, scholars, merchants, farmers, and others. One of these "castes" is the warrior's, but it is important to point out that the warrior's responsibility is precisely that of *maintaining rita*, preserving the interrelated cosmic and social order. Although important subsequent developments have richly supplemented this ancient Vedic wisdom, the pervasive notion of the right ordering of life remains enormously influential in Hindu thinking.

After the Vedic period, the next major stage of Hindu religious history is identified with the *Upanishads* (800–500 B.C.E.), the teachings of which constitute what is sometimes called *classical Hinduism*, or the *high tradition*. In the *Upanishads* the central notion is *dharma*, meaning righteousness, religion, law, or duty—that which is morally binding for all human beings according to their respective *jati* (birth). *Dharma* thus includes the full range of one's social and moral obligations, and it is from the concept of *dharma* that those principles and values are derived which contribute to the resolution of tensions in both one's personal and social life.

The other key concept of the *Upanishads* is the ultimate identity between *Atman* and *Brahman*: between the neuter spiritual force that sustains the universe and the self. In fact, this identity is so complete that in most classical interpretations, belief in the existence of a separate individual personality is held to be illusory. This unity is epitomized by the famous *Upanishadic* phrase *Tat tvam asi*, which is sometimes translated into English as "that thou art." This formula radically undercuts the illusion of selfhood and points to the ultimate oneness of that which appears to be separate or in conflict.

How have Hindu scholars mined these teachings to address human conflict? They have derived rules of conduct at two levels. First is the behavior expected of ordinary people, who are exhorted to follow their *dharma*. Such fidelity will both minimize social antagonism and ensure a good rebirth, until eventually the drop of water returns to the primal sea and no further rebirth is needed. Second is the conduct expected of the more informed person, which requires the person's pursuit of a spiritual discipline (*yoga*), and thereby the gradual elimination of all selfish actions. Both paths lead ultimately to the One.

Like any other human vision that becomes embroiled in the political arena of human reality and its strenuous pressure on the otherwise ideal teachings of harmony and peace, Hinduism has had its share of tension in history. When Hinduism first came to be associated with political power and to dominate social life, some attempts at religious uniformism led to persecution between Shaivite Hindus and Vaishnavite Hindus; but sectarian diversity and caste multiplicity eventually came to be accepted. Hinduism thus emerged as essentially free of religious intolerance.

In its bearing toward other faiths, Hinduism's main characteristics are twofold: tolerance and absorption. Over the centuries, Hindus have displayed a remarkable capacity for integrating aspects of other religious traditions into their own framework. The following admonition by the famous Hindu scholar Keshub Chunder Sen (1838–84) exemplifies this approach:

How the Hindu absorbs the Christian; how the Christian assimilates the Hindu! Cultivate this communion, my brethren, and continually absorb all that is good and noble in each other. Do not hate, do not exclude others, as the sectarians do, but include and absorb all humanity and all truth.

Accordingly, India was a natural haven for religious sects of all sorts. A number of persecuted groups—such as the Jacobite Christians, Jews, Zoro-astrians, and Shiite sects of more than one variety—have sought asylum in Hindu India. This tolerant diversity was maintained, however, by insulating the several religious communities from one another, which prevented close social interaction. Thus, the potential for dialogue—or confrontation—has always been present. Indian religious thought developed a firm tradition of universalism—the idea that all the various religious forms represent diverse paths to the one Truth, paths that are all in some degree valid. Although such a universalism was not unique to India, it certainly became a practical means for facilitating relations among the various religious communities.

Such a universalism was not naturally satisfactory to all Hindus nor to all Muslims, however. Eventually the universalist approach was set aside by a communalist approach that tended to emphasize the confessional community within a given area rather than the territorial nation as a whole. Communalism thus divided India into a Hindu and a Muslim nation, with each having its own culture and social structure. More than anything else, communalism demanded separate *political* structures to express the two distinct social structures, which ultimately led to the horrors of communal violence. Once the British withdrew as colonial overlords, political communalism led many educated Hindus and Muslims to either search for a spiritual meaning or to sink into hopeless disillusionment with regard to the value of religious belief.

As noted later in this discussion of other world religions, one can see here at the heart of the Hindu vision both its sources for restraint and justice and some causes for tension and confrontation. The absorption of insights from other religions seems natural to the Hindu, but it is often rejected by representatives of other faiths. It is especially difficult for monotheistic religious traditions such as Christianity and Islam to accept this "anything can be included" basis for religious interaction. These more particularistic traditions, though they may respect and even admire the tolerance of Hinduism, tend to be suspicious of its genius for digesting and incorporating all that enters its realm. Still, the underlying Hindu insight—that what appears to be divided is at some level essentially one, and that conflict lies at the level of perception, not of reality—can sometimes (but obviously not always) serve as a valuable corrective when a conflict seems to defy resolution. Especially for Westerners, whose intellectual traditions tend to feature opposing forces (God and world, insider and outsider, class struggle, thesis and antithesis), it is sometimes salutary to see that what appears at first to be irresolvable animosities can turn out, on closer examination, to be attributable to different ways of perceiving.

In the contemporary world, it is Mahatma Gandhi who incarnates the Hindu approach to conflict resolution most clearly. Of course, Gandhi was deeply influenced by Christian teachings. He once remarked that when he first read the Sermon on the Mount, "it went straight to my heart." One reason Jesus' words touched Gandhi so deeply may be that they evoked associations with his very Hindu conviction that even the bitterest enmity can be made to give way to reconciliation if the actors can be led to *see* the situation differently.

Despite the undeniable Christian influences on his thinking, Gandhi remained a Hindu throughout his life. In fact, it is in his uncanny capacity to tolerate differences and to absorb insights from other faiths that we see his essential Hinduism at work. His underlying belief was that the key to overcoming enmity was to make a friend of the enemy. He always approached social conflict with a candor designed to assure those on the other side that he did not wish to disgrace or humiliate them. He believed that hostilities among people arose not from some permanent stain of sin but from a mistaken perception of what was ultimately good for all parties. One can see in this point of view reflections of both the ancient Vedic emphasis on order and the Upanishadic notion of the ultimate oneness of that which appears to be disparate or conflictual. Gandhi's actions were premised on the belief that even the most hostile opponent could be "taught" by confronting him with patient, nonviolent suffering.

Gandhi significantly influenced the ministry of Martin Luther King, Jr., and the examples of these two men, in turn, helped shape the nonviolent revolutions that shook Eastern Europe in 1989. That both King and Gandhi died by assassination shows how high a price can be exacted by the consistent application of a religiously based ethic to social hostility. The fact that Gandhi died at the hand of a fellow Hindu who believed the Mahatma was abusing the tradition is both a tragic denouement to his life story and a reminder of the deep moral ambiguity present in all religious traditions.

Gandhi's martyrdom on the altar of Hindu-Muslim unity highlights a facet of modern Hindu thought that has consciously and constantly supported the view that each religion is sufficient for its believer. It thus tends to discourage proselytization. "This proselytization," Gandhi declared, "will mean no peace in the world." Gandhi preferred vertical to horizontal conversion—that is when people rejoice in "seeing Hindus become better Hindus and Mussalmans become better Mussalmans and Christians become better Christians," instead of wanting Hindus to become Muslims, Muslims to become Christians, and so on.

BUDDHISM

Tangle within, without, lo! in the toils
Entangled is the race of sentient beings
Hence would I ask thee, Gotama, of this:
Who is it can from this tangle disembroil?
      Kindred Sayings, 1:20, Pali Canon

One of the most intriguing features of Buddhism for anyone interested in religious sources for conflict resolution is that it arose precisely as a method for coping with just such dilemmas. The opening verse of the Visuddhimarga in the Pali Canon, quoted above, bears witness to this characteristic.

Gotama, the Buddha (563?–483? BCE), was born in India into a Hindu society divided by the contradictory teachings and disparate metaphysical theories of diverse schools of thought and practice. The story of his childhood discovery of human conditions and states of aging, illness, and death enshrines the motivation for his spiritual quest. Especially for the purposes of this chapter, it is important to recall that as he set out on this search, Gotama was equally troubled by the baffling cacophony of religious answers he heard. To cope with this confusion, he advocated an approach to religion and to life informed by three simple principles: compassion, "critical tolerance," and the wisdom that can come only from experience (*prajna*).

Critical tolerance means that one must begin by giving those with whom one differs, even on very vital questions, the benefit of the doubt; it is an attitude shaped by compassion. One accepts all one honestly can of the other's position. The real key to the encounter with fundamental disagreement, however, is the experiential one. The Buddha taught that no teaching or idea—his own included—should be accepted simply because it is taught by an authority or is said to be revealed. It must be "empirically tested" in life and through the practice of rigorous meditation.

In everyday behavior, Buddha was an eloquent advocate of the "middle way." He spurned both external asceticism and self-indulgence, exemplifying a life of balance, sobriety, and gentleness. His lifestyle eschewed fanaticism, and his teachings suggest that our stubborn desire to win the argument, to shape the other person to our preferences, and to be in control all spring from an ego that has not yet learned the disciplines of nonattachment and nonaggression.

Does this demanding ethic have any relevance in the world of organized power within which statesmen and politicians operate? To cast some light on this question, one can look to the man who is often held to be the best example of the Buddhist ruler, the great Indian king Ashoka (269–232 BCE). The story goes that just as Ashoka was feeling the pangs of regret that arose from the suffering he had caused by his far-flung conquests, he also heard the Enlightened One's teachings. As a result, he left behind his Hindu upbringing and became a Buddhist. He then went on to try to forge a kingdom in which the various religions could dwell together peaceably. Even more importantly, he decided that his commitment to the "middle way" of the Buddha, although it allowed for self-defense, excluded all wars of aggression.

Ashoka's career is important because it marks a turning point. In his lifework, the Buddha's demanding moral and spiritual teachings, which had previously been practiced mainly by monks because they were considered too difficult for those involved in the troubling ambiguities of governance, were shown to represent an ethic that could also guide public policy.

Ashoka's reign raises another question about religion and conflict, however. As a convert, he displayed the zeal converts characteristically do and, while tolerating other paths, adopted a goal of converting all of India to the Buddha's way. He erected stupas and sent out missionaries, to places as distant as Egypt, Syria, and Greece. His own brother headed the mission to Sri Lanka, where Buddhism remains the principal religion today, centuries after it virtually disappeared from the land of its birth.

The Buddhist "conquest" of southeast Asia, however, took its toll. Today in Sri Lanka one can witness some of the negative effects of using a religion, even such an essentially pacifistic one as Buddhism, to bolster a national and ethnic ideology. The question thus posed is how religious values can inform the actual policymaking of a state without losing some vital aspect of their spiritual essence. How can a ruler (or government) draw on a religious tradition without imposing his (or its) values on religious and cultural minorities? It has been the strong conviction of secularistic political thinkers that basing public policy on religious values nearly always causes division and rancor, but this opinion is based on the belief (for which there is more than a little evidence) that religion is *essentially* divisive. However, there is also evidence to suggest that when religion is *appropriately* related to the public sphere, it can contribute to healing.

There can be little doubt that despite nineteenth-century predictions of its imminent demise, Buddhism is a vital spiritual force in the world today. After its virtual disappearance from India, it has continued to inform cultures of southeast Asia, Tibet, China, and Japan. In the past 150 years, Buddhist teachers have made a distinct impact on the West, especially in artistic and intellectual circles. Since Buddhists do not insist on belief in a deity as essential to their worldview, they may be in a better position than some other traditions to help a skeptical postmodern world in its struggle toward enlightenment. Further, Buddhism is able to enter into fusion and synthesis with other religious traditions more easily than many of its counterparts. Its interaction with Japanese Shintoism is a good example. The cultural and religious synthesis in Japan is so seamless at most points that it is sometimes impossible to distinguish between the two traditions. Japanese people happily practice both with no sense of contradiction.

The Buddhist idea of critical tolerance is likely to become increasingly significant in a religiously pluralistic world. Buddhism does not confuse tolerance with the uncritical acceptance of the other person's point of view. For Buddhism, tolerance represents that space from within which its own doctrines, as well as those of others, can be examined without prejudice on the basis of their inherent truth or value.

Buddhism carries with it an ineradicable ethos—a unique core of meanings and values that usually, but not always, mandates a reasonable, temperate, and balanced approach to conflict. When Buddhist monks immolated themselves in front of their pagodas to protest the Vietnam war 25 years ago, their actions caught the eye of informed observers in part because they were so uncharacteristic. Such a radical gesture dramatized their utter desperation. In any case, the ancient and supple wisdom of Gotama, who was troubled by the tragedies of the human condition and by the contradictory nostrums offered for its healing, is likely to continue offering a rich depository of insights for a long time to come.

ISLAM

In the Name of God, the Merciful, the
  Compassionate —

Praise belongs to God, Lord of all Being,
the All-merciful, the All-compassionate, the
  Master of the Day of Doom.

Thee only we serve; to Thee alone we pray for
  succor.
Guide us in the straight path,
the path of those whom Thou hast blessed,
not of those against whom Thou art wrathful,
nor of those who are astray.

                              Koran, opening chapter

Islam makes particularly pressing the question being posed here: Can religious traditions provide a resource for resolving tensions among peoples? We live at a time when the once culturally and politically powerful Islamic realm has entered a period of religious and political renewal. This energetic resurgence of Islam as an alternative to secular ideologies is occurring not just in the traditional ambience of the Arab world, but also in Asia and Africa—indeed, on a global scale. In news accounts from Trinidad to Iran to the Philippines, this activist Islam is in the headlines, often portrayed as representing a ruthless urge for power and domination—hardly the characteristics one would look to as sources of reconciliation.

At the same time, there is perhaps no other time in modern history when sincerely religious Muslims, Jews, and Christians are seeking so searchingly for the means to resolve conflict by highlighting the universally recognizable principles of their respective exclusivist religious heritages.

Islam, the last of the Abrahamic religions, was proclaimed by the Prophet Muhammad (570–632 c.e.) in the seventh century in Arabia. When Muhammad was growing up in Mecca, he was aware of the social inequities and injustices that existed in a tribal society dominated by a few powerful chiefs. The growth of Mecca as a commercial center had weakened the humanism of tribal societies to a point where the weakest members and the downtrodden were left with no security. Islam emerged in the midst of a serious socioeconomic imbalance between the rich and the poor and at a time of tension between the extreme forms of self-centered individualism (which rejected responsibility to others in society) and tribal bigotry (which failed to take into account the existence of individual human dignity beyond the tribal bond).

Consequently, Islam (meaning "submission to the will of God") became synonymous with a struggle to establish a monotheistic faith and to create an ethical public order that embodied divine justice and mercy. Muhammad was both a prophet and a statesman who instituted a series of reforms to create a community based on religious affiliation. This dual role of the founder of Islam also marked a distinctive feature of Islamic faith, which has not conceded absolute separation between the religious and temporal spheres of human activity and has insisted on the ideal of unity of civil and moral authority under a divinely enacted legal system, the Sharia. The Sharia provided Muslims with a divinely approved blueprint for human conduct that was inherently and essentially religious. It dealt with every aspect of conscience, from interpersonal relations to an individual's relationship with God. On the interpersonal level, questions of ethical content were treated in every possible sphere of human activity, including governance.

In the promulgation of the Sharia, an inevitable tension was generated with those who did not share its commitment to create or maintain the Islamic polity. Moreover, under the Sharia, the Islamic polity could not bestow full equality to those who held other beliefs and practiced other forms of worship. It did, however, accord to the followers of other monotheistic faiths—Jews, Christians, and Zoro-astrians—a degree of practical and theoretical tolerance.

The most authoritative source of Islamic views regarding interfaith and inter-personal relations is the Koran, which Muslims believe to have been revealed to the Prophet Muhammad by God himself. The central tenet of Islam is the affirmation of the divine unity, the Oneness of God, which constitutes the integrity of human existence for the person individually and as a member of society. The Koran teaches that all men and women are naturally both moral and spiritual, having been endowed by an innate disposition to know the difference between good and evil. More importantly, they have an inclination toward God, regardless of the particular spiritual tradition that one follows.

One also finds within Islamic teachings, however, a note of sharp criticism directed against distortions of religion, especially the various forms of "idolatry" and "associationism" (ascribing divinity to things or persons that are merely God's creatures). Muhammad taught his followers to respect the religious prophets and teachers who came before him, from Abraham to Jesus, but he himself is believed by Muslims to be the "Seal of the Prophets," the last bearer of the divinely inspired message before the final day of judgment. Muslims therefore believe they have a moral responsibility to set up divine scales of justice on earth that will lead to the creation of an ideal sphere of moral and spiritual existence for humanity. This requirement has made Islam one of the most activist faiths in history, resulting, among other things, in the conquests of the areas between the Nile and the Oxus by Muslims.

Thus, there is at the core of activist Islam a tension between its unqualified affirmation of the integrity of all human beings in the matter of negotiating their spiritual destiny, as taught by the Koran, and its historical commitment to bring ·under its dominion the entire earth as the "sphere of *islam*."

As noted in the case of Hinduism, historically when the confessional religions came to be associated with power and to dominate social life, there were persecu-tions and confrontations with those who did not share the dominant faith's claim to exclusive truth. In the case of Islam, the intricate relationship between the religion itself and power is based on the requisites of accepting the faith and taking up the moral challenge of creating a public order on earth that reflects the divine will.

Hence, the course of Islamic history was conditioned by the human response to the divine challenge to rise above self-centered pettiness and to work toward the ethical public order. This path toward moral and ethical perfection has been both universalistic in its appeal to justice and equity on earth and particularistic in its demand to adhere to the particular revelation given to the prophet. The latter demand was the consequence of the historical circumstances in which *islam*, the universal message delivered to humanity by all the prophets of God, became particularized under specific conditions of the early community of Islam.

To be sure, this particularization was accepted by the Koran as both a human necessity and a divine mystery when it proclaimed:

> The truth comes from thy Lord; then be not among the doubters. Every man has his direct to which he turns; so be you forward in good works. Wherever you may be, God will bring you all together; surely God is powerful over everything. (Koran, 2:145)

Moreover, it was undesirable for human beings to coerce one another in matters of religion, as is made explicit in the following passage:

> Say [O Muhammad]: O unbelievers, I serve not what you serve and you are not serving what I serve, nor am I serving what you have served, neither are you serving what I serve. To you your religion, and to me my religion! (109:1–5)

A later message, "No compulsion is there in religion" (2:258), also excludes coercion in matters of faith. Religious faith can only be genuine if it is entered into freely. Since Islam was related to the civil order, however, it was deemed proper to require people living under its political dominion to comply with the social norms of the Sharia, the sacred law. This compliance with Islamic public order has been the major source of conflict in areas where religious minorities are not granted the same civil and political rights that accrue to the Muslim majority. Thus, the Sharia reflects a premodern world order in which, at least theoretically, the universal norms of Islam are to be promulgated as the law of the land.

Establishment of a modern international order made up of nation-states has put enormous pressure on Muslim intellectuals to rethink the philosophical underpinnings of the Koran that speak to universal moral principles touching all human beings, regardless of their particular religious tradition. The recognition of universal moral virtues with which all human beings are endowed thus allows for religious pluralism and respect, not only for fellow monotheists but also for followers of any other religious tradition. The function of divine revelation is to supplement the common ethical sense (Koran, 91:8).

To a Western reader this important concept of "the common ethical sense" (*al-ma'ruf*) calls to mind the philosophical idea of natural law, or natural moral reason, which has played such an important part in the history of Western moral philosophy and predates the Christian era. The idea is also found in Christianity, as in St. Paul's Epistle to the Romans, in which he insists that all people are endowed with the capacity to know right from wrong. The concept then wends its way through Western theological and philosophical thought up to the contemporary period.

It is important to note that the Koran regards this innate capacity for moral goodness ingrained in the human psyche as leading to a rationally derived guidance that transcends the revelations, which are the other major source for human guidance. In fact, the Koran portrays the religious diversity of the human family not as an accident but as something that has been willed by God:

> If God had willed he would have made you one nation. But He did not do so, that he may try you in what has come to you [as guidance].

> So, compete with one another in good works; Unto God shall you return; altogether; and He will tell you the Truth about what you have been disputing. (5:48)

Contrary to the negative depiction of Muslims as inspired by a fanatical, one-sided, and irrational religion, both in its original sources and in its authoritative teachings, Islam emphasizes elements that can be drawn upon to resolve tensions among groups and nations. The Koran does not merely affirm the validity of religious pluralism, asking in effect for a contest in goodness and fidelity that God himself will eventually adjudicate; it also insists on the common moral wisdom of the human race. Nevertheless, much of the history of Islam has inclined toward exclusivism, intolerance, and, at times, proselytization by the sword.

A historical figure who exemplifies the salient moral principles of Islam is Akbar (1542–1605), the greatest of the Mogul emperors of India. Skilled in the arts of war and diplomacy, Akbar enlarged the Mogul realm to include the whole of northern India. Although he was illiterate, he knew his kingdom would suffer from fissures and hatred unless the various religions were reconciled, so he made his courts at Delhi and Agra centers for interreligious and intercultural conversation. He surrounded himself with Muslim scholars, along with Hindu Brahmins and Jesuits (who by this time had found their way to Asia). He disallowed persecution of any sort, even setting aside the legal death penalty for conversion away from Islam, and he contributed financially to building temples for various faiths. In this way he put into practice a universalist orientation toward religion in general, which formed an important component of the interfaith cultural climate in Indian cities.

His fatal mistake in the area of religious interaction was his attempt to promulgate a syncretistic admixture of the various religions of India, with himself as its prophet. This so-called divine faith (*Din-i-Ilahi*) never took hold, but even today, both Muslims and Hindus frequently recall the example of Akbar when religious strife becomes particularly severe. Akbar's career serves as a useful example both of the side of Islam that is informed by its tolerance and of the disappointment that accompanies the efforts of emperors who also try to be prophets.

In the contemporary period, the Muslim political figure who best exemplifies the Islamic teaching on the oneness of all peoples is the late President Anwar Sadat of Egypt. Although he came to power in the political tradition of President Gamal

Abdel Nasser, as an Arab populist, Sadat eventually took courageous steps to end the long hostility that had separated his Muslim nation from the Jewish state of Israel. His celebrated visit to Jerusalem and his subsequent conversations with Israeli and American representatives led eventually to a "framework for peace" between two nations that had long been at war. Biographers of Sadat believe that none of this would have been possible without his faith and moral fortitude. His example counteracts the notion that Islamic leaders are inevitably pushed by their religion toward narrowness and provincialism.

There is every indication that the current Islamic resurgence will continue and that various expressions of Muslim values will color the perspectives of significant numbers of people. Those committed to the peaceful resolution of conflicts should make themselves aware of the internal complexity of the Islamic worldview and of the often untapped resource it offers for adjudicating differences.

SIKHISM

He who established this creation, recognize Him
as the true Word and do not imagine Him to be far
distant. He who meditates on the Name finds
peace. Without the Name the game (of life) is lost.
Adi Granth, p. 795

Recent events in India—the battles around the Sikhs' Golden Temple in Amritsar and the involvement of Sikhs in the assassination of Indira Gandhi—would seem to make Sikhism an unlikely candidate as a wellspring of conciliatory impulses. But nothing is simple, including the short but convoluted history of *Sat Nam* (the "True Name," the official title of the Sikh religion). Further, Sikh history provides a striking example of how historical circumstances can shape, and in this case almost invert, a religion's original character.

Two persons are generally credited with originating *Sat Nam*. The great fifteenth-century mystic and poet, Kabir (1440–1518 c.e.) was raised in Benares. He is said to have been the son of a Muslim father and a Hindu mother, which, in turn, may have influenced his lifelong attempt to blend the two faiths or at least to overcome the animosities between them. His was a universal vision, seeing all men as brothers before God. He denounced idols, questioned the authority of both Hindu and Muslim scriptures, and sang of finding God in "whatever I see."

Guru Nanak Dev (1469–1539 c.e.), was significantly influenced by Kabir and is generally considered the founder of Sikhism. Like Kabir, Nanak tried throughout his life to overcome the antagonism between Hinduism and Islam. After an early manhood spent in study and attempting to sort out rival religious claims, Nanak left his family and all worldly occupation and fled to the forest, where he had a vision that he summed up in a brief aphorism: "There is neither Hindu, nor Muslim." He spent the next 40 years trying to fill in the content of this sweeping claim.

After Nanak's death, his followers were persecuted, especially by the Moguls. Their response was to fight back and to exalt, with increasing emphasis, the military virtues of courage, endurance, and tenacity. Since the time of the Sikh leader Gobind Singh (1675–1708), every Sikh has been required to wear a topknot in his uncut hair (a symbol of defiance of enemies in battle) and to carry a *kirpan* (short dagger) at all times. Sikhs are often sought out as bodyguards for public personages. *Sat Nam*, to the outside observer, seems to combine an elevated mysticism ("Hail to Him, the primal, the pure, without beginning, the indestructible, the same in every age") and zealous particularism (Sikhs traditionally greet each other with a war cry).

Sikhism is a useful reminder that the historical experience of a religious community can often shape its values as much or more than the ideas of its founder. This, in turn, suggests that any comparative study of religions in the interest of drawing upon them for conciliatory values must avoid a kind of "functional fundamentalism" that overemphasizes canonical sources at the expense of religious history. The values of a tradition arise from both.

JUDAISM

And He shall judge between the nations,
And shall decide for many peoples;
And they shall beat their swords into plowshares,
And their spears into pruning-hooks;
Nation shall not lift up sword against nation,
Neither shall they learn war anymore.

Isaiah II:4

Judaism holds a unique place in religious history. Although it counts less than 13 million adherents in the world today, it provides the loam of stories and history out of which two of the much larger traditions—Christianity and Islam—have grown. Moreover, after nearly two millennia of statelessness and general persecution, during which Jews spread out to nearly every corner of the globe and fashioned a supple and enduring tradition, it has become in modern times the official religion of a small but powerful and influential state. For these reasons, it is important to ask the central question of this chapter of Judaism as well: What values does it offer to conflict resolution in a violent and divided world?

As we have seen in the other faiths already discussed, Judaism also carries within itself a tension between particularism and universalism. The Hebrew scriptures teach that God created the progenitors of all people—not just Jews—and that God has a redemptive purpose for all nations. The universal dimension of Judaism may best be symbolized by the story of God's promise to Noah, sealed with the rainbow sign. This was a universal gesture, made by God to all Earth's inhabitants—not just the people, but the plants and animals and Earth itself. To fulfill his purpose for all peoples, however, God went on—so the

Israelite faith holds—to choose a particular people and command them to be a "light to the nations."

Jews have not always succeeded in holding these two polar elements of their polyphonic tradition together (as, indeed, no other tradition has either). Even within the Jewish Bible, the more universal tones of Jeremiah and Isaiah coexist with the particularistic ones of Ezra and Nehemiah. Nor have the sages and rabbis agreed: Philo, Maimonides, Moses Mendelsohn, Martin Buber, and Abraham Joshua Heschel sound various notes on the universal/particular scale.

The issue is hardly a theoretical one. Since the establishment of Israel as a Jewish state and its government's decision to make Orthodoxy in effect the only officially recognized form of Judaism there, the debate within the Jewish community about what Judaism is and how it should inform public policy—in Israel and wherever else Jews may live—has become ever more intense. How can a faith that makes the large universal claims Judaism does function as the "civil religion" of one nation without losing this universalism? Conversely, how, after the grim reminder of the holocaust, can a religion that is also the faith of a particular people among others continue to protect itself from extinction without the seeming *sine qua non* of sovereign statehood (a question Sikhs are also pressing in India)?

Thus, though small by comparison to the large faith families, both Sikhism and Judaism remind us that the effort to retrieve resources for conflict resolution from any religious tradition is a daunting one. Religions exist in this plane, on earth, and this means they involve themselves in the unavoidable contingencies and contradictions of history. Still, they continue to enshrine and inculcate values one ignores at one's peril.

FINAL THOUGHTS

This brief survey of world religions has revealed that each contains within itself an internal tension with respect to how conflicts among human beings can best be resolved: there are both harmonizing and confrontational elements in each tradition. Christianity is no exception. The radical "love thine enemy" ethic of Jesus stands in dramatic contrast to the sorry history of the Crusades, the conquistadors, and the Spanish Inquisition. Clearly, these debates are not only fought out among theologians. They incarnate themselves in social movements that involve varying approaches to dealing with hostility and misunderstanding.

Paradoxically, the twentieth century, despite its miserable record of death and destruction, has also produced eloquent spokesmen from the conflict-resolving sides of the great traditions. The lives of Mahatma Gandhi, Thich-Nhat Hanh, the Dalai Lama, Anwar Sadat, Abraham Heschel, and Martin Luther King, Jr. offer clear proof that all religious traditions can provide sustenance and guidance in coping with the destructive aspects of human animosity.

It is easy to smile at the religious provincialism of the crusty Presbyterian elder, John Foster Dulles. On closer examination, through, the inept invitation to his Muslim and Jewish colleagues to work together like Christian gentlemen hints at an accurate insight. In his own way, he realized that there come moments in the affairs of men and nations when only the reference to a larger moral universe that transcends the specific particularities of the contending parties can move a dispute beyond dead water. He recognized, if somewhat awkwardly, that politics is not an autonomous sphere. As both the visionaries and the practitioners recalled in this survey demonstrate, statecraft subsists within a more encompassing realm of moral values and the underlying religious worldviews from which these values spring. If Mr. Dulles's vocabulary was too insular, at least his instinct was global.

To marshall the resources of the religions of the world in the service of human community and tension management is an ambitious undertaking. It does *not*, however, call for some artful synthesizing of the discrete faiths of humankind—which would be impossible and ill-advised. Rather, it calls for rigorous study and critical analysis that recognizes the variety of worldviews alive today, the areas in which they differ, and the points at which they intersect. It also suggests that in the ongoing internal debate *within* each of the traditions, there is a need to strengthen the universal aspects, while at the same time maintaining the specific rites and symbols without which no religion can touch the depths of human need. It is more than the work of a lifetime.

Contributors—Masao Abe is Professor Emeritus, Nara University, Japan. Moshe Idel is Professor of Religion, Department of Jewish Thought, Hebrew University of Jerusalem, Israel. Harjot Oberoi is Associate Professor in Asian Studies, University of British Columbia, Canada. Abdulaziz Sachedina is Professor of Religious Studies at the University of Virginia, United States. Arvind Sharma is the Birks Professor of Comparative Religion at McGill University in Canada.

Bibliography

Breslauer, S. David. *The Ecumenical Perspective and the Modernization of Jewish Religion* (Missoula, Mont.: Scholars Press, 1978).

Coward, Harold. *Pluralism—Challenge to World Religions* (Maryknoll, N. Y.: Orbis Books, 1985).

Cox, Harvey. *Many Mansions: A Christian's Encounter with Other Faiths* (Boston: Beacon Press, 1989).

Danjal, Beryl. *Sikhism* (London: Batsford, 1987).

D'Costa, Gavin. *Theology and Religious Pluralism* (Oxford: Basil Blackwell, 1986).

Drummond, R. H. *Gautama the Buddah: An Essay in Religious Understanding* (Grand Rapids, Mich.: Eerdmans, 1974).

Ellsberg, Robert, ed. *Gandhi on Christianity* (Maryknoll, N.Y.: Orbis Books, 1991).

Lemaitre, Solange *Ramakrishna and the Vitality of Hinduism*, trans. Charles L. Markman (Woodstock, N. Y.: Overlook Press, 1984).

Maduro, Otto. *Religion and Social Conflicts* (Maryknoll, N.Y.: Orbis Books, 1979).

Marshall, George. *Buddah, the Quest for Serenity* (Boston: Beacon Press, 1978).

McLeod, W. H. *Who Is a Sikh?: The Problem of Sikh Identity Today* (Oxford: Clarendon Press, 1989).

Mitchell, Stephen. *The Enlightened Heart: An Anthology of Sacred Poetry* (New York: Harper and Row, 1989).

Nasr, Seyyed Hossein. *Ideals and Realities in Islam* (London: Allen and Univen, 1966).

O'Connell, Joseph T., Milton Israel, and Willard G. Oxtoby, eds. *Sikh History and Religion in the 20th Century* (New Delhi: Monohar Publications, 1990).

Panikker, Raimundo. *Myth, Faith and Hermeneutics* (Leominster, Eng.: Fowler Wright, 1979).

Parrinder, Geoffrey. *Encountering World Religions* (New York: Crossroads, 1987).

Sachedina, Abdulaziz, David Little, and J. E. Kelsey. *Human Rights and the Conflict of Cultures: Western and Islamic Perspectives on Religious Liberty* (Columbia: University of South Carolina Press, 1988).

Singh, Gopal, *A History of the Sikh People 1469–1988* (New Delhi: World Book Center, 1988).

Singh, Rajwant. *The Sikhs: Their Literature on Culture, History and Philosophy, Politics, Religion and Traditions* (Delhi: Indian Bibliographies Bureau, 1989).

Smartha, S., ed. *Living Faiths and Ultimate Goals* (Geneva: World Council of Churches, 1974).

Smith, W. C. *The Meaning and End of Religion: A New Approach to the Religious Traditions of Mankind* (London: SPCK, 1978).

Sri Rahula, Walpola. *What the Buddha Taught* (New York: Grove Press, 1974).

Whaling, F., ed. *The World's Religious Traditions: Current Perspectives in Religious Studies* (Edinburgh: T. & T. Clark, 1984).

III ▪ IMPLICATIONS

13 ▪

Implications for the Foreign Policy Community

STANTON BURNETT

Only a great fool would call the new political science diabolic: it has no attributes peculiar to fallen angels. It is not even Machiavellian, for Machiavelli's teaching was graceful, subtle, and colorful. Nor is it Neronian. Nevertheless one may say of it that it fiddles while Rome burns. It is excused by two facts: it does not know that it fiddles, and it does not know that Rome burns.

Leo Strauss

The United States had some stake, and some role, in a few of the cases in this book. Washington's connection with part of South Africa's recent history is discussed later in this chapter. The United States, by its advocacy of European regional groupings—some including North America, some not—helped institutionalize Franco-German reconciliation. And, as leader of the West during the Cold War, the United States offered a secondary pole of attraction (after West Germany and Western Europe) for East Germans thirsting for change.

In general, however, the cases have not dealt with those headline stories in which postwar American foreign policy was a principal protagonist. Even well-informed American readers have probably found here cases, or aspects of cases, with which they are relatively unfamiliar.

In some of the arenas known to all, such as Vietnam, Lebanon, and Iran, however, the group that guided this research overall believed that the question of the profundity of Washington's understanding of spiritual factors could justly be raised. None of these are uncontroversial, even among the participants in this research. Chapters 2 and 3 are based on serious study of the cases involved, but space did not permit all the apparatus of evidence to accompany each mention.

But the authors in this volume are not indicting U.S. diplomacy. We write about it because it is ours, and because of the hope we invest in the demonstrated seriousness and flexibility of its officials. Conventional understanding of the controversial cases is enough, therefore, to make the point about the missing ingredient. In Lebanon, to take one example, one can find those who have no criticism of American understanding and policy and put the entire burden for the bombing disaster on mistakes by the U.S. Marine Corps. To many of us, however, this interpretation is insufficient, and thus the suggestion is made in the opening chapters that there were failures to understand the character of the parties to the conflict, especially the meaning and nuances of the religious beliefs involved, and that these led to an unfortunate approach to the whole problem of Lebanon.

But one must acknowledge that there are two other possibilities. One is that the American diplomats involved, both on the scene and in Washington, had a perfect understanding and drew exactly the right conclusions, but failed to influence decision making at the top. Since many of the principals have written or commented on those days, one would expect that there would by now have been some evidence of this had it been the case. The other possibility is that the understanding all up and down the line was perfect, and that the actions taken were attuned to all the key factors, including the religious factors. If *that* were the case, then what official Washington told the American people about Lebanon was knowingly false. In a political culture that seems these days to react more sharply to cover-ups than to the original malfeasance being covered, such a proposition would open a large, economy-size can of worms.

So the case studies offered here reveal neither a consistently important American presence in the political mix of those situations nor damage done by its absence. The world is obviously not clamoring for Washington or other capitals to shanghai platoons of clerics into their service in order to support a global pacification mission.

Yet the cases do highlight a compelling reason for a reassessment of the tradition and intellectual habit of dogmatic secularism described by Edward Luttwak (Chapter 2). American policy-making and diplomacy have every interest in understanding the potential role of spiritual factors in the resolution of conflict, an idea that may seem hopelessly idealistic to a practicing politician or diplomat without the historical record offered by the cases to demonstrate that such a role was actual and effective in important past instances. He or she does not need faith in faith, only faith in history and analysis.

The participants in this research saw the work in larger, different contexts depending on their background. For some, this work was part of the overall relationship between religion and politics, one whose negative side produces so many disturbing headlines that deliberate effort is required to contemplate other aspects of the connection. The term *religion* is here inadequate to express the range of interest; this research stretches beyond the formal institutions of religion and searches for something deeper that responds more appropriately to a word such as *spiritual*.

For others, the research fits into the context of the challenge American diplomacy has frequently failed to meet: that of doing its homework, of engaging in serious and profound study of the cultures, not just the politics and economy, of other nations. The reasons for this, stretching from factors in American history to State Department personnel practices, are discussed later. But the failure is that of achieving an adequate familiarity with the religions, philosophical movements, arts, and manners that are the key to a level of diplomatic effectiveness to which we too seldom aspire.

The initial focus of the research project was on U.S. diplomacy because of the background of some participants, not because rigorous analysis found it deficient. But, with the doing of the work, the focus became increasingly broad, so that the implications are rich for actors in domestic and international politics around the world. With an increasingly interdependent world, groups of people from clans to nation-states must find new ways of conducting their relationships. And the implications of this research cannot be confined to diplomacy: they were and are needed in Selma, Alabama; in Ulster; and between the Tutsi and the Hutus in Burundi—as well as within Tajikistan and Somalia.

Finally, for a third group of participants, including some in the first two groups, the study was an effort to get a scholarly grasp on areas that had been inadequately analyzed by the mainstream of Western international relations (IR, in the trade) scholarship, a neglect as easy to explain as it is available for remedy.

THE COSTS OF DISREGARDING RELIGIOUS FACTORS: INTELLIGENCE

The taxpayers in Iowa—presumably willing to support a diplomatic establishment that does what is necessary to defend America's vital interests abroad, suspecting that the folks in those big embassies may be living a little high at their expense, occasionally grateful for a grain agreement with Russia or for getting a son out of jail in Cancun—may not be keenly interested in the advanced study by their hired representatives into the arcana of exotic cultures. They would probably approve of the fact that the country team in that big embassy rarely asks the cultural attaché for a contribution to its reporting cables, unless it needs a paragraph on a riot at the local university. Washington's responsibility to those taxpayers requires a hard-headed appraisal of whether we really pay a price for the "missing dimension" analyzed here. Every victim of conflicts that were intensified or prolonged because of the blindness to spiritual factors on the part of the United States and other leading countries would be a line item in that cost.

The starting point for resolving a conflict is understanding it. The case study conflicts in this book are not religious controversies. But some of them (and many conflicts that one can foresee, both internationally and within states) have religion as the defining characteristic of at least one of the contending communities. Thus the character of the conflict is misunderstood when religion is not accurately taken into account. A blue ribbon conference on "The Foreign Service in 2001," staged by Georgetown University's Institute for the Study of Diplomacy (ISD) at the Department of State in December 1991, predicted that "identifying the root causes of and avoiding local wars will be reason enough for maintaining an extensive foreign service political reporting and analysis apparatus."[1] It is Barry Rubin's judgment (Chapter 3) that Washington has often misunderstood political controversies between communities whose behavior cannot be

understood, predicted, or used positively in conflict resolution without an understanding of the spiritual factors guiding their behavior. In conflicts of this kind (as
distinguished, still, from religious controversies), Rubin contends that "religion
as the prime communal identity has, until recently, been too often neglected"
(p. 21 in this volume).

Inadequate recognition of the defining character of spiritual elements is especially likely to occur, and to be especially costly, in the Third World. Weak and
ineffective governments (or governments strong and effective only in criminal
activities) are often transformed in diplomatic reporting into communities whose
binding fabric is weak. Yet the real warp and woof of the social fabric, sometimes
almost invisible to modern Western eyes, is provided by religious institutions and
spiritual phenomena woven deep into the culture. When this thread is missed,
diplomacy based on the assumption that a weak government equals a weak
community is flawed from the outset.

In West Irian, U.S. reporting refused to treat the religious basis for the stormy
relationship between Indonesian authorities and Javanese settlers (both Muslim),
the indigenous animists, and the Christians. Reporting of the *Intifadah* misses the
point when Left-to-Right places on the conventional political spectrum are used to
characterize the varieties of Islam in conflict among the Palestinians.

In Iran there was, from time to time, some recognition of religious factors by
American diplomacy. The U.S. embassy made an attempt in 1955–56 to reach out
to the mullahs, although it failed through a failure of understanding. It tried a set of
invitations to mullahs within the International Visitors Program, the highlight of
which was a conference at Princeton, a totally misbegotten approach for this
group. It was so inappropriate as a way of dealing with the mullahs that the result
was that Washington was perceived as trying to modify Islamic fundamentalism.
It confirmed the mullahs' prejudices about the United States. This particular effort
was driven by John Foster Dulles, who was trying to do something about the arc of
countries south of the Soviet Union. The context was entirely Cold War, not a
religious dialogue. American diplomacy made no serious connection with religious leaders in either Iran or Pakistan.[2] Luttwak cites the failure of the CIA to
support a single proposal for following the religious dimension of Iranian politics
as one case in a pattern of distortion caused by official America's "secularizing
reductivism," defining the struggle by way of conventional Western political and
economic categories. When U.S. reporting did focus on religious factors, it
contrasted "pious" with "modern."

In Vietnam, in the fall of 1971, the United States urged the Catholics and
Buddhists to put up an electoral candidate against President Thieu. The CIA had
especially good contacts with both groups. But American talks with the Buddhists
were enigmatic at best. The Catholics seemed easier: they were perceived as the
hard-liners. The Americans were looking at both groups as basically political,
with no profound understanding of the religious content of either group's effort.[3]
Officials in the United States viewed the whole situation exclusively in political
terms.[4] Much about this period remains controversial, but it is safe to say that
while U.S. officials saw what was going on with religious groups, they neither

grasped their full significance nor knew how to "use" the strong and varied spiritual presence in the situation.[5]

Even in Poland, where understanding should be easier for Americans, failure to take accurate account of the religious factor affected the performance of U.S. diplomacy. The United States, especially the CIA, did have some connections with the Polish Catholic church, but all overt contacts were under tight government surveillance. In 1969, during the tenure of Ambassador Walter Stoessel, the embassy spent months deciding whether Stoessel should pay a courtesy call on the Polish primate. When the visit finally happened, it was very, and merely, formal. When John Gronouski was ambassador in Warsaw (1965–68), he went to church regularly, a different church in a different town each time. The display in all this was obvious, since the Voice Of America would broadcast the advance schedule into Poland. But the connection was so superficial that the embassy was not in a position to be active or even predictive relative to the church's role when the political pot started bubbling in Poland. By comparison, some embassy officers were circumventing the regime's constraints to have regular meetings in Gdansk and elsewhere with union activists who were soon to be, along with the church, part of the explosive mixture that changed Polish history.[6]

For reasons explored later, the experiences of Iran, Vietnam, and Lebanon have not produced the corrective in these patterns of thought that one might have expected. The missed beat goes on.

Later in this chapter evidence will be offered for the increase, rather than the decline, of the importance of spiritual factors in defining communities and relationships between them. The intelligence costs of leaving this element out of consideration will similarly increase.

The diplomatic system of reporting and analysis serves three purposes: understanding, action, and prediction. Diplomats typically loathe that last word, yet Washington continually prods them to risk their professional necks by doing it. (Many necks are saved because nobody bothers to remember past predictions— forgetfulness is the flotation device of diplomats, scholars, and journalists.) This difficulty in diplomacy is a subset of the overall weak predictive capability of materialistic determinism and other popular twentieth-century modes of analysis: neither Marx nor Adam Smith would have done a very good job of anticipating the actions of nations and other communities over the last 30 years. They would make even less out of the scrambled map emerging in Europe.

THE COSTS OF DISREGARDING RELIGIOUS FACTORS: ACTION

The missing or diminishing of the religious element in diplomatic reporting (as well as American media reporting read by, and often inspired by, American officials) led naturally to failures in action and policy. It could scarcely be otherwise. Because it is difficult to measure what might have been, toting up the precise action costs is impossible, even confining ourselves to a few situations in which U.S. national interests were heavily in play. But the study's participants believed that failure to gain and use knowledge of pertinent elements of foreign cultures globally has come at a high price.

Thus, in Vietnam, it seems clear that Washington moved to support leadership that had a Buddhist identity at far too late a date, only after immolations had rendered the religious factor impossible for U.S. officials to ignore. In Iran, reforms were urged on the shah that broadened the political base of his regime but did not extend to or pacify the lethal part of the opposition that was based on religion (Chapter 2 in this volume). The concept of the superior survivability of broad-based regimes came from Western secular politics and ignored the rules by which Khomeini was playing the political game. Doggedly following this secular concept is likely to be inappropriate wherever a prism created by spiritual factors substitutes for the Western secular prism. Washington's refusal to listen to the Nicaraguan church on the potential for revolution in the country, its failure to estimate correctly the strength of the clerical and lay forces of the Nicaraguan Christian Democratic party, the consequent failure to work with the church, and then the failure to see the role (strongly pro-Sandinistan) being played by young clerics among the people, were among the factors that contributed to the original victory of the Sandinistas (Chapter 3 in this volume). (U.S. treatment of the Nicaraguan Christian Democratic party as just another lay party, ignoring the role of religion in both its aims and its connections, is symptomatic of its treatment of Christian Democratic parties elsewhere.)

Luttwak, in his section on "ignoring the intractable," suggests that blindness to spiritual elements has frequently led U.S. diplomacy to hope and action when despair and inaction would have been more appropriate. Optimism may be an attractive American characteristic, but nobody ever suggested Candide as the model for effective diplomacy, and ignorant optimism can be deadly.

THE RECORD OF SUCCESS: SPOTTY BUT TELLING

The fact that from time to time American diplomacy has taken proper account of spiritual factors in its understanding and action makes the failures and their costs more impressive.

Terms such as *U.S. diplomacy* are fiction: they stand for a body of system and action produced by a large number of complicated men and women. Those people—political officeholders, foreign service officers, and administration and congressional leaders—may have produced the patterns in which religion is a mostly missing element, but in individual instances some of them did their homework, observed without blinders, and acted with greater sophistication than their institutional norm.

Official U.S. representatives in South Africa played a role, especially through the 1980s, which would bring some pride to Americans if it were better known. Libraries were kept open and programs were run in Soweto and other key black townships despite strong counterpressures from the regime. The most prominent religious connection, even in an actual physical sense (the man stood almost seven feet tall) was Edward J. Perkins, whose service as U.S. ambassador to Pretoria (1986–89) included regular attendance at churches in the black townships, where his presence, and the support it implied, could not be missed.

The most concrete U.S. support for reform – the Comprehensive Anti-Apartheid Act of 1986 – is described by Douglas Johnston in Chapter 9. South African churchmen were part of the pressure for action in the United States, a case where foreign religious figures influenced U.S. politics so effectively that the 1986 act could garner the votes to override a presidential veto. But there was no overt U.S. policy line encouraging either side to give a more prominent role to religious figures and institutions through those difficult times.[7]

The belated success of mid-level U.S. diplomats in getting Washington policy-makers to understand the Catholic role in the revolt against the Marcos regime led to tardy but appropriate U.S. action in the Philippines. The Reagan administration, following its predecessor's pattern until late in the game, failed to give proper weight to the church-supported opposition to Marcos, an alternative to both the regime and the communist opposition (Chapter 3 in this volume). (Washington was confronting a moving target: the positions of the church and of Cardinal Sin evolved during this period.)[8]

The Philippine example is especially germane to the hope that U.S. diplomacy will, in the future, more effectively understand religious/spiritual factors and bring them to bear in the search for solutions. Had the United States not transformed its vision of the possibilities in the Philippines, Rubin suggests that the church and other moderates might have "been driven to support the Marxist-Leninist New People's Army in order to get rid of Marcos" (p. 30 in this volume).

WHY THE MISSING DIMENSION IS MISSING: CAUSES OF THE FAILURE

Luttwak's chapter in this volume is devoted entirely to one area of causation: habit and ideology. It is not the only explanation, but Luttwak, in describing the synergistic philosophical brothers – dogmatic secularism and materialistic determinism – has put his finger on the roots of a set of attitudes that, in themselves, would be enough to lead U.S. diplomacy[9] into a state of indifference to the spiritual elements described in this study. Luttwak traces the path by which this philosophical juncture was reached, starting with the restrictive prejudices of the Enlightenment. The impact of these prejudices on the scientific study of politics and international relations was to create a "learned repugnance" toward contending intellectually with that which is religious or spiritual. It is true that the religious can become, even in post-Enlightenment eyes, political when some theological dispute, whose content is not taken seriously by outsiders, escalates to conflict proportions. Even then, the conflict can be seen as significant while the religious concerns that trigger it are still seen as trivial. (See also Chapter 3 on the relation between the religious and the political.)

While the Luttwak explanation would suffice, it has worked in combination with other strong reinforcing factors, four of which will be suggested in this section. The first is mixed in with the factors Luttwak mentions; it is that of *expectations about the future*. Secularism and materialism led naturally to, and probably stemmed partly from, the assumption that religion is a declining force in most societies, that people who are defined as "modern" will have increasing power and influence. The characteristics of modern in this stereotyping are Western thought and lifestyle.

Two causes for the relative failure of American diplomacy to take account of spiritual factors are unrelated to the body of thought in which it operates. One, the second of our list, is the almost-uniquely[10] U.S. pattern of *amateurism as an approach to some important overseas assignments*. The high percentage of non-professional political appointments to "country"[11] ambassadorships has long been a cause célèbre in Washington, kept alive by two of the three aggrieved parties: the career diplomats who are the losers and the party out of government. The conclusion of the Institute for the Study of Diplomacy (ISD) conference was that "underqualified foreign policy makers are a luxury that a competitive nation cannot afford."[12]

Third, even more significant in its impact than the haphazard effect of the appointment of political appointees to major ambassadorships were some recent *assignment and other personnel practices* in the major U.S. foreign affairs agencies. The "globalization of assignments" initiated under Secretary of State Henry Kissinger had a serious intent: to assure that officers with potential for broader responsibilities had broader experience. This, in turn, involved moving diplomats around faster and farther; an officer would have difficulty obtaining another tour, even years later, in a country of previous service. The result was a costly loss of area and country expertise. Even the language level at key posts declined.[13] While good diplomats may continue to be able to understand and report on front-page political events in their host country, the likelihood of a more profound effectiveness risks being lost: the ability to understand sectors of host-country society that involve the cultural and spiritual life of the country, and to be effective in using these elements for conflict resolution.

The ISD report says flatly: "The world's complexity can no longer be ignored." In elucidating this point, the report predicts that "the decision to intervene in foreign conflicts will be based more often on complex moral or ethical grounds."[14] Given this position, it is striking that religion, either as the basis for an ethical system or as a wellspring of positive intervention in conflict, is nowhere mentioned. Though not a surprise, this underscores the fact that calling religion a missing dimension in U.S. statecraft is no exaggeration.

The fourth cause that merits attention is the *intellectual framework* within which most Americans in the field are introduced to the scholarly literature of international relations. Long dominated by the Realist school and its progeny in IR theory, the branch of modern American social sciences that treats this field provides the introductory education for most American diplomats and the others— journalists, politicians, and analysts—who most influence diplomatic thinking.

It is tempting to retain the quotation marks around "Realist" that were once so common, because it was precisely because of its difficult relation to political reality that doubts about this ontology crept into international scholarship. More striking even than its failures at prediction and the poverty of its descriptions were the departure of some of its leading scholars from its own conceptual framework when they wanted to talk seriously about international issues.[15] The family tree of the Realist school extends from the Enlightenment and Auguste Comte through Max Weber and the school's arrival on the scene as a reaction to the lack of scientific rigor in earlier commentaries on international relations. In its thirst to imitate the physical sciences (and to gain, therefore, the success and prestige the physical sciences have in our society), the Realist school, along with its offspring and principal competitors, was dogmatically, unflinchingly secular. Its denial of human—including religious and spiritual—factors was a mere part of its denial of all cultural factors as significant in the shaping of the behavior of states (the only actors on display). Hans Morgenthau will occasionally pay lip service to strange beliefs that might cloud men's minds, but these are, of course, not subject to analysis or coherent explanation. There is no room for that in the pure air through which his billiard-ball states slide as they seek to maximize power in bouncing off other balls. American diplomats, raised in the Enlightenment secularism of the Realist school, are unprepared to see spiritual aspects of problems and possible solutions or, for that matter, to cope (as more than a colorful aside) with the whole cultural richness, including the intellectual life and structure of belief of the *people* (not just the institutions) with whom they deal abroad. It is true and encouraging that many diplomats in the field have long ago recognized that the Realist scholars do not describe the world that they see around them. We have seen expectations about the future, the casual approach to some appointments to ambassadorships and other high offices, assignment practices that at times discourage area specialization, and, most important, the entire intellectual tradition and current training within which both U.S. diplomacy and the preparation of its main players exist. Small wonder, then, that religion has become a missing ingredient in U.S. statecraft.

IMPLICATIONS FOR THE PRACTICE OF TRADITIONAL U.S. DIPLOMACY

The benefits of escaping dogmatic secularism need not delay us: it is the other side of the coin from the costs of that straitjacket. Nothing but good can come from seeing a society whole, from understanding its most salient cultural characteristics. That this intelligence and this understanding are the essential precursors to enlightened action is also obvious.

But the political life, local or global, presents itself as a series of conflicts and problems—about too many claimants for too few resources and about irrational appetites for turf, in either its literal or figurative meaning. When an American comedian gave his list of the reasons why Saddam Hussein invaded Kuwait, the one at the top was that "a man can never have too much sand."

Some of the cases in this book are about "winning" conflicts, some are about ending or preventing political conflict, and one (Franco-German postwar reconciliation) is about forgiveness and forging a productive relationship between previous belligerents. The question is whether the diplomat or policymaker desiring to help bring about prevention, resolution, reconciliation, or victory over oppression will avail himself of the insights and possibilities that may be offered by spiritual elements, or whether the practice of unilaterally depriving our diplomacy of these assets will continue.

To put the matter in cold terms, the long-term strategic benefits of understanding the cases in this book and the insights they provide are not precisely calculable but are clearly enormous. Strategic thinking needs information, analysis, and insight— insight from all of the relevant sources contributing to an understanding of human interaction. It needs the capacity to predict, but prediction about the person or the community that is playing by different rules, including some we do not understand, will suffer regular failure. As will be seen in the section at the end of this chapter, one certain prediction is that which maintains that an incapacity to see, understand, and make proper use of spiritual/religious factors will involve even higher future costs because of an increase in the number of conflicts and instances of political turmoil in which these phenomena will be an important part of either the problem or the possible solution, usually both. U.S. diplomacy, by consciously widening its vision, can achieve much greater suppleness and effectiveness.

HOW TO BRING ABOUT CHANGE

What has been described is an entire *mindset*, and change must start there, with the body of theory that produces the practitioners of the art of international relations. This means considering the implications for the Realist school (discussed later). Beyond that, it means a reconsideration of Max Weber. Without entering the thicket of the perpetual methodological debate within Western political science, two questions about Weber's distinction between facts and values must be raised.

Fortunately, the easiest is the most immediately necessary: Does the fact that social scientists who follow Weber place "values" outside their range of analysis mean that values must be outside the consideration of practicing diplomats? If the answer were simply that diplomats can certainly observe value-based behavior, even Weber would render his blessing. But the fact that modern sociology (and its offspring, modern political science) lacks tools of analysis for important parts of the life of men and nations should not impede sober consideration and serious "use" by diplomats of this whole range of ethical, religious, spiritual, philosophical, and mythical phenomena, which are important to political actors and potentially helpful intervenors.

The harder question, not immediately necessary but absolutely unavoidable in time, is whether all the considerations swept together under the Weberian rubric of "values" are, in fact, beyond systematic analysis.[16] To reconsider this question means to return to the central question of an earlier political science: What is the best regime? Within this question is that of how a person should live. And with this question, we are at the point of so raising the gaze of parties to a conflict that all things become possible. For now, these questions that were tossed out the back door by the Enlightenment sneak back in through the windows of the minds and souls of the men and women who may be found at, or brought to, the negotiating table.[17]

On the heels of, even intertwined with, this change of mindset, are changes in *procedures, organization, and priorities*. Luttwak's approach in Chapter 2 is direct: he proposes the assignment of religion attachés to those diplomatic missions where religion has major consequence. At other posts, responsibility "to monitor religious movements and maintain contact with religious leaders" could be made a charge of the cultural attaché. In fact, this is already done at a few posts, depending on the predisposition of the public affairs officer, the immediate superior of the cultural attaché.

That is where the emphasis proposed by Harold Saunders becomes especially apt.[18] His experience in negotiation taught the costs of narrowness; so he posits the virtues of broadening both conception and practice. His view is that modern diplomacy must move toward a *totality of interaction* between bodies politic. This is in direct contrast with Morgenthau's pristine billiard-ball nation-states. Iconoclastically, Saunders is especially keen on a focus on people, not just institutions, counter to the normal diplomatic practice of dealing with institutions (with individuals defined principally in their institutional context).

Several participants in the research project reported in this volume were veterans of U.S. diplomacy, and they were in no sense calling for a downgrading of the role of a professional foreign service. They were calling for a broadened, enlightened, enriched version of that work, one that is able to add this largely missing ingredient, and other aspects of cultural understanding and cooperation, to the traditional stew. Saunders, however, is talking mainly about a new partnership between professionals and policymakers within government and between governments and people outside of government.

If diplomatic broadening is to be serious and enduring, *training and assignments* needs are clear. Language training for service abroad must be cranked up a notch. This is expensive for the foreign affairs agencies and burdensome for the diplomat-students themselves. The same can be said of more profound "area studies," taught by those capable of broadening the current range of considerations, before officers go abroad. But the cost and burden can be sliced by about half by planning, early in an officer's career, for a pattern of assignments that give the officer two or more tours of duty in the same country or region.

The ISD report says simply that the service must be staffed sufficiently to allow training time, estimating that this will require a 16 percent increase in the officer corps. In ranking the importance of subject areas for the training, "language and area expertise" are at the top.[19] This seriousness of purpose about cultural understanding would bring into the officer's compass the religious and spiritual life of the host country, and an awareness of the possibilities therein.[20]

IMPLICATIONS FOR THE PRACTICE OF
PUBLIC DIPLOMACY

"Public diplomacy" in American scholarship and practice embraces all the dialogue and transactions that occur outside the corridors of embassies and foreign ministries, whose "audience" includes all but those officially charged with diplomatic intercourse with U.S. representatives. Public diplomacy has gone through looping meanders in its postwar history, from that hard repetition of U.S. policy (and accompanying drum rolls) that edged close to propaganda (although the professionals regularly succeeded in pulling it back from that brink) to mere neutered impresarioship (especially during the Carter administration), involving the building of a platform to present an indiscriminate parade of supposedly representative Americans and American ideas. Occasionally these meanderings have come to rest at a point where the mission was seen clearly as that of civilized persuasion—a type of advocacy based on dialogue, respect for the interlocutor, and an absolute abjuring of manipulation.[21]

It is during these latter fortunate periods that there is likely to be the best comprehension of the relation between public diplomacy and the spiritual ingredient of statecraft. Public diplomacy has the charge to penetrate the culture of the host country beyond the political and governmental institutions; the embassy's contacts in the religious and academic worlds are normally contacts of the public affairs team (U.S. Information Service in most countries). There is a greater focus on people rather than on institutions than in other parts of the embassy, except perhaps the consular section. And at times of political tension, there are even greater possibilities. In Poland and other Warsaw Pact countries, USIS officers fraternized in circles that caused some neuralgia for the regime, but not the outright explosion that the same contacts by an embassy political officer would have caused.

A political officer on a rebellious university campus is an interference in the country's internal affairs; a cultural officer in the same place is doing his normal labor. The great difference in expectations, and therefore acceptability, goes to Saunders's concern for breadth. The conclusion is not that America's diplomacy should lean more heavily on the current public diplomacy establishment, but that the political sections (and chiefs of mission) and the State Department offices to which they report, should seek to broaden their contacts and cultural penetration.

CONCEPTUAL IMPLICATIONS

There will be no attempt here to construct a fresh theoretical framework because a satisfactory framework already exists, as we shall see. As for the study's relation to what has been orthodoxy in much of post–World War II international relations (IR) theory, that is a simple comparison between the tenets of the Realist school and the disruptive facts about how states and their representatives, let alone parties to other kinds of conflict, *do* behave, as recorded in the case studies. Either those events did not happen and the parties did not behave in the manner recounted, or a spanner, just one more, has been thrown into the gears of the Realist machine.

To be brief, since the groundwork has been laid above, one starts with the difficulty posed to post-Weberian social science, in fact to Weber's methodology itself. The challenge does not come from the motives driving the actors: Weberian science is perfectly capable of studying behavior triggered by any sort of quirk in the minds of men and women. (It should be, of course, *several* men and women so sociology can go about its quantification. Personal idiosyncrasies are the domain of psychology, not sociology.) The challenge comes from the idea that the source of those motives, called *values* in Weber and thereafter, are more than just inexplicable yearnings and may themselves be subject to analysis.[22]

Since modern Weberian social scientists confine themselves to the study of behavior, modern IR seeks to build a structure of theory about the behavior of its chosen animal, the nation-state. But IR theory is not about real nation-states; it is about a hypothetical construct called "nation-state" whose relationship to nation-states-in-being was problematical from the beginning. There are, to be sure, mentions of actual existing countries in the Realists' standard texts, but they have uncomfortably rough and shaggy edges, a serious problem for a billiard ball. And there is never enough of anything for successful quantification: never enough wars, enough borders, enough treaties, or enough alliances; never the easy abundance of the economist, who never lacks for transactions. The nation-state is also unsatisfactory as a laboratory animal, closing a path open to some psychologists.

But the enterprise of building a great theoretical machine needs parts that fit together. So plain English, a messy tool if there ever was one, is replaced by jargon, which has a real utility for consistency in communication.[23] The political phenomenon, rich in history and implication, is replaced by the nonpolitical, manageable construct. And, most important for our purposes, the nation-state, for which men bleed, is replaced by the "nation-state," which has no existence outside the theoretical machine. This is proper procedure for the scientific task at hand, which is not to observe accurately and penetrate the richness of political life, but to construct the theoretical machine.

The question this book raises about the relation of this scientific enterprise to real statecraft is not that of the scientific philistine who, simply because some of the practitioners of the art have disappeared behind a curtain of theory, jargon, and numbers, decides to play Strepsiades[24] and burn down the think tank. The question raised is precisely the opposite: whether IR theory should not be much more than it is, should have both the suppleness and the close relationship to the real phenomena that would permit it to take account of, even to see, the phenomena (including behavior) discussed in this volume.

Morgenthau saw the problem we raise, but dismissed it:

The supranational forces, such as universal religions, humanitarianism, cosmopolitanism, and all the other personal ties, institutions, and organizations that bind individuals together across national boundaries, are infinitely weaker today than the forces that unite peoples within a particular national boundary and separate them from the rest of humanity.[25]

One could bog down in a debate as to whether contemporary instances of unruly Kurds and Macedonians verify Morgenthau's statement. Are they nation-states, nation-states-in-embryo, or something else? Or is nation-state the condition to which they aspire? The debate is unnecessary here because, in any event, Morgenthau is describing a phenomenon of a very limited historical time and place. (The classical *polis* is clearly not a nation-state.) In most of the world it is a mere import from Europe, a conceptual product of European imperialism absolutely disharmonious with the preexisting political culture and showing signs around the globe of not having planted roots as deeply as those of the beliefs and perceptions that gripped the people before they enjoyed the benefits of being invaded.

In much of the Third World, both the nation-state and nationalism are either absent or new; they are clearly not part of a universal human political condition, and they face mighty competitors. In Europe itself, is the nation-state primary in Northern Ireland, throughout Eastern Europe, or in the shards of the Soviet Union? Even if the fair rejoinder is that these are really embryo nation-states, it is clear that religion and ethnos are defining nations, not the other way around.

A corollary to seeing the world as a billiard table populated by nation-states is the definition of the objective of (all) nations, the engine that propels them, in an equally schematic way: power or, in Morgenthau's terms, "interest defined in terms of power,"[26] which comes to the same thing. This is not power as a means related to some end: power *is* the end. The modern claim that the classics failed to understand the concept of power is only partly correct. They found the pursuit of power unrelated to some other objective as simply irrational. Not so Morgenthau: "Whatever the ultimate aims of international politics, power is always the immediate aim."[27] In this theoretical construct, however, it is also the ultimate aim. Despite lip service to other human appetites, they make no appearance in the theory itself. There is, of course, something to this idea. But in modern IR studies, it is treated as a constant, as though springing from the well of human nature. If that were the case, then much of what is recorded in the case studies simply could not have happened. The repeated spectacle of political leaders finding some other propeller for their actions, something other than simple maximization of power, occurs too many times in the case studies reported here to be the illusion of one or two scholars. They force the conclusion that there are political leaders around the world who are somehow behaving in a manner that the Realist school does not recognize.

The phenomenon (of a geopolitical game played by single-minded actors seeking only maximization of power), which was nowhere ever as simply predominant as IR theory would have it, is characteristic of statesmen of a particular time and place, whose greatest apparent victory was to plant the seed in the minds of some scholars that man never acted any differently. This is the particular and limited period when an important part of the political leadership of Britain (with Gladstone and others in dissent) sought simply to expand the amount of British-Empire pink on the map of the world. Since, by the middle of the colonial period, most of the places left to grab were, so far as these Londoners knew, without economic value (except to keep some young men employed as troops to take and hold them), and the image of some civilizing mission among the heathens was never as convincing to Englishmen as it was to Frenchmen (churchmen aside), the only benefit those stretches of pink could offer was some imagined increase in national power. The map rooms in London dramatized the goals; the Prussian general staff, on the other hand, displayed the organizational machinery best designed to support goals of power-maximization untrammeled by other objectives.[28] These and a few other European salons were the principal incubators of geopolitics. Often discussed as though it were universal, it is instead a discrete chunk of history.

One other characteristic of the artificial world created by modern IR fundamental to the Realist theory is the idea that states must be willing to go to war with each other. Without that, threat, deterrence, domination-and-submission, alliances, balances—nothing works. The threat must be perceived by the other players, requiring the investment in the machinery of war that makes it credible. The point here is not that some of the parties in the case studies were not willing to make war (or revolution, or civil war); it is rather the obvious inapplicability of this critical generalization to all parties. What is happening in instances of reconciliation, such as the Franco-German postwar history analyzed in this volume, is the erosion of the willingness to make war (which, in these and some other cases, starts with citizens before it reaches governments—keeping in mind that what is at issue is the general, long-term unwillingness to make war, not just a transient state of peace between governments). These are not just events in the life of states. For in IR theory, they constitute the *denaturing* of the states. The billiard balls roll off the table and, if they were consequential balls, the game is over. Since the whole game existed only in the scientific imagination anyway, the sun will still come up the next morning.

The case studies in this book challenge an important sector of the behaviorist orthodoxy in the social sciences. The principal actors appear, in most cases, not to be nation-states. The actors, through their political leaders, do not behave in ways that theory holds they should behave. These leaders are driven by "values," a poor modern word for the beliefs and altered levels of thinking and believing that are in evidence here. This fact makes no problem for modern theory. But a satisfactory understanding of the cases requires a level of analysis and understanding of those beliefs that lies outside the understanding of Weberian science.

ADVANTAGES AND LIMITATIONS OF THE CLASSICAL APPROACH

There has been more destruction than construction thus far in this discussion of the relation between scholarship and practice, because our diagnosis is that the conceptual framework of (and training of future diplomats by) the contemporary academic discipline of international relations as it is taught in most schools is part of the problem, has helped keep the missing ingredient missing.

An alternative approach has not been offered here because a sufficient conceptual foundation already exists and is available as a beginning. The Enlightenment, and the great enterprise of social scientists to imitate the methods (and the success and prestige) of the physical sciences, was a reaction to an earlier political science. But before Francis Bacon there was no conviction that "torturing" nature—that is, manipulating and engineering it—was a beneficent act.[29] Bacon put his foundation down on the lot that had been cleared by Machiavelli, whose assault on the epistemology of the classical study of politics may not have been a logical success but was the big winner historically. What these founders of modern thought displaced was a way of observing, not torturing, nature that has many of the characteristics necessary for comprehending (and making available to the political life) the possibilities inherent in spiritual and religious factors.

There was, for example, no separation of "state" and "society" in classical thought. There is only the *polis*: the character of the citizens and the character of the regime are inextricable. The classics saw the *polis* in all its richness, in direct contrast to a social science that must narrow and re-make political phenomena so that they can (a) receive a label in a jargon that will match perfectly the terms used for other items and (b) slide comfortably into the scientific machine being constructed. The state is to the *polis* as the stick figure of Economic Man is to anybody we know. The classical understanding would be comfortable with what Hal Saunders is suggesting: diplomacy that is *polis*-to-*polis*.

Classical authors such as Plato, Aristotle, and Xenophon believed that the question of what is good and bad, "values" as we imprecise moderns label it, was too serious to be shrugged off. To see men as laboratory rats whose behavior (*only* the behavior) is recorded, while some black box inside them that is calling the shots remains sealed, would seem willfully obscurantist to the classics. Said simply, study and diplomacy based on the idea that conflict resolution might be preferable to conflict escalation, or that peace might be preferred to war, can find no support in the value-free sciences. A study that supports the breadth of considerations raised in this book must engage the larger, contextual, wholesale questions. It must understand that the character of a conflict is changed when the parties are able to look up, to see larger and loftier considerations.

Finally, the principal method and the central question of classical political science are both wonderfully suited to the serious consideration of the spiritual in the political life. The method is that of a dialogue in which two or more parties, each with imperfect knowledge, engage in a joint inquiry that raises all of them to a higher level of knowledge. And the central question—what is the best regime?— translates to the question of how a man should live in the *polis*, which translates to the question of how a man should live. Nothing is more characteristic of the case studies in this volume than the successful effort to lead parties in a dispute to focus on what the classics called "first things"—the fundamental and supremely important aspects of human life. There is a natural harmony between the characteristics of the classical approach to the study of politics and the innovations in the practice of politics described here.

The limitations must also be noted: they lie in the relation between classical thought and organized religion. The classics knew civic religion, religion tied to the *polis* and to patriotism, and therefore a religion that does the opposite of softening those elements. The more important limitation of the classical approach is that it can offer no analysis of the revealed word.[30] That is a very serious limitation, but it is a limitation shared fully with contemporary social sciences.

THE PRIORITIES OF FUTURE STATECRAFT

The research project discussed in this volume started with the observation that an important element was frequently missing from American diplomacy: a serious and effective relationship to spiritual factors that might possibly be brought to bear on the mitigation or resolution of conflict (either international or within current states), and on reconciliation. But it did not start with a full-scale analysis that demonstrated this observed insufficiency. If seen in the context of the need to do better in understanding and working effectively with overseas cultures, then the agreement of most serving professionals in the U.S. foreign affairs establishment is assured. The characteristic desire of U.S. diplomats to improve the quality of their service gives hope that they will be enthusiastically open to the considerations of this study.

One reason why spiritual factors have usually been ignored by U.S. diplomacy is the sense of the movement of history held by modern policymakers and diplomats. A team investigating the U.S. intelligence failure to predict the revolution in Iran found, for example, a feeling of many officers that they were doing the best job for the U.S. national interest by focusing on "the future" — on the Iranians who seemed to constitute the Iran of the future, the ones in business suits carrying attaché cases. Equal focus should have been given to bearded medieval characters sitting on prayer rugs. As it turned out, the future did indeed wear strange clothes.

This book has demonstrated a need to consider other actors, other influences and motivations, other approaches to negotiation and strategy. And, as the cases show, this *is* emerging, not (yet) as a systematic effort by foreign ministries to achieve greater breadth and effectiveness, but out of the struggle of mankind to find paths out of impasse. Necessity is the mother of these inventions; their other parent is the indomitable determination shown by some of the actors in the case studies to appeal to unusual (i.e., outside politics-as-usual) realms when the alternative is despair and bloodshed.

So on both the problem side and the solution side, what is analyzed here can be quite confidently predicted to grow in importance. First, spiritual elements are rarely successfully repressed. As Rubin says: "The importance of religious institutions is guaranteed because they and their personnel are usually relatively immune from repression" (p. 24). Second, the continuing failure of Third World countries to develop a strong state apparatus frequently hands to, or leaves with, religious institutions the role of providing the binding strength of the political community. In the last few years, headlines have focused on the way Muslim and Hindu groups have filled this role. But they are not alone. Rubin shows that in Latin America, the political question is not whether Christianity will be a powerful force in the years ahead, but whether moderate or radical theological thinking will have the upper hand. And "in parts of Africa and Asia, Catholicism and Protestantism have become new sources of identity that provide a basis for political communities" (p. 32). Rubin also finds foreign alignments in West Africa being heavily influenced by Christian and Muslim commitments. In South Africa, it is Christianity that competes with Marx within the ANC: it is impossible to picture the future of that country without a strong role being played by some of its religious leaders.

The ISD report predicts that, a decade from now, "more diplomacy will be preventive and interventionist."[31] United States diplomacy will be in the conflict-resolution business; the question is how much it will tie its own hands. The report goes on to predict that "international discourse will increasingly focus on normative issues."[32] Spiritual factors must, with no room for doubt, play an increasing role in the resolution of political conflict because of the absence of an alternative. Marx has fallen of his own insufficiencies. Inventive demagogues might find a rallying cry for a few years at a time, in the guise of lofty thinking, for a Sukarno or a Mobutu. And nationalism is still very much with us, but it more often intensifies than reduces conflict. Modernity itself does not produce, in the place of a guiding idea system, much beyond material abundance in some places, desperation and envy in others, and economic theories to explain both.

If political leaders and statesmen around the globe are insufficiently broad in their vision and in the people and considerations they are willing to bring to the table, they will be unable to be of much help for most of tomorrow's serious conflicts. Some of them may not be bothered by this failure, because that same narrowness will have prevented them from understanding the true terms of the conflict in the first place. Candide as the model of the modern statesman will gaze uncomprehendingly at the conflagration before which he lies helpless.

Notes

1. *The Foreign Service in 2001*, Report of the Institute for the Study of Diplomacy, School of Foreign Service, Georgetown University, August 1992, 21, cited hereafter in the text as "ISD Report."

2. Statement by Wilson Dizard in a meeting of the steering group of the CSIS project that produced this volume. Dizard is a senior associate in international communications at the Center for Strategic and International Studies (CSIS). As a former foreign service officer, he was directly involved in U.S. programs in both countries.

3. Dizard, who was in the Political Section of the U.S. Embassy in Saigon at the time.

4. This is the overall estimation of Gerrit Gong, director of Asian studies at CSIS.

5. Ibid. This is what can be said on the basis of facts currently available. It is by no means certain that a better understanding or manipulation of the religious dynamics would have led to a favorable outcome, only that the odds would have been improved.

6. Much of this also comes from Dizard, who was the USIS chief in Warsaw in 1968–70.

7. Helen Kitchen, director of African studies at CSIS, finds that U.S. diplomacy, true to its dogmatic secularism, generally did not engage the religious element in its search for solutions in South Africa, even with Desmond Tutu playing U.S. politics like a piano and even in a country where over three-quarters of the people are active churchgoers. Steven McDonald, executive vice president of the African-American Institute, says that there was no aspect of U.S. policy that related to South Africa's churches. He notes that even Afrikaans-speaking officers in the U.S. embassy had no significant relationship with the Dutch Reformed church; when individual church leaders rose to *political* prominence, for whatever reason, *then* attention was paid.

8. Interview with Gong. He notes some surprises in this period, such as the attendance of the U.S. ambassador at Ninoy Aquino's funeral.

9. This is generally true of Western diplomacy as well, although the secularism of U.S. diplomacy exceeds the others.

10. A few Latin American countries offer a partial exception to the rule.

11. The commentary here refers only to bilateral ambassadorships, where the United States and another country exchange diplomatic missions. The record of specialized ambassadorships—to multilateral organizations, to negotiations, and ambassadors-at-large—is quite different.

12. *Foreign Service in 2001*, 39. Until very recently the amateurism-quotient numbers were especially high. Under former President George Bush, progress was made in increasing the number of professional appointments from 1990 on. But the numbers do not tell the story. The situation is actually *worse*; appointments to the major posts where U.S. interests are most profoundly engaged are heavily amateur-ridden, while foreign service officers predominate at outposts where the main task is to show the flag so that the host country, inconsequential on the world's geopolitical atlas, is not offended by the absence. In fairness, a number of these "amateurs" are of such a stature that the term is clearly a misleading characterization. It is also the case that some political appointees either reveal an unexpected talent for diplomacy or recognize their incompetence and leave the work of diplomacy to others on the embassy staff. Other situations don't fare so well and call into serious question our Russian-roulette approach to important ambassadorial posts.

13. Former Ambassador L. Paul Bremer III, who headed a 1989 study group on the foreign service, reports that "we found that language-designated posts were being encumbered by fewer and fewer [language-capable officers]. Even between 1985 and 1988, in every single region of the world the number of people who had the languages had fallen. In some bureaus it was less than 50 percent" (*Foreign Service in 2001*, 43).

14. Ibid., 4.

15. The most celebrated case is Hans Morgenthau on Vietnam. There is an interesting parallel in the great richness of Max Weber's footnotes and asides—the commentary by a scholar of humane letters too big for the confines of his own methodology.

16. Such systematic analysis is found in the Christian tradition (Thomas Aquinas et al.), the Arab tradition (Alfarabi and Abu'l-Walid Muhammad Ibn Rushd, known to Latins as Averroes), and, of course, among Plato, Aristotle, and other old Athenian pagans. It is the denial of this effort, treating "values" as *unexaminable givens*, that is the novelty of modernity.

17. The same considerations have, historically and today, also driven men to the barricades.

18. Harold H. Saunders, former assistant secretary of state for Near Eastern and South Asian affairs, was a participant in this research project from the beginning. See his "An

Historic Challenge to Rethink How Nations Relate," in *The Psychodynamics of International Relationships: Volume I. Concepts and Theories*, eds. Vamik D. Volkan, Demetrios A. Julius, and Joseph V. Montville (Lexington, Mass.: Lexington Books, 1990), Chapter 1; also idem, *The Concept of Relationship: A Perspective on the Future Between the United States and the Successor States to the Soviet Union* (Columbus: Ohio State University, Mershon Center, 1992.)

19. *Foreign Services in 2001*, 43-44. Former Ambassador (and former president of the U.S. Institute of Peace) Samuel W. Lewis was plainspoken about the kind of training that is needed: "As I become more and more sensitive to the complexities and unpredictabilities of this era in world politics, the more I'm driven back in the direction of the traditional tools of analysis, historical comprehension, language skills."

20. It should go without saying that the spiritual life of a country is not confined to indigenous religious institutions, but includes everything from foreign clerics to the relationship of people on the scene to organizations such as Moral Re-Armament and the World Council of Churches. It includes the latest book on Islam read by a Hindu leader in the country and the religious awakening that the prime minister experienced during an early stint in prison.

21. Since *propaganda* is used here with all the freight of connotation that it carries in the United States, manipulation is the characteristic of propaganda that distinguishes it from more civilized forms of advocacy and dialogue. One argues with friends, but one does not manipulate them, does not propagandize them. "Propaganda" does not carry this freight in European usage.

22. Of course even classical political science stops at the wall of the revealed word. This problem, noted later as a limitation to the classical approach, is what makes dialogue between philosophy and religion ultimately impossible. The best Thomas Aquinas could do was to suggest that, by their own routes, philosophy and religion wound up at the identical spot with regard to the principal political questions.

23. This is an important point that may need a further word of elucidation. To take as an example the physical science most obviously close to sciences studying man—biology—we find the use of Latin as a jargon, which has the virtues of worldwide agreed usage, consistency, and clarity. Anything less than the devising of, and slavish adherence to, an agreed jargon would be impossibly inefficient for exactly the enterprise of building a scientific structure. But biology can use this jargon without paying a price in accuracy of description because of one critical distinction between biology and the study of politics, or of human history in general. In biology, the variations among individual beasts or individual organs and processes, bearing the same Latin name—if they are truly individual differences and not distinctions among groups that therefore call for further morphological classification and more labeling by more jargon—are totally inconsequential. Differences between mongrel cats that are crucial to a child are, if they fall within an allowable morphological range, without biological significance. The result is that the jargon works, without any loss of the particular kind of accuracy-in-description that would affect the work. One problem with the uniqueness of the mongrel cat (that cat which, to the child, is like no other cat in the world, and to the biologist is essentially, on every score that counts scientifically, like a large number of other cats) is that of numbers. None of the physical sciences, nor such arenas of quantification as survey research and economics, are comfortable with cells with only one item in them. But a social scientific endeavor that, for theory construction, must treat Japan or France or Angola as scientifically identical, if not with each other then at least with some other countries, is fundamentally incapable of accuracy about any of those countries. Social scientists, historians, and journalists must, of course,

make generalizations, as do our case study investigators. But there is no suggestion here that Zimbabwe or Sudan or the Miskito Indians or Robert Mugabe or Ian Smith can be properly understood as identical to any other entity. They are alone in their cells, and the only path to understanding is not, of course, to avoid generalization, but also not to lose analytical touch with their uniqueness.

24. In Aristophanes' *The Clouds*, the basket in which the young Socrates rides is destroyed by a father angered by what his son has been taught. Amusingly, some English translations actually call the basket a "think tank."

25. Hans Morgenthau, *Politics Among Nations* (New York: Knopf, 1950), 312. This sentence, published first in 1948, was repeated without change in the editions of 1954, 1967, 1972, and 1985, although many other elements of the same chapter were revised. Morgenthau's belief in its correctness obviously endured.

26. Ibid., 5.

27. Ibid., 312.

28. An account of the historically circumscribed character of geopolitics can be found in the latest book by Edward Luttwak entitled *The Endangered American Dream* (New York: Simon and Schuster, 1993).

29. Thus Prometheus was considered dangerous.

30. To put it simply, the Socratic dialogue is blocked whenever someone suggests a source of critical knowledge unavailable to the other participants in the dialogue.

31. *Foreign Service in 2001*, 4.

32. Ibid., 7. The report is silent on religious and spiritual factors.

14 ·

Implications for Religious Communities: Buddhism, Islam, Hinduism, and Christianity

WILLIAM VENDLEY AND DAVID LITTLE

O mankind! . . . we made you into nations and
tribes that you may know and cooperate with one
another.

Koran 49:13

The central implication of the case studies in this volume is quite straightforward: religious communities should recognize the role they can play in peacemaking and exercise that role much more than they usually do. Peacemaking presents both a significant opportunity and a major challenge to religious communities.

The underlying assumption of this book is that the case histories—the various "stories" that have been told—have a persuasive power of their own: they can serve as parables of what religiously motivated individuals and groups can accomplish in conflict situations. Like other parables, they have the power to prompt those who are receptive to new ways of thinking and acting. These examples of ways that religious actors have contributed to conflict resolution and to nonviolent social and political change should serve to inspire others to seize similar opportunities. Such opportunities are both more frequent and more manageable than commonly thought.

The cases also reveal some of the complexities in the histories of religious communities and in their responses to conflict. Such complexities—including the divergent interpretations of religious teachings and the often-contradictory forms of action taken in conflict situations—pose the greatest challenge to religious communities in pursuit of a more deliberate peacemaking role. On the other hand, the ways in which various communities have dealt with such dilemmas and have tapped both theological and human resources in supporting positive steps toward peace help clarify potential peacemaking activities. As illustrated in the Philippines (Chapter 8) and South Africa (Chapter 9) cases, pursuit of a constructive peacemaking role may require a reversal of existing approaches to conflict, in addition to a reevaluation of the central importance of certain foundational religious narratives to the conflict in question.

RELIGION, PRIMARY LANGUAGE, AND PEACEMAKING

"We tell ourselves stories in order to live," writes Joan Didion.[1] Human life is somehow given its most elemental identity by stories or narratives through the overarching coherence they provide to the diversity of human experience. Both individuals and the communities that form them are shaped in an elemental way by narrative.

The same holds true for religious communities. Each religion is constituted by a set of stories that make up its central identity. In effect, these narratives constitute the seedbed of a religious tradition that can be transmitted and developed across time. Religious traditions can be passed on orally or by means of sacred texts, learned commentaries, and a variety of other carriers of meaning, such as prayer, meditation, ritual, music, song, and dance. In turn, each tradition's collection of stories, narratives, religious customs, and artistic expressions can be usefully understood as that religion's *primary language*.[2]

Religious primary language establishes and defines a religious community.[3] It constitutes the community's living memory, provides for the possibility of shared experience and interpretation of reality, and offers a fertile foundation for that community's passage through time—orienting it to the past, the present, and the future.[4] The strength and fecundity of primary language can be seen in its ability to secure the religious identities of believers and reorient them in the constantly changing vicissitudes of history.

Understanding a religious community's primary language is a key to grasping that community's potential for peacemaking. First, primary language discloses the depth dimension of a religious community's experience; it establishes that community's horizon of ultimate concern or caring, even in the face of injustice or suffering. Second, it creates a shared ethical space for a community of believers and provides norms and principles for a moral stance in life. Third, primary language provides moral warrants for resistance against unjust conditions, including those conditions that give rise to conflict. Finally, it offers normative symbols of the religious meaning of peace and the human responsibility to strive for peace.[5]

Moreover, these four functions of many religions' primary languages are intrinsically universal in their intent. Consequently, believers of such religions often view their moral norms as guidelines for behavior toward all humans beings, including those who are their opponents in conflict. It should be noted, however, that not all religious communities' primary languages are universal in intent, and even those that are often find themselves burdened with histories of having "demonized" others.

Virtually all primary religious languages engage in some sort of questioning about what is wrong with the present state of affairs (pathology) and about what religious means should be applied to remedy that condition (soteriology). The former concept relates to a religious interpretation of the human experience of tragedy, suffering, and failure; the latter refers to salvation or the religious means of addressing pathology. When religious communities confront threats to peace, they creatively employ symbols of pathology and soteriology to interpret and deal with the circumstances they face.

Taking Christianity as an illustration, the following stories are examples of pathology: the temptation and fall of Adam and Eve; Cain's murder of Abel; the tower of Babel; the temptation to return to the security of slavery in Egypt and the rejection of the Ten Commandments; breaking God's sacred covenant; rejecting God's call to conversion as it is made present through the speeches of prophets; and the betrayal and crucifixion of Jesus. Across time, Christians have pondered these and many other stories in the Bible while attempting to come to grips with the root causes and characteristics of evil. These stories have provided Christians with a way of integrating the experiences of suffering, tragedy, evil, and moral failure inherent in conflict and war.

Linked with and corresponding to these stories of pathology are a series of soteriological stories—episodes in the overarching narrative of salvation. The following stories are examples of the Christian primary language of salvation: the essential goodness of creation as portrayed in Genesis; God leading Abraham in faith; calling the Hebrews out of slavery in Egypt; God forming a people in the desert and offering them a covenant; sending the prophets to call the community back to fidelity to God's covenant; offering mercy and forgiveness for the community that strayed from God's covenant; and establishing a new covenant in Jesus. The latter is understood as the forgiveness of sin and the beginning of the reigning of God's mercy on earth. Over time, this language has provided Christians with the ability to sustain their identities and live in hope, confident of God's goodness, even when confronted with tragedy and evil. This language of salvation, which enjoins all Christians to love their enemies, constitutes the principal religious resource for Christian peacemaking.

When confronted with actual conflict then, religious communities typically engage in two related and highly creative sets of activities.[6] First, they *turn back* to the roots of their own histories to "consult" their central religious stories. To be grasped, a situation of conflict must be interpreted in relation to the community's primary language. Perhaps not all stories will appear immediately helpful in interpreting the new problem at hand, so the community is driven further back in search of a more usable past. Which story, which chapter of a story, which teachings or practices embodied in at least some episode of the tradition's overarching narrative can orient contemporary believers in relation to the particular conflict in question? This task of turning back involves working out a connection, discovering a correlation, between its religious narratives and the new situation of conflict.

Second, the religious community must also *move forward*. It cannot be content to merely repeat what it hears from its past. It must find a way to "say anew" what it has heard from its tradition with regard to the conflict at hand. To effectively say anew what it means to be a Hindu, Buddhist, Jew, Christian, Muslim, or member of another religion in a given conflict requires dynamically creative acts that orient believers affectively, cognitively, morally, and spiritually to that conflict. This process is not limited merely to the spoken or written word, but encompasses the total religious response, including the numerous attitudes and actions that address the various dimensions of the conflict.

A NEED FOR SELF-EXAMINATION

Religious traditions are storehouses of diverse and sometimes contradictory messages. Their symbols and stories have often been interpreted in very different ways. If religious communities are to realize their potential for peacemaking, they will need to reexamine their primary language self-critically in light of the examples supplied in this book. They will need to search their scriptural and doctrinal foundations and their own histories to discover the motivation, guidance, and resources for making peace.

Religious communities will have to take a long, hard look at themselves and, when appropriate, admit that not everything said in their tradition points in the direction of peace, but rather some of it actually produces strife. This fact will need to be acknowledged before those elements in the tradition that inspire and promote peace can be identified and effectively pressed into action.

The challenge for religious people committed to making peace, then, is to disentangle the themes of conflict in their traditions from the themes of peace and to employ the latter, while disregarding or modifying the former. This is a painful process. Confession and contrition for the infirmities of religion are inherently difficult to undertake, but the process is necessary, nevertheless.

AMBIVALENT IMPERATIVES

A Buddhist Example

Much in Buddhism favors the cause of peacemaking. The well-known emphases on nonviolence, on persuasion rather than force and coercion to convey the teachings of the Buddha, and on the readiness to "bear with" opponents rather than to dominate them—all lead to a spirit of tolerance and forbearance, which is a crucial condition for creating peace. Harvey Cox and his colleagues deal with these qualities extensively in Chapter 12 of this volume. As they point out, there can be a dark side to Buddhism, too.

In the island republic of Sri Lanka, where Buddhism is the dominant religion, an ancient series of chronicles written by Buddhist monks glorifies the image of the warrior king rather than the ideas of tolerance and forbearance. It is recorded that in the second century B.C.E., King Duttagamani ("Gamani, the ferocious") went to war with a non-Buddhist king, bearing a relic of the Buddha on his spear. He eventually won a bloody victory, but when, as a good Buddhist, he expressed remorse for all the people he had killed, he was informed by some monks that he need only worry about two of the victims, who happened to be Buddhists. No mercy was due the others, said the monks, because the non-Buddhists were "not more to be esteemed than beasts."[7]

Such an acceptance of violence, if not the glorification of it, has been adopted by some modern Buddhist nationalists in Sri Lanka, where it has been used as a source of encouragement in the conflict with minority groups. Given the rich peaceful tradition of Buddhism, there is significant opportunity for Sri Lankan Buddhists to lay the bellicose themes aside and to recover the tolerant, open-hearted tradition of King Ashoka, the famous Indian king who sought to promote religious tolerance as a basis for creating inclusive, peaceful conditions in his troubled country (Chapter 12). Righteous living, according to King Ashoka, had a common source: "Modesty of speech, one must not exalt one's creed by discrediting . . . others. . . . Concord is good only insofar as all listen to each other's creeds and love to listen to them."[8]

An Islamic Example

Islam displays a similar ambivalence. Islamic revelation provides its own diagnosis of the conditions that obstruct the realization of peace, which is the divine goal for humanity. Human civilization, the Koran maintains, is the record of the perpetual struggle (*jihad*) against human self-centeredness and self-cultivated pettiness, the two principal sources of conflict and the attendant destruction that flows from it. According to Islam, the root cause for the human failure to work toward the establishment of an ethical order on earth that would guarantee peace and harmony is mankind's incomplete submission to the divine will. Only through true submission can humanity recognize its primordial nature, which is oriented toward peace and endowed with God-conscious cognition and volition. The enemy within needs to be conquered before external threats to the creation of a just and peaceful society can be overcome.[9]

Religion and public order are closely connected for Muslims. Sacred law, or Sharia, is taken to govern public life, but according to certain conventional interpretations of Sharia, tolerance of non-Muslims is often sharply restricted. Even other monotheists, who, unlike polytheists, have often been permitted a degree of religious freedom, are nevertheless denied full civil and political equality with the Muslim majority. Past efforts of the National Islamic Front in the Sudan to impose Sharia upon unwilling citizens, Muslim and non-Muslim alike, is a vivid contemporary example of this tendency.

Even as there are questionable elements in Islamic practice, there are central teachings in the Islamic tradition that are relevant to peacemaking. These are well explored in Chapter 12 and represent a major resource for dispute resolution in the years ahead.

A Hindu Example

Recent events in India—particularly the destruction by Hindu extremists of a sixteenth-century Muslim mosque in Ayodhya and the subsequent violence between Hindus and Muslims—illustrate the potential for intolerance among Hindus. Encouraged by Hindu nationalists, militants contend that Ayodhya is a sacred site of ancient significance and thus deserves to be set aside exclusively for Hindu use. Regaining control of what is considered to be the birthplace of a prominent Hindu deity, they argue, is one way of reinstating Hinduism and reducing the influence of "alien" religions, such as Islam.

In contrast, the primary language of Hinduism provides an interpretation of reality that would, if properly applied, dissolve the miasma of intolerance generated by extremists. In Hinduism, the root cause of human bondage and conflict is seen to be *avidya* or ignorance. This primordial ignorance leads one to imagine or perceive the existence of an independent, substantial world of real objects, persons, and processes. This perception is grounded in some pervasive error that impels us to take the unreal for the real and the real for the unreal.

Maya, the mysterious power of *Brahman*, the Absolute One, by which the world of multiplicity comes into existence, deludes us into taking the phenomenal world as reality. *Maya* seduces us to take ourselves to be what we ordinarily think we are—a unity of physical organization, mental capacity, emotional activity, and volitional life. It is *maya* that has the power of producing such illusory notions as "I," "me," or "mine." Thus, all memories and cognitions, precepts and logics, attachments and aversions, hopes and fears are grounded in *maya*.

This pathology of primordial ignorance can be overcome only by the "saving" knowledge that *Brahman*, the Absolute, alone is real, that the world is illusory, and that the true Self within us in not different from *Brahman*. The true Self, the *Atman*, is pure, undifferentiated, self-shining consciousness: timeless, spaceless, unthinkable, indescribable, and not different from *Brahman*, the Absolute. In the experience of the identity of *Atman*, the Self, and *Brahman*, the Absolute, one realizes *sat*, pure being, *chit*, pure consciousness, and *ananda*, pure bliss. It is the experience in which the separation of self and non-self, of ego and world, is transcended, and complete Self-realization and Self-knowledge are obtained. It is the state in which one is liberated from the bondage and illusion that is the root cause of conflict.[10]

Contrary to the Ayodhya experience, this understanding has contributed to a high degree of tolerance toward other religions as illustrated by Hinduism's willingness at various times to welcome into its embrace a variety of persecuted religious groups.

A Christian Example

The South Africa case study illustrates especially well the ambiguity of a religious community's interpretation of its own primary language in relation to questions of racial division. It is a dramatic example of the contradictory messages that have been derived from the Christian religion. Initially, the Dutch Reformed church (DRC) played a central role in inspiring and justifying the policy of apartheid. In this process, the biblical story of the tower of Babel figured prominently: the idea that the various peoples of the world were estranged from one another by divine decree was used to legitimize a total separation of the races. Starting in the 1960s, however, the DRC gradually revised its thinking on the subject until finally, in 1990, it joined with other denominations in declaring that apartheid was in direct conflict with the fundamental precepts of the Christian tradition.

Shifts in positions on apartheid and in theological orientation progressed in tandem. The central relevance of the biblical story of Babel for apartheid was called into question.[11] In its place, Christian communities appealed to other, and arguably more central, narratives within the Christian tradition that could be interpreted as calls to reject apartheid. Both the Genesis account of Adam, in which humanity is recognized as being made in the image and likeness of God,[12] and other major narratives of both testaments, in which God's peace is recognized to involve a rightness in all relationships among people,[13] contain teachings that effectively undermine the concept of apartheid.

Based on the changing and conflicting interpretations of its primary scriptural and traditional language, the DRC served, at first, to produce and legitimate the conditions of racial strife in South Africa, then to help ameliorate those conditions, and finally to create the opportunity for a just peace. These variations and conflicts within a single denomination exemplify comparable tensions over questions of justice and peace within churches throughout the whole of Christendom.

THE BROADER POSSIBILITIES FOR PEACEMAKING

The case studies, together with the previously cited examples, reveal a need for religious communities to search their traditions for teachings that promote peace and to engage in critical self-examination of their respective approaches to conflict. In one way or another, religious communities are always engaged in some form of action in this regard. Even a stance of nonaction is a form of action, as illustrated by the role of the Catholic church in the Philippines prior to the events discussed in Chapter 8.

With religions around the world reaching into virtually every city or village, there are innumerable religiously motivated "agents" available for peacemaking. The types of religious actors within the Christian community represented by the case studies in this volume (together with the case vignettes in Chapter 15) are indicative of the potential for peacemaking that exists:

- international ecumenical body (e.g., the World Council of Churches)
- international denominational organization (e.g., the Vatican)
- national ecumenical body (e.g., the South African Council of Churches)
- national denominational group (e.g., the Evangelische Kirche in East Germany)
- national nondenominational group (e.g., Moral Re-Armament in Rhodesia)
- ad hoc ecumenical group (e.g., the Conciliation Commission in Nicaragua)
- ad hoc denominational group (e.g., the Quaker team in Nigeria)
- individual representing a denomination or religious tradition (e.g., Anglican Archbishop Desmond Tutu in South Africa)

- individual acting independently (e.g., prayer fellowship member General David Jones in the Kenya-Somalia dispute—see Chapter 15)

Such a list must be viewed as merely suggestive of a much larger range of possibilities: there are other types of religious agents not represented in the case materials in this book, and a comparable listing might be anticipated for each of the other non-Christian religious traditions, as well.

Peacemaking Functions

In principle, religious agents can engage in a wide variety of functions relative to peacemaking. They can function as activists (parties to the conflict) by working as a force for nonviolent change or in support of an emerging political consensus. Examples of activists in the above sense can be found in the Philippines, South Africa, and East Germany (Chapter 7) cases. Religious agents can also work as advocates (parties in support of one side in a conflict) by providing sanctuary for internal opposition groups, engaging in truth-telling, or applying pressure from outside the political system. Examples of these advocacy functions, respectively, are provided by the Protestant churches in East Germany; the Catholic church in Rhodesia; and the World Council of Churches, the World Alliance of Reformed Churches, and Pope John Paul II in South Africa.

In addition to partisan roles, there is a wide variety of third-party functions that religious agents can perform, including peace process advocacy, opening lines of communication between the parties in conflict, conciliation, and mediation. Examples of the first three functions can be found in the work of the Quakers in Rhodesia (Chapter 10) and Nigeria (Chapter 6), while mediation was performed by the Conciliation Commission in Nicaragua (Chapter 5). Religious agents can also act as observers as they did in the election-monitoring activities performed by priests and nuns in the Philippines. Finally, although not represented in the cases, they can conceivably serve as enforcers, or guarantors, of some aspect of a political settlement.[14]

Clearly, the cases suggest that peacemaking opportunities for religiously motivated actors are both numerous and significant. It follows that religious communities should feel challenged to prepare themselves for pursuing these possibilities. Internal reflection and self-criticism regarding religious meanings and practices are necessary first steps. Next comes an examination and adjustment of the tradition's forms of practice in relation to peacemaking. Finally, there should be a wide dissemination of the tradition's peace-oriented teachings to its members and a purposeful effort to educate and train them in the art and science of conflict resolution. The growing body of literature and practical expertise in the field of conflict resolution needs to be adapted and appropriately applied by religious communities at all levels of society.

Finally, the painful history of religious conflicts suggests the need for religious communities to learn to cooperate in support of peace. There is evidence that many of them are prepared to do so. An early but illustrative example occurred in

1970, when some 250 senior leaders representing 10 major world religions and coming from 40 different countries met in Kyoto, Japan, at the first World Conference on Religion and Peace. As they sat down together, facing the urgent issues of peace of that time, they concluded that many of the beliefs that united them were more important than those that were divisive. As reflected in their joint declaration, they found a number of points of moral common ground:

- a conviction of the fundamental unity of the human family, and the equality and dignity of all human beings
- a sense of the sacredness of the individual person and his or her conscience
- a sense of the value of human community
- a realization that might is not right; that human power is not self-sufficient and absolute
- a belief that love, compassion, selflessness, and the force of inner truthfulness and of the spirit have ultimately greater power than hate, enmity, and self-interest
- a sense of obligation to stand on the side of the oppressed as against the oppressor
- a profound hope that good will prevail[15]

On the basis of these shared convictions, the participants expressed their belief that a special charge has been given to all men and women of religion to work for peace and that religious people have often betrayed their religious ideals and commitments to peace. In their words, "it is not religion that has failed the cause of peace, but religious people."[16] Even if this betrayal remains a permanent possibility rooted in the frailty of the human character, the call for peacemaking in religious primary languages nevertheless endures. Fidelity to that call will demand courage and creativity.

Notes

1. Joan Didion, *The White Album* (New York: Simon and Schuster, 1979), 11.

2. Our use of the words *story* and *narrative* does not render formal judgment on the truth claims of a given religion's stories or narratives.

3. For religious communities, *secondary languages* are forms of secular discourse used to express the moral concerns that are rooted in their respective primary languages. Many religious communities today feel challenged by religious and secular pluralism to express themselves in a secondary or secular form of discourse. They feel compelled to "speak their concerns" in the public square by translating—or better, transposing—their ethical sensibilities into a secular, public language. Martin Luther King, Jr., for example, successfully transposed his Christian convictions regarding the dignity of all persons into a form of nonsectarian public speech addressed to all Americans by using the secular concept of civil rights. In addition, Dr. King's use of secondary language provided a means for reaching agreement on civil rights with different religious and ideological groups, as well as a basis for cooperative action. For more on this topic, see William F. Vendley, "Religious Differences and Shared Care: The Need for Primary and Secondary Language," *Church and Society* (September/October 1992), 16–29.

4. Paul Ricoeur notes that our experience of time has a narrative structure. We experience time as a story with a past, a present, and a future (Paul Ricoeur, *Time and Narrative*, vol. 1 [Chicago: University of Chicago Press, 1984], 52).

5. For a related and helpful understanding of the function of religion, see Hans King, *Global Responsibility: In Search of New World Ethic* (New York: Crossroad, 1991), 53–54.

6. Although these two types of activity may not be consciously distinguished by all religious communities, in practice they will engage in them, at least to a limited degree, if the communities are functioning at all in relation to contemporary problems.

7. Mahanama (a Thervada Buddhist monk), *Mahavamasa*, ch. 25 verses 109–111 (Sri Lankan Buddhist Chronicle, circa sixth century A.D.).

8. Cited in M. Searle Bates, *Religious Liberty: An Inquiry* (New York: Harper, 1945), 267–68.

9. Dr. Abdulaziz Sachedina's assistance with this section is gratefully acknowledged.

10. Dr. Anand Mohan's assistance with this section is gratefully acknowledged.

11. See, for example, Section 2.5.1 of the "Rustenburg Declaration," National Conference of Churches in South Africa, November 1990.

12. Ibid., Section 4.2.4.1.

13. Ibid., Section 4.3.1.

14. If the types of religious actors are listed along one axis and their specific peace-making functions along another axis, a useful grid can be constructed to chart the diversity of peacemaking agents and range of functions. This five-part typology of conflict intervention roles is drawn from James Laue and Gerald Cormick, "The Ethics of Intervention in Community Disputes," in *The Ethics of Social Intervention*, ed. Herbert C. Kelman and Donald P. Warwick (Washington, D.C.: Halsted Press, 1978), 205–32. The contribution of Cynthia Sampson in drawing up these lists of agents and functions is gratefully acknowledged.

15. Homer A. Jack, ed., *Religion for Peace: Proceedings of the Kyoto Conference on Religion and Peace* (New Delhi: Gandhi Peace Foundation, 1973), ix-x.

16. Ibid. x.

15 ▪

Looking Ahead: Toward a New Paradigm

DOUGLAS JOHNSTON

It is not for you to complete the work, but neither are you free to desist from doing it.

Rabbi Tarfon

For all their diversities, there are certain properties that most of the major religions hold in common: the premise that self-centeredness is the source of most unhappiness, that help is needed to overcome this condition, and that there is a "divine ground" from which humankind has sprung and in relation to which one's true worth is to be sought. Finally, and perhaps most important, they also contain some version of the Golden Rule.[1] These represent significant commonalities on which to build in promoting interfaith dialogue and the nonviolent resolution of differences.

On the other hand, the recent prominence of religious figures in conflict resolution should not encourage overly high expectations. What is needed, rather, is a sober appreciation of the continuities of history and the critical role of political, military, and economic factors in creating the conditions that induce decisionmakers to seek—or at least cooperate with—spiritually inspired mediation or conciliation efforts.

On average, there are more than 100 armed conflicts in the world in any given year.[2] Many of these are characterized by seemingly "irrational" motives—motives that outsiders cannot relate to material aims. Others are conflicts in which the parties to the dispute believe that only the application of force can make a difference, whether by resolving the matter through conquest, inducing negotiations, or establishing a new balance of power in which the opposing forces effectively offset one another. The fact that many conflicts take place because of a clash of interests, and not merely as a result of misunderstanding, is a sobering reality that must be acknowledged by those who seek nonviolent solutions. Nevertheless, as demonstrated in some of the case studies in this book, spiritually based mediation and conciliation can, under the right circumstances, achieve genuine breakthroughs to peace.

Capitalizing on this potential, however, is a delicate undertaking. The application of religious factors to political problems is inherently complex and fraught with peril; hence the Western predilection for maintaining a complete separation between the two. But the potential for overcoming the shortcomings of conventional diplomacy in some situations by introducing religious or spiritual factors appears to be substantial. It suggests that foreign policy professionals and religious practitioners should study the possibilities and seek to facilitate and reinforce one another's efforts to resolve conflict wherever it appears sensible to do so.

As one explores the application of spiritual approaches to present and future disputes, the types of religious groups and institutions depicted in the case studies must be recognized as significant assets. To be sure, the spectrum of peacemaking initiatives depicted in the cases presented in Chapters 4 through 10 is neither comprehensive in scope nor exhaustive in its typology. It is at most a partial sampling of a wider range of experience and a still wider range of possibilities. As Chapters 13 and 14 emphasize, exploiting the full potential of spiritually based peacemaking will require both new openings for religious actors (a challenge to the foreign affairs community) and increased efforts on their parts (a challenge to religious communities).

THE ROLE OF THE INDIVIDUAL

Touched on in some of the case studies but deserving of further mention and closer examination is the role of spiritually motivated individuals operating independently of an institutional base. The individual may be one of the principals in a conflict, a religious figure, or a layperson. The potential contribution of the solitary person operating from a sense of personal conviction is not necessarily less than that of someone who operates under an institutional umbrella. It may, in fact, be greater. The examples below are offered as illustrations.

Spiritual "First Parties" (The Sudan: 1972)

A poignant example of how a personal spiritual commitment at the principal-actor level can influence the outcome of a conflict is that offered by Joseph Lagu during the first Sudanese civil war between the Muslim-dominated north and the largely animist and Christian south. By way of background, fighting started soon after Sudan's independence in 1956 as the South attempted to secede from what could only be described as a northern-dominated state. As the conflict evolved, the stakes grew higher with the involvement on one side or the other of Ethiopia, Uganda, Egypt, Israel, Libya, Algeria, Iraq, and the Soviet Union. At least four different contests were manifest in Sudan: north versus south, Christian versus Muslim, East versus West, and Arab versus Israeli.[3]

It was within this larger context that Joseph Lagu, leader of the rebel forces in the south, was confronted with a specific and, as events would later prove, highly significant dilemma. In 1971 a plane filled with northern Sudanese civilians crash-landed in rebel territory, and the 29 survivors were captured by Lagu's soldiers. Only 14 days earlier, government troops had attacked a rebel village and burned down a church, killing a number of the worshipers within. Thus the temptation for revenge was all but overpowering. After wrestling with the decision over the course of a restless night, Lagu ordered the captured civilians freed.

According to Lagu, he was heavily influenced by a question that he posed to himself: "What would Christ have me do?" In response to this question, he had several thoughts. His first was of Christ feeding the multitudes when they were in need. His second was of the scriptural admonition concerning the number of times that one should forgive one's enemy—70 times seven. His last thought was of some advice a chaplain had given him when he was a young man: "If I ever had a thought in the cool hours of morning, I should act on it and not dilute it by consulting others. God was talking to me, not them."[4]

As he struggled with the decision, Lagu became convinced that a gesture of generosity rather than a retaliatory response might turn his prisoners into ambassadors for peace. That is precisely what happened as news of his humanitarian gesture spread and effectively undermined the government's accusations that the rebels were no more than "savages and thieves." It was shortly thereafter that mediation between the two sides was initiated by representatives from the World Council of Churches (WCC) and the All Africa Conference of Churches (AACC). Both sides in the conflict were in need of relief aid (which the WCC and AACC were in charge of supplying), and neither felt that it had the military strength to continue the war. So the realpolitik "planets" of material need and military stalemate had already acquired a degree of alignment. But it was Lagu's transformational thoughts and action that helped establish the level of trust needed to facilitate the later breakthrough to peace.

Subsequent events in Sudan, though moving beyond the realm of the spiritually motivated individual, are also instructive. The fact that an ecumenical Christian team was accepted by Muslims in an intermediary role is unusual in itself. It was facilitated by the fact that the team had no political agenda, only an expressed concern for peacemaking and reconciliation. It is noteworthy, however, that the ensuing Addis Ababa settlement of 1972, which granted autonomy to the south, is now criticized by some Muslim commentators who accuse the Christian mediators of having had a political agenda after all, i.e., autonomy for the south (in spite of the genuine feelings of remorse expressed by both sides at the time of the settlement).[5]

Implementation of the Addis Ababa settlement eroded over the course of the next decade until the agreement itself was abrogated by President Gaafar Nimeri in 1983. It is generally thought that an unsuccessful coup attempt against Nimeri by the northern opposition in 1976 ultimately led him to appoint a number of opponents of southern autonomy to his government, including Hassan al-Turabi, leader of the Muslim Brotherhood. Later, Nimeri declared Sudan an Islamic state, with himself as the imam.[6] He next attempted to impose Sharia law throughout the entire country, encompassing Muslims and non-Muslims alike. By 1983 civil war had broken out again.[7] (Ironically, it was General Lagu who had helped to thwart the 1976 coup by threatening to march north against the opposition forces.)

While it might be expected that a settlement based on a genuine reconciliation of differences would last longer than one that is politically imposed, the Sudanese experience suggests the need for institutionalized follow-through at the grass-roots level. If the transformation that takes place around the bargaining table is not replicated within the respective constituencies, the durability of any agreement is likely to erode over time.

Religious Figures Operating Independently (East Germany: 1989)

At times, church officials operating in a purely personal capacity, quite apart from their institutional affiliation and authority, have also influenced the course of human history. A possible instance of this took place in the mid-1970s when the Vatican's secretary of state, Cardinal Casaroli, had a series of private philosophical discussions with Klaus Gysi, East Germany's first ambassador to Italy. The Cardinal confronted Gysi about the persecution of the Christian churches in his country. Gysi at first responded along classic Marxist lines, but Casaroli persevered, insisting that the hearts of men would always be tied to religion "because of the human need to fill a spiritual and moral vacuum (something that classic Marxism could not do)."[8] The cardinal, knowing of East Germany's desire to improve its standing with the West, also emphasized the direct correlation between the state's treatment of Christians and its external image.[9]

Gysi conveyed these thoughts to the East German head of state, Erich Honecker. Soon thereafter, the churches were given greater freedoms, including the right to construct church buildings in new housing districts (a tacit recognition that the church would be around for some time to come).[10] The relationship between these new freedoms and Casaroli's dialogue with Gysi is not totally clear. It appears noteworthy, however, that as religious dissent increased and the state granted additional concessions, Honecker named Gysi state secretary for religious affairs (reportedly to force him to deal with a problem he had helped create).[11] Gysi appears to have then become a force for change in his own right and to have played at least an indirect role in opening the churches to opposition elements.[12] Thus, the personal intervention of Cardinal Casaroli may have played a significant, albeit unrecognized, role in opening the way for the East German revolution.

Spiritually Motivated Laypersons (Kenya/Somalia: 1984)

Beyond the vagaries of chance that produce leaders like General Lagu and General Gowon of Nigeria, who have deep spiritual convictions of their own, there are the opportunities offered by time and circumstance in which spiritually motivated laypersons act on a personal basis to inspire positive action among policymakers. This type of activity is encouraged and well represented by the network of individuals associated with the National Prayer Breakfast, which is held annually in Washington, D.C., and in numerous other capitals around the world.

This global network of colleagues and friends places a singular emphasis on the centrality of Christ's teachings but does not confine that emphasis to a Christian context. It feels that regardless of how one views Christ—as the son of God, as one of many gods, or simply as a great prophet—the profundity of his message to "love thine enemy" remains.

Other distinguishing characteristics of the network include a focus on people in positions of leadership at all levels of society, the encouragement of those leaders to meet together in small fellowship groups as a way of reinforcing one another in serving the disadvantaged, and a strong emphasis on personal transformation. Representative of how this movement works is the role played by U.S. Air Force General David Jones in 1981 as he sought to help resolve a long-standing border dispute between Kenya and Somalia. At the time, Jones was chairman of the Joint Chiefs of Staff.

Major conflict had erupted between Kenya and Somalia in 1963 over the Northern Frontier District (NFD), the northern third of present-day Kenya (Figure 15.1). Somalia, which had achieved its independence several years earlier, insisted that the NFD should be under its control because the majority of the district's inhabitants were Muslim tribesmen of Somali extraction who wanted to become part of a "Greater Somalia."[13] Although Kenya was a Christian country, the British felt obliged to honor the artificial boundaries of the British East African Protectorate[14] and ceded the NFD to Kenya when they granted it independence in 1963.

From 1963 to 1967, the Somali tribes in northern Kenya attempted to secede from the new state. The Kenyan government took strong measures to suppress the rebellion and ultimately succeeded in doing so. Talks took place between the two sides in 1967, and the war was officially terminated. However, border hostilities continued. In September 1979, Daniel arap Moi, who had succeeded Jomo Kenyatta the year before as president of Kenya, met with President Mohamed Siad Barre of Somalia to discuss their differences, but nothing of consequence came of it. They met again on at least one other occasion; this time without either leader discussing their mutual conflict.[15] As President Siad Barre later indicated, addressing these problems at the political level would have been interpreted as weakness and tantamount to political suicide.[16]

In 1981 an American and his son who were involved with the National Prayer Breakfast landed at the airport in Mogadishu, the capital of Somalia, en route to visit President Moi in Kenya. During their brief stopover, they paid a call on Siad Barre at his home where they "discussed the power, importance, and results of men and women meeting in the spirit of Christ around the world."[17] After describing a number of situations in which various leaders had been able to work out their problems when meeting on such a basis, the visitors rose to return to their plane. Siad Barre asked where they were going. They replied, "to Kenya to see President Moi." Siad Barre then told them of his country's border disputes with Kenya and asked them to tell President Moi that he would be willing to meet "in the spirit of Christ" to work out their problems. The Americans subsequently conveyed Siad Barre's message to Moi who, although noncommittal, found it "interesting."[18] Upon their return to the United States, the Americans shared their story with General Jones, a close friend who was involved with a Pentagon fellowship group.

Figure 15.1. Kenya and Somalia

A few months later, Siad Barre, in the United States on an official visit, called on Jones at the Pentagon to discuss his country's military needs. After completing their formal discussions, Jones, remembering the earlier story, asked the Somali leader if he would be willing to join Jones and a few of his friends at a fellowship breakfast the following morning. Siad Barre, unaware that Jones knew of his recent conversation with his American visitors, was initially taken aback but agreed to participate.[19]

On May 29, 1981, a small but diverse group assembled for breakfast. Among others, it included representatives from the prayer breakfast groups in the U.S. Senate and House of Representatives.[20] Following readings from the Koran and the Old and New Testaments, several of the participants shared their feelings about the importance of meeting in fellowship. They described difficult personal situations in which their colleagues had provided valuable support, despite the fact that they shared deep political differences.

As the group talked further about various problems around the world, Siad Barre echoed his earlier concern about the difficulties between his country and Kenya and the long-standing bitterness that had prevented any dialogue on the subject. After he had spoken, Jones pointed his finger at Siad Barre, and said, "Mr. President, you should go see President Moi before your countries are at war." In contrast to his earlier signal to the American and his son, Siad Barre said such a meeting would be impossible; his staff would not understand it, nor would his people. Jones persisted and said, "You must go. What if the meeting could take place in secrecy? What if separate helicopters could bring each of you to an American aircraft carrier for a rendezvous at sea? No one would have to know about it."

Jones next turned to Robert Murray, then under secretary of the U.S. Navy and a fellow member of the Pentagon fellowship group, and asked if either of the two aircraft carriers in the region could be made available. Murray responded, "The carrier of your choice!" After listening to this, Siad Barre leaned back in his chair, reflected for a moment, then looked at Jones and said, "General, I have decided two things. When I return to my country, I will start a small fellowship group in my government. Second, I will go see President Moi."[21]

The following month, Siad Barre and Moi met "in a spirit of fellowship" following an OAU meeting in Nairobi (at which Siad Barre paved the way for reconciliation by announcing that Somalia was not seeking any territorial gain from Kenya).[22] A joint communiqué following the two leaders' private talks conveyed a mutual commitment to promote better understanding and collaboration between their countries.[23] At subsequent meetings in August, Somalia offered to help Kenya control insurgents along their common border, and both sides agreed to cooperate in suppressing bandit activity. Trade was also resumed across the border.[24] As President Moi said when queried as to the significance of the meeting with Siad Barre, "Before the meeting, we had wars; after the meeting, no more wars."[25]

The influence of other factors should also be noted, however. Following the suppression of the initial rebellion, Moi had taken steps to develop an extensive infrastructure of roads, hospitals, and the like in the contested region, an area that had been largely isolated and neglected under colonial rule. This effort was helpful in defusing secessionist passions and had the long-term effect of assimilating Somalis into Kenya's mainstream—to the point where Somali tribesmen came to occupy some of the more senior positions in the Kenyan government.[26]

Perhaps even more compelling at the time was the fact that Siad Barre was anxious to consolidate his position internally after an unsuccessful attack on

Ethiopia. For his part, Moi was concerned about ideological encirclement of his own country in light of socialist Tanzania's close ties to Ethiopia and its increasing influence in Uganda.[27] Thus, both countries had significant incentive to seek an agreement. It was in this context that the efforts of General Jones and his colleagues were able to produce results.

Later events in Kenya and Somalia attest to the fact that this settlement of differences between the two leaders was anything but a "Damascus experience"[28] for either of them. The bloodshed attending Siad Barre's fall from power and the unrest associated with Moi's resistance to implementing multiparty democracy in his own country attest to the failings and associated difficulties each has subsequently experienced. But that should not detract from the fact that lives and property were undoubtedly spared as a result of their willingness to act at a given point in time in response to a spiritual catalyst. Nor does it diminish the value of inspired intervention on the part of the spiritually motivated layperson operating out of a personal commitment to peace.

Bottom Line

What each of the above vignettes demonstrates is that individual men and women imbued with a spiritual commitment can become effective instruments of reconciliation, regardless of their political or religious leanings. This represents a highly important resource as one looks to a future that is likely to be marked by disorder and uncertainty.

THE PLANETS UNALIGNED

Beyond those conflict situations described in the case studies of earlier chapters in which some form of closure was achieved, similar religious factors are at work in a number of ongoing conflicts that have yet to be resolved. Three places where religious or spiritual approaches have been tried, with varying degrees of success, are Northern Ireland, Sri Lanka, and the Punjab in India. A brief examination of these efforts may prove instructive in suggesting additional approaches to conflicts that arise across religious divides.

Northern Ireland

The history of the conflict in Northern Ireland is well known. The social and cultural strife in that country stems from a complex ethnicity produced by successive Celtic, Roman, and later Saxon invasions. Many observers view the conflict as a religious confrontation between Catholics and Protestants, but Northern Ireland is not a battleground for classic religious warfare in which one party seeks to force the conversion of the other. Beneath the religious labels are economic disparities, rival national identities, and conflicting political objectives.[29]

The attitudes and perceptions of both groups are shaped by mutually exclusive goals. The Catholics want a united state with the British out, while the Protestants fear being subsumed by the Catholics in a united Ireland. In effect, the two sides' deep-seated suspicions, fueled by vicious cycles of violence and revenge, have become self-fulfilling prophecies.[30]

Despite its many attempts to do so, the British government has been unable to present itself as an objective party in resolving the conflict. Even its most recent peace initiative of December 1993, in which British Prime Minister John Major and Irish Prime Minister Albert Reynolds issued a joint declaration calling for talks and popular plebescites on Northern Ireland's future, has given rise to suspicions about British motives. As a result, a number of clergy and church lay leaders have stepped in to fill the vacuum. Indeed, some have been active from as far back as 1968 in their attempts to defuse hostilities. Two efforts in the mid-1970s particularly stand out.

The Feakle Initiative of 1974, organized by officers of the Irish Council of Churches, brought representatives of Sinn Fein, the legal political arm of the Irish Republican Army (IRA), together with representatives of the British government to conduct negotiations. Among other accomplishments, these negotiations resulted in a short-lived cease-fire lasting from Christmas of 1974 until Easter of 1975.[31] During this same period, a Leaders Peace Campaign was initiated by other church officials. This public campaign of newspaper advertisements, rallies, and petitions resulted in meetings between Catholic and Protestant church leaders and government officials from the Republic of Ireland, Northern Ireland, and the United Kingdom.[32]

Despite the fact that these early efforts soon broke down, throughout the 1980s and into the 1990s church leaders have persisted in their attempts to bring the opposing parties together to build confidence and provide a context for reconciliation. Even with the renewal of violence in late 1991 and the fall of 1993, unprecedented in intensity since the mid-1970s, many church efforts have continued apace. These range from providing relief services to public campaigns for peace and understanding.

Some of the more notable initiatives include the activities of the Corrymeela peace center, involving Catholics and Protestants committed to reconciliation and peace; regular meetings of the highest officials of the four largest churches;[33] and the efforts of the Irish Council of Churches Advisory Forum on Human Rights (sometimes working jointly with the Roman Catholic Justice and Peace Commission), which deals with issues of punishment, imprisonment, and the rights of victims.

The paradox remains, however, that while religious persons and groups continue to be active in promoting peace, outside analysts consider religious institutions to be major contributors to the ongoing tensions in Northern Ireland.[34] Although institutional church leaders meet, issue statements against violence, and urge prayers for peace, many of these same leaders are criticized for resisting peace initiatives that might alter their own institutions, such as the formation of ecumenical bodies involving both Catholics and Protestants, integrated schooling, or mixed public housing.[35]

Northern Ireland thus presents a microcosm for understanding the role of religion as both a source of conflict and as a means for resolving conflict. It is not a matter of "the church" standing apart from the turmoil. The majority of the people in Northern Ireland have an active connection with a church, and the churches reflect many of the same divisions that plague the society. In such a situation, there can be no simple separation of politics and religion. Church initiatives that effectively address the psychological barriers between the two sides may thus be an important prerequisite to any breakthrough in the political stalemate. To a great extent, though, the churches, like their congregations, have become captives of their own traditions and thus over-identified with a single culture. A degree of distancing may therefore be required if they are to effectively serve both cultures in a reconciling capacity.

Sri Lanka

Since the mid-1950s, a divisive form of populist nationalism has prevailed in Sri Lanka in which the Buddhist Sinhala majority has characteristically excluded the Hindu Tamils from most facets of Sri Lankan society, including the functions of government. As a result of this discrimination, civil war broke out in 1983 between the Sinhalese and various Tamil rebel groups, of which the largest and most powerful has been the Liberation Tigers of Tamil Eelam. The ensuing violence has resulted in a de facto separation of the island into two regions: the north, from which the Tamils operate, and the rest of the country over which the Sinhalese predominate.

In 1987, as the Sinhalese appeared to be gaining the upper hand, the government of India put considerable pressure on Sri Lanka to accept an Indian-mediated peace agreement and the establishment of an Indian peacekeeping force. By February 1988, India had committed 50,000 troops to such a force; but they encountered stiff resistance from the Tamil rebels who refused to give up their armed struggle. In August 1989, as Indian casualties mounted and domestic political support in India waned, the two countries agreed to a withdrawal of Indian forces by the end of March 1990. Although the withdrawal was completed on schedule, violence between the Tamils and Sinhalese has continued.

A religious group (which shall remain nameless to protect the confidentiality of its involvement) has been attempting to find ways to bring the fighting to an end. It has injected itself where official efforts at diplomacy have failed and has had some success in bridging the communications gap between the two sides. The group itself, which enjoys a high degree of credibility with both parties, continues to persevere despite adverse conditions and the added complications posed by the recent formation of a Sinhalese Marxist insurgency. Its involvement demonstrates the potential usefulness of actors from an "uninvolved" religion addressing differences between other religious groups.

The Punjab

A prime example of the ethnic and sectarian strife found in many parts of Indian society is the conflict between the Sikhs and the Hindus in the northern province of

Punjab. Over the years, a Sikh separatist movement has attempted to establish an independent state in the Punjab. The central Indian government, which is dominated by the Congress party, believes that India, a broad conglomeration of ethnic groups speaking a myriad of languages, will quickly unravel if it grants independence to the Punjab.[36]

The situation took an interesting turn with the involvement of a Jain monk, Acharya Muni Sushil Kumar, who is dedicated to nonviolence. He toured the areas of the Punjab most affected by the violence in 1986, and in the spring of 1987 issued an appeal for peace in the region, calling on the various Sikh leaders as well as Prime Minister Rajiv Gandhi to end the violence.

In May 1987 Kumar met with the leaders of the militant Sikhs who were occupying the Golden Temple at Amritsar, after having prevailed upon Prime Minister Gandhi to withdraw his police forces during the times they were meeting. (They had surrounded the site since 1984). This meeting created an opportunity for Kumar to facilitate a dialogue between the Sikhs and the central government that resulted in the formulation of a four-point peace plan calling for (a) the release of political prisoners from both sides, (b) the rehabilitation of army deserters, (c) a permanent withdrawal of the Central Reserve Police Force from the Punjab, and (d) the dismissal of all court cases against underground youths.[37] The plan itself was never implemented because the Punjab state government systematically undermined the peace process, apparently fearing a loss of prestige if religious leaders were to succeed where it had failed.[38]

In January 1988 Kumar succeeded in establishing communication with all of the militant Sikh leaders in the Punjab and arranged a meeting for them to settle their differences. Soon thereafter, one of the leaders was assassinated, and the meeting was canceled. In February Kumar appealed to the central government to release imprisoned priests from the Golden Temple. Gandhi responded favorably, announcing his intention to move forward in accordance with the Indian constitution. Leaders of the Sikh militant groups also pledged their support for Kumar's initiative, and the priests were subsequently released.

Although Kumar's efforts proved inconclusive, an uneasy peace has subsequently been established through harsh police tactics on the part of the recently elected congress party government (September 1992). Kumar's initiative, however, demonstrates the potential for a religious figure to promote dialogue between people with strongly differing opinions and worldviews. In this case, an avowed apostle of nonviolence met with terrorists and engaged them in dialogue with a central government, which theretofore had refused to communicate.

A CASE FOR SYNERGY

Nation-state negotiations and the interactions of official diplomats (track I) are consistent with the basic paradigm of international relations set forth by Hans Morgenthau in his classic work, *Politics Among Nations*, first published in 1948. As illustrated by some of the case studies in this book, there are numerous interactions that also take place at the unofficial track II level, many of them to positive effect.

Although there are situations where one track or the other will clearly represent the preferred course, conflict prevention or resolution does not have to be a single-track process. In the mounting disorder of the "new world order" of the 1990s, foreign policy (and religious) practitioners will need to use every approach available to them, including synergistic combinations of tracks I and II. Using the two tracks in combination can sometimes reduce, if not eliminate, the limits to what can be achieved when using only one in isolation. The peace treaty of October 4, 1992, which ended 16 years of civil war in Mozambique, is proof that under the right circumstances a combined whole can, in fact, exceed the sum of its parts.

Mozambique

In 1962 the Frente de Libertacão de Mozambique (Frelimo) was founded to free Mozambique from Portuguese colonial rule. With Portugal's defeat in 1975, Frelimo became the natural power base from which an independent Mozambique was born. Within six months of achieving independence, however, an insurgency was launched by the Resistencia de Nacional Mocambicana (Renamo), an organization formed with the support of Rhodesia. Renamo's purpose was to pressure the new government into halting its support of Robert Mugabe's Mozambique-based Zimbabwe African National Liberation Army. By 1977 the increasingly radical orientation of the Frelimo leadership led it to adopt Marxism-Leninism as its guiding ideology and to sign a 20-year treaty of friendship with the Soviet Union. It also established alliances with several East European governments and Cuba.[39]

These alliances were viewed by the government of Rhodesia as a strategic threat to its interests, and Rhodesian intelligence assumed direct control of the Renamo insurgency. When Rhodesia, renamed Zimbabwe, achieved independence in 1980, control was shifted to South African military intelligence, and Renamo shifted its headquarters to the Transvaal, the South African province immediately adjacent to Mozambique. Over the course of the next decade, the civil war took a significant toll, with nearly a million lives lost, another 4.5 million persons displaced or rendered homeless, and about $15 billion in damage to property and infrastructure.[40]

The ascendence of Joaquim Chissano to the presidency in 1986, following the death of President Samora Machel, represented a turning point in Frelimo's approach. Chissano believed that only negotiations could end Mozambique's plight. Accordingly, he set about isolating Renamo from its South African military and diplomatic support and establishing a framework for negotiations that would appeal to Renamo as well as to his own constituency.[41] In addition, Chissano continued to relax the tight restrictions on the churches of Mozambique (an initiative begun by Machel shortly before his death).

In concert with Chissano's new diplomatic efforts and at his request, Mozambique's Catholic and Protestant churches undertook an agenda of dialogue, reconciliation, and peacemaking. The initiative that emerged on the Catholic side stemmed from an old friendship between Mozambican Archbishop Jaime Goncalves and the Community of St. Egidio (CSE), a Rome-based lay Catholic organization dedicated to serving the poor and the elderly. CSE had been active since the late 1970s in working to reduce religious persecution in Mozambique and in opening up a church-state dialogue. Because of the devastation of Mozambique's civil war, CSE had also been working with Mozambican bishops in seeking international humanitarian and development aid for the country. It soon became apparent, however, that it would be impossible to provide effective assistance until there was peace. Thus began a lengthy and trying effort to end the war, with the Community of St. Egidio taking the lead on a track II basis.

Meanwhile, Chissano was proceeding on track I. In 1989 Afonso Dhlakama, Renamo's military and political leader, announced his willingness to negotiate an end to the fighting if Frelimo would agree to four conditions: a multiparty constitution, a free market economy, free elections within two years, and the creation of a new national military. Chissano accepted Dhlakama's overtures to negotiate, although not on Dhlakama's terms, and then asked a small delegation of Mozambican clerics,[42] including Archbishop Goncalves, to determine the appropriate contacts within Renamo for conducting negotiations. Chissano subsequently invited President Moi of Kenya and President Mugabe of Zimbabwe to mediate formal talks between the two sides. Following an initial attempt at mediation in August 1989, both Moi and Mugabe lost their credibility with Frelimo and Renamo, respectively (for different reasons), so the track I effort stalled.

At this point, the Community of St. Egidio, together with Goncalves and Mario Raffaelli, a representative from the Italian government,[43] offered to host talks between the two sides. Chissano and Dhlakama both agreed, primarily because the Catholic church enjoyed good credibility with each side.[44] Also helpful in this decision was the fact that Goncalves had by this time acquired a formidable reputation as an effective intermediary.[45] As described by a member of CSE:

> Bishop Goncalves has taken for himself the task of solving the problem and stopping the war. That means that sometimes it's not only the structure or the numbers we count, but also the attitude of one single person can be important, in this case, the attitude of Bishop Goncalves himself.[46]

Together with CSE's founder and leader, Andrea Riccardi, and CSE member Don Matteo Zuppi, a parish priest in Rome known for his commitment to helping the poor, Goncalves and Raffaelli joined forces as mediators for the more than two years of negotiations that followed.

The first meeting took place in July 1990, after which 10 additional rounds of talks were required before the two sides agreed to end the war. Along the way, the Vatican, the Italian government, and the governments of several other countries, including the United States, provided moral support. For the final round, the mediators invited five official observers, one each from the United States, Portugal, France, the United Kingdom, and the United Nations. It had become apparent that the weight of the international community would be required to guarantee fair multiparty elections and effective implementation of the settlement's other provisions. In even more immediate terms, additional resources and expertise were needed to design and monitor a cease-fire, and to deal with other technical aspects of the agreement. Thus, the track II mediators began to pass the baton to track I representatives.

Following the October 4 settlement, Riccardi attributed the mediation team's success to the fact that it had no vested interest in the political outcome. He further noted that "the peace talks also worked because of the very climate of trust that was built up. In many of the diplomatic initiatives, the human element was lacking. . . . Of course, these people had their political interests and differences, but we also saw human values being reawakened in them, and that was important."[47]

In the Mozambique situation, the religious actors appear to have been ideally suited to the critical task of getting the parties to the bargaining table, persevering in the lengthy process of establishing trust (with and among the parties), and moving the process to the point of establishing the terms of settlement. The case demonstrates the limits of a track II effort and the potential offered by a constructive interface with track I. It was only through collaboration of the unofficial and official diplomats that the full scope of the peace process could be realized.

Any number of approaches might be considered in resolving present and future conflicts, but the use of track II in seriatim with track I appears to be one of the more useful. Respected religious figures provide a level of reassurance that official diplomats are often hard-pressed to equal. By the same token, the parties to a settlement will inevitably look to the economic and military capabilities of the international community to provide the necessary political and security guarantees.

The possibilities for exploiting synergism such as that achieved in Mozambique are limited only by the confines of one's imagination—and the specific circumstances of any given conflict. A note of caution is in order, however. To the extent that a Track II religious or spiritual effort at peacemaking comes to be identified with any particular government, it may run the risk of political "contamination" in the eyes of one or more of the parties. So for official diplomats, it becomes a matter of encouraging such activities where appropriate, perhaps coordinating with them, but not controlling them.

The Former Yugoslavia

As one looks at trouble spots around the globe, one sees no end to the opportunities for applying dispute-resolution capabilities enhanced by a sophisticated spiritual awareness. Beyond the functional combinations of tracks I and II diplomacy suggested above, there are the added possibilities offered by interfaith dialogue. One area of the world where this approach might offer a degree of hope is in the republics of the former Yugoslavia. The civil war there now ranks as the longest running conflict on the European continent since World War II. Thus far, the war's tempo and seemingly unbreakable cycle of communal violence and revenge have thwarted all attempts to halt the fighting.

The immediate causes of the conflict are numerous and complex. Initially, repudiation of the Serb-dominated Communist party in republican elections led to resentment and fear of oppression among the Serbs in areas where they were in a minority. These fears were exacerbated by a resurgence of Croatian authoritarianism under President Franjo Tudjman (including the use of symbols identified with fascism), which evoked memories of the Croatian massacres of Serbs during World War II. Serbian leader Slobadan Milošević, in turn, used this as a rationale for stirring up ethnic passions in Croatia, Slovenia, and Bosnia-Herzegovina (Figure 15.2). Finally, the Serb-dominated Yugoslav army, fearing a complete disintegration of the country and a corresponding loss of status, attempted to hold the federation together by force. These causes collectively translated into an intense campaign by the Serbs to reclaim territory which they consider to be part of a Greater Serbia (at the expense of Croatia, Bosnia-Herzegovina, and potentially other neighboring republics).

Because religion constitutes one of the principal ingredients of ethnic identity among the peoples of the former Yugoslavia, it will undoubtedly be one of the keys to any settlement that eventually emerges. Religion has also contributed to the conflict, as some religious groups have openly identified themselves with political parties and even in some instances taken up arms. The Serbian Orthodox church, for example, has been strongly identified with the drive for a Greater Serbia.

At the same time, Serbian Orthodox Patriarch Pavle of Belgrade, the spiritual

Figure 15.2. The Former Yugoslavia

leader of 12 million Serbian Orthodox Christians worldwide, has openly deplored the military leadership in Serbia and the newly independent republics: "The leaders of the Serbians, Muslims, and Croatians were all Tito's generals before and under the influence of an atheistic ideology. And for that reason they came so easily to that inhuman desire to fight the war."[48] In September 1992 the patriarch joined with Cardinal Franjo Kuharić, the Roman Catholic Primate of Croatia, in issuing an appeal to secular leaders to end the violence. The two church leaders condemned the practice of "ethnic cleansing" and the "blasphemous destruction of all prayer and holy places, Christian and Muslim."[49]

Despite the deep resentments between the ethnic groups of the former Yugoslav federation, the potential for religious leaders to bring their collective influence to bear in a helpful way would appear substantial and worth pursuing.[50] Pursuit, however, will not be without its challenges.

The Orthodox, Catholic, and Muslim traditions have coexisted in this region for centuries and have often engaged in interfaith dialogue on at least two levels. First, there are the spontaneous conversations that have taken place naturally among the local religious communities within ethnically mixed regions. And on a more formal level, there have been a number of attempts at dialogue between various religious leaders. To the extent that religious bodies have aligned themselves politically with their respective ethnic groups in the present conflict, however, these earlier channels of communication have broken down.[51] A related complication exists as a result of the breakdown in trust that has taken place among many of those who have not only engaged in dialogue in the past but who were once close friends. As a result, a degree of desensitization has developed in which external appeals to work together toward halting the violence tend to fall on deaf ears.

Pax Christi, the International Fellowship of Reconciliation, and the Council of Churches for Britain and Ireland are currently attempting to facilitate peace-making efforts at the grass-roots level.[52] Meanwhile, the World Council of Churches (WCC), the Conference of European Churches (CEC), and the Council of the European Bishops' Conference (Roman Catholic) are having some success in bringing religious leaders together to discuss the role they might play in ending the strife.[53] At the middle levels of the indigenous denominations, the International Conciliation Service of the Mennonite Central Committee (U.S.) and the Life and Peace Institute of Sweden are working to develop a dialogue process that can recreate an atmosphere of cooperation and trust.[54] Past attempts by the Catholic church in Slovenia to act as an unofficial intermediary between Croatian Catholics and Serbian Orthodox Christians suggest a special role for the Slovenes in promoting future interfaith dialogue.[55] To the extent that the more conciliatory elements within these religious bodies have access to the levers of social communication, such as the media and educational institutions, any attempts at peacemaking arising from such dialogue will naturally be enhanced.

Once this kind of groundwork has been laid, it may become possible to pursue conciliation on a track II basis, with an eye toward mediation on track I. Again, there are any number of approaches that might be attempted, but each of them assumes a degree of rational behavior on the part of the protagonists and a corresponding ability to control their respective armed forces. Thus far, neither of these conditions exists. The planets are clearly misaligned.

A FINAL NOTE

Ordinarily, negotiated settlements become possible when the parties fear the consequences of continued conflict more than they fear the consequences of a settlement. Merely getting to the negotiating table itself is extremely important, since it is only through interaction, dialogue, and debate that understanding can develop. It is within such a process that the parties to a conflict are able to delineate and compare the actual differences in their positions, differences that in the cold light of day often prove to be not so very different.

Perhaps the most compelling argument for involving religious actors as intermediaries in the peacemaking process is that offered by Joseph Montville, a leading architect of the concept of track II diplomacy:

> If one single quality has to be chosen to account for the influence that religiously identified third parties have, it would be their ability to inspire trust. One might think that is an obvious answer and, indeed, an easy quality to find in, say, any gentleman or well-bred lawyer or diplomat. But ethnic or sectarian conflict has a special aspect in that people have endured aggression and loss simply because of their membership in an identity group. They are dehumanized, despised, raped, pillaged, and murdered for no other reason than who they are, not for anything they have done.
>
> Until these people have suffered aggression and loss, they probably have a sense of fairness and predictability in life that allows them to get on without any particular daily foreboding. After their attack and loss, or the unreconciled and unmourned loss of their forebears, they feel distinctly distrustful of all outsiders. Their lessons in life have been that they can be killed because of their ethnic identity and, therefore, only members of their ethnic group can be trusted (and even some of them are suspect).
>
> Into the lives of these victimized people come religious outsiders, who in varying ways convey a sense of understanding and empathy for their fears and who have established reputations for honesty, discretion, and integrity. They are disinterested in the conflict except for their sadness over the human losses associated with it. And even the religiously motivated third parties have to work "on site" with their new friends to prove through daily interaction that their reputations are justified and that they can be trusted to care about the life and death and future of the group they hope to help.[56]

Among the ongoing conflicts referred to in this chapter, one finds Christians fighting Christians, Hindus fighting Buddhists, Sikhs fighting Hindus, and Christians fighting Muslims. While religion itself may not be the primary catalyst for any of these disputes, it is clearly a complicating factor. By the same token, the use of a religious rationale to justify a conflict creates opportunities for spiritually motivated peacemakers. They can appeal to the parties on the basis of universal religious principles or on the basis of the specific warrants for conflict resolution that exist in each religion's theology. Yet, despite the best of efforts, such appeals may fall on deaf ears. By the time this book is published, any or all of these heretofore unresolved conflicts may have run their course. Indeed, it seems likely that the Yugoslavian situation will have played itself out on a tragic and inconclusive note. If so, then one may be relegated to looking to the Franco-German case study as a model for achieving a degree of reconciliation in the aftermath.

In today's world of ethnic strife and high-technology weaponry, orthodox concepts of security based on a competition of armaments will no longer be adequate. Increasingly, security will become a function of the strength and durability of national and international relationships. This eventuality suggests a need to move toward a new paradigm for international relations. The challenge is to reach beyond the state-centric focus of the power-politics model to accommodate nongovernmental interactions at the subnational and individual levels. The case studies in this book illustrate that there is a distinct role for nongovernmental actors in building and changing relationships through dialogue and conflict resolution processes. The Franco-German initiative with its early contribution to European unity is a particularly compelling example.

It is at the unofficial level that many of the pressures that frustrate policymakers and often lead to conflict can be addressed with greater open-mindedness and effectiveness. As noted by Michael Banks of the Centre for the Analysis of Conflict, the international relations paradigm that has prevailed throughout the Cold War carries with it a distinct liability insofar as the practice of conflict resolution is concerned. It tends to promote a status quo mentality that leads "more towards the partisan manipulation of a conflict than towards its impartial mediation. Intellectually, there is a pervasive rigidity of attitude that holds back the spontaneous creation of new ideas. It also obstructs an open-minded discussion of ideas that originate outside it."[57]

In short, today's model leans heavily on the recycling of old approaches and adapting them to fit new problems, problems which they are ill-designed to accommodate. Because diplomacy typically tries to resolve conflicts according to a patent interest, there is a need to go beyond the normal mechanisms to uncover and deal with the sources of conflict by rebuilding relationships and making concessionary adjustments wherever possible. In this context, reconciliation born of spiritual conviction can play a critical role by inspiring conflicting parties to move beyond the normal human reaction of responding in kind, of returning violence for violence. And therein lies an extraordinary challenge. It is hoped that this book will help encourage and equip the policy-making and religious communities to meet this challenge.

Notes

1. Huston Smith, *The Religions of Man* (New York: Harper and Row, 1958), 310.
2. Peter Wallenstein, ed., *States in Armed Conflict 1988* (Uppsala, Sweden: Uppsala University, Department of Peace and Conflict Research, 1989), 1.
3. Personal communication from Joseph Lagu, October 29, 1992.
4. Interview with Joseph Lagu, Caux, Switzerland, August 14, 1992.

5. The mediators introduced explicit religious content into the deliberations by way of sermons and prayers. These were drawn from the Old Testament and, thus, also from the Koran (presentation by Hizkias Assefa, then-professor of management and international affairs at LaRoche College, University of Pittsburgh, and author of *Mediation of Civil Wars: Approaches and Strategies—The Sudan Conflict* [Boulder, Colo.: Westview, 1987], to the Religion and Conflict Resolution Project Steering Group, Center for Strategic and International Studies [C. Sampson, Memorandum for the Record, February 8, 1990, 10]).

6. A title accorded various religious or temporal leaders claiming descent from Muhammad.

7. The justification for imposing Sharia law in all of its seeming harshness is mystifying to many in the West. Perhaps instructive is a rationale recently provided by al-Turabi himself. He describes the need for the Sharia as transcending purely religious considerations:

> We do not have a basis in Moslem culture for ethics or for morality except in religion. And our society has been experiencing so much communication, people are being displaced, moved from one place to another. And as they move, their customs no longer hold because customs are environmentally based. It is only those who observe you and who know you personally who can compel you to behave conventionally. Once you go to urban areas or you move to other places because of economic transformation, or war or drought or whatever, the customs cannot serve you. You need more universal values, more human norms, so to speak. But also in the field of political power and political institutions, especially after the Sharia was disestablished by colonialists, we lost completely a sense of a higher law or we lost the idea that politics is part of religion and part of morality. . . . The Sharia for many centuries provided us with a higher law than any other functions of government. But the Sharia is not law. It is a system of norms. Some of them are legal, others are morals for society to execute, to implement. Still, some are only conscientious. And in Islam these different ways are preserved, the limits are known but law cannot transgress on morality.   (Address at the Center for Strategic and International Studies, May 12, 1992.)

8. Telephone interview with Cardinal Casaroli, with interpretation by David Leishman, October 20, 1992.

9. Interview with Rudolph Dekker, a former West German parliamentarian who had discussed this incident with Klaus Gysi, December 5, 1992.

10. Robert F. Goeckel, *The Lutheran Church and the East German State: Political Conflict and Change Under Ulbricht and Honecker* (Ithaca, N.Y.: Cornell University Press, 1990), 243.

11. Interview with Dekker.

12. William Brehm, an American businessman who enjoys a close friendship with Gysi, has summed up his impressions of Gysi's role in an unpublished document, "Summary of My Meetings with Dr. Gysi," on file at the Center for Strategic and International Studies, November 11, 1992, 7.

> These things seem clear to me: At some point in his career Dr. Gysi concluded that the GDR brand of socialism did not work and would not deliver on its promises. Then, at some point in his government responsibilities, Dr. Gysi decided to allow meetings in the churches. Most believe that the GDR revolution started at such meetings. I believe Dr. Gysi knew exactly what he was doing.

13. The term Greater Somalia encompasses Somalia, Djibouti, part of Ethiopia, part of Uganda, and the Northern Frontier District in Kenya.

14. The boundaries were established at the Berlin Conference of 1895, when the colonial powers of Africa met to divide up the continent among themselves.

15. The meeting took place in 1981 at an Organization of African Unity conference in Kenya (interview with Hussein Mohamed, minister for state in the Office of the President of Kenya, Nairobi, February 15, 1991).

16. Siad Barre made this statement at a May 29, 1981, breakfast meeting with General David Jones and others (interview with David Jones, Arlington, Virginia, September 6, 1992).

17. Interview with the American visitor, who asked to remain unnamed, Arlington, Virginia, September 6, 1992. The reason for routing their journey through Mogadishu was because the American had wanted to show his son the relevance of Christ in a non-Christian environment. Neither of them had ever met Siad Barre before, so the meeting was arranged through the Somalian finance minister by U.S. Congressman Don Bonker in his capacity as chairman of the International Economic Policy and Trade Subcommittee of the House Foreign Affairs Committee (interview with former Congressman Bonker, Washington, D.C., November 19, 1992).

18. Interview with the American visitor.

19. Interview with Jones.

20. In addition to Jones and Siad Barre, those present included General Lew Allen, USAF; Frederick Benson, vice-president of the American Paper Institute; Congressman Don Bonker of Washington; William Brehm, chairman of SRA International; Douglas Coe, an associate of the National Prayer Breakfast; Under Secretary of the Navy Robert Murray; Senator Don Nickles of Oklahoma; and Ambassador Mahmoud Haji Nur, Embassy of Somalia.

21. This account is based on separate interviews with William Brehm, Robert Murray, and Frederick Benson in Arlington, Virginia, October 30, 1992, November 6, 1992, and November 8, 1992, respectively. Although President Siad Barre did not form a fellowship group that met regularly, he did convene his prime minister, a vice president, the defense minister, and several other officials on subsequent occasions when the American revisited Mogadishu (interview with the American visitor).

22. Pranay B. Gupte, "Somali President Ready for Ogaden Peace Talks," *New York Times*, June 30, 1981, 3.

23. Ibid.

24. Colin Legum, ed., *Africa Contemporary Record, Annual Survey and Documents 1981–1982* (New York and London: African Publishing Co., 1981), B268.

25. Interview with President Moi, Arlington, Virginia, January 31, 1990, on the occasion of his attendance at the National Prayer Breakfast in Washington, D.C.

26. Mohamud Mohamed, chief of staff of the armed forces, and his brother Hussein Mohamed, minister for state in the Office of the President, are two examples.

27. "Supping with the Devil," *Economist* (September 15, 1979), 58.

28. A reference to St. Paul's life-changing encounter with Christ on the road to Damascus.

29. Edward Moxon-Browne, *Nation, Class and Creed in Northern Ireland* (Gower, England: Hants Aldershot, 1983), 3.

30. John McGarry and Brendan O'Leary, "Northern Ireland's Future: What Is to Be Done?" *Conflict Quarterly* (Summer 1990), 47.

31. Lyne Shivers and David Bowman, *More Than the Troubles: A Common Sense View of the Northern Ireland Conflict* (Philadelphia: New Society Publishers, 1984), 142.

32. Ibid.

33. These officials include the Catholic cardinal archbishop of Armagh, the archbishop of the Anglican church of Ireland, the president and general secretary of the Methodist

church of Ireland, and the moderator and general secretary of the Presbyterian church of Ireland. Their most recent initiative was a joint call for foreign economic investment and enforcement of workplace anti-discrimination laws (Gustar Niebuhr, "Ireland's Major Churches Join in Economic Appeal," *Washington Post*, January 14, 1994, A29).

34. See, for example, Moxon-Browne, *Nation, Class and Creed*, 3.

35. Thomas L. Jones, "Northern Ireland," unpublished paper on file at the Center for Strategic and International Studies, February 28, 1991, 3–4.

36. James C. Clad, "India in Crisis and Transition," *Washington Quarterly* (Winter 1992), 93–94.

37. Jay Raina, "Peace Prospects Bright in Punjab," *Hindustan Times*, May 12, 1987, 3.

38. "Guruji's Peace Mission in Punjab," *Siddhachalam Newsletter* (July 1987), 3.

39. Witney W. Schneidman, "Conflict Resolution in Mozambique: A Status Report," *CSIS Africa Notes*, no. 121 (February 28, 1991), 1.

40. Ibid., 2.

41. Ibid., 7.

42. The other delegation members were Cardinal Alexandre Maria dos Santos, the archbishop of Maputo, and the Reverend Osias Mucache, a Presbyterian pastor.

43. Mario Raffaelli is a socialist parliamentarian from northern Italy and a former under secretary in the Italian Foreign Ministry. He also served as the Council on Security and Cooperation in Europe (CSCE) mediator of the Nagorno-Karabakh conflict.

44. Schneidman, "Conflict Resolution in Mozambique," 7.

45. Ibid.

46. Presentation by Claudio Betti, U.S. Institute of Peace Workshop on Conflict Resolution, Washington, D.C., July 13, 1992.

47. As quoted by Clare Pedrick, "Unlikely Negotiators Help Mozambique Find Peace," *Washington Post*, October 10, 1992, G1.

48. Rick Allen, "Serbian Patriarch Appeals for Understanding," *Washington Post*, October 10, 1992, G1.

49. Ibid.

50. As noted by former U.S. Assistant Secretary of State Richard Schifter in an address of several years ago:

> Last year, in the course of a visit to Belgrade, I had the opportunity to meet with an Orthodox archimandrite, a Roman Catholic priest, and an Islamic mufti. We discussed the problem of interethnic strife, and I asked what religious leaders can do to help ameliorate it. All three of them agreed that it would indeed make sense for religious leaders to play that role, but added that they had never done so in the past.

(Richard Schifter, "To Hate All the People Your Relatives Hate," presentation at the U.S. Institute of Peace Conference on Ethnic Conflict Resolution Under Law, Washington, D.C., June 12, 1991).

51. David A. Steele, "Report on Yugoslav Trip of August 1992," unpublished paper on file at the Center for Strategic and International Studies, October 2, 1992.

52. Pax Christi conducted a fact-finding trip in April 1992 (John Paul Lederach, "Trip Report to Mennonite Central Committee," January 26–February 8, 1992, 1–2). The International Fellowship of Reconciliation held a seminar on nonviolence in Zagreb during the summer of 1992 for teachers, religious workers, and peace activists (N. Gerald Shenk, "A Peace Conference in War-Torn Croatia," Eastern Mennonite Theological Seminary, Harrisonburg, Virginia, 1–2). The Council of Churches for Britain and Ireland held a consultation in May 1992 on the role of the churches in the Yugoslav crisis. At the meeting, Catholic, Orthodox, and Protestant representatives from churches in Britain, Ireland, and

the former Yugoslav republics explored possibilities for third-party involvement on the part of external religious bodies (Council of Churches for Britain and Ireland, "British and Irish Churches Confer on Yugoslav Crisis," press release, May 7, 1992, 1–3).

53. These groups have used their "power to convene" to bring together the hierarchical leadership. Representative of such gatherings have been two Catholic-Orthodox dialogues held in Switzerland in January and September, 1992. In addition, an ecumenical and interfaith round table was held in December 1993, which included Orthodox, Catholic, Protestant, Muslim, and Jewish participants from all levels of religious involvement in Croatia, Serbia, and Bosnia-Herzegovina.

54. Further details of the results of this dialogue process can be found in a forthcoming report authored by David Steele entitled "Evaluation of Roundtable Discussion: The Role of Religion in the Conflicts in Serbia, Croatia, and Bosnia-Herzegovina" in *Religion and Conflicts in the Former Yugoslavian Republics*, ed. N. Gerald Shenk (Uppsala, Sweden: Life and Peace Institute, 1994), 75–93. Both Steele and Shenk are facilitators of this dialogue process.

55. Past contacts were especially effective between the theological faculties in Ljubljana and Belgrade. At present there is dialogue within Slovenia between the Orthodox and Catholic churches. There has also been some dialogue in Serbia where the Catholic archbishop is a Slovene. But there is little communication between Serbia and Slovenia. Furthermore, Croatian Catholics have indicated they are suspicious of Slovenian Catholic contacts with the Serbian Orthodox church (interviews by David Steele with Archbishop Mgr. Alojzij Sustar, vice president, Catholic Bishops' Conference, Ljubljana, August 18, 1992; Father Franci Petric, journalist with *Druzina*, Ljubljana, August 18, 1992; and Father Drago Klemencic, deputy editor-in-chief of informative programming, TV Slovenia, Ljubljana, August 19, 1992).

56. Joseph Montville memorandum to Douglas Johnston, Center for Strategic and International Studies, undated [1992]. Joseph Montville has been a member of the Religion and Conflict Resolution Steering Group from its inception. He coined the term *track two diplomacy* in 1981 (William D. Davidson and Joseph V. Montville, "Foreign Policy According to Freud," *Foreign Policy*, no 45 [Winter 1981–82], 145–57). He further developed the concept in "The Arrow and the Olive Branch: A Case for Track Two Diplomacy," in *Conflict Resolution: Track Two Diplomacy*, eds. John W. McDonald and Diane B. Bendahmane, Foreign Service Institute, U.S. Department of State, 1987; and idem, "Transnationalism and the Role of Track Two Diplomacy," in *Approaches to Peace: An Intellectual Map*, eds. W. Scott Thompson and Kenneth M. Jensen with Richard N. Smith and Kimber M. Schraub (Washington D.C.: U.S. Institute of Peace, 1991), 253–69.

57. Michael Banks, "The International Relations Discipline: Asset or Liability for Conflict Resolution," in *International Conflict Resolution, Theory and Practice*, eds. Edward E. Azar and John W. Burton (Sussex, England: Wheatsheaf Books, 1986), 24.

Index ▪